# THE

# FIRST ROMANOVS.

## (1613—1725.)

A HISTORY OF MOSCOVITE CIVILISATION AND
THE RISE OF MODERN RUSSIA UNDER PETER
THE GREAT AND HIS FORERUNNERS.

By R. NISBET BAIN.

*WITH ILLUSTRATIONS.*

LONDON:

ARCHIBALD CONSTABLE & CO., LTD.,

16, JAMES STREET, HAYMARKET.

1905.

BRADBURY, AGNEW, & CO LD., PRINTERS,
LONDON AND TONBRIDGE.

Petrus Magnus
Russorum Imperator
Pater Patriæ

Peter the Great at the Age of 41

To

MY MOTHER.

in vast land-locked lakes, and whose most salient feature is a monotonous sameness. Obviously the nation which should occupy, for want of a better territory, this immense and remote eastern wilderness, must start at a disadvantage in the race for empire as compared with the nations which were fortunate enough to be the first to occupy the more favoured western lands with their contiguity to the sea, their natural boundaries, their more temperate climate, and their superior facilities of internal communication, to say nothing of the intercourse and the com-petition of close neighbourhood which so powerfully contributed to lay the foundations of modern civilisation. The nation which Mother Nature, from the very outset, thus treated in so step-motherly a fashion was the Russian nation. Vastness of territory and paucity of population, too much land and too few hands to cultivate it profitably—these were the primary conditions which prevented the normal development of barbarous Russia. Land was almost valueless and feudalism impossible in a country where the prince and his comrades* roamed perpetually from place to place, levying tribute in kind from the surrounding savages, and varying the pleasures of the chase with an occasional raid upon the weak and wealthy Royal City,† as the Slavs called Constantinople. And here an extraordinary circumstance must not be overlooked. At a later day, when the descendants of the primeval House of Rurik multiplied into a dozen principalities, they contrived to appropriate all the land, so that the boyars, or nobles, had no opportunity of forming a landed aristocracy interested in curtailing the authority of the prince, as was the case in the west. The very liberty enjoyed by the boyars of transferring their allegiance at will from one prince to another perpetuated their landless condition. Thus, for some centuries, the whole eastern plain was a primitive world of fluid forms. But, sooner or later, the course of history follows the lie of the best land, and so also in the eastern plain. Russian history begins in the watery ways leading from the Baltic to the Black Sea, especially in the central Dnieper district, where lay the best land of all. But now were seen the disadvantages of a boundless plain where no barrier could be erected against the incursions of

*Druzhina.          † Tsargrad.

# THE FIRST ROMANOVS.

## CHAPTER I.

### INTRODUCTORY.

A CURIOUS observer scrutinising, for the first time, the map of Europe, must inevitably be struck by the singular contrast presented by the physical conformation of its eastern and its western halves. The western half is remarkable for its long, irregular, indented coast-line, ramified by peninsulas and diversified by islands, while numerous mountain ranges intersect its fertile plains and naturally subdivide them into so many distinct and independent units. The sea, too, is not very remote from even its most central portions, and broad, navigable rivers supply an easy means of access thereto on the north, south, and west. Entirely different are the natural features of Eastern Europe. There we find endless plains, whose rivers terminate

# LIST OF ILLUSTRATIONS.

———•———

# CONTENTS.

# CONTENTS.

———◆———

her people, he saw to be so different from ours that it was vain to apply our standards to her." Be that as it may, it is an indisputable historical fact that Russia owes everything to the Tsars —her prosperity, her greatness, her Empire, her very existence. The Tsars have made many mistakes, and the mistakes of an autocracy must always be more glaringly obvious than the mistakes of any other form of government ; but any impartial critic, taking a broad historical view of the one hundred and ninety-eight years during which the Romanovs have held sway, must admit that no other European dynasty has so conscientiously, and on the whole so successfully, done its duty.

R. NISBET BAIN.

*February,* 1905.

the Great ; we are even learning to know something about Ivan the Terrible. But seventeenth century Moscovy is still, to most of us, a *terra incognita*. The talismanic keys which alone can unlock for us its treasures are the Russian and Polish languages, and, unfortunately, the very few among us who possess these talismans seem willing to use them for almost every purpose except the purpose of historical research.

I may remark as to Peter the Great that in these pages he has been treated, not biographically, but historically. He is regarded, primarily, as the last and greatest of a series of native pioneers who lightened his task by preparing the way for him— men like Orduin-Nashchokin, Artamon Matyeev, Nikon, Rtish-chev, Pososhkov, and Vasily Golitsuin—all of whom, in their degree, as we shall see, contributed to lay the foundations of modern Russia. Many anecdotes concerning Peter, which may readily be found elsewhere, must not, therefore, be looked for in these pages. But no detail, however trivial, which can explain the policy or illuminate the character of the first Russian Emperor has been omitted. The Great Northern War, more-over, and the one-and-twenty years of European diplomacy of which it was the focus, have for the first time been examined by the double light of Scandinavian and Slavonic documents in order that the fullest justice might be done to both the pro-tagonists in the titanic struggle, and also that the effect of the struggle on their contemporaries (for it resulted in the establish-ment of modern Europe), might be more impartially and comprehensively set forth.

People sometimes talk glibly enough of the necessity for Russia of constitutional government in the Western sense of the word. Such amiable enthusiasts would do well to ponder the words of one whose very *obiter dicta* on any historical sub-ject must ever be authoritative, and who took a peculiarly keen and intelligent interest in Russian affairs—I allude to the late Dr. Mandell Creighton. We are told in the recently published biography of the great bishop that: "What he had observed and heard convinced him of the absurdity of Englishmen attempting to suggest schemes of reform for Russia or to solve her problems. Her conditions, her civilisation, the character of

# INTRODUCTION.

———◆———

IT will be my endeavour, in the following pages, to describe the
social, ecclesiastical, and political conditions of Eastern Europe
from 1613 to 1725, and trace the gradual transformation, during
the seventeenth century, of the semi-monastic, semi-barbarous
Tsardom of Moscovy into the modern Russian State. The
emergence of the unlooked-for and unwelcome Empire of the
Tsars in the Old World was an event not inferior in importance
to the discovery of the unsuspected Continents of the New, and
the manner of its advent was even stranger than the advent
itself. Like all periods of sudden transition, the century which
divides the age of Ivan the Great from the age of Peter the
Great has its own peculiar interest, abounding, as it does, in
singular contradictions and picturesque contrasts. Throughout
this period, East and West, savagery and civilisation strive
incessantly for the mastery, and sinister and colossal shapes,
fit representatives of wildly contending, elemental forces, flit
phantasmagorically across the dirty ways of the twilight scene.

And, if it is one of the most interesting, this seventeenth
century in Moscovy is also one of the most important periods
of modern European history, for, explored with intelligence and
patience, it can be made to yield up the deep-lying explanations
of many things that trouble or bewilder us in the Tsar's domains
to-day, e.g., the backwardness of the people, the veneration for
the Throne, the venality and inefficiency of the public service,
the vices and the failures, the ambitions and the exploits, of
Holy Russia.

Finally, the subject possesses the rare and crowning merit
of almost absolute novelty. We have some few manuals of
Russian history ; we know something, by this time, of Peter

the martial nomads, who from the seventh to the fifteenth century passed regularly from Asia to Europe. The savage Tatar hordes drove the Russian princes out of the fertile southern steppes to the north-eastern forest region of the Upper Volga, where greater tranquillity was only enjoyable in a harder climate and on a far more barren soil. Almost simultaneously the still unchristianised Lithuanian princes, a whole series or born military geniuses, subjugated Western Russia, and ancient Kiev, the mother of Russian cities, which had in her the promise of a second Byzantium, dwindled down to a townlet of churches with the environments of a cemetery. A new order of things began for the unfortunate Russian nation. Driven from the fertile south-western districts to the secluded and inhospitable north-east, communication with Europe and civilisation was interrupted, not, as so many suppose, by the subsequent invasion of the Tatars, but by the far more powerful, because permanent, influences of necessity and environment. Everything now followed the flow of the Volga, and, consequently, took an easterly direction. The Russian, the last and uttermost of the Christian nations, separated from his brethren and pushed further and further into the eastern wilderness, was forced, for generations, to live outside the European family to which he naturally belonged. Nations need the fellowship of nations for their proper development just as individuals need the fellowship of individuals ; when, then, all such fellowship was suddenly cut off, the consequences to the Russian nation could not fail to be disastrous. Moreover, Russia did not even possess the usual and subsidiary advantages of infant states. Her sparse population was scattered, over immense and ever-increasing areas, in thousands of large villages ; and history has taught us that it is only when men congregate in those larger and closer communities which we call cities that such rudiments of progress as the brisk exchange of wares, the subdivision of labour, community of interests and the public spirit thence ensuing, find a congenial soil. All these common initial advantages were for a long time denied to ancient Moscovy.

The peculiar situation of Moscovy, as we must henceforth call Eastern Russia (for, gradually, the Grand Duchy of Moscovy subjugated or absorbed all the surrounding principalities), naturally conditioned the form of its government. By the end of the first half of the fifteenth century two salient political factors confront us at Moscow: a wealthy Grand Duke, who owns all the land, the sole means of maintenance, and a poor and numerous aristocracy composed partly of the old *Druzhina* of boyars, no longer nomadic but attached to the Court, and partly of immigrant *knyazes*, or princes, descendants of Rurik,* or Gedemin, but now nothing more than needy competitors with the boyars. The boyars and the *knyazes* were the dependants of the Grand Duke in the most literal sense of the word. We may say of the mediæval kings of France and Spain that they attracted the great nobles from castle to court, but of no period of Russian history can this be said, for the simple reason that the boyars and *knyazes* never had castles to dwell in. When Ivan III. married a Greek princess, born in Italy, and the Grand Dukes of Moscovy expanded into Tsars,† or Kings, the distance between the subject aristocracy and their sovereigns became remoter still. The boyars rebelled against the insulting change, but the crafty Greek lady prevailed, and her son, educated according to her principles, duly ascended the throne. Again the boyars rebelled ; but the struggle, if bloodier, was even briefer than before, and the depressed patricians emerged from it the submissive slaves of the *Veliki Gosudar*.‡ In all Moscovy there was only one potentate which at any time threatened to be a rival of the Tsar, and that was the semi-republic of Great Novgorod. But wealthy Novgorod, with her tumultuous popular assemblies, her unwieldy machinery of government and her inadequate means of defence, was, even at the best of times, an anomaly in an empire of villages, and she fell, because her down-trodden lower classes were forced to apply to Moscow for the common justice denied them by the tyrannous oligarchs of their own city. It was the well-deserved reputation for relatively fair dealing and good government which

---

* Rurik, the semi-mythical ancestor of the Russian; Gedemin, the historical progenitor of the Lithuanian Grand Dukes.

† The title was first used officially by Ivan III.'s son, Vasily III.

‡ Great Sovereign.

ultimately drew the hearts and minds of the people of the remote provinces to the Tsars at Moscow.

Thus, by a process so gradual, so natural, as to appear inevitable and unalterable, the *Gosudar* became the focus and the motive power of the national life and the national ambition. But the Tsar was more than autocratic, he was sacrosanct. To understand how this came about we must go back to the origin of Moscovite Christianity. It was a misfortune for the pagan Russians that they were converted by the decadent Greek branch of the universal church. The all-embracing asceticism of Byzantium, based upon the duty of renouncing utterly an incurably corrupt world, was, perhaps, the last remaining means of salvation for the effete society of the luxurious imperial city; but to impose such a regimen upon a simple race of vigorous barbarians was like applying to healthy growing children a rule of life only suitable for profligate repentant dotards. And, unfortunately, this regimen was applied with all the severity of uncompromising fanaticism. Elsewhere I shall endeavour to demonstrate the pernicious effects of "Byzantinism" on the social, political, and spiritual life of the Russian people. Here I would merely indicate its responsibility for that perverse ideal of domestic life which dominated Moscovy from about the fourteenth to the end of the seventeenth century.

Domestic life in old Moscovy was of a semi-monastic character. The father of the family was everything—"the master," * "the great one,"† "the real one,"‡ "the abbot,"§ of the establishment, responsible at the judgment day for the behaviour of the rest of the household, the immature inferior creatures committed to his charge. His will was a law from which there was no appeal.

Absolute obedience to him, "with slavish fear," was the counsel of perfection enjoined upon his "children," and the term children included his wife and all who dwelt beneath his roof.|| The model household was conducted according to strict canonical rules. Every hour of the day had its appointed prayers; the simplest domestic business was accompanied by

---

* *Gosudar.*　　† *Bolshoi.*　　‡ *Nastoyashy.*　　§ *Igumen.*
|| Zabyelin: "Domashnui Buit," etc.

obeisances and genuflexions ; daily attendance at church was of
universal obligation, and the ambition of every devout rich man
was to leave behind him, as a lasting memorial of his devotion
and his penitence, a church or chapel of a magnificence corresponding to his means.   Thus the social and religious life of the
people were indissolubly blended, and if every pious man was
venerated as "the abbot" and *gosudar* of his own household,
how much more so the Tsar, who, as the Gosudar of gosudars,
was over all?   This was especially the case when the Tsars
happened to be men of irreproachable morality and unimpeachable piety, as were the first sovereigns of the House of Romanov.

This indivisibility of the secular and the religious life in
ancient Moscovy was symbolised by the *Kreml*,* the centre
and heart of Moscow, a huge conglomeration of large and
beautiful churches, in the midst of which, like an abbot's cell
in a monastery, rose the Tsar's palace, itself a motley unsym-
metrical mass of buildings, including the public offices, built at
various periods, according as they were wanted.   The *Kreml*,
with the adjoining *Kitai-Gorod*, or China-town, was surrounded
by a strong and lofty crenulated stone wall, which made it in
those days a fortress of the first rank.   If every rich Moscovite
felt bound to leave behind him a memorial chapel, it is intelligible that the richest man in the realm, the Tsar, would be
especially distinguished by his zeal for ecclesiastical architecture
and decoration.   Hence the innumerable churches which surrounded his residence, and the frequent processions to the
shrines of celebrated adjacent monasteries on the various great
festivals.   Thus, on September 1st, the festival of St. Simeon
*Lyetoprovodets*,† the church and the world together kept New
Year's Day in the square between the churches of the Archangel
Michael and the Annunciation.   The peculiar festival of the
Patriarch of Moscow was the day of St. Peter the Thaumaturge
(December 21st), the first resident metropolitan of Moscow who
did so much to magnify and embellish the city, which was kept
with great solemnity.   On the 19th the patriarch proceeded to
the Tsar's palace to invite the Tsar, the Tsarevich, and the

* *Kreml*, erroneously *Kremlin*—" inner citadel."
† " Bringer in of the New Year."

magnates to a banquet at the patriarch's palace, after attending divine service at the cathedral of the Assumption. On this occasion custom demanded that the host should bless his guests and present them with gifts, usually drinking-cups, rich vestments, gems and precious sables. On Christmas Day it was the Tsar's turn to play the host. On that day, at the fourth hour before dawn, he proceeded to the prison-house to distribute alms to poor prisoners, stopping on his way at the hospital for poor wounded soldiers on a like errand. At the third hour of the night loud ringing began in the Tsar's ante-chamber, where the *protopopes*, or deans, *popes*, or priests, and deacons of all the churches met "to glorify Christ" by singing carols. On the festival itself, after dinner, the Tsar sent "a whole table" to the patriarch, and two dishes, with corresponding bumpers, to the lesser civil and ecclesiastical dignitaries. Another ceremony peculiar to the Eastern Church was "the Jordan," or blessing of the water, at the feast of the Epiphany. On that day, escorted by twelve companies of the *stryeltsui*, or musketeers, in flowered silk robes, the Tsar emerged from the *Kreml*, in full regalia, supported by his chamberlains, and immediately followed by the *postchuchi*, or tappers, with towel and stool. After the *postchuchi* came the Court magnates, the more illustrious of them in costly furs, the rest in cloth of gold, and finally, the soldiers in ceremonial *feryazi*, ample sleeveless, collarless garments, reaching down to their heels. On the ice of the Moskva the procession was solemnly received by the patriarch with his attendant prelates, richly robed, with banners, crosses and censers. After a preliminary service, which to foreigners not inured to the arctic climate seemed a trifle long, the patriarch gave the whole assembly his blessing, the gospel for the day of Christ's baptism was duly sung; the patriarch, supported by two deans, proceeded to a large hole cut into the ice, the water within which had all the while been stirred continually to prevent it from freezing, and stepping into a little floating wooden structure covered with tapestry, blew thrice crosswise over the water, crossed it thrice, and then, taking his crucifix, thrice dipped it slowly into the water, each time letting the water dripping from the end of it fall into a

little silver vessel by his side, and the ceremony was complete.
Finally, omitting more familiar festivals, the Tsar, on Palm
Sunday, participated in a religious ceremony which no Russian
in modern times has ever seen. Proceeding from the church of
the Assumption to the beautiful gate of St. Saviour, with ikons
and crosses borne before and after him, the Tsar and his boyars
made their way through the crowded streets between a double
row of *stryeltsui* to the *Lobnoe Myesto*, or Golgotha, where the
patriarch joined them and distributed palms and willow branches.
The gospel for the day was then read, and the patriarch, holding
the cross in his right hand and the gospels in his left, bade his
clergy go and loosen the ass and bring it to the steps of the
Golgotha. The ass having been brought, the patriarch solemnly
mounted it, and the Tsar leading it along by the end of its
bridle, first handing his sceptre, willow branch, consecrated
candles and napkin to his attendants, the procession returned
to the Uspensky church, headed by huge willow branches in
state sledges, each sledge being drawn by six dark-grey
horses, the *stryeltsui* meanwhile spreading their garments in
the way.

But perhaps there is no more striking instance of the solidarity
of the public and the religious life of old Moscovy than the
elaborate ceremonies on the occasion of a declaration of war.
Take the typical case of the war with Poland, which was proclaimed by Tsar Alexius in 1653. The official address to the
troops began with these words : " It is written that every good
gift and every perfect gift cometh from above, from the Father
of Lights, and greater love hath no man than that he lay down his
life for his friend." Therefore the generals were to receive their
inspirations from on high, and the soldiers were to lay down
their lives for their father the Tsar and their brethren of the
orthodox faith. At the solemn supplication for victory in the
church of the Annunciation it was proclaimed that the Great
Gosudar, hoping in God and the Most Holy Virgin and in the
Moscow Thaumaturges, and having taken counsel of "our Father
and Great Gosudar the Most Holy Patriarch Nikon " (notice
the equality of the chief spiritual and the chief temporal power)
and of the whole sacred synod, and of the boyars, had decreed

and determined to go against his enemy, the King of Poland. After the patriarch had celebrated mass and blessed the generals and officers, the Tsar and the patriarch together proceeded to the ikon of the Mother of God of Vladimir, and the Tsar handed the *voivodsky ukaz*, or plan of campaign, to the patriarch, who placed it, on an altar-cloth, on the *kiota* or glass frame containing the ikon. The generals, thereupon, drew near, and the patriarch thus addressed them : " Take this *ukaz* from the throne of the Lord God and be of unchanging confidence, for God Himself hath said that if ye have faith but as a grain of mustard-seed ye shall move mountains. Go forth, therefore, joyously and courageously, in the name of the Holy Church of God, and of the pious Gosudar ! But and if ye do not obey this *ukaz* of the Gosudar, may your fate be that of Ananias and Sapphira." The Tsar then left the church, leaning on the arms of the boyars, but paused on the steps outside to invite the officers to break bread with him. When they had assembled, he solemnly reminded them of their religious duties during the ensuing campaign. Above all, they were to be merciful to their soldiers as they would answer for it to God, while the subalterns were charged to obey their *voivodes* as if they were the Tsar himself, "living moreover, in all purity and cleanliness as ye know not the day or the hour in which your souls shall be required of you." Meanwhile the *klyuchar*, or keeper of the vestments, having made ready the *khlyeb bogoroditsuin*, or bread of the Mother of God (consecrated wafers in honour of the Blessed Virgin), with the accompaniment of the usual ritual prayers and hymns, drew near and presented it to the Tsar, who partook of "the most holy bread with godly fear." The "cup of the Mother of God " was then also presented to him, and after reverently drinking therefrom thrice, he summoned the generals in order of precedence, who received of the cup from him and retired, after kissing his hand, with due obeisances. The Tsar then took his usual place at the table, all the boyars and *voivodes* still standing before him, and after regaling them with red and white mead, and with vodka, he again exhorted them to be true sons of the Church, especially urging them to communicate themselves, and to compel their soldiers to do so. " And this I tell you

boldly," he concluded, "if ye participate at the deathless table,
the angels of the Lord will encamp about your hosts." Then
came the solemn leave-taking. The commander-in-chief "drew
near to the Tsar's hand," and the Tsar taking his head in both
hands pressed it to his breast, "because of his sincerity, and of
the dignity of his grey hairs, and of his religious and illustrious
character, being wise in the Holy Scriptures and fortunate in
war and a terror to his enemies." Moved to tears by such con-
descension, the *voivode* did obeisance to the ground thirty times
in succession. After dismissing the officers, the Tsar proceeded
to dismiss the soldiers likewise, giving them cups of white mead
with his own hand, the soldiers, in turn, assuring their sovereign
that they would die for him, whereupon the pious and affectionate prince wept for emotion and solemnly assured them
that God, for their good will, would grant them life instead of
death. And so the army departed for a thirteen years' war
in which, unfortunately, the strategy of the Moscovite generals
in the field was by no means as remarkable as their piety
out of it.

But now let us follow the Tsar to Court and see him transact
business, and learn at the same time to know the names and
the offices of his chief servants who had the inestimable privilege
of "beholding his bright eyes," to use the semi-oriental Court
jargon of the period.

Early every morning the gentry and nobility of old Moscovy
were obliged to assemble at Court, the old men coming in
carriages or sledges, according to the time of year, the young
men on horseback. Everyone dismounted some little distance
from the Tsarish Court, and approached the *krasnoe kruil'tso*,
or "red staircase," leading from the great square *na verkh*, or
"upstairs," to the innermost apartments of the Tsar. But only
a select few had the right to go so far and so high. The less
important *molodine*, or "young people,"* remained at the foot
of the staircase awaiting commands from "upstairs." Among
these are to be noticed some of the five hundred *stolniki*, or
chamberlains, the children of fathers in high positions but not of
the first rank, whose office at Court it is to carry dishes to the

* Young in rank, not necessarily in age.

Tsar's table on solemn occasions. They also supplied most of the ordinary envoys to foreign parts, the *voivodes*, or rulers of towns and provinces, and the members of the *prikazes*, or public offices. The *stolniki* were also called *ploshchadniki*, or "people of the square,"* in contradistinction to the *komnatniki*, or "people of the apartments,"† the children of more illustrious parents who served the Tsar in his private apartments. Along with the *stolniki* on the staircase, we also find many of the two thousand eight hundred *stryapchie*, who were employed on less important missions, and the *d'yaki* and *podyachi*, "scribes" and "sub-scribes," men of lowly birth but skilled in affairs, and becoming more and more indispensable with the spread of civilisation. The *d'yaki* and *podyachi* numbered two thousand at least, and forty of them were constantly in attendance at Court. Flitting continually up and down the staircase are the *zhilt'sui*, or gentlemen-ushers, also employed as couriers. All the "young people" respectfully make way for the *boyare*, the *okolnichie*, and the *dumnuie d'yaki* who do not stop on the staircase, but gravely ascend it on their way to the Tsar's ante-chamber. They represent the three highest grades of Russian officialdom. The word *boyar*‡ is as old as the Russian language, the dignity existing in the days when the Russian princes were nomadic chieftains, and the boyars their close comrades and trusty counsellors. The *okolnichie*§ first appeared at a much later date, when a regular Court had become established. They were pre-eminently courtiers, and acted at first as masters of the ceremonies, introducers of ambassadors, and grand heralds. But at a later day they held no particular office, but simply ranked as the second class of the official hierarchy, the boyars being the first. The third grade was held by those who had not yet attained to the *boyartsvo* or boyardom, and yet were members of the Tsar's Council, the *dumnuie dvoryane*, or "nobles of the Council." Attached to these three first grades were the four *dumnuie d'yaki*, or clerks of the Council, erroneously identified by many contemporary foreigners with the imperial chancellors elsewhere, because, practically, they conducted the

* *Ploshchad.*      † *Komnatnui.*      ‡ *Rus. boyarın,* pl *boyare,*
§ *I.e.,* those near the Tsar's person.

whole business of the Council, and being men of great experience, and relatively learned, were the Tsar's principal advisers,
and necessarily enjoyed great influence in a state where the
wielders of the sword could not always handle the pen.   The
*dumnuie d'yaki* first rose to eminence in the reign of Ivan the
Terrible, who, constantly suspicious of the nobles, confided
more and more in these astute upstarts, and in course of time
they came to be regarded as oracles of statecraft.   But in the
Tsar's ante-chamber also there were degrees of privilege and
precedence.   Thus the *blizhnie boyare,* or " near boyars," stood
a little closer to the door of the *komnata,* or "bedchamber,"
than the other boyars, awaiting a favourable opportunity of
entry—a privilege denied to the rest, who had to remain outside.
But at last the outsiders also received the reward of their
patience.   The doors of the bedchamber were thrown open
and the Tsar entered and sat down in a large armchair in the
*peredny ugol,* or " chief corner," where the lamps burned before
the holy ikons, whereupon all present did obeisance to the ground.
The Tsar then beckoned to those with whom he would take
counsel, any absentees being summoned to his presence forthwith,
and severely rebuked for their want of respect.   Those whom the
Tsar did not honour with his conversation drew discreetly aside
while he talked with their more favoured brethren.   Then other
boyars came forward and prostrated themselves to the ground
before the Tsar.   These were petitioners begging leave to
attend christenings, marriages, or other family feasts at their
country-houses.   In all such cases the Tsar carefully inquired
after the health of the boyar and every member of his family,
and gifts were exchanged between them, the Gosudar being
regarded not merely as the master, but also as the father of
his people.   The reception over, the Tsar dined in state with
his whole Court, and after the usual siesta, the rest of the afternoon was devoted to business, each of the *prikazui,* or public
offices, having its allotted day.   Business of unusual importance
was transacted in a general assembly of all the boyars, called
" The Session of the Great Gosudar and his Boyars," the boyars
sitting at a little distance from the Tsar on rows of benches
according to rank, first the boyars, then the *okol'nichie* and then

the *dumnuie dvoryane*, while the *dumnuie d'yaki*, really the most important people there, remained standing unless the Tsar bade them be seated. The Tsar opened the session by asking the opinions of the boyars, but many of them, as a contemporary chronicler quaintly tells us, only "stroked their beards and answered not a word, inasmuch as the Tsar graciously makes many to be boyars not because of their learning, but because of their high birth, wherefore many boyars are ignorant of letters." On very urgent occasions, such as the beginning of a war when extraordinary subsidies were required, *sovyetnuie lyudi*, or "national councils," consisting of representatives of all classes, including the merchants and artificers, were held under the presidency of the Tsar, that they might assess their own burdens and thus have no excuse for subsequent complaint. During the troublous and disastrous seventeenth century, the liberality of these extraordinary popular assemblies had to be appealed to pretty frequently, as we shall see.

All ordinary routine business, on the other hand, was done in the *prikazui*. The difficulty of determining the origin of these, the most salient and characteristic instruments of old Moscovite administration, is due to their very simplicity. From time to time the Gosudar of the day *prikazuival*, or directed, one of his servants to see to this or that affair, gave him a scribe and a sub-scribe to assist him with the necessary clerical work—and a *prikaz*, or "directory," sprang at once into existence. The expenses of the *prikazui* were defrayed by certain towns or districts allotted to them for the purpose, and as the business of administration became more and more extensive and complicated, the numbers of the *prikazui* increased proportionally in the most natural and casual way, often with the oddest results. At the end of the seventeenth century we find more than forty of these *prikazui* in full working order and controlling everything, from the administration of the national finances and the direction of foreign affairs to the furnishing of the Tsar's table, wardrobe, and funeral. Thus the *Kazennui Prikaz*, or "Directory of the Treasury," presided over by a treasurer and two *d'yaki*, looked after the Tsar's gold and silver plate, furs, silk, and cloth, and supplied him with presents for distinguished foreigners or his own

meritorious servants.   Here, too, were to be found the hundred
furriers and tailors employed to make all his clothes, as well as
the costumes of his courtiers and the uniforms of his *stryeltsui*,
except his gloves and stockings, which were supplied by the nuns
of the Novodyevich Convent, who were famous for their skill
in those handicrafts.   The early Romanov Tsars, being both
pious and liberal, were never tired of lavishing gifts of rich silk
stuffs and still richer furs upon visitors from all parts of the realm,
and it was one of the chief duties of the *Kazennui Prikaz* to
honour His Majesty's gracious orders upon his treasury.*   But
who provided the money for the purchase of all these endless
stores of precious gifts?   *That* was the business of the *Prikaz
Bolshago Dvortsa*, or "Directory of the Great Court," where sat
a *boyar*, or an *okol'nichy*, a *dumnui dvoryanin* and two or three
*d'yaki*.   The revenues of more than forty towns were assigned
to this *prikaz*, as well as of eight of the trade sections of Moscow,
viz., the coppersmiths, the tinsmiths, and blacksmiths, the fish-
mongers, the carpenters, the tentmakers, the potters and the
brickmakers, and the taxes derived from these sources were
expended, *inter alia*, in the maintenance of the Tsar's Court.
The "Directory of the Great Court" also had the charge of the
Tsar's thirty cellars, from which it annually supplied him with
one hundred barrels of wine, and four to five hundred of mead
and beer; looked after his three hundred granaries, his fifty
vegetable gardens, and his innumerable orchards; and saw to it
that he regularly received his nuts from Tula or Kaluga, and his
grapes from his vineyards at Astrakhan.   It also dispensed
dishes, by way of gifts, from the Tsar's table to the boyars and
others, and so much was this a matter of course that any
dignitary not receiving his usual dole, appeared next day at
Court, inquired for the pantler, and "with curses" asked him:
"What is the meaning of this?   The Tsar is not angry with me,
wherefore this dishonour?"   Whereupon inquiries would be
made, account-books scrutinised, and the forgetful pantlers and
scullions put in prison for twenty-four hours, or beaten with rods.
Every day three thousand dishes were set on the Tsar's table or

* More than 18,000 clergy are said to have applied to Tsar Alexius for cloth
and furs.

hospitably distributed, the cost of the fish-meats alone amounting in a single year to £100,000.

The *Konyushenny Prikaz*, or "Stable Directory," looked after the Tsar's forty thousand horses. The *Prikaz Tainuikh Dyel'*, or "Directory of Secret Affairs," was under the Tsar's personal control, and it was here that he conducted his private unofficial correspondence. It also had the charge of his falcons, which were fed from a "pigeon court" especially provided for them, containing 100,000 nests. Finally this *prikaz* had a sinister connection with secret affairs of a very different sort, in which the torture-chamber played a leading part. But of this more anon.

The *Posol'sky Prikaz*, or "Ambassadorial Directory," was "over the affairs of the surrounding states," as the Moscovites contemptuously lumped together the rest of Europe. At first it was of very small importance, little more than a passport-issuing office in fact, as foreign affairs were generally settled "upstairs" by the Tsar and his boyars. Not until the period of the Peace of Andrussovo (1669) was the conduct of foreign affairs formally committed to a particular boyar, who took the magnificent title of "Guardian of the great sovereign embassies and of the great sovereign seal." Various remote but important districts had their especial *prikazui*, e.g., the Siberian, the Malo-Russian and the Vladimir Directories. The *Pomyestnoi Prikaz*,\* as its name implies, had the control of the imperial domains. The *Razryadny Prikaz*, or "Directory of Ranks," superintended the administration of the civil and military services, despite the fact that each fresh division of the national forces received its own *prikaz* as it arose. Thus we find the *Stryeletsky Prikaz*, or "Musketeer Directory"; the *Reitarsky Prikaz*, or "Cavalry Directory"; the *Pushkarsky Prikaz*, or "Artillery Directory." The *Schetny Prikaz*, or "Directory of Accounts," regulated the imports and exports; and the *Razboiny Prikaz*, or "Freebooter Directory," caught and punished criminals, of whom robbers and freebooters were then the chiefest. Finally, there were a number of petty *prikazui* with special functions like the *Panikhidny Prikaz*, or "Directory of Masses for the Dead," which saw to it that the proper number of masses for the repose of the Tsar's soul was duly sung.

---

\* From *pomyesti*, an estate.

What strikes one most about the *prikazui* is their primitive, haphazard, character.   In this respect, however, they were true Moscovite institutions, for everything in old Moscovy was more or less casual and patriarchal.   No new thing was ever accepted there unless its rejection threatened instant disaster, and tradition, even in the middle of the seventeenth century, was in some matters a greater autocrat than the Tsar himself.   This tyranny of custom was most noticeable in the theory of the family, which was responsible for the vicious principle known as *myestnichestvo*, or " priority of place," and all its ruinous consequences.

In Moscovy the family was everything, the individual nothing ; nay, more, the individual was unthinkable apart from his family. The elders of every family, the magnates, as we should call them, were responsible for the behaviour of all the younger members of the same family, and bound to punish their misconduct, with stripes and imprisonment if necessary, even when they had reached man's estate.   Further, if one member of a family were condemned to pay a heavy fine, all the other members had to contribute to pay it off, and the elevation or degradation of one member of a family was the elevation or degradation of all the other members.   This principle of family solidarity was carried out to its last consequences.  Ivan Ivanovich, for instance, would refuse to serve under Semen Semenovich if any single member of Ivan's family had ever held a higher position than any single member of Semen's family, otherwise Ivan was held to have dishonoured his whole family, and the honour of the family had to be upheld at whatever cost of suffering to the individuals composing it.   Thus it came about that the Moscovite boyar, slavishly obsequious as he might be to the Great Gosudar in all other things, would rather quit the Tsar's table than sit below any other boyar of inferior family ; rather endure imprisonment, *batogi*,\* or even the terrible *knout* itself than put himself *bez myest'ye*, "out of place," as the phrase went, on any public or ceremonial occasion.   There was no help for it.   He was obliged to stand on his dignity, otherwise all right-minded people of his own order would have regarded him as a renegade, and existence under such a slur would soon have become intolerable.   There

* Flogging with rods.

were sixteen very great families in Moscovy, all of them boyars by prescription; there were sixteen great families who had passed through the intermediate rank of *okolnichy* before they became boyars; but though families of princely rank, descendants of ancient sovereign dynasties, were to be found in both groups alike, any member of any of the families in the first group would have died in torments rather than have yielded precedence to any member of any of the families in the second group, though their actual official rank might be much higher. To such a point was this principle of "priority" at length carried that the members of one family would resort to the most desperate expedients rather than yield precedence to another family, even when it was obviously entitled thereto. Thus in 1663, at a great banquet at the Tsar's table, when Prince George Trubetskoy was placed higher than Nikita Sheremetev, the Sheremetevs, though well aware that the Trubetskoys were an older family than themselves, found it so hard to give way that the eldest member of the Sheremetev family actually petitioned the Tsar against the honour shown to Trubetskoy; but the petition was angrily dismissed. At another banquet at the Tsar's table, on Palm Sunday, 1614, Prince Boris Luikov, rather than give place to the Tsar's uncle, Ivan Nikitich Romanov, refused to sit down, went home, and, though twice summoned to answer for his conduct, refused to come, declaring that the Tsar might punish him with death, but he "would not be less than Ivan Nikitich." Shortly afterwards, on the occasion of the reception of the Persian ambassador, a *ruind*, or guard of honour, could not be formed because the boyars who were to compose it could not agree as to precedence. At last the Tsar, losing patience, sent to inquire the reason of the delay, when it was found that Ivan Chepchyugov declared it would be "out of place" for him to serve with Prince Vasily Romodonovsky, who was not only of a more ancient family but old enough to be his grandfather. Ultimately Chepchyugov was well birched, and forced to apologise humbly to Romodonovsky. Even the great national hero, Demetrius Pozharsky, who had so valiantly saved Moscovy from the Polish yoke, refused, on one occasion, to admit the pre-eminence of the newly-boyared Michael Saltuikov.

R.                                                                                    C

Out of deference to Pozharsky the affair was thoroughly gone into, when it was discovered that Saltuikov's ancestors were undoubtedly superior to Pozharsky's. Pozharsky had nothing to say for himself, so he took to his bed and feigned serious illness. Four years later, when Pozharsky himself was lying at Kaluga on the point of death, the *stolnik*, George Tatishchev, on being ordered to visit him, refused to go, with the usual excuse that it would be "out of place" for him to do so. A severe application of the knout, however, induced the defaulter to change his mind, and he had to convey to Pozharsky not only the Tsar's condolences, but his own apologies. It is obvious how prejudicial to the public service this *myestnechestvo* was bound to be ; during warfare, in particular, it frequently paralysed all military operations. It was no uncommon thing for sub-ordinate officers to refuse to conduct troops to the nearest general because of the inferiority of his family, and petition that they might be sent instead to some other general of higher birth. For the same reason one general often refused to serve under another general even though the Tsar had appointed him generalissimo. The only remedy devisable against this claim for privileged insubordination was for the Tsar to pro-claim beforehand that so long as the war lasted, and so long only, all the officers without exception were to be *bez myestye*, "out of place"—in other words, family rank was not to count during hostilities.

A hard, impassable line, with all the burdens on one side and all the privileges on the other, sharply separated the noble from the non-noble classes in Moscovy. We have seen that in ancient Russia there was no such thing as a feudal system in the Western sense of the term, but when, at last, the princes became rooted to the soil, and Moscow absorbed all the other princi-palities, the members of the old nomadic *druzhina*, or "body-guard," became the *slushnuie lyudi*, or "serving people," of the Tsar, and were bound to render him military service when-ever called upon to do so, receiving in return *pomyest'ya*, or freehold estates, whence their name of *pomyestschchi*, or fief-holders. As the only recognised military order in the realm, they were the Tsar's *muzhui*, or "men," the rest of the population being mere *mushiki,** "little people," whose business it was "to nourish" all the "big people"—in other words, bear all the expense of government and administration, whence also their name of *tyagluie lyudi,* or "people who paid the taxes." These *tyagluie lyudi* were subdivided into numerous classes, according as they dwelt inside or outside the *gorod.*

In the seventeenth century the word *gorod†* still retained its original meaning of an enclosure. Fortresses of all sorts were absolutely necessary in a country so exposed to attack from all sides as was Moscovy, the manning and defending the walls of the *gorod* was one of the chief duties of the population, and the erection of a fortress was the preliminary act of colonisation in every new settlement as the Tsardom encroached on the savage eastern and southern steppes. In the reign of Alexius (1645/76), twenty at least of these *gorodui* were of stone or brick, not including the strong, walled monasteries, often the surest of refuges ; but the majority were of wood, or earth, or of both combined. In remote and dangerous border settlements the *gorod* never developed into a town, but remained a naked fortress, *e.g.,* Cherny Yar and Tsaritsuin. The *gorod* was thus the nucleus of every true town, which gradually grew up around it. Within the *gorod* were the chief buildings, the church, the *prikaznaya izba,* or residence of the *voivoda,* or governor, the powder magazine, the Government granaries, the clergy house, the barracks of the *stryeltsui,* or musketeers, the prison, the "siege mansions" of the country gentry, whither they resorted with their families in troublous times, and similar asylums for the poorer people. Outside the *gorod,* but immediately adjoining it, were the *posadui,* or suburbs, where dwelt the chapmen and artificers. The central feature of the *posad* was the great square, where on certain days the tradespeople exhibited their wares for sale, and around it stood the "guest court," or abode of foreign merchants, the offices of the tax collectors, the wine and spirit magazines, and the *zemskaya izba,* or land office, where local affairs were discussed and settled by the people of the suburb, together with the elders of the outside peasant communities.

* *Lit.* manikins.
† Philologically, the same word as the Scandinavian *gaard.*

Frequently, in exposed situations, the *posadui* also were fenced about with walls and ditches.   Besides the *posadui*, or suburbs, many of the larger towns had *slobodui*, or outlying settlements, attached to them, inhabited by the lesser gentry, or their dependants, or by privileged foreign merchants or mechanics. Thus at Moscow there were the settlements of the *stryeltsui*, the Germans, the saddlers, the potters, and many more.   In secure and well-frequented trade centres like Novgorod, Pskov, and Astrakhan, the suburbs and settlements spread so widely that the *gorod* proper, or *kreml** as it was generally called, became a mere point (though the most important and salient point) in a vast congeries of buildings.   This was notably the case at Moscow, whose vastness and beauty profoundly impressed every visitor who, suddenly, and for the first time, surveyed it from the surrounding heights, the *Vorob'evui Gorui*, or "Sparrow Hills," for instance.   As far as the eye could reach extended the dark masses of its myriads of wooden houses, relieved, at frequent intervals, by the bright gables of the boyars' *khoromui*, or huge timber mansions in the midst of their bright green gardens, and surmounted by countless churches and belfries, whose parti-coloured, gilded cupolas sparkled in the sunlight, while above everything, and the centre of everything, towered the imposing *kreml*, enclosing within its snow-white walls and turreted bastions a whole forest of cathedral churches, whose golden poppy-heads shone like burning lights against the deep blue sky. But a closer inspection of the city was invariably disappointing. Viewed from afar, the disillusioned foreigner would say, it was as magnificent as Jerusalem ; examined in detail it was as poor as Bethlehem.   In the centre of the city, adjoining the *kreml* of which it was an extension, lay the *Kitai-gorod*, or "China town,"* surrounded by a thick and lofty brick wall, whence it derived its name of *Krasnoi* or "Red town."   South of the combined *kreml* and *Kitai-gorod*, and washed by the waters of the Moskva and the Neglinnaya, lay the suburb named *Byel-gorod*, or "White town," from its white wall of circumvallation. These three portions of the city were enclosed by another suburb, the *Zemlyanoi-gorod*, or "Earthen town,"† so called

* Citadel.     † Also called *Skorodom*, or "Soon-Built." *See* Frontispiece.

MOSCOW IN THE XVII CENTURY.

A. THE KREML.   B. CHINA TOWN.   C. WHITE TOWN.   D. EARTHEN TOWN; ALSO CALLED SKORODOM, OR "QUICKLY BUILT.   E. THE SUBURB OF THE STRYELTSUI OR MUSKETEERS.   12. THE GERMAN CHURCH.   14. THE GERMAN CEMETERY.   THE BEGINNINGS OF THE GERMAN SETTLEMENT

from its circle of earthworks.   Eastwards of the *Zemlyanoi gorod* lay the *Stryeletska Sloboda*, or "Musketeer Settlement." The *Nymetskaya sloboda*, or "German\* settlement," where foreigners of all sorts resided, was outside the walls.

The first personage in the *gorod* was the *voevoda*, or governor. His principal duty was to see to the collection of the imperial revenues, but he was also the judge in all civil cases, and the commanding military officer of his district, responsible alike for the defence of the *gorod*, and the supply of the proper quota of troops to the imperial army.

The office of *voevoda* was not very highly esteemed.   Wealthy people naturally regarded removal from Moscow to some distant *voevodstvo* as little better than an honourable exile.   Such posts were generally reserved for inferior or impoverished *sluzhnuie lyudi*.   The *voevoda* received no salary, but was "nourished" by the people of his district, who were obliged to supply him, his staff of *dyaki* and *sub-dyaki*, and his household with food and stores, often in such quantities that, after supplying all his wants, he was able, by selling the surplus at a considerable profit, to lay up a little fortune by the time his three years' term of office was out, especially as he was also entitled to receive fees from all petitioners at his Court, to say nothing of bribes and forced loans.   Innumerable proverbs testify to the injustice and rapacity of the *voevoda*.   Complainants against him had, however, the right of petitioning the *Razryadny Prikaz*, the headquarters of the *voevodui*, or the Gosudar himself, and this right was very freely exercised in old Moscovy both by individuals and by whole communities.   A special public department, the *Chelo-bitenny Prikaz*, or "Directory of Petitions" was appointed to receive such petitions, and thus the Government was enabled, to some extent, to counteract the notorious maladministration and venality of the *voevodui* and *sluzhnuie lyudi*.

The next important official of each district was the *gubnoi starosta*, who was over all criminal affairs.   He had charge of the jails and torture-chambers, but perhaps his most urgent duty

\* The word *Nyemets*, *lit.* a dumb person, or one who could not speak Russian, originally meant every foreigner, but subsequently was limited to people of the Germanic stock.   Thus the Moscovite chroniclers speak of the "Swedish Germans," the "Danish Germans," etc.

was to keep within manageable limits the local vagabonds and
freebooters. He was elected by the gentry, while the inferior
*starostas*, who had to provide for the maintenance of the *voevoda*
and his family were elected by the people of the *posad* and the
surrounding peasantry, who met every year for the purpose in
the *zemskaya izba*. This system of popular local government
was originated by Ivan IV., in the hope of thereby stimulating
public spirit and interesting the people in the work of
administration. But the social conditions of the sixteenth
and seventeenth centuries were unfavourable to the experiment. The poor, ignorant lower orders soon became the mere
slaves of the *voevoda*, though he was forbidden by law to be
present at their assemblies, and it became more and more
difficult to persuade them to act as *zemskie starostas*, or presidents
of the county council, as in their official capacity they were held
responsible for the whole burden of taxation and had to make
up any deficiencies out of their own already sufficiently scanty
private means.

The *tyagluie lyudi*, or "tax-paying people," consisted of the
inhabitants of the *posad*, or trading classes, and the incomparably
more numerous *krest'yane*,* or "peasants," living under the *mir*,
or communal land system, or on the domains of the Gosudar, the
monasteries, or the *pomyestschiki* or land-owners. It was a difficult matter to collect revenue in old Moscovy. So grievous were
the burdens of the tax-payers, that they seized every opportunity
of eluding them by flying to the forest or the steppe and adopting
the easy, careless life of a cossack or freebooter, synonymous
terms in those days. The treasury, at its wits' end for money,
adopted the most rigorous measures to prevent this exodus. In
the middle of the seventeenth century the peasantry was chained
to the soil, and the "suburb people" to their suburbs, the death
penalty being imposed (in 1658) on all who flitted from place to
place. But how was it possible to catch the fugitives in a land,
four-fifths of which was forest or morass? The savage ordinance
remained a dead letter, and served only to emphasise the helplessness of the Government. The position of the "tax-paying
people" was the more helpless, as all privileged and lucrative

* *Lit.* "Christians," as is plain from the older form of the word, *Khristinui.*

offices were practically closed to them, while they were compelled to serve gratis as collectors of tolls, taxes, and imposts of all sorts, or as sworn salesmen, beer and spirit farmers—thankless and even dangerous charges which, as often as not, exposed them to severe punishment in case of default of payment of the pre-assessed sums due from them to the treasury.    They were also the unpaid road-menders, bridge-builders, overseers and police officers of their districts.    They had, as we have already seen, to support the *voevoda* and his family, and all the *voevoda's* sub-ordinate officials and *their* families, supplying them with the very paper they wrote on, and the ink they wrote with.    In war time, as, for instance, during the thirteen years' war with Poland, besides surrendering from a twentieth to a fifth part of all their property, the " tax-paying people " had to supply the soldiers with all necessary stores, as well as with the carts, horses and drivers for their transport ; they also paid for the release of all prisoners, and were responsible for the maintenance of the post stations.    In a word, they paid for everything, and when, in desperation, they protested they could pay no more, they were flogged into compliance at the whipping-post, and this last resource failing, as it often did, their farms or booths were confiscated to the Gosudar.    It is only fair to add that the Government did its best to relieve the tax-payers from what they felt to be the heaviest burden of all, the capricious tyranny of its own officials ; and in those places near to Moscow the *voevodui* and their scribes, generally speaking, " nourished themselves " with moderation because there the Tsar was accessible to the never-neglected petitions of his people.    But in the more distant regions where, as the Russian proverb put it, " God is very high up and the Tsar very far off," the *kormlenshchiki*, or " nourished people," as the quaint phrase went, had free play, and strange and terrible things happened, especially where the *zemsky starosta*, or representative of the people, as frequently was the case, fawned on the *voevoda* instead of " barking at him."    Very often, too, the " lesser people " of the *posad* or the *mir* were obliged to petition the Tsar against the oppression of the " better people," who, whenever they could safely do so, attempted to shift the heavier part of the burden of taxation on to the shoulders of their poorer and weaker brethren.

The misery of the people was made still more miserable by the narrow puritanism of a Government which was, perhaps, the closest approximation to a pure theocracy attainable by human perversity. From the first the Greek Church in Russia had looked askance at every sort of diversion except a moderate table ; but, for some centuries, monastic asceticism was regarded simply as a counsel of perfection highly commendable in the abstract, but by no means of universal application. Even so late as the beginning of the fifteenth century the civil power discreetly stood aside while the people rose up to play. But the standpoint of the Church was never for a moment doubtful, and it is well illustrated by an incident recorded in the life of St. Nifont. The Prince of the Devils, so the legend runs, was one day walking past the House of God with twelve other devils, who, sad and envious at the singing of the people inside, reproached their prince for his carelessness. "If Christ be so praised, our power will soon be clean gone," said they. "Fear not," replied the Prince of the Devils, "in a very little time all this psalm-singing will be over, and the people will fall to with their harps and fiddles and dancing and carousing. Then we shall be greatly exalted, and hell will open her jaws wide for the whole lot of them !" The Church banned all music, profane songs, dances, and games as sheer idolatry, akin to fornication. Draughts and chess were anathematised because they were supposed to be of Chaldean, cards because they were known to be of Latin origin. Dancing bears, hunting dogs and hunting birds, together with jesters, mountebanks and minstrels who "used shameless words" (to wit, all popular, poetical expressions), were also pronounced accursed. Nevertheless, till the middle of the sixteenth century, the people were allowed "to go a-whoring after their own inventions," and then two momentous things happened. In 1551 the Synod of Moscow published its *Stoglav*, or hundred articles, severely condemning amongst other things all popular amusements, while about the same time, Silvester, a priest of Novgorod, published his *Domostroi*, or "Domestic Economy," which aimed at making every household

a monastery, and soon became authoritative in the highest
circles.   But a rule of perfection cannot be universally enforced
in a day even by an autocracy, and it was not till the middle of
the seventeenth century that punitive edicts, in the spirit of the
*Stoglav* and the *Domostroi*, were actually issued.   In 1648 the
young God-fearing Tsar Alexius, then in his nineteenth year,
acting under the influence of the fanatical patriarch Joasaf I. and
his chaplain Vonafitev, began a war of extirpation against the
" diabolical " amusements of the people.   In that year an *ukaz*
was read in every church and market-place in the realm, commanding that all musical instruments were to be broken up and
burnt, and all mountebanks and jugglers were to be whipped for
plying their godless trade, with rods for a first, with the knout
for a second offence.   How sweeping and indiscriminate this
edict really was may be gathered from the nature of some
of its prohibitions.   The people were ordered to go to church
on all Sundays and festivals ; they were forbidden to admit
jesters or soothsayers into their houses ; they were not to gaze
at the moon on the first days of each month ; they were not
to bathe in lakes or rivers during thunderstorms ; they were
by no means to play at cards, draughts, or knuckle-bones ;
they were not to lead about or encourage dancing bears or
dogs ; they were not to sing "devilish " (*i.e.,* popular) songs,
or utter filthy jests ; not to box,* or swing on swings, or leap
on tables, or wear masks.   Thus no distinction was made
between superstitious observances, brutal pastimes, and popular
spectacles ; every sort of diversion was regarded as an orgie.
And yet, oddly enough, the universal and disgusting vice of
drunkenness was left unpunished.   In 1687 the patriarch issued
an encyclical threatening all persistent offenders against the
*ukaz* of 1648 with excommunication in this world and damna-
tion in the next.   It is recorded that in one year, in Moscow
alone, five waggon-loads of musical instruments were collected
and burnt at the usual place of execution behind the marshes.
In 1660 a still fiercer edict confirmed the *ukaz* of 1648, and
ordered that all violators of its provisions should be brought

---

* This particular prohibition was not unwise, as the *kulachky boi,* or "fist
fights," of Moscovy were very brutal and, generally, fatal affairs.

before the *Monastuirsky Prikaz*, or "Monasterial Directory," and summarily punished.

At Court a more liberal spirit timidly asserted itself. There ecclesiastical puritanism found it expedient grudgingly to tolerate what elsewhere it rigorously proscribed, and in the very focus of the religious life of Moscovy the *potyeshna palata*, or "pleasure hall," was an indispensable adjunct of the Tsar's establishment. Here draughts, chess and cards, accursed beyond these privileged limits, were freely indulged in, and a guild of turners, the *shakmatniki*, or "chessmen makers," earned their living by keeping the Court supplied with draughts and chess-men. Nay, the "devilish" organs and other musical instruments let their voices be heard at Court, and thousands assembled outside to listen. We hear of organ players at the Moscovite Court as early as 1490. Tsar Michael's *strement*, or organ, built for him by Johan and Melchoir Lunn, two Dutch masters, was richly coloured and gilded, and a cuckoo and a nightingale on the top of it came out and sang of their own accord. For this masterpiece the Lunns received the relatively enormous sum of 2,676 rubles.* The more frivolous fiddle disappeared from Court in 1626 ; but the *domra*, a stringed instrument on which the *domrachi*, or "minstrels," sang the popular songs of old time heroes, persisted till 1648. The *guselniki*, or itinerant harpers, were only occasional visitors at Court, but must have been highly valued, for we know from the public accounts of the period that they were paid double as much as the *domrachi*. Still more acceptable were the *bakharei*, or "story-tellers," learned in the lore of the old folk-tale, of which the Russian nation possesses such precious stores. In the latter years of his reign, the conscience-stricken Ivan the Terrible could not sleep at night without the ministrations of his *bakharei*, and three of them, all very old men and quite blind, took it in turns, every night, to soothe the tyrant to slumber with their stories. But if the Tsar were in a merry mood, he sent for his fools and jesters, who were the chief delight of "the pleasure hall." The official duty of the fools was to provoke laughter by any means, witty or

* The value of a ruble in Tsar Michael's reign, 1613/48, was estimated at 10s. English.

foolish, so long as it was extravagant or extraordinary. They acted as a sort of moral safety-valve for the society of the day, which, outwardly grave and reverend, was inwardly bubbling over with artificially repressed animal spirits. The fool, as a fool, had the utmost license of expression, and, cynical or absurd as his wit very often was, in that stifling atmosphere of Byzantine stagnation it had, nevertheless, all the bracing effect of a current of fresh air. The fools were of two kinds—mentally deficient persons, kept as curiosities, like the almost equally amusing dwarfs, negroes, apes and parrots ; and humourists of real talent, who were to their audience what comedy and comic literature are to us. The fools of Tsar Michael must have been of the idiotic order, as we hear of them being taken in Holy Week to various monasteries to fast, which would have been unnecessary had they been sensible fools. The fools were of both sexes, and even the abbesses of great monasteries, generally princesses, were not above being entertained by them. Manka, the female fool of Tsar Michael's mother, was very famous, and on her death a memorial hospital was built by her mistress. The usual dress of a jester was a red or yellow *odnoryadka*, an upper sleeveless garment of Tatar cut, with an under-linen caftan, a girdle of red or green cloth, and a fox-skin cap, often with pointed ears. The famous Polish jester, Yushka, received from Tsar Michael, in 1626, a black velvet jerkin with a velvet collar, a bright red atlas caftan with a gold collar, and red cloth trousers with copper buttons. Dwarfs, as rare sports of nature, a species of living doll, were also highly prized. They appealed to the coarse inhuman sense of humour of a semi-savage state of society. Tsar Michael had sixteen dwarfs, Tsar Alexius even more, and Peter the Great, when a child, had six Court dwarfs to play with, and delighted in the society of dwarfs to the day of his death. The dwarfs were dressed in very bright colours, to show them off, preferably sky-blue and crimson, with red or yellow shoes. They were kept apart from the fools in rooms of their own, and had charge of the Court parrots. There is a curious petition extant from the dwarf Ivashka, who, during the great plague at Moscow in 1659, when the deserted city was a wilderness of snow-drifts, was left behind in the *Kreml* in charge "of four parrots and one old one," which he fed for twenty weeks on almond-cakes, and "kept alive and well." "And as regards my patience and the feeding of thy sovereign birds," wrote the dwarf to the Tsar, "is it not all known unto the oven-heater Alexander Boshkov, who visited me every day and examined thy sovereign birds." It is pleasant to learn that Ivashka received the twenty rubles compensation which he had asked for his trouble. We also hear of other curios in the shape of negroes, calmucks, and natural monsters. Tsar Michael had a negro called Muratka, who lived with the fool Moryaga. Tsar Alexius's negro Savelli was taught his letters and his "hours" by the *dyak* Koverin. The Tsarevna Martha was very proud of a legless little girl who was also an excellent teller of tales, while one of the wonders of Tsar Alexius's Court was the armless ikon painter Nikiforov. Another great celebrity was the variety artist, Ivan Loduigui, who amused the Court for ten years. He also taught rope-dancing and drum-beating, for which he received payment in cloth and furs. There is a record of his quarrel with the Tsar's jesters, who tore off the silver buttons of the *odnoryadka* he had received as an Easter gift, for which damage he was compensated by a splendid suit of Persian silk. In Tsar Michael's last days, when age, sickness, and the stern admonitions of the clergy tended to turn the thoughts of the gentle and pious monarch more and more away from this world, we hear far less of "the pleasure halls" and their motley inhabitants, while, during the first twenty years of the reign of his son and successor, the God-fearing Alexius, the inner pastimes of the Court either vanished altogether or put on a semi-clerical garb. The singers, players, and jugglers were banished from Court; the dwarfs and jesters were reserved for only very special occasions; but the Tsar had not the heart to do away with the aged story-tellers, so he kept them at Court in special apartments along with the cripples, the pilgrims, and the very poor, whom every rich Moscovite was bound in those days to maintain as part of his household if he would "save his soul." Alexius entertained a whole hospital of these infirm and needy pensioners. They were called "the upstairs beadsmen," or "the upstairs poor," and the Tsar would often spend whole hours among

them, listening to their talk.    This renunciation was all the
easier as the Tsar had many outdoor amusements to fall back
upon in the shape of hunting and hawking.    There was also the
*medvyez'ya potyeka*, or "bear sport," of several kinds.    The
comic variety was played by means of tame, or "Court bears,"
as they were called, who performed with trained goats.    Still
more stimulating were the bear-fights between *dikie*, or savage
bears, and expert bear-fighters, who encountered the animal in an
enclosed pit with spears or forks.    The most famous bear-
fighters of the seventeenth century were Kondraty Korchanin
and Alexius Merkulev, who for twenty years afforded the Court
excellent sport with little harm to themselves, and the huntsman,
"Blind Andrew," who was paid four times as much as the
others for his exploits because he was blind.    The gentry very
frequently fought bears to amuse the Gosudar, *e.g.*, Ivan
Gundurov in 1628 and Prince Cherkasky in 1631.

If the Tsar was privileged in the matter of amusements, the
ordinary Russian had to be content with the pleasures of the
table.    Junketing was his sole canonical pastime, so to speak,
and he made the most of it, with the natural result that banquets,
which invariably began with an edifying religious ceremony,
usually ended in drunken orgies.    The pious Alexius himself
freely unbent at his own table.    Thus we read that on October 21st,
1674, he gave a grand supper in his "pleasure hall" to his
boyars, clerks of the council, and his confessor, when after
eating "beyond measure," the company were entertained by
German minstrels who played on organs, drums, trumpets and
lutes.    Finally, the Tsar and his guests drank themselves
drunken and staggered from table to bed at an early hour
in the morning.    It is true that this relaxation happened in
the progressive period of Alexius's reign, when he had somewhat emancipated himself from clerical influence, but if such a
virtuous prince could so far forget himself, we can imagine the
sort of thing which would go on in less conscientious house-
holds.    And in truth, travellers were horrified at the habitual
and bestial drunkenness of the Moscovites.    "In no other
country in the world," says the Serb Krijanic, "is such disgusting drunkenness to be found as in Russia.    Men and

women, priests and laymen, roll or wallow about in the muddy
streets, and many drink themselves to death. Spaniards, Turks,
and Italians are thrifty and temperate, Germans are thrifty and
intemperate, but the Russians are both unthrifty and drunken,
and love riotous living." Three-quarters of a century later we
have similar testimony from the Dane Juel. He tells us that at
banquets people ate and drank ten times more than was necessary, and whenever he took a walk he came upon drunken
people fast asleep on the frozen lakes and rivers, or in the snow-
drifts, reminding him of nothing so much as the slain on a
battle-field. At Eastertide in particular, most men got drunk
three or four times a day, and ran about the streets crying
" Christ is risen ! " " so that the noise of singing, swearing, and
excess of all kinds is indescribable, and you will hardly find a
sober man anywhere." And it must be borne in mind that
Krijanic and Juel are friendly witnesses, pre-determined to make
the best of a nation from whom they expected great things.

And unfortunately, in every other respect, the morality of
seventeenth century Moscovy fell far below the by no means
lofty standpoint of contemporary Western Europe. We have
unimpeachable contemporary evidence for asserting that nowhere,
not even in the indulgent East, were unnatural vices regarded
with such careless complacency as among the Moscovites. " Go
and learn shame and temperance from the Turks," Krijanic
apostrophises them. " Those infidels are guilty of similar
offences ; but they have some shame, they do not talk or boast
of them, for fear of punishment, while in Russia people openly
jest about things for which in the Western lands they would be
burnt alive."

Another sign of the lawlessness of the times was the lack of
public security. At Moscow, so late as the reign of Peter the
Great, it was unsafe for the inhabitants to leave their houses
after nightfall, and in Peter's time police regulations were
enforced far more vigorously than they were or could be in
the days of his father, Tsar Alexius. In Western Europe,
during the Middle Ages, many a rock-built castle was a menace
to the passing traveller, but in seventeenth century Moscovy the
same thing might have been said of every large country-house,

not because the boyar who owned it levied blackmail upon wayfarers, but because his hundreds of idle and ill-paid servants were wont to fleece passers-by on their own account during his absence ; while freebooters were so numerous and so audacious that merchants feared to travel along the public roads without a strong escort of *stryeltsui.* Thus we hear that the people of Prince Yury Romodanovsky on one occasion enticed the *starosta* of the goldsmiths' guild into their master's courtyard, beat him to death, killed twenty of his comrades and appropriated all their wares. Again, the mansion of Prince Boris Golitsuin, near Dmitrovka, was so notorious a den of thieves that no man of substance durst pass that way. At last things grew so bad that in 1671 an *ukaz* was issued ordering all the roads within fifty miles of Moscow to be cleared of the bandits who infested them, and by the vigorous application of the wheel and the impalement stake some improvement was effected.

Good manners and good morals by no means go together. The aged Talleyrand used frequently to declare, with a sigh, that the unfortunate mortal who had not lived before 1789 knew not what life really was, for he had never seen society in its most exquisite perfection. Yet this quintessential refinement was but the surface iridescence of an underlying *cloaca* of moral corruption When, however, both manners and morals spring from a common pride and ignorance, they will of course be equally inferior, and this was emphatically the case in Moscovy. The ignorance, coarseness, and insolence of the Moscovites disgusted everyone who approached them. Their very garments were ugly and inconvenient, fettering all free movement and tending to sloth and indolence, while their long unkempt hair gave them a ridiculous appearance, "like wild men of the woods." Their habits at table were extremely filthy. They dipped their fingers indiscriminately into plates and dishes, and drank greedily out of unclean vessels. Christian IV. of Denmark said of their ambassadors on one occasion : "If these people come again we must build them a pigstye, for nobody can live in any house that they have occupied till six months afterwards because of the stench they leave behind them." The boyar Ushakov, and the *dyak* Zaborovsky, sent on an embassy to Vienna in 1613,

grossly insulted all the women they met, and got so drunk that
they nearly set on fire the quarters assigned to them.    In
Holland, the same gentlemen in their tipsy brawls used
language "which could bring nought but dishonour on the
Gosudar," as one of their staff reported.    So disgusted was the
Kaiser with their boorish conduct that he refused to give the
usual golden chains and portraits to "such worthless dogs," and
another embassy had to be sent to him in the following year,
with the Gosudar's apologies.    Even more scandalous was the
conduct of the Russian ambassador to the Court of Christina of
Sweden, to whom his own master wrote : " You do wicked things
in a foreign country of which it is a shame to speak."    As these
" wicked things " included homicide, it cannot be said that the
Tsar exaggerated.    It may be added that foreign ambassadors
to Moscovy were often treated with outrageous insolence.    In
1618 Shah Abbas complained that his envoys were penned up
like cattle.    In 1616, during the negotiations which led to the
Peace of Stolbowa, the    Moscovite envoy Mezetsky openly
accused the Swedish general of withholding the pay of his
soldiers till after the battle, that he might pocket the portion
of the fallen.    During the first half of the seventeenth century
the various envoys from France, Holland, and Denmark were
treated more like convicts than ambassadors, and complained
bitterly and justly of the chicanery of the Russian negotiators.
So little were polite usages understood, that if, instead of being
ordered about, a Moscovite were asked "Would you please to do
this or that?" he would leave it undone altogether, and justify
himself afterwards by declaring that it had been left to his own
choice to do it or not.    Krijanic repeatedly reminds us how
difficult it is to make the Moscovite do anything without using
force, and the humane Juel, a century later, assures us that it
never answers to be too courteous or indulgent in Russia.
Under these circumstances it is not surprising to find men of
superior energy, well aware of the sloth and obstinacy of their
countrymen, frequently taking the law into their own hands.
Thus, in 1620, when a lying petitioner had been condemned to
be knouted by the boyars, the famous *Dumny dyak,** Tomila

* Clerk of the Council.

Lugovsky, suddenly arose, and exclaiming, "Why wait for that?" belaboured the delinquent with a stout cudgel in full council with the complete approval of his colleagues. And Lugovsky was not only a secretary of state, but one of the most honourable and capable men in the Tsardom!

But it is in the family life of old Moscovy that the backwardness of the period is most painfully apparent. This was mainly due to the peculiar position occupied by the women. They were regarded as purely domestic creatures whose chastity would, in some mysterious way, be tainted by any appearance in public. The only exceptions to this rule were the "widow-mothers" with young children, who, till their eldest sons came of age, acted as the heads of their families, and performed many of the functions otherwise regarded as the exclusive prerogative of the men. But the "widow-mother" was, after all, only an occasional and exceptional phenomenon.* In general the Moscovite women were looked upon as permanently immature creatures, and kept under perpetual tutelage. The wife was not the equal of her husband but his pupil. As the first of his domestics she was responsible indeed for the government of his household, and, so far as she did her duty in that respect, might be regarded as her husband's right hand, yet his own hand fell very heavily upon her if she in any way ran counter to his superior wisdom. In case of disobedience he was empowered to chastise her ("unmercifully" in the case of obstinate impenitence), but he was to do it privately. He was also to avoid striking her on the ear, or the eye, or "under the breast with his fist," nor was he to kick her or beat her "with any instrument of wood or iron"; but, short of this, there seems to have been no restriction to his right to inflict corporal punishment upon her whenever he thought fit so to do. The Moscovite lady's complete seclusion from the world was, however, of comparatively late origin. We hear of the *terem*, or "women's quarters," indeed, as early as the eleventh century, but up to the end of the fifteenth century the fair Moscovites seem to have had a considerable amount of liberty, though the monastic ideal of a

---

* A widow without children was regarded on the other hand as even less than an ordinary woman; she was *bogodyelna*, or God's orphan, and a monastery received her.

R.                                                                                    D

perfect household was gaining ground continually. At last the *terem* became a fortress as well as a monastery, and by the beginning of the sixteenth century the domestic incarceration of women was an accomplished and peremptory fact. They were now allowed only to receive visits from their near relatives ; when they travelled it was by night in closely shut vehicles ; even when they went to church they were guarded as jealously as nuns. Only as a mark of extraordinary hospitality would the master of the house occasionally open the doors of his *terem* and reveal to the friends assembled round his table the hidden treasures of his innermost apartments. Then, at his command, his wife and his married daughters came forth in their richest vestments, and, standing in the " chief corner," where the lamps shone before the ikons, made the *malui obuichai*, or " lesser obeisance,* to the guests, who, rising in their places, responded with the *bolshui obuichai*, or " greater obeisance."† Then the master of the house, after doing obeisance to his guests, would beg them to honour him by kissing his wife, while they politely insisted on his first setting them the example. Then the host would kiss his wife on the lips, while the guests saluted her cheeks, each one bowing to the ground to her after his salutation, while she, in her turn, rendered the lesser obeisance to each of them. Then she waited upon the guests with various sorts of wine and spirits, doing obeisance and touching each glass with her lips before presenting it, till all were served, whereupon with a concluding obeisance she vanished once more within her own apartments. As to the general mode of life of the model ladyhouseholder of the early seventeenth century, we shall find an outline of it in the curious and interesting biography of the saintly Julia Lazarenka. Left an orphan by her mother, she was brought up in the house of a worldly aunt, where from the first she exhibited all the virtues insisted upon by the *Domostroi*. Her kinsfolk would have brought her up in the usual way by making her eat and drink from morning to night, but she gave herself up entirely to prayer and fasting—" withdrawn from mirth and all pastimes "—and had a great fondness for weaving and spinning. " All night long her candle never ceased burning,

* *I.t.*, to the girdle.        † To the ground.

for she would be sitting up sewing and stitching for the sick, the widows, and the orphans." As the parish church was two miles from her village, she was unable to visit it till her marriage day. Every member of her household was well clothed and fed ; every one had work allotted him according to his strength ; she never called anyone "by any common name," and would never let any of her domestics pour water over her hands or unloose her shoes, preferring to do such menial offices herself. Only when guests were present did she suffer her servants to stand before her and serve her for the honour of the family ; but when the guests were gone she took up again her daily burden. "When I myself am such a poor creature," she would say, "why should I suffer other people, who are also God's creatures, to stand before me?" "And though she did not know her letters," adds her chronicler, "she always loved to listen to the reading of holy books." The wealthy boyarinya Morozova, whose tragic story will occupy us later,* is a still more illustrious example of a wise house-holder who was also a great saint and martyr, and such women were the very salt of their society, by their example rebuking and arresting corruption. Unfortunately they must, in the nature of things, have been rare exceptions. Perpetual tutelage and an absolute want of culture were almost invincible obstacles to anything like the development of a free and healthy social life in old Moscovy. Moral influences apart, those who have been the longest beneath the yoke of servitude make the most exacting of taskmasters. Thus the attitude of a coarse and recently emancipated young Moscovite towards a weaker and more timid creature than himself, suddenly placed under his absolute control, whom he called his wife, was not likely to be particularly gentle, especially if he had been promised a Rachel and obtained a Leah, a by no means infrequent con-tingency, for, as old Kotoshikin reminds us, "nowhere in the world is there such trickery with regard to maids as in the state of Moscovy."† Domestic misery was bound to happen in nine cases out of ten, when the morally undeveloped wife was thus placed at the mercy of her morally undeveloped husband, and domestic tyranny frequently led to efforts on both sides to sever

* See Chapter V.　　　　† *Sochineniya.* Ed. Grot.

D 2

the unnatural yoke either by violent means, or, at the best, by
the more peaceful process of the tonsure.   Husband-murdering
was frequent in Moscovy, despite the terrible deterrent penalty
of burying alive.   Characteristically enough, the Russian Code,
up to and beyond the middle of the seventeenth century, is
silent as to the punishment to be meted out to a wife murderer.
In 1674, however, a test case arose.   A peasant of the Totemsky
district, Bazhenov by name, murdered his wife for robbing him
of a piece of linen, and then, seized by remorse, gave himself up.
The local authorities, much puzzled, sent the case up to Moscow,
where, after a long search for precedents, it was discovered that
a *stryelets* who had once upon a time killed his wife in a fit of
passion, had had his right hand and his left foot chopped off,
so Bazhenov was treated in the same way.

Such, in the briefest outline, was the state of Moscovy during
the seventeenth century.   It is a dark and distressing picture,
pointing as it does to a condition of things perilously near to
moral and political bankruptcy.   But the fact remains that
Moscovy did not fail, that she emerged from her ruins, regained
her natural boundaries, and succeeded, in the face of heart-
breaking blunders and apparently insurmountable obstacles, in
winning her proper place in the world, as the chief representative
of the Slavonic races.   Such an unlooked-for and complete
renaissance implies the existence, deep down in the heart of
the nation, of a force, a virtue, as incalculable and as inexhaustible
as the natural resources of the country itself.   How that force
was released, developed, and disciplined into a great reforming,
conquering principle, which created a new nation and laid the
foundations of a world-empire hardly inferior to our own, it will
be my endeavour to set forth in the ensuing pages.

TSAR MICHAEL.

# THE GREAT ANARCHY.

## CHAPTER II.

### TSAR MICHAEL AND THE PATRIARCH PHILARET.
#### 1613/45.

Pozharsky and Minin drive out the Poles—Michael Romanov chosen Tsar—
Intense Misery of the Nation—Poverty of the Tsar—Suppression of Zarucki
and other Bandits—Negotiations with the Swedes—Peace of Stolbovo—
Moscovite Missions to Vienna and Stambul—War with Poland—Truce of
Deulina—Return of Philaret—His Early Career—The Diarchy—Marriage
of the Tsar—Philaret's Administration—The Archimandrite Dionisy and the
*i ognem* Controversy—Army Reform— The *Stryeltsui*— Importation of
Foreign Officers—The Chocim War and the Second Polish War—Death
of Philaret—Relations with the Porte—The Azov Affair—The Wooing of
Prince Waldemar—Death of Tsar Michael.

AT the beginning of the seventeenth century the Tsardom of
Moscovy seemed to be in the throes of political dissolution.
With the "withering away of the last flower of the land of
Russia," as the old chronicle pathetically describes the death
of Tsar Theodore I. (1598), the line of Rurik, which had ruled
Russia for centuries, came abruptly to an end; and within the
next thirteen years no fewer than four usurpers (two of them,
Boris Gudunov and the pseudo-Demetrius, men of genius
unhappily born out of their time) flit like shadows across a
scene of ever-darkening turbulence. With the disappearance
(1610) of the last of these usurpers, Vasily IV. (Shuisky), into
a monastery, the horrors of an interregnum were added to
Moscovy's other disasters, and during the next three years her
ever hostile neighbours, Sweden and Poland, disputed with each
other for the possession of the disintegrated realm. But
deliverance was at hand. In Kuz'ma Minin, a butcher of
Nizhny-Novgorod, and his comrade the boyarin Prince
Demetrius Pozharsky, stimulated and supported by the power
of the Church as represented by the noble-minded Archimandrite
Dionisy, Moscovy found, at last, liberators from the yoke of
the mercenary and the alien. On October 24, 1612, the

remnant of the Polish garrison surrendered to Pozharsky, and
on the following day the triumphant Russians, preceded by the
clergy carrying the crosses and ikons, passed through the open
gates of the *kreml'* and gave thanks to God in the church of
the Assumption. Circular letters were immediately sent forth
to all parts of the Tsardom inviting freely elected deputies from
every class of the population to assemble at Moscow ; and after
three whole days spent in fasting and supplication, this national
assembly met to elect a native Tsar. The magnates could not
agree among themselves as to a candidate, but the gentry and
the common people were from the first in favour of the youthful
Michael Theodorovich Romanov. The Romanovs, though
they appear in Russian history as early as the last quarter of
the thirteenth century, were by no means the most ancient
or illustrious patricians in Moscovy, but no other noble house
had such a clean and blameless record. And the family was
popular as well as pure. Michael's grandmother, the saintly
Anastasia Romanova, the first of Ivan the Terrible's seven
consorts, and Michael's grandfather, Nikita Romanov, Ivan's
most valiant captain, still lived in the popular memory, while
his father, Archbishop Philaret, whom Sigismund of Poland had
treacherously detained as a hostage during the last three years,
was justly regarded as a martyr for patriotism and orthodoxy.
Had not Philaret been a churchman there can be little doubt
that he would have been elected Tsar, but failing him, the
electors decided in favour of his son. On February 21 the
national Council proceeded to the Red Square to submit the
candidate to the choice of the people, but their announcement
was anticipated by the shout of the thousands assembled there,
who cried with one voice: "Let Michael Theodorovich Romanov
be the Tsar-Gosudar of the realm of Moscovy and the whole
state of Russia!" Thus the first Romanov Tsar was unanimously elected by the deliberate choice of the whole Russian
nation.

And the possibility of such an election was an even more
remarkable and encouraging fact than the election itself. It
was the symptom of awakening public spirit, the presage of a
better order of things. The people of Moscovy had learnt from

terrible experience the meaning and the consequences of discord and division. They now proved that they possessed sufficient moral strength and courage to profit by their discipline. They had risen superior to all personal or local considerations, and, after purging the capital of foreign foes, had placed themselves unreservedly beneath the sceptre of an autocracy as being the best conceivable government for themselves under the circumstances. Their choice, at such a time, of an inexperienced youth of sixteen to be their Tsar, demonstrated that it was not so much the person of the monarch as the principle of monarchy for which they voted. It is not too much to say that the renaissance of Russia dates from the quinquennium (1613/18) during which the great men of the realm exclusively devoted themselves to the patriotic duty of guiding the footsteps of their young Gosudar, and rallying all the recuperative elements of the nation around the newly established throne.

And now, having elected a Tsar, the next thing was to find him. Not till March 13/24 did the delegates of the Council discover the young prince in the Ipatievsky Monastery near Kostroma under the guardianship of his mother, Martha Romanovna. On the following day they proceeded in solemn procession to the monastery and besought Michael not to despise the tears and groans of orthodox Christian Russia, which by the will of God had elected him Gosudar, but hasten to his Tsarish throne at Moscow and deliver the remnant of his people from their tribulations. But neither mother nor son would accept the dangerous gift. Michael, " with tears and great wrath," repulsed the petitioners. Martha protested that her son was too young and tender for so difficult an office, and bitterly laid upon the disloyalty of the boyars in the past all the blame for the present dilapidation of the realm. From the third to the ninth hour the boyars entreated Michael to accept the throne, and he only yielded at the last moment when they solemnly declared that if he persisted in his refusal they would hold him responsible to God for the utter destruction of Moscovy. Then he suffered them to kiss his hand and promised to come to Moscow.

Michael may well be pardoned for his hesitation. Rarely has

any European country been in such desperate straits as Russia was in 1613. The Swedes occupied all her Baltic provinces, as well as Novgorod, her commercial metropolis. The Poles held all her western and most of her central provinces. Savage hordes of Tatars and Cossacks swarmed in every direction, leaving a smoking wilderness behind them. In the extreme north thousands of native freebooters and vagabonds pillaged, burnt, and slew. In the extreme south-east Zarucki, the last of a long line of pretenders, aimed at carving out a kingdom of his own on the Volga. From every quarter of the Tsardom came tales of woe. The *voevodui* of Archangel and Cholmogory reported that throughout the whole district all the churches of God had been profaned, all the cattle killed, all the villages burnt, and those of the inhabitants who had escaped from the freebooters were freezing and starving to death in the forests and morasses. On the banks of the Onega alone nearly 3,000 mangled and mutilated corpses strewed the ground.*

Travellers entering Moscovy from the west had tales of equal horror to tell. They found every village between Reval and Novgorod destroyed by the Cossacks, and before they could shelter from the extreme cold in the ruined wayside huts, they had to empty them of the corpses of their former owners, often the terrible stench drove them back again to the snowdrifts. But Tsar Michael had no need to be told of the misery of his people; he could see it with his own eyes. On his way from Kostroma to Moscow, every day he encountered hundreds of people of all classes robbed to the skin, maimed, bleeding, and blinded, or covered with bruises and sores. On reaching the great Troitskaya Monastery, some seventy-five miles from the capital, he refused to go any further till something had been done to stay this effusion of blood. But in truth it was not so much horror as penury that detained him. Not only was he unable adequately to mount and equip his retinue and attendants, but the boyars could not provide suitable quarters for him at the *kreml'*, because the palaces were without roofs and windows and there was no money in the treasury to pay carpenters for repairing them. In his

* Sipovsky: "Rodnaya Starina," III., 1.

extremity Michael was compelled to beg the wealthy mercantile house of Strogonov, "for the sake of Christian peace and quiet," to lend him money, corn, fish, salt, cloth, and all manner of wares to pay, feed, and clothe his soldiers. At last, on May 2/13 the Tsar was brought into Moscow by the whole of the male population, which had gone forth to meet him, and on July 11/22 he was solemnly crowned in the church of the Assumption. It was on this occasion that the brave butcher Kuz'ma Minin was ennobled by the Tsar.

The first care of Michael and his Council was to clear the land of robbers. The material means for doing so were obtained by a general contribution in money and kind, collected with the utmost difficulty by agents accompanied by soldiers, and additionally fortified by the authority of the Church, which threatened the backward and the disobedient with excommunication. The attempt to re-establish law and order was naturally resented by all the native freebooters, whose very element was anarchy. The most dangerous and audacious of these ruffians was the Cossack Zarucki, calling himself Tsar Demetrius Ivanovich, who had married Marina, the widowed Tsaritsa of the pseudo-Demetrius, conquered Astrakhan, and set up a court of misrule there. It was his practice to ride about the city with a bodyguard of 500 Nogai Tatars, on a charger whose silver stirrups were made from the censers of pillaged churches, and he levied blackmail indiscriminately on the Russian and Persian merchants in the bazaars, with the usual accompaniment of torture and murder. He meant to extend his sway by capturing Kazan and Samara, but was defeated and taken prisoner on June 16/27, 1614, and impaled at Moscow. Three months later a large Cossack host, which had advanced against Moscow itself, was routed and dispersed on the banks of the Luzha by the boyars Luikov and Boyashev. For some years to come robber bands were to continue to pillage the central and south-eastern provinces of Moscovy, but after the fall of Zarucki, and the rout on the Luzha, they ceased to be a peril to the state.

The aliens, who occupied between them one half of the Tsardom, had next to be got rid of, and, as it now became clear that the Poles would be the most difficult to dislodge, it was resolved to treat with the Swedes first.

Sweden had originally intervened in Moscovite affairs as the ally of Tsar Vasily Shuisky, who, by a secret clause in the Treaty of Viborg (February 28, 1609), had promised her, by way of compensation, the province of Kexholm. But when the Poles conveyed Vasily a prisoner to Warsaw, and proclaimed their own Korolowicz, or Crown Prince, Wladislaus, Tsar of Moscovy, in the very *kreml*, Sweden had no longer any legal status in the country, and was compelled to look after her own interests, for, as a Protestant state, she could not view with indifference Russia and Poland united beneath the hostile sceptre of the Catholic line of the House of Vasa, which claimed Sweden likewise. Accordingly she proceeded to appropriate the defenceless Baltic provinces of Moscovy which lay ready to her hand. In the summer of 1611, Great Novgorod, in the beginning of 1612 Nöteborg, the key of the Neva, fell, and by the end of the year she had also secured Yama and Gdov, on the eastern shore of Lake Peipus, and Narva and Ivangorod, in Ingria. So hopeless did the prospects of Russia seem at this time to the Russians themselves that Novgorod was willing to recognise Prince Charles Philip, Gustavus Adolphus's younger brother, as the Grand Duke of a separate Russian state, extending from the Baltic to the White Sea, and united with Sweden as Lithuania was with Poland.* The election of Michael Romanov dispelled this dream of a Scandinavian Empire. Naturally enough, Novgorod, despite the presence within her *kreml'* of a Swedish governor, now looked to Moscow for orders. "You would destroy our souls, but we will not be separated from the realm of Moscovy,"† was the fearless reply of Prince Nikifor Meshchersky, the representative of the Novgorodians, when the Swedish governor, Evert Horn, demanded from him an oath of allegiance, not to Charles Philip, who had, in the meantime, abdicated the throne of Novgorod, but to Gustavus Adolphus, as King of Sweden. Meanwhile Tsar Michael had not been idle. In June, 1613, Aleksyei Zyuzin had been sent to England

* Veibull : "Sveriges Storhetstid," pp. 52—69.
† Solovev: "Istoria Rossy," vol. IX., chap. I.

for assistance. James I. received the envoy with great courtesy, and despatched a special envoy, John Merrick, to mediate between Sweden and Moscovy. He arrived in 1614, by which time Sweden was almost as anxious for peace as Moscovy. Her position at Novgorod, amongst a hostile and patriotic population, was growing every day more precarious, and the failure of Gustavus Adolphus to take Pskov, the bulwark of Moscovy against Lithuania, heroically defended against him by Vasily Petrovich Morozov and Theodore Buturlin from July to October, 1615, lent double weight to the warnings of Oxenstjerna, who declared, peremptorily, that placed as they were betwixt numberless enemies and faithless friends, with many debts and little money, it was not merely unreasonable, but impossible, to wage war with Moscovy and Poland at the same time.* The negotiations lasted, with frequent interruptions and perambulations, from January 14, 1616, to February 17, 1617. At first the Swedes demanded the whole of the vast province of Novgorod, besides Ingria and Kexholm, while the Moscovites would not concede an inch of territory. Merrick, stimulated by the vain hope of obtaining subsequently from the Tsar for England free trade with Persia by way of the Volga, access to the East Indies *viâ* the river Ob, the monopoly of the seal fisheries in Nova Zemlya, and other minor privileges, did his utmost to obtain tolerable terms for Moscovy. On September 25 he offered Sweden the fortresses of Ivangorod, Yama, Koporye, and 100,000 rubles, so as not utterly to shut Moscovy off from the sea, but the Swedish plenipotentiaries stood out for the coast on both sides of the Neva. Only with great difficulty did he persuade them to relinquish even Novgorod, Rusa, Gdov, and Porkhan. Finally, on March 10, 1617, the definitive treaty was signed at the now extinct town of Stolbovo, to the satisfaction of both parties. At Moscow, "the surrender of a few places," even though they included Nöteborg, the key of Finland, at the junction of the Neva with Ladoga, and three other fortresses in Ingria, was regarded as a trifling matter compared with the retrocession of Great Novgorod, and the recognition of Michael as Tsar of Moscovy. The Moscovite Government does not

* Oxenstjerna's letter to Evert Horn, cited by Solovev : "Istoria," XI., 1.

seem to have recognised the fact that the total loss of the Baltic sea-board meant the domination of Sweden in the north. Gustavus Adolphus, like Peter the Great at a later day, had an open eye for its immense importance. " I hope to God," he declared to the Swedish Riksdag in 1617, "that it will be difficult for the Russians to skip across that brook* in future;" and we are told that had he taken Pskov as well as Novgorod he meant to have shifted the capital of his empire from Stockholm to Narva, as being more central.†

Meanwhile Moscovy was at open war with Poland. Negotiations, opened in September, 1615, under the mediation of the Imperial ambassador, Erasmus Gandelius, had been broken off in January, 1616, amidst fierce recriminations, the Moscovites absolutely refusing to accept Wladislaus Vasa as Tsar, and the Poles as obstinately declining to recognise Michael Romanov. Every effort had been made by the Tsar to incite the Kaiser and the Porte against Poland, and many humiliations had been endured by the Moscovite ambassadors both at Vienna and Stambul. At first the Kaiser had ignored Michael's very existence, and in August, 1614, Ivan Thomin appeared at Vienna to express, in the Tsar's name, surprise "that you, our brother, should have treated us so contrary to all custom by sending us a letter addressed to nobody." When Thomin presented his sovereign's salutation to the Kaiser, Matthias, instead of rising at the mention of the Tsar's name, simply raised the corner of his hat, wherefore Thomin, in taking his leave, bowed only to the girdle instead of to the ground. The master of the ceremonies, aghast at such an act of disrespect, asked Thomin how he durst insult the Emperor by asking him to rise at the name of the Tsar. "Had you used such language to the Emperor Rudolf," he added, "you would have been thrown out of the window." Thomin replied, with spirit, that he had acted according to the Tsar's instructions, and that ambassadors ought not to be treated as slaves. He was detained at Vienna eighteen months that the Austrian ministers might see how the Tsar's affairs progressed , but his firmness produced such a good effect that, subsequently, the Emperor explained that gout in the feet

* *I.e.*, the Baltic.　　† Veibull : "Sveriges Storhetstid," p. 69.

had prevented him from rising, and he even asked the ambassador whether Tsar Michael would be disposed to accept the hand of one of the Austrian archduchesses in marriage. It was now Thomin's turn to stand on his dignity. " The Tsar's intentions," he replied, " are in the hands of God and known to God alone." On the arrival of another Moscovite envoy, Lukyan Myasny, in June, 1616, the Kaiser was mollified by a present of a precious lynx-skin and forty sables. The ambassadors returned in 1616 with the reassuring tidings that Matthias meant to give no assistance whatever to the King of Poland.

" Soft furniture," as the precious pelts of Moscovy were called in the diplomatic jargon of the day, were also of material assistance to the negotiators who were dispatched to the court of Sultan Achmed of Turkey in August, 1615, to urge the Porte to invade Poland from the south, while Moscovy attacked her from the west. At first the raids of the Don Cossacks, who were just then engaged in one of their periodical piratical expeditions against Sinope and Trebizond, so enraged the Grand Vizier that he threatened the Moscovite envoys with death. They pleaded, as usual, that the Don Cossacks were escaped criminals and freebooters over whom the Tsar had no control; but it took no fewer than seven forties of sable-skins to persuade the Vizier of the correctness of their arguments, and no sooner had he been won over than he was superseded by Halil Pasha, who had to be bought in the same way, but proved far more difficult to convince, and consequently ten times dearer than his predecessor. At last, after a detention of thirty months, the ambassadors were allowed to return home with the joyful intelligence that a large Turkish army was assembling on the Polish frontier with the intention of attacking the fortress of Hotin.

Nevertheless, Moscovy had to bear the brunt of the struggle with Poland alone. The new Sultan, Osman, though burning to avenge himself on Poland for the ravages of the Cossacks, was actually embroiled in a war with Persia, so the Polish Republic, leaving her undefended southern borders to the care of Providence,* in April, 1617, voted supplies for one year to the Korolowicz Wladislaus, and sent him forth with the heroic

* Sokolowski: " Dzieje Polski," pp. 849—851.

veteran Karol Chodkiewicz as his mentor, to conquer and
incorporate Moscovy. " I depart," said the chivalrous youth,
after Gustavus Adolphus certainly the most amiable prince of
the House of Vasa, " I depart having in view, first of all, the
glory of the Lord my God and of the Holy Catholic Religion,
and then the honour of the Republic, which hath nourished me
hitherto and now sends me forth on the path of glory, and I will
show my gratitude by conquering Northern Europe and adding
it to her territories."* Terror fell upon the commandants of
Central Russia at his approach. Dorobuzh opened her gates
to him, as Tsar of Moscovy, in September, and in October
he made his triumphal entry into Vyazma. From thence he
sent a letter to Moscow by the renegade Adadurov, reminding
the boyars that they had already sworn fealty to him as a minor,
and informing them that he was now coming to claim his sceptre.
To all who should obey him he would show mercy, not excluding
even " Michael the son of Philaret." This letter produced no
effect. The cowardly *voevodui*, who had fled to Moscow proclaiming that all was lost, had already been knouted and
banished to Siberia. Moscow was placed in a state of defence.
The national hero, Demetrius Mikhailovich Pozharsky, took the
field against the Poles, and his cousin, Prince Demetrius Petrovich,
was sent to hold Tver. After wintering at Vyazma, Wladislaus,
against the advice of the experienced Chodkiewicz, advanced
upon Moscow ; but his progress was retarded by the mutiny of
his unpaid troops, the Polish Diet, with its usual fatal parsimony,
having sent reinforcements without the still more necessary
money and supplies. Nevertheless, despite all the efforts of
Pozharsky to prevent it, Wladislaus effected his junction on the
Oka with 20,000 Cossacks whom the Hetman Sahajdaczny had
hurried to his assistance, and on October 1/12, 1618, he made a
night assault upon Moscow which was repulsed with heavy loss
to the Poles. Dread of the approaching winter, and the miserable
condition of his half-clothed, half-starved, and more than half-
mutinous army, then compelled Wladislaus to open negotiations
with the Moscovites. At first the Poles demanded instant and
unconditional surrender. The Moscovites should make haste,

* Solovev : " Istoria Rossy," vol. IX., chap. I.

they sneered, as otherwise they would have nothing left but earth and water. The boyars steadily refused to admit the claims of Wladislaus, but an increasing ferment among the inhabitants of Moscow and the desertion of 3,000 Don Cossacks so far depressed them that they sent plenipotentiaries to the village of Deulina, three versts from the Troitskaya Monastery, and after negotia· tions protracted from Nov. 23/Dec. 4, 1618, to Feb. 2/13, 1619, during which the Moscovites were humiliated to the uttermost, a truce of fourteen years and six months was concluded, each party surrendering too much to consent to a definitive peace. The Poles provisionally recognised Michael as Tsar of Moscovy, while Michael surrendered to the Republic a large tract of his central provinces extending from Byelaya in the north to Chernigov to the south, both inclusive, with the fortresses and towns of Smolensk, Starodub, and Novgorod Svyersky; thus bringing the Polish frontier appreciably nearer Moscow. The Truce of Deulina is interesting historically as marking the furthest extension of Poland eastwards.

The most important result of the Truce of Deulina was the return from exile of the Tsar's father, the Metropolitan of Rostov.

Theodore Romanov, the second son of the boyarin Nikita Romanovich, was born about 1553. The handsome, high-spirited youth, who won the hearts of the people by his frank *bonhomie* and the respect of the learned by his erudition (he was one of the half-dozen Moscovites of his day who knew a little Latin), seemed from the first to be marked out for a high career. During the reign of his first cousin, Theodore I.* Theodore Romanov equally distinguished himself as a soldier and as a diplomatist, fighting against the Swedes in 1590, and conducting negotiations with the ambassadors of Kaiser Rudolf in 1593/4. On the death of the childless Tsar in 1598 he was the popular candidate for the vacant throne, and it was even rumoured that Theodore on his death-bed had appointed his cousin his successor. Nevertheless, he acquiesced in the election of Boris Gudunov and shared the disgrace of his too powerful family, three years later, when Boris compelled both him and

* Theodore I. was the son of Anastasia Romanova, Theodore Romanov's aunt.

his wife, Ksenia Chestovaya, to take monastic vows under the names of Philaret and Martha respectively, Michael, their sole surviving son, being at the same time imprisoned with his aunt, Nastasia, at Byelozera. Philaret, as we must now call him, was kept in the strictest confinement in the Antoniev Monastery, where he was exposed to every conceivable indignity; but when, in 1608, that genial impostor the first pseudo-Demetrius overthrew the Godunovs, he released Philaret and made him Metropolitan of Rostov (1605). Philaret, in 1609, fell into the hands of the Thief of Tushino, as the second pseudo-Demetrius is generally called, who named him Patriarch of all Russia, and he actually exercised the patriarchal office over the very limited area which acknowledged the pretender. On the flight of the second pseudo-Demetrius, Philaret found his way, in 1610, to Moscow, and was sent from thence on an embassy to King Sigismund, of Poland, at Smolensk, but refusing to acknowledge either that potentate or his son Wladislaus, Tsar of Moscovy, he was detained and transported to Lithuania, where for the next eight years he remained an unwilling guest in the mansion of the Sapiehas.* The tidings of his son's election was, at first, by no means welcome to him, and he hinted pretty plainly that a better Gosudar might easily have been chosen from among the other boyar families. Whether his disapprobation was due to pique or anxiety it is difficult to determine. Anyhow, on returning to Moscovy he both gratified his own ambition and served his country by reigning conjointly with Michael.

On June 14/28 Tsar Michael and his boyars, escorted by crowds of people, went forth from Moscow to welcome Philaret. Five miles from the city, on the banks of the river Pryesna, father and son met again after a separation of nine years. The meeting was an affecting one. Both the Tsar and the archbishop went down on their knees and remained in that position for a long time dissolved in tears. Ten days later, Philaret submitted to be enthroned as Patriarch by Theophanes, Patriarch of Jerusalem, and the prelates of the Russian Church, and henceforth, till his death in 1633, the established government of Moscovy was a diarchy. During these fourteen years there were two actual

* See Kizevetter : "Filaret."

Gosudars, Michael Theodorovich, and his father the Most Holy Patriarch Philaret Nikitich. Theoretically they were co-regents. Foreign ambassadors presented their credentials to them together and simultaneously, the only distinction being that while the Tsar occupied his throne, the patriarch, in equally resplendent robes, sat at his right hand in a golden chair. Each potentate replied separately to the ambassadors,[*] and gave and accepted separate gifts. In private letters Philaret invariably addressed his son as " Your Majesty," and the name of Michael preceded that of his father in all public documents ; but, on the other hand, Philaret frequently transacted affairs of state alone and without even consulting the Tsar.[†] Naturally, the domination of the experienced and energetic patriarch was deeply resented by the *clique* of courtiers who had hitherto been nearest to the young Tsar, but who, if influence should be accompanied by ability, had no right to be near him at all. These dispossessed self-seekers loudly exclaimed against the ambition and the cruelty of Philaret, who, they said, oppressed the boyars and terrorised the Tsar himself. But all those who hated anarchy and loved good government welcomed the advent to power of an enlightened statesman who protected the weak against the tyranny of the strong, and was gracious to all men of learning and ability irrespective of birth or rank.[‡]

The first care of the patriarch was to secure the succession by getting the Tsar married. Before his arrival Michael had been betrothed to Maria Khlopova, but just as she was about to be proclaimed Tsaritsa she was suddenly discovered to be an incurable invalid, and consequently injurious to the Tsar's health, whereupon the unfortunate girl, and her whole family, were incontinently banished to Siberia. Philaret was bent upon raising the dignity of the new dynasty by securing a consort for his son from a foreign sovereign house, and embassies were sent to Copenhagen and Stockholm for the purpose. But Christian IV. of Denmark refused even to receive the Moscovite envoy, while

* " Verhaal van de nederlandsche gezanten Burgh en Veltdrich," 1630 31, which contains a very full account of an audience with Michael and Philaret.

† Kizevetter.

‡ Solovev : " Istoria Rossy," tom. IX., chap. I.

Gustavus Adolphus, on hearing that his sister-in-law, Catherine of Brandenburg, the lady selected by Philaret, would first have to be re-baptised into the orthodox Church, declared, with a bigotry not inferior to that of Philaret's, that the princess should not sacrifice her soul's salvation even for the Tsardom of Moscovy. Philaret then fell back upon the original bride, who, in the meantime, had cautiously crept back from Tobolsk to Nizhny Novgorod. Suspecting treachery, he ordered the state of her health to be examined medically, when it came to light that her pretended illness had been a trick of the rival Saltuikov family, who had temporarily injured her digestion by hocussing her vodka.* The Saltuikovs were promptly banished to Siberia for "interrupting the Tsar's wedding and pleasure," and the whole incident serves to show us what sort of people surrounded the young Tsar before the arrival of his father. The victimised lady received a handsome maintenance by way of compensation, but the Tsar, to please his mother, married, instead of her, the Princess Maria Dolgorukaya, who died within a year of her espousals, whereupon he gave his hand to Eudoxia Stryeshnevaya, the daughter of a small squire, who thus became the matriarch of the Imperial Romanovs.

Philaret's administration must be judged rather by its intentions than its results. The dilapidation of the land was too great, its resources were too inadequate, to admit of anything more than an attempt to lay the foundations of a better order of things, and this Philaret conscientiously endeavoured to do. His first care was to replenish the treasury by means of a more equable system of assessing and collecting the taxes. Petitions from all quarters of the land had revealed a shocking state of tryanny and peculation. The tax collectors had habitually exempted those who were rich enough to bribe them from their due share of the public burdens by overtaxing the poorer people. This abuse was partially remedied by the compilation of new land registries and the appointment of tax assessors from among the taxpayers themselves. The necessities of the Government were so great that money had to be raised by every possible means. In return for small loans, English merchants were

* Solovev: "Istoria Rossy," tom. IX., chap. I.

allowed to trade* in Russia toll free, to the great detriment of
the poor and struggling native traders; the inns and public-
houses were made Government monopolies and farmed out to
speculators from Moscow, and fresh imposts, often of the most
inquisitorial and vexatious character, such as the taxes on trading
booths, laundries and watering-places for cattle, were levied on
the already overtaxed people. The most important measures
of domestic reform were the extension of the *prikaz*† system
so as to make the administration more definite and precise, and
the chaining of the peasantry to the soil. This latter measure
was directed against the increasing migration of the peasants
both in the interests of the smaller proprietors, who complained
that their serfs were in the habit of flying to " the strong
people,"‡ who refused to surrender them, so that the former
masters were no longer able to cultivate their estates; and also
and specially in the interests of the Government itself, which often
lost thereby thousands of taxpayers, inasmuch as the peasants
frequently abandoned their land and their families altogether,
fled to the steppes or the forests, and there took to the more
lucrative trade of freebooter. A perambulatory commission was
appointed by Philaret to inquire into the condition of the various
districts, remit taxation wherever necessary, but at the same time
to use every effort to bring the fugitive serfs back to their original
dwelling-places. Hitherto, the rights of the oppressed peasantry
had to some extent been safeguarded by the fixing a time
limit within which they might be recovered by their former
owners. By the *ukaz* of 1597 this had been fixed at five years,
subsequently it was extended to nine, eleven, and at last to
twenty years. But now, yielding to the earnest solicitations of
the gentry, the Government authorised them to recover their
fugitives without any time limit being fixed. On the other hand,
the taxation of those of the Tsar's *slyuzhnuie lyudi*, who lived in
the *posad*, was the first step towards the proportional taxation
of the hitherto privileged classes.

The severe economical policy of Philaret was entirely due to
the distress of a Government which was obliged to raise as much

* But they were not to export silk or import tobacco.
† See Chapter I.                    ‡ *I.e.*, the larger proprietors.

money as possible by whatever means. In other respects his administration was obviously progressive, and this especially applies to his efforts on behalf of education and Church discipline. It is true that, as compared with the great reformers of the next reign, Nikon, Orduin-Nashchokin and Matvyeev, he was a strict conservative. His zeal for the purity of orthodoxy sometimes led him into regrettable excesses, as, for instance, his insistence on the re-baptism of converts from Catholicism, and his burning (1627) of the "Uchitelnoe Evangelie" of Kirill Stavrovetsky, which really contained nothing heretical.[*] On the other hand, he encouraged the publication of theological works; formed the nucleus of the subsequently famous Patriarchal Library, and instituted a special department for the revision of liturgical books. Numerous were the new editions published for distribution among churches and monasteries, or for sale in the book booths of Moscow, many of them edited, or revised, by the patriarch himself. He also commanded that every archbishop should establish a seminary in his palace, and he himself founded a Greco-Latin institute in the Chudov Monastery. It was Philaret, too, who renewed the relations of Moscow with the Eastern orthodox Churches, and encouraged learned Greeks to settle at Moscow to instruct the orthodox clergy. How necessary the vigorous intervention of this severe but equitable archpastor in Church matters really was may be gathered from the curious story of the *i ognem*[†] controversy which agitated Moscow at the beginning of Tsar Michael's reign.

If there was one man in Russia at the beginning of the seventeenth century who deserved the respect and gratitude of his fellow-countrymen, it was David Theodorovich Zobnikovsky, in religion Dionisy, archimandrite of the great Troitskaya Monastery. In the darkest hour of the anarchy it was he who had inspired the heroic defence of the monastery for sixteen months (1610/11) against the all-conquering Poles, which gave Pozharsky and Minin time to collect the army of liberation. which ultimately saved the capital and the Tsardom along with it. When the Poles burnt Moscow, all the printing presses were destroyed, and the printers scattered; but no sooner was Tsar

---

[*] Smirnov: "Filaret Nikitich Romanov."     [†] "And with fire."

Michael seated firmly on his throne than he restored the typographers, recalled the master-printer Thofanov and his journeymen from Nizhny Novgorod, and at the same time appointed a committee to revise the corrupt text of the *Trebnik* or Breviary, and the other service-books of the Russian Church, at the head of which he placed Dionisy, whose learning was equal to his piety. Amongst other things, Dionisy amended the formula for the consecration of water. In the old *Trebnik* the sentence ran thus · "Come, O Lord! and sanctify this water with Thy Holy Spirit and with fire." Dionisy at once perceived that the phrase, "and with fire" was an interpolation due to the ignorance of former revisors, and accordingly struck it out. Some of his less erudite colleagues did not agree with him on this point, but all might have been well had not Dionisy possessed two dangerous enemies in his own monastery, to wit, the chief cantor, Login, and the *ustavshchik*, or chief lector and choir-master, Philaret. Both of these men were celebrities in their way. Login was famous for a voice of unsurpassable power and beauty. His singing and reading attracted crowds to the monastery, and the brethren looked up to him with awe and wonder. That he habitually spoilt the sense of the verses he sang by his extravagantly long-drawn-out cadences was, naturally, a matter of indifference to one, who like himself, regarded all knowledge, specially a knowledge of grammar, as so much heresy. Philaret, the choirmaster, owed his reputation to a purely external adornment (he had a very long beard of silvery whiteness, a possession regarded with superstitious reverence in old Moscovy), and to the fact that he had been choirmaster in the monastery for nearly half a century. Login and Philaret were close allies, and regarded their brethren as so much dirt beneath their feet. They were in the habit of cursing and swearing, kicking and cuffing the monks and the clergy on no provocation, and when their ecclesiastical superior, the archimandrite, himself the humblest as well as the bravest of men, most mildly remonstrated with them on the error of their ways, they turned their combined fury against him. But what aggravated these worthies most of all was the interference of Dionisy with what they regarded as their own peculiar functions.

They held that he had no business to chant or read in church
at all when they were there. What follows would be incredible
were it not vouched for by legal evidence. Once, at early mass,
when Dionisy was proceeding to read part of the service, Login
rushed at him and tore the book so violently out of his hand
that the lectern was overturned, to the great scandal of the congregation. Dionisy merely crossed himself, returned to his place
in the choir, and sat down in silence. Login then read the
appointed passages himself, but his rage was still hot within
him, and when he had finished his portion of Scripture he walked
up to the archimandrite and fell to cursing him for a fool and
heretic. "Cease, Login," said Dionisy, shaking his staff at
him, "do not interrupt divine service and disturb the brethren."
Even this gentle rebuke, from one generally too gentle to rebuke
at all, so infuriated Login, that he snatched the staff out of the
archimandrite's hands, broke it in four pieces, and flung it in his
face. But Login did not stop here. He was proud of his learning
as well as of his voice, and considered himself a theological
expert because he had once corrected a few proof-sheets. The
alteration made by Dionisy in the *Trebnik* revolted this champion of orthodoxy. "He does not confess that the Holy Ghost
comes with fire," he cried, and in conjunction with the choir-
master, Philaret, and the deacon, Markell, he actually denounced
Dionisy to the *locum-tenens* of the patriarchate, John, Metropolitan of Krutitsk (for Archbishop Philaret was still in captivity),
as a dangerous heretic. The examination, which lasted four
days, showed that the judge was as stupidly ignorant as the
accusers. Dionisy was pronounced heretical, and when he
refused to purchase his liberty by allowing his monastery to be
despoiled, he was treated like a common felon. Stripped to his
shirt, fettered and manacled, he was placed upon a wretched
hack and led through a jeering crowd, which pelted him with
sand and mud. Then he was shut up in a shed all through a
hot July day without so much as a cup of water to refresh
him, and the crowd battered him with bludgeons, while the
Metropolitan of Krutitsk, sitting at dinner in an upper apartment, looked on. This outrage on the most saintly monk
in Moscovy was largely due to a rumour spread among the

people that Dionisy was the promoter of a new heresy which would banish fire from the world, whereupon all the smiths and other handicraftsmen who could not do without fire clamoured for his death. Finally he was shut up in the Novospassky Monastery and condemned to a penance of a thousand obeisances. But his imprisonment was of short duration. On the return of Philaret with the Patriarch of Jerusalem, the case was reopened and thoroughly investigated. The Greek prelate demonstrated that the words " and with fire," were not in the Greek, and ought not to be in the Moscovite service-books, whereupon Dionisy was honourably reinstated, while "the rascally, tippling chorister, Login," received the reward of his ignorant presumption.*

Another great service rendered by Philaret to his country was the reorganisation of the army with the help of foreign officers, experience having proved to demonstration that the timid and insufficient Moscovite levies were incapable, single-handed, of coping successfully, not merely with the disciplined mercenaries of the northern and western Powers, but even with the amateur chivalry of Poland, or the still more lightly equipped Tatar hordes. The Moscovite gentry had lost its ancient martial instincts, while still remaining the military caste of Moscovy. The gentry had come to regard their settled peaceful life on their estates, where they were now lords paramount, as their normal state of existence, and the occasional summons to warfare, their sole obligation, as an extraordinary and unwelcome interruption. Moreover, the wars of the seventeenth century, which invariably ended in disaster, were not of a character to inspire these backward warriors with confidence in themselves or their leaders. Contemporary writers like Kotoshokin† not inaptly compare the Moscovite armies of their day to herds of cattle. The infantry, encumbered rather than armed with heavy, obsolete blunderbusses, the so-called *pishchal,* which they knew not how to use properly, or with blunt and clumsy spears and axes, rarely ventured to attack an enemy unless they outnumbered

---

* Comp. Solovev: "Istoria Rossy," IX., 1; Skvortsov: " Dionisy Zobni-kovsky."

† " O Rossy v tsartsvovanie Aleksiya Mikhailovicha."

him four to one, while the cavalry was "a shameful thing to look upon." Mounted on sorry hacks, and armed with clumsy carbines or simply with the *saadak*,* they considered it a great victory if they managed to kill two or three Tatars. That is to say, if they fought at all, for the one aim of the Moscovite soldier was to get home as quickly as possible. " God grant us some slight wound which will not hurt much, that we may obtain a reward from the great Gosudar!" was their most fervent battle-cry. To escape military service the *sluzhuie lyudi* were capable of any baseness. In vain a whole series of statutes threatened deserters with the knout, exile, and confiscation ; the most terrible threats were unavailing, and the *voivodui* were constantly complaining of shameless and wholesale desertion in the course of every campaign. Krijanic is still more severe. " The Turks and Tatars," he says, " though they run away, do not allow themselves to be killed for nothing, but defend themselves to their last breath. But our soldiers, when they run, do not attempt to defend themselves, but allow themselves to be cut to pieces."† Yet we know from another, if somewhat later, reliable source,‡ that the Russian infantry, when properly trained, would " follow its German officers through fire and water, though the Russian cavalry readily turns its back."

The gentry formed the bulk of the Tsar's forces, the peasants and tradespeople were rarely recruited, being far too valuable to the state as taxpayers. Homeless vagabonds were, however, often formed into companies of light troops called *sheldaki*, close akin to the Cossacks, while in the *stryeltsui*, or musketeers, the Tsar possessed a peculiar and superior sort of militia, composed of able-bodied volunteers outside the agricultural class. In times of peace the *stryeltsui* lived in their own quarters on the outskirts of the towns, with their wives and families, carrying on various trades toll free, and at the same time acting as police and firemen. In Moscow alone there were 20,000 of them divided into twenty *prikazui*, or companies. The

---

* A bow with its quiver of arrows.
† Krijanic: " Russkoe Gosudarstvo v polovinye, XVII., v."
‡ Rinhuber : " Relation du Voyage en Russie, en 1684." (*Ger.*)

pick of them formed the *stremennuie*, or stirrup corps,* in other words, the Tsar's body-guards. The *stryeltsui* had a fixed salary as well as a special allowance for clothes and salt. Their chief officers, the *golovuie*, or colonels, the *polugolovuie*, or lieutenant-colonels, and the *sotniki*, or captains, were always selected from among the nobles. The proved inefficiency of the Russian fighting men compelled Tsar Michael, like Tsar Boris before him, to introduce foreign mercenaries to teach the native levies European methods, and be their instructors in the art of warfare generally. As early as 1614 foreign soldiers began to enter Tsar Michael's service. The Irish captain who defended Byelaya against the Moscovites went over to them with his whole company after the place surrendered. In 1624 we find in the Russian service no fewer than 445 foreign officers, of whom 168 were Poles, 113 Germans, and 64 Irish. There were also Greeks, Wallachs, and Serbs. These officers were divided into two classes, the *pomyestnie*, who received landed estates, and the *korenovuie*, who received money for their services. Recruiting officers were also sent abroad to enlist foreign soldiers, but the most orthodox of governments looked askance at Catholic mercenaries, as is evident from the following instructions to one of their agents : " Hire soldiers in the realm of Sweden and other realms with the exception of the French and others of the Roman faith." Amongst the foreign officers who drilled the Moscovite regiments at this period, the most conspicuous are the Scots Leslie, Keith and Matthison, the Englishmen Fox and Sanderson, and the Germans, Fuchs and Samuel and Jakob Scharl. Every foreign colonel got 400, every lieutenant-colonel 200, every major 100, every doctor 60, every chaplain 30, and every common soldier 4½ German dollars a month.†

Tsar Michael's army was an improvement upon all previous Moscovite armies, but when it came to be tested in the Second Polish War, the chief event of Michael's later years, its inadequacy was most painfully demonstrated.

The Peace of Deulina was but a temporary interruption of hostilities postponed by mutual consent. Poland, harassed simultaneously by the Swedes in the north, and the Turks in

* From *stremya*, a stirrup     † Solovev: "Istoria Rossy," IX., 1.

the south, was forced to leave her rebellious vassal, as she still
regarded Moscovy, unpunished for a time, while Moscovy eagerly
awaited the first opportunity of regaining provinces which had
belonged to her from time immemorial and had only been
extorted from her helplessness. The opportunity seemed to have
come when in August, 1621, Thomas Cantacuzene, the special
envoy of Sultan Osman, arrived at Moscow. He announced
that the Sultan was about to attack Lithuania with all the forces
of the Ottoman Empire, and he brought with him letters from
the Patriarch of Constantinople, encouraging the Tsar to strike
at once. Simultaneously, Gustavus Adolphus invited Michael
to co-operate with the Protestant Powers against the papal
league and its threatening project of a world-wide dominion, by
attacking the Poles as the common enemies of the Lutheran and
the Orthodox faiths. A national assembly was at once summoned
to Moscow (October, 1621), and the Tsar laid before it the proposi-
tions of his allies. The assembly begged the Gosudar to stand
firm for the Church of God, and the honour of the realm, and
promised to assist him to the utmost of its ability. The *boyare*
and *dvoryane* were actually despatched to the provinces to levy
troops ; an ultimatum was forwarded to the Poles, and war
appeared to be on the threshold, when the unwelcome tidings of
a Turkish disaster reached Moscow. Sultan Osman, like a
second Xerxes, sweeping together from Europe, Asia, and
Africa, a host of 160,000 fighting men, * myriads of elephants,
camels, and mules and innumerable artillery of huge calibre,†
set out from Stambul to subjugate Poland once for all. His
progress was barred at the Moldavian fortress of Chocim, by the
Grand Hetman‡ of Poland, Jan Karol Chodkiewicz, one of
heroic Poland's greatest captains, who had entrenched himself
on the Dniester with 65,000 men. The veteran hero died during
the siege (September 24), but he lived long enough to hurl back a
dozen assaults, and so break the spirit of the Turkish host, that
on the first fall of autumn snow, Osman opened negotiations,

---

* Including camp-followers the army numbered 300,000. See Tretiak:
" Historya wojny chocimskej."
† Some of the cannon balls weighed 55 lb
‡ Commander-in-chief.

and on October 9 a treaty was signed so humiliating to the Ottoman Empire that the Sultan was assassinated by the janissaries on
his return to his capital.   This unexpected Polish victory stayed
the hand of the Tsar for ten years, during which time the
Moscovites strained every effort to strengthen their position.
The illness of the old Polish King, Sigismund III., brought
matters to a head.   In 1631, Alexander Leslie was sent to
Sweden to hire 5,000 infantry, and persuade as many smiths,
bullet casters, wheelwrights and carpenters as possible to come
to Moscow.   Two other emissaries to the same country purchased 10,000 muskets with the necessary ammunition.   At the
end of the same year there were 66,000 hired mercenaries in
Moscow, and the leading *voivodui* were busy inspecting troops
in the provinces.*   In April, 1632, King Sigismund died at last,
and the consequent interregnum encouraged the Tsar to break
the Peace of Deulina without ceremony.   Another of those
national assemblies which were the great feature of Michael's
reign, and pointed to weakness and irresolution in the central
Government, voted large subsidies in money and kind, and
Michael Shein and Artemy Izmailov were sent to recover the
lost towns, with 32,000 men and 158 guns, speedily reinforced
to twice that number.   At first everything went well, and Shein,
who had had some military experience, " picked up fortresses as
if they were birds'-nests."   Serpyeisk surrendered on Oct. 12/23,
Dorogobuzh six days later, and sixteen smaller places followed
their example.   Then Shein sat down before Smolensk and
besieged it for eight months.   It was on the point of surrendering, for the garrison was small and ill-equipped, when the new
King of Poland, Wladislaus IV., immediately after his election,
hastened to the relief of his chief eastern fortress with 16,000
Poles, and 15,000 Cossacks.   Shein had distributed his troops
in three immense entrenched camps on both sides of the Dnieper,
the walls of which, according to an eye-witness, were as strong,
vast and lofty as the walls of Smolensk itself, and defended
besides by forts and blockhouses.†   After a series of bloody
assaults lasting Aug. 7—22, Wladislaus captured two of the

---

* Solovev. "Istoria Rossy," vol. IX., 1, 2.
† Sokolowski : "Dzieje Polski." pp. 879—881.

Moscovite camps, occupied the surrounding hills, and besieged Shein for four months in his main camp, while the Crown Hetman Kazanowski defeated a relief army advancing from Dorogobuzh.     By the end of October the Moscovites began to suffer hunger, and discipline was so relaxed that Sanders, one of Shein's foreign officers, was shot dead by his colleague Leslie for accusing him of treachery in Shein's presence.    Finally, on February 26, 1634, Shein, who had received nothing from Moscow but promises of help which never came, and yielding to the clamours of his foreign officers, surrendered to the Poles (February 26, 1634).    On March 1, the Moscovite army "without music or the beating of drums, and with arms reversed," issued forth by companies, and laid 122 banners at the feet of the Polish King, who sat proudly on horseback beneath the triumphant white eagle standard, sword in hand, surrounded by a brilliant retinue of palatines and castellans.    The Moscovite army, after surrendering all its arms and artillery, was suffered to depart on parole, but not before the aged Shein and his fellow-generals had humbly done obeisance to the Polish King.    On 'reaching Moscow the unfortunate old man, who seems to have done his best under great difficulties, was beheaded along with his second-in-command, Izmailov, while the other generals were sent to Siberia, all of them obviously the scapegoats of a terrified Government, confronted by an impossible task.    Meanwhile the Poles, themselves half dead with cold and hunger, were besieging the fortress of Byelaya, which resisted so stoutly that Radziwill, the Chancellor of Lithuania, said henceforth it should be called, not Byelaya,* but Krasnaya.†    So great was the dearth of food in the Polish camp that the King himself ate only half a chicken for dinner in order that he might save the other half for supper, while bread, even at the royal table, was a luxury.‡    And now, too, disquieting news from the south disposed him to secure his Moscovite conquests by a permanent peace.    The Turks were again in arms against the Republic, and though the Grand Hetman of the Crown, Stanislaus Koniecpolski, in the summer of 1633, had defeated them at Paniowce, it was rumoured that Sultan Amurath IV., after publicly insulting the Polish special

* White.        † Red.        ‡ Solovev: "Istoria Rossy," vol. IX., 1, 2.

envoy Trzebinski at a public audience, had placed himself at the
head of a new army, and was already at Adrianople. Negotiations were accordingly opened with the Moscovites on the river
Polyanovka in March, 1634, but it was not till May 17/28 that
the treaty was signed. The Poles conceded the title of Tsar to
Michael, but refused the epithet "of all Russia," arguing, reason-
ably enough, that as Russian provinces* were to be found
both in the Moscovite and Polish states, Michael should call
himself "Tsar of his own Russia." Territorially the Poles
were very much in the same position as after the Truce of
Deulina, as they had little more than recovered what the Moscovites had won at the beginning of the campaign. The Tsar,
moreover, renounced all his rights to Livonia, Esthonia and Courland, and paid a war indemnity of 200,000 rubles. Wladislaus,
on the other hand, relinquished all his rights to the Moscovite
crown.

A national assembly had sanctioned the Second Polish War,
and another national assembly submissively voted for peace
when Tsar Michael explained that failure was due to the wholesale desertion of the Moscovite soldiers, and to the insufficiency
of the subsidies, which had come in more slowly and scantily
than at any previous period of his reign. It is doubtful, however,
whether the war would have been concluded so hastily, but for
the death of the patriarch Philaret, who expired, at the age of
eighty, in October, 1633. His death was the withdrawal of the
strongest prop from a Government feeble enough even when
supported by all the weight of his authority. Joasaf I., his
successor on the patriarchal throne, was utterly insignificant.
It is also certain that Shein would never have been sacrificed had
his old comrade and fellow-exile in Poland† survived for another
twelvemonth, nor can we imagine the energetic old statesman
abandoning the Don Cossacks as his successors did in the curious
affair of Azov, when Moscovy's paralysing dread of the Sublime
Porte prevented her from getting for nothing a valuable possession

* Thus Red and Black Russia belonged at this period to Poland, while White
Russia was half in Poland and half in Moscovy.

† Philaret, Shein and Prince Golitisuin had been seized by King Sigismund at
the same time.

which Peter the Great, sixty years later, only gained after an
enormous outlay of blood and treasure.

The Moscovites of the seventeenth century were always
nervously anxious to avoid a rupture with the terrible Turk.
The chief object of their numerous embassies from 1620 onwards
was to apologise for the raids of the semi-independent Don
Cossacks who periodically swept the Black Sea in their *strugi,**
and even penetrated to the environs of Stambul. The Tsar's
envoys used to assuage the wrath of the Grand Vizier by means
of precious pelts, in those days the principal secret-service fund
of the Moscovite state. In 1622, the envoys Konduirev and
Bormasov nearly lost their ears and noses because they had only
indifferent sables to offer, while the Grand Vizier Hussein
demanded black fox-skins. "You bring me nothing!" he cried.
"Sables grow in Moscovy and are sent from thence to all
kingdoms. In Lithuania sables do not grow, they come from
Moscovy, yet the Lithuanian envoy sent me fifty forties of sables
and more."† In 1630, there was a more than usually violent
outbreak of Cossack piracy, and the inhabitants of the Euxine
coast lands complained to the Sultan that life was impossible
because of the Cossacks. In that one year they destroyed
Iconium, attacked Sinope, and ravaged the whole Anatolian
coast. When rebuked by the Tsar's ambassadors, the Cossacks
turned upon them and beat them to death, so that not infrequently the Moscovites themselves had to implore the Sultan to
send his warriors against these orthodox freebooters. In 1637,
things came to a crisis. On April 21/May 1 of that year, 3,400
Don Cossacks and 100 Zaporozhian Cossacks set out on a formal
expedition against the Turkish fortress of Azov, murdered *en
route* a Turkish envoy, and on June 18/19 took the fortress by
storm and massacred all its Mussulman inhabitants. Then,
proud of their exploit, they sent a courier to Moscow to proclaim
it. The Tsar was mightily alarmed. Instead of praising he
reproved the Cossacks for their foolhardiness and wrote an
abject letter to the Sultan, repudiating all responsibility for this
unauthorised act of a "lot of runaway thieves and rascals."

* Large flat-bottomed boats, each capable of containing forty men.
† Solovev: "Istoria Rossy."

Indeed his orthodox Majesty went so far as to say that he would not move a finger to save them from extermination.  The Persian war, and the death of Murad IV. compelled the Turks to leave Azov in the hands of the Cossacks for nearly five years; but in 1641 Sultan Ibrahim I. set out to recapture the fortress at the head of 240,000 men and 100 guns.  The whole Cossack army was less than 10,000* strong, including 800 amazons, but they shut themselves up in Azov, and offered the most determined resistance.  Not a single man deserted to the Turks, not the most exquisite tortures could extract a word of information from a single prisoner, and after being repulsed in twenty-four assaults, and losing 24,000 men, the Sultan raised the siege Sept. 26/Oct. 7.  The Cossacks thereupon again offered Azov to the Tsar.  This time, Michael, much impressed by the astounding success of their audacity, commended their valour and steadfastness in the cause of the orthodox faith, and sent them a present of 5,000 rubles ; but he durst not take on himself the dire responsibility of accepting an ex-Turkish fortress from a band of freebooters, so a national assembly was summoned in January, 1642, to decide the matter.  The boldest of the *boyare* strongly advised the Tsar to retain Azov, as it would give him the command of the surrounding steppes.  The deputies of sixteen of the largest towns were of the same opinion, and declared outright that to re-surrender to the Mahommedans this border stronghold, so providentially put into orthodox hands, would assuredly bring down the wrath of God upon the whole Empire.  They then boldly inveighed against the selfishness of the rich privileged classes and the corruption and peculation of the official caste, especially the *dyaki;* proposed a general census of all the property in the Tsardom, and insisted that all classes, including the higher clergy, should be taxed according to their means.  If everyone contributed as he ought, they argued, Azov could easily be held against all enemies.  Yet there was something to be said on the other side.  In March, 1642, a Turkish envoy arrived at Moscow with an ultimatum, and the well-informed Vasily Lupul, Hospodar of Moldavia, advised the Tsar of the

---

* According to some accounts there were only 5,637; according to others, more than 14,000.

risk he would run of a Turkish invasion if he retained Azov, and assured him authoritatively that the Sultan had sworn in the event of a war with Russia to massacre the whole orthodox population of his Empire. Vasily also reminded Michael of the proverbial inconstancy and flightiness of the Cossacks, who had ever been a broken reed to those who leaned upon them, and nowhere was this fact better appreciated than in Moscow. Taking all things into consideration, not omitting the circumstance that the fortifications of Azov were so dilapidated that they could only be repaired at a cost to which the treasury was quite unequal, the Tsar thought it best to command the Cossacks to abandon the fortress. This they did, but not before they had utterly razed it to the ground, so that when the Turkish army reoccupied its site in April, they found nothing but a heap of ruins in the desert steppe.

But if the timidity of the Moscovite Government sometimes constrained it to forego its own advantages and disappoint the hopes of the most patriotic section of the nation, its misplaced zeal for orthodoxy, in purely immaterial matters, occasionally plunged it into the most ridiculous and embarrassing situations, as witness the grotesque comedy of the wooing of Prince Waldemar.

The strong desire of the Tsar to dignify his dynasty by contracting matrimonial alliances with sovereign houses abroad, induced him in April, 1642, to send a special embassy to Copenhagen, offering the hand of his daughter Irene to Prince Waldemar, son of King Christian IV.* The envoys were somewhat fettered by their instructions. For example, if asked for the portrait of the princess, the usual preliminary in such cases, they were to reply that it was not the custom of the sovereigns of Russia to imperil the health of their imperial daughters by having their portraits taken, nor was it even necessary, inasmuch as in the realm of Moscovy "the eyes of the sovereign Tsarevnas are beheld by none save the *boyare* who are near akin to them." With such an introduction, it is not surprising to hear that the envoys were not treated very courteously, especially as the Danish Court already had a grudge against the Court of Moscovy for

* For the whole story in detail, see Solovev: "Istoria," etc., IX., 4.

refusing to grant trade monopolies to Danish merchants. The negotiations foundered on the refusal of Christian IV. to allow his son to qualify for the hand of the Tsarevna by conversion to the orthodox Church.    In December a second ambassador, the Dane Peter Marselis, who had resided for some time in Russia, arrived at Copenhagen, to apologise for the blunders of his predecessors and assure Christian IV. that Waldemar would be treated by the Tsar as a son, and would not be compelled to accept the orthodox faith.    After much debate, Christian allowed his son to depart for Moscovy with a retinue of 300 persons, on the express condition that he was to have the free exercise of his religion, " an honourable and glorious appanage, and precedence in rank over everyone except the Tsar and the Tsarevich." Waldemar arrived at Moscow on Jan. 21/31, 1644, and the patriarch immediately pestered him concerning his faith.    The prince, much irritated at this evasion of the Marselis treaty, threatened to return home instantly if such persecution were repeated.    From his high Lutheran standpoint he looked down upon the orthodox.    " I am better lettered than any priest," he said ; " I have read the Bible through five times and recollect every letter of it, and I am ready to argue with the Tsar and the patriarch concerning the Scriptures whenever they like," but further than this he would not go.    And now began a peculiar, persistent inquisition.    On Feb. 13/24 the Tsar formally urged Waldemar to accept the orthodox faith, or he could not marry his daughter.    Waldemar professed himself ready to shed his blood for the Tsar, but threatened instant departure if any attempt were made to tamper with his faith.    He also reminded Michael of the solemn promise given through Marselis that he should have the free exercise of his religion.    Michael replied that force would of course not be used, but he never undertook not to try to convert his future son-in-law.    He also refused to let the prince go, as such a course would be "indecent and dishonourable."    For the next six weeks the controversy went on, and then the guards round Waldemar's house were doubled, and he was detained a close prisoner.    When another month had passed the Patriarch addressed to the unfortunate prince a long letter, urging him not to forfeit the friendship of the Tsar by

R.                                                                                                F refusing to submit to the threefold immersion of the Holy Orthodox Conciliar and Apostolic Church. "We know you *call* yourselves Christians," naively remarked the Patriarch, "but you do not in all things hold the right faith of Christ." As a final inducement, he cheerfully offered to take upon himself all the responsibility of Waldemar's conversion should the latter regard such a thing in the light of a sin, whereupon Waldemar adroitly countered by suggesting that as the Patriarch was so accommodating as to take upon himself the sin of Waldemar's apostasy from Lutheranism, he might just as well be responsible for Irene's apostasy from orthodoxy instead, and so let them be married without more ado. All through April to the beginning of May the argument went on, and then the Danish ministers asked for their and Waldemar's passports, which the Tsar refused on the ground that Waldemar now stood to him in the place of a son, and therefore could not honourably be sent away. Driven to desperation, Waldemar's followers vainly attempted to break out of Moscow by force at midnight, killing one of the *stryeltsui* and wounding six more, but this only led to their closer incarceration. May, June, and July passed in fruitless efforts to convert Waldemar by a whole array of Court priests and prelates. In the autumn Waldemar bribed a Lithuanian named Basistov to convey him disguised to Denmark through Poland, but the plot was detected and Basistov was seized and tortured. At the end of November came letters from Christian IV., peremptorily demanding the fulfilment of the Tsar's promises or the release of his son ; but Michael held on to Waldemar as if there were not another marriageable prince in the universe. At the beginning of January, 1645, the captive, who had now been detained a prisoner for more than twelve months, addressed to Michael a final appeal in the most bitter terms, protesting that his Tsarish Majesty was dishonouring himself in the eyes of the whole civilised world, by treating free men worse than even Turks and Tatars for their own good name's sake would ever dare to treat them, and declaring that if the Danes were not released forthwith, they would attempt to escape sword in hand if it cost them their lives. To the Polish envoy, Konski, who advised submission, Waldemar fiercely declared that if the Tsar threatened him with all the thunderbolts of Jove he would not betray his conscience. But the obstinacy of Pharaoh King of Egypt in a bad cause was as nothing compared with the obstinacy of Tsar Michael Theodorovich in a good one, and he absolutely refused to let the children of Luther go. Not till the accession of his son and successor Alexius did Waldemar and his companions regain their freedom. But the day of deliverance was now close at hand, and as a matter of fact Tsar Michael was very much more to be pitied than Prince Waldemar. This very year, the tender affectionate nature of the mildest of all the Tsars had suffered severely from domestic bereavement; in the course of a few weeks death had wrested from him his two eldest sons, Ivan and Vasily, and his failure to marry his daughter Irene honourably and without offence of conscience, was an additional mortification, and the probable cause of his death. He wept so continuously that the surgeons who attended him declared, with perfect gravity, that the accumulation of tears in his stomach, liver and spleen, had deprived these organs of their natural warmth and chilled his blood, giving rise to all sorts of evil humours. Most probably the cause of death was dropsy aggravated by intense mental depression. On July 12, 1645, his name-day, the Tsar attended mass at the Court chapel. During the service he fell down in a fit, and was removed to his apartments in a dying condition. On recovering consciousness he summoned his surviving son, the Tsarevich Alexius, then in his sixteenth year, and, in the presence of the Patriarch, the Tsaritsa, and the Tsarevich's uncle, Boris Ivanovich Morozov, appointed Alexius his successor, at the same time tearfully entreating Morozov to guard the young prince as the apple of his eye. Michael was not perhaps a great, but he was certainly a good, ruler. The universal belief in his honesty and conscientiousness was fully justified, and during his reign the downtrodden and overburdened Russian people looked to the throne alone for relief and justice, nor looked in vain.

# CHAPTER III.

## The Uniates and the Cossacks.
### 1580—1651.

Poland and her Constitution—The Jesuits and the Question of the Union of the Roman and Greek Churches—Gross Disorders in the Orthodox Church of Lithuania—The Bishops—The Laity—Intervention of the Patriarch Jeremiah II.—Beginning of the Movement Romewards—Negotiations of the Orthodox Bishops with the Polish Government—Despatch of Delegates to Rome—Rage of the Orthodox Laity—"*Ruthenis Receptis*"—Fierce Resistance of Ostrogski—Synod of Bresc—Murder of Bishop Kuncewicz—Orthodox Church established by Law—The Cossacks—Their Origin and Distribution—The Zaporozhians—Their Mode of Self-Government—Their Quarrels with Poland—Their Rebellions and Humiliation—Bogdan Chmielnicki—Driven into Rebellion by the Pans—Defeats the Potockis at "Yellow Waters" and "Hard Plank"—Horrible Outrages of the Cossacks in the Ukraine—Chmielnicki's Victory at Pilyava—Negotiations with John Casimir—Instability and Insolence of Chmielnicki—The Ukraine Plundered and Terrorised—Battle and Compact of Zborow—Chmielnicki a Sovereign Prince—He is defeated at Bereszteczko—An Independent Cossackdom henceforth impossible.

THE Treaties of Stolbovo and Polyankova had thrown Moscovy further back towards the East than she had ever been thrown before. She was now altogether cut off from the Baltic ; the great watercourses of the Dnieper and the Desna had become the exclusive property of Poland, and a whole group of her ancient possessions, notably the venerable Kiev, the mother of the Russian cities, had passed into the hands of the detested Latins. Nevertheless, the sacrifices had given Moscovy some measure of that peace and order for the want of which she was perishing, and she was thereby enabled gradually to recruit her strength for future efforts and ventures. For the next twenty-five years, however, she may be said to have lain in a heavy though not always tranquil slumber, knowing but little of what was going on in the world around her, and of small account in the councils of Europe. During this period, her fate was being decided for her elsewhere, and it is to Western Russia, or Lithuania, that we must look for the causes which led to the gradual awakening of the Moscovite Colossus.

At the beginning of the seventeenth century, Lithuania was the name given to the eastern portion of the Polish Republic which embraced the whole of the vast plain lying between Courland, Moldavia, the upper Desna and the Bug, a territory nearly half as large again as France before 1870. By the Union of Lublin (1569) the Polish and Lithuanian Governments were permanently and completely united. After this great event, Lithuania must, for all practical purposes, be regarded as an integral portion of ·the Polish Republic. By far the greater portion of Lithuania consisted of Russian territory, that is to say, territory which had been wrested, from time to time, from the independent Russian princes in the fourteenth and fifteenth centuries. The inhabitants of these provinces spoke a dialect* closely akin to the language of Moscovy, and, like the subjects of the Tsar, were staunch adherents of the Greek orthodox Church. The Tsars of Moscovy never abandoned the hope of recovering these portions of the original old Russian land, but at the beginning of the seventeenth century, this hope seemed but a forlorn one, for, to all appearance, Poland was destined to remain the leading Slavonic power, and as such all Europe regarded her.

But, in reality, the period of Poland's greatness was over and her swift and irremediable decline had already begun. The primary cause of the ruin of the most chivalrous of republics was her incurably vicious constitution. On the death of the last Jagiello, in 1572, the Polish crown had been made purely elective, and the chief authority in the state was vested in the *Sejm*, or Diet, a tumultuous assembly of landed gentlemen (the towns had long since ceased to be represented therein), every member of which enjoyed the unassailable privilege of instantaneously dissolving it by interposing his individual veto, whereupon all Acts of Parliament previously passed, even those upon which the veto in question had no bearing, became *ipso facto* null and void.

The first instance of a Diet that thus dissolved itself occurred

* Generally called Ruthenian or Little Russian.

in 1536, but it was not till the end of the sixteenth century that
this *liberum veto* was employed so frequently that the whole
machinery of government came to a standstill. The more pro-
vident of the Polish statesmen struggled hard against this abuse
in vain; every attempt to abolish it was mischievously circum-
vented or fiercely resisted. At last the Poles hit upon a corrective
more mischievous than the original evil. This was the right
accorded to every member of the Diet to form an armed Con-
federation to support the views of the majority or the minority
of the *Sejm*, as the case might be. Thus the Government of
Poland gradually drifted into what can only be called a constitutional anarchy tempered by civil war. The boundless egoism of
the *szlachta*,* or gentry, whose interest in political affairs was
purely personal, or, at the very best, purely local, was an additional impediment to good government. In private life the
Polish *szlachcic*† was recklessly hospitable—he would encumber
his estate to feast his friend. But whenever called upon to contribute to the necessities of the state, he immediately drew his
purse-strings tightly, and became the meanest of men. Absolutely incapable of a broad political outlook, ignorant of the
very rudiments of statecraft, the grey-coated Polish squires
could never be made to understand that no government in the
world can be carried on without money. Still worse, he would
never learn from adversity. Frequently, after refusing voluntarily to pay a few thousands for strengthening the national
defences (and the geographical position of Poland exposed her
every moment to attack from every quarter) he was obliged to
pay as many millions to save his country (and his own estates
along with it), from calamities mainly due to his own
improvidence and parsimony.

When the Diet was not sitting, Poland was ruled by the Senate,
a council of magnates and great officers of state. But the *panowie*‡
or Pans, were responsible to the *Sejm* for everything they did,
while the so-called King, who presided over their deliberations,
was a mere state decoration. If he were a great warrior, he was
permitted to lead the armies of the republic to victory at his own
expense : but he could neither levy taxes, nor declare war, nor

* Gentry—*geschlacht*.    † A member of the *szlachta*, gentleman.    ‡ Lords.

contract alliances without being previously authorised so to do by the *Sejm*. Even treaties with foreign Powers were concluded in the name of the King and the republic conjointly. Thus there was practically no control over the incalculable caprices of an ignorant, suspicious, and close-fisted assembly of country gentlemen, too often the unconscious dupes, or the shameless hirelings of self-seeking politicians and foreign Powers. The one national asset was the splendid valour of the *szlachta* which, when intelligently guided, had so often saved the republic from ruin, but there were ominous signs that even this last resource was diminishing both in quantity and quality.

The centrifugal and disintegrating tendencies inherent in the Polish constitution were checked, to some extent, by the last two princes of the House of Jagiello, who reigned from 1506 to 1572. That period was a peculiarly perilous one for the statesmen of the republic. The rise and progress of the Reformation in Poland more than once threatened the disruption of the state, but Sigismund I. and Sigismund II., with rare sagacity, held the balance evenly between the contending confessions till the Polish nation's inveterate dislike of everything German prevailed over the Polish gentry's passing differences with their own priests and they became zealous Catholics once more. But in fact Protestantism, outside the Prussian provinces, had never taken firm root in Polish soil, and the attitude of the various sects towards each other had always been more fratricidal than fraternal. The arrival of the Jesuits coincided with and completed the Catholic reaction. First introduced into the diocese of Wilna, within forty years of the establishment of their order, by Bishop Waleryan Protaszewicz, their success was instantaneous and extraordinary. The splendour of their churches, the eloquence of their preaching, the excellence of the education they offered to all men irrespective of class or creed, attracted general attention, and their triumph over Protestantism was assured when the Lithuanian magnates, the Radziwills, the Sapiehas, and the Chodkiewiscy, who had hitherto professed Calvinism, became their spiritual children.

Having conquered the Lutherans and Calvinists, the Jesuits next turned their attention to the Greek orthodox Church, their one remaining spiritual rival in the territories of the republic. Unfortunately for them and for Poland, the facility of their past victory over the heretics blinded them to the difficulties of their coming contest with the schismatics. The Jagiello princes had very wisely left their orthodox subjects alone. Their policy was to strengthen by every means the union between Poland and Lithuania, and their statesmanlike instincts told them that any attempt violently to bring together the Roman Church in Poland and the orthodox Church in Lithuania would only intro- duce discord where harmony was so essential. The Jesuits thought differently. Their great argument was that the union of the two Churches would consolidate the union of the two states, and this argument is set forth with extraordinary force and eloquence in the famous book of the greatest of the Polish Jesuits, Peter Skarga, entitled " O jednosci Kosciola Bozego." * In the third part of this work Skarga argues that the three principal obstacles to the proper discipline of the Russian Church in Poland were (1) the parochial clergy, who, as married men, thought of their families before their flocks, and, as unlearned men, could not properly instruct others ; (2) the bar- barous Slavonic idiom, which was not and never could be a learned language like Latin and Greek, the sole sources of en- lightenment ; and (3) the pitiable subjection of the weak clerical order of Lithuania to the strong and wealthy laymen. To remedy this state of things he proposed a provisional union between the Roman and Greek Churches on three conditions : (1) that the Archbishop of Kiev, the metropolitan of the West Russian Church, should henceforth be consecrated by the Pope instead of by the Patriarch of Constantinople ; (2) that the Russians should agree with Rome in all the essential articles of the Christian faith and acknowledge the supremacy of the see of Rome ; and (3) that the external ceremonies and the liturgical language of the Russian Church should remain intact. A conditional union was considered preferable to an absolute

* "On the Unity of the Church of God." Printed in 1590 and dedicated to Sigismund III.

submission as being the easier way of undermining the obstinate attachment of the orthodox congregations to their ancient faith.*

Whatever we may think of Skarga's somewhat premature condemnation of the Slavonic language, his indictment of the orthodox clergy, so far from exceeding, fell far short of the mark. The flagrant abuses of the orthodox Church in Poland were due, primarily, to external and therefore uncontrollable political causes. She derived from the patriarchate of Constantinople; and the patriarchate of Constantinople, absolutely dependent as it was on the caprices of the Padishah, was habitually put up for sale to the highest bidder by the favourites of the seraglio. Thus orthodoxy was tainted at its very source; the rascality of the Greek clergy soon became a by-word throughout the orthodox world, and so low did the reputation of the patriarchal see fall among the Lithuanians, that from the end of the fifteenth century they had been content to receive their metropolitans and bishops from the King of Poland, without paying any regard to their own official archpastor at Stambul. But Warsaw was a long way from Lithuania; local influence grew ever stronger as the authority of the central Government grew weaker; and at last the disposal of Church preferment fell almost entirely into the hands of the wealthy Lithuanian magnates, who ruled like little princes in their own provinces. The Glinscy, the Ostrogscy, set bishops on their episcopal thrones; other magnates procured for their clients nominations to vacant sees from the royal chancellery; and small squires, or encumbered noblemen, some of whom had never even taken orders and were ignorant of all spiritual matters, sought a career or a competency in the orthodox Church of Lithuania.†

Moreover, these Russian‡ dioceses were fat and far extending, and it was no easy matter to dispossess the greedy self-seekers who had once got hold of them. In no other country did might so triumphantly flout right as in the Polish Republic. Every bishop was a law unto himself, and within a very few hours he

---

* Solovev: "Istoria Rossy." X.. 1.    † Sokolowski: "Dzieje Polski," 803.
‡ *I.e.*, the Russian provinces of Poland.

could convert his palace into an impregnable stronghold. But a few instances will show us best what manner of men these sturdy "fathers in God" really were. In 1585 the *Sejm* addressed a letter of remonstrance to Onesiphor Dievoczka, Metropolitan of Kiev. According to this curious document the primate of the orthodox Church, instead of protecting his flock from the wolves, seems to have helped the wolves to prey upon them. It is pointed out to him that during his pastorate, abuses have multiplied, churches have been closed, the blessed sacrament has been locked up, no church bells have been rung, and the people have not been able to pray in their own churches—in short, "things that were never done in the worst days of the pagan emperors are being done daily during the pastorate of your grace!" He is further charged with using church plate for the service of his own table, and converting chasubles and epitrachilia into jerkins, girdles and mantles. Twenty years earlier (1565) the rival candidates for the see of Vladimir-Bresc fought the matter out in good old feudal fashion, and the bishop's palace was carried by assault. The royal writ-servers on this occasion were beaten and trampled upon inside the cathedral, and the successful competitor, Theodore Lazowski, threatened that he would cut the carcass of his rival, Borzobogaty, into pieces and feed his dogs with it if he ever put his foot in Bresc again. Another bishop designate, Ivan Krasinsky, who happened to be a layman, had first to be *forced* by his metropolitan to take priest's orders. As Bishop of Luck he treated the property of the diocese as if it were his own private estate, dowered his daughter out of it and permitted his sons to provide for themselves by plundering churches and appropriating monasteries. The lesser clergy, with few exceptions, naturally followed the example of their ecclesiastical superiors. All contemporary evidence describes the condition of the Russian Church in Poland in the darkest colours. Prince Constantine Ostrogski, the chief pillar of the orthodox Church, bitterly complained that the common people hungered in vain for the Word of God while Melecy Smotrzycki, Archbishop of Polock, declared that he could not lay his hand on three orthodox preachers, and that but for the aid of

Catholic *postillas* there would have been no preaching at all.*

Gross ignorance was inevitably followed by coarse manners and low morality. The secular clergy, who were permitted to marry once, on taking orders, abused the privilege by marrying twice or thrice, while the monks, in defiance of their rule of celibacy, lived openly with their concubines, and provided for their numerous families out of the revenues of the religious houses.† At this crisis the unhappy Russian Church in Lithuania was saved from dissolution only by the energy and devotion of the laity. Foremost among them was Prince Constantine Ostrogski. As liberal and pious as he was wealthy, Ostrogski had done his utmost to reform the orthodox clergy, and raise their moral dignity. In 1580 he founded an academy on his estate at Ostrog, in 1587 he established a high school at Kiev, similar institutions sprang up under his protection at Lemberg, Wilna, Jaroslaw, and Bresc, and it was on his initiative that the Bible was translated into the Slavonic language. Ostrogski was supported by a few of the other magnates, but his chief allies were the middle-class, lay guilds, or confraternities, of Lemberg, Kiev, Wilna, and the other large towns of Lithuania, in which the old communal system had been still further strengthened by the privileges of the *Magdeburg Recht.* These guilds exhibited an extraordinary vitality, founding schools, establishing printing presses, and working generally in the interests of orthodoxy. Such was the situation when, in 1588, Jeremiah II., Patriarch of Constantinople, passed through Poland on his way to Moscovy. He was bombarded by complaints from every quarter against the bishops and clergy, and these complaints were mingled with threats that if he did not reform the abuses of the orthodox Church, the orthodox themselves would be obliged to seek salvation at Rome. The Patriarch, on his return from Moscovy, moved by these representations, summoned two synods, the first at Wilna and the second at Bresc; but the reformation, so ardently desired, stopped short at petty formalities, and the expedients devised by Jeremiah for restoring the discipline of the Church did far

* Sokolowski: "Dzieje Polski," 803.　　† Solovev: "Istoria Rossy," X., 1.

more harm than good, and raised a perfect storm of protest.
He did, indeed, depose the infamous Dievocza from the metropolitan see of Kiev, and appointed in his stead Michael Rahoza,
Archimandrite of Minsk, the nominee of the laity ; but at the
same time he elevated to the dignity of exarch, Cyril Terlecki,
Bishop of Luck, thus creating a new ecclesiastical authority
superior to that of the metropolitan. And as if this were not
sufficient to divide and dismember the hierarchy of the orthodox
Russian Church in Poland, the patriarch withdrew the great
guilds of Lemberg and Wilna from the jurisdiction of the
bishops, conferred upon them the title of *Stauropigialic*,* and
granted them supervisory functions, in certain cases, over both
bishops and clergy. Trouble began ere yet the patriarch had
quitted Lithuanian soil. Everyone was dissatisfied with the
results of his intervention. The bishops were jealous of the
*Stauropigialic* guilds, and the aristocratic laity shared this
jealousy. The metropolitan resented the establishment over
his own head of an exarch, and the exarch was embarrassed,
rather than flattered, by an usurped authority which he could
not safely exercise. So profound was the dissatisfaction of the
Lithuanian orthodox with the Jeremian reforms, that the best
men among them, both lay and clerical, began to look longingly
towards Rome. Solovev has, somewhat unfairly, represented the
origin of the Uniate Church of Poland as due entirely to the
ambition of the prelates, and their jealousy of the laity. No
doubt the prospect of taking their places in the Polish senate,
as the equals of the Roman Catholic bishops, was a flattering
prospect to the more worldly of these prelates ; no doubt,
too, they regarded the abnormally privileged position of the
lay guilds as an encroachment upon their episcopal jurisdiction,
from which Rome alone could deliver them. But it is equally
certain that they were genuinely distressed at the disorder of
the orthodox Church, and keenly alive to the fact that the
corrupt and futile oriental patriarchs could do nothing to help
it. It must also be remembered that, with the exception of

---

* That is to say, under the direct and immediate control of the Patriarch of
Constantinople. Compare Solovev, "Istoria Rossy," X., 1, and Sokolowski,
"Dzieje Polski," 804, 805.

Gedeon Balaban, Bishop of Lemberg, they were earnest, conscientious men of a very different calibre to the robber-bishops of the preceding generation. The metropolitan Rahoza, if timid and vacillating, was a pious man "of relatively blameless life"; Ipaty Pociej, Bishop of Vladimir, ex-castellan of Bresc, had voluntarily relinquished one of the highest offices in the state to take the tonsure ; the exarch Cyril Terlecki, though of a more worldly complexion, was justly renowned for his ability and learning. All these men were anxious to do their duty, and their duty seemed to lead them to Rome. Unfortunately, they made the great mistake of ignoring the laity, and especially the leader of the laity, Prince Constantine Ostrogski. If ever a layman had the right to be consulted on Church questions, that layman was Ostrogski. We have already seen what inestimable services he had rendered to the orthodox Church, and his immense wealth (his estate covered 242 square miles, and he was the patron of 600 livings) had always been at the service of learning and religion. Nay, more, Ostrogski himself was in favour of union with Rome. On June 21 July 1, 1593, he wrote to his intimate friend, Pociej, that he saw in such a union the sole remaining means of salvation for the orthodox Church of Lithuania, but, unfortunately, he stipulated for the previous consent thereto of the Churches of Moscovy, Wallachia, and the East! Such a condition precedent would never have been proposed by anyone with an ounce of statesmanship in his composition ; it was impossible—unthinkable ; and this the bishops very well knew. Yet they not only made no attempt to argue the matter out with Ostrogski, but, while consulting him privately about the best means of bringing about a union with Rome, they had already, unknown to him, arranged the matter their own way with the Polish Government, which, naturally, was very desirous (especially after the erection of the independent patriarchate of Moscow in 1589) to separate its Russian subjects from the Russians of Moscovy. After long preliminary negotiations with the King and his chancellor, Zamoiski, extending over some years, the orthodox bishops took the decisive step, and, at a synod held at Bresc on June 14, 1595, they drew up two addresses, one to the Pope and the other to the King, in which they declared their willingness to accede to the Union of Florence on condition that their ceremonies and discipline were left intact, and Terlecki and Pociej were sent as delegates to Rome to offer the submission of the orthodox Church in Poland to the apostolic see. Then, and then only, was Ostrogski told of what had been done.

The fury of Prince Constantine was volcanic. He who, five years before, sitting humbly at the feet of the bishops, had pronounced the union desirable, now, in a circular addressed to the orthodox laity of Lithuania, denounced the union actually accomplished as the devilish deed of half a dozen Judases, plotting together accursedly against their natural pastors, the most holy patriarchs. "Treating us orthodox laity as if we were dumb brute beasts,"* continues the irate patrician, "they have arbitrarily determined to depart from the true faith and drag us after them to perdition. Instead of being the light of the world, they had become a thick darkness and a scandal "—and he urges the orthodox to unite with him and stand firm together for the true religion of Christ. Much must be forgiven to an octogenarian autocrat crossed for the first time in his life in the matter nearest to his heart, but, unfortunately, he proceeded from words to deeds which in any other country but Poland would have been regarded as rank rebellion, and promptly punished as such.

Meanwhile the delegates of the bishops had reached Rome, where a splendid reception awaited them. Three days after their arrival Clement VIII. received them in private audience, like a tender father welcoming his children with unspeakable affection. They were lodged close to the palace of his holiness in magnificent apartments and supplied by the Pope's benevolence with all things in abundance. When they pressed for an interview the Holy Father replied : " Nay, my children, rest awhile from your journey!" Not till three months after their arrival (December 23) were they granted a solemn audience, in the Hall of Constantine, by his holiness, surrounded by the Roman Senate, the cardinals, archbishops, and the ambassadors of the Catholic Powers. After kissing the Pope's foot, the delegates presented their letters, which were read, first in Slavonic and afterwards in

* Letter of Ostrogski, cited by Solovev, "Istoria Rossy," X., 1.

Latin, whereupon Clement VIII., through one of his chamberlains, answered them kindly and gratefully. Then the delegates
swore obedience to the holy see on the Gospels, in the name of
the metropolitan and all the orthodox bishops of Lithuania.
This done, the Pope bade them draw nearer. They must know,
he said, that it was not his desire to rule over them, but to bear
their burdens, and with that he dismissed them. On Christmas
Eve the delegates attended mass in the new cathedral of St.
Peter, and early in the new year Clement published the bull
"*Magnus Dominus et laudabilis nimis*," announcing to the world
the union of the Russian with the Catholic Church, and commanded gold and silver medals to be struck with the inscription
"*Ruthenis receptis*," to commemorate the great event.

The delegates, joyful and triumphant, quitted Rome in March,
1596, and on returning home found all Lithuania in an uproar.
It must have seemed to them like a descent from the mountain
of the beatitudes to the dwellings of the demoniacs. The veteran
Ostrogski had already taken the field against them, and he exhausted all the resources of popular agitation to destroy their
work. He terrified the vacillating metropolitan Rahoza, formed
a close union with the *Stauropigialic* guilds, and, during the Diet
of 1596, at the head of a formidable minority, fiercely opposed
the King himself, while orthodox preachers, like Stephen
Zyzania, perambulated the country, denouncing the bishops as
traitors, and stirring up the orthodox population against them.
At the Synod of Bresc, held on October 9, 1596, to confirm the
union, the two parties met face to face. Those who refused to
accept the union were solemnly excommunicated by the Uniate
bishops, while the Uniate bishops and their followers were simultaneously placed under the ban of the orthodox Church by
Nicepheros, *protosingel* of the Patriarch of Constantinople,
whom Ostrogski had hurried to Bresc to give some sort of
ecclesiastical sanction to his operations. Thus the immediate
result of the union was the division of the West Russian Church
into Uniates and "Disunited," but the orthodox party was now
in a much worse position than before, because it was no longer
recognised by the Polish Government, and had to contend
against the united forces of the Uniates and the Catholics. But

Ostrogski did not abandon the struggle, and it was due to his efforts that the Warsaw Diet of 1607 granted a "constitution" to the "Disunited," which gave them a quasi-legal status, and at the same time confirmed the rights and the privileges of the guilds. The death of Ostrogski in the following year was a great blow to the orthodox, and the Uniates redoubled their efforts to "convert" the "Disunited." We obtain a glimpse of the methods they employed from a letter of remonstrance addressed by Sapieha, the Chancellor of Lithuania, to Josephat Kuncewicz, Archbishop of Polock, the most fanatical of the Uniate propagandists. "Your actions,"* writes the chancellor, "seem dictated rather by anger and ambition than by love for your neighbour. The whole Ukraine complains of you. You are scattering abroad sparks of discord, which threaten us with a general conflagration. You talk of converting the renegades, so as to have one fold and one shepherd, but the precept: *compel* them to come in! has never been applied in the Polish Republic. You demand that the schismatics be driven from the realm. God preserve us from committing such an illegality! Far better would it be for us to be rid of our unruly allies, the Uniates, for never have we had such discords as those caused by this blessed union! The very Jews and Tatars are not prevented from having their synagogues and mosques in the King's domains, and you would close Christian churches!" Kuznetsky persisted, however, in his propaganda, and in November, 1623, he was murdered in the streets of Witebsk by the outraged orthodox population. An inquiry into the matter by Sapieha led to the execution of the Burgomaster of Witebsk and eighteen citizens, the disenfranchisement of the town, the removal of its bells and the destruction of its two orthodox churches. Here, however, Sapieha stopped short, and no notice was taken of a savage epistle from Pope Urban VIII., declaring that compassion in such cases was cruelty, and that the plague of schism should be extirpated by fire and sword. Thus Poland once more vindicated her character as a non-persecuting power in an age of intolerance. In process of time, too, the position of the "Disunited" improved. The courage with which they endured the stress of persecution

* Quoted *in extenso* by Solovev, "Istoria," X., 1, here much condensed.

strengthened their self-reliance and self-respect, and the deputies whom they sent to the Diet obtained fresh privileges for them from that nonchalant assembly. Thus the Diet of 1631, despite the opposition of the Curia, fully recognised the orthodox Church in Poland as a separate and independent establishment, with bishoprics at Lemburg, Przemysl, and Mohilev, and a metropolitan at Kiev, and confirmed them in the possession of all their property. The patriotic and statesmanlike Wladislaus IV., who actually arranged a *Colloquium Charitativum*, at Thorn, between the Catholics and all the Dissidents in 1644, would have gone a step further and given the orthodox a patriarchate of their own, but his laudable efforts foundered on the determined opposition of Pope Urban VIII.*

The indulgence shown by Poland to the Russian Church in Lithuania was due, not so much to an abstract love of liberty, or to religious indifference, though both motives undoubtedly co-operated, as to a desire to avoid offending, as far as possible, the susceptibilities of an important part of her orthodox population, whose services she could ill afford to dispense with. I allude to the Cossacks of the Ukraine. But before proceeding to describe the peculiar relations existing between the republic and her semi-independent vassals, the Cossacks, a word of explanation is necessary as to the origin and early history of these audacious and picturesque freebooters.

At the beginning of the sixteenth century the illimitable steppe of South-eastern Europe, extending from the Dniester to the Urals, had no settled population. Hunters and fishermen frequented its innumerable rivers, from spring to autumn, returning home laden with rich store of fish and pelts, while runaway serfs occasionally settled, in small communities, beneath the shelter of the line of fortresses built, from time to time, to guard the southern frontiers of Poland and Moscovy. The perpetual incursions of the Tatar hordes of Budjak and the Crimea made the *Ukrain*,† as that borderland was called, unsafe to dwell in; but gradually, as the lot of the serf, both in Poland and Moscovy,

* Sokolowski : "Dzieje Polski," 895, 896.
† *Ukrain* is the Ruthenian word for a border, or boundary, corresponding with the Russian *okrain*.

R.                                                                          G

grew more and more intolerable, the more energetic spirits
among the peasantry threw off the burdensome yoke of the
Pans and the Gosudar alike, and sought an untrammelled,
adventurous life in the free steppe.  There, at any rate, the
fugitives found plenty to eat and little to do.  The climate of the
Ukrain, for seven months out of the twelve, was superb.  Its
famous black soil, the most fertile in Europe, could produce fifty,
seventy, and even a hundred-fold.  The succulent wild grass of
the steppe grew so high that horses grazing in it were invisible
a dozen yards off, and only the tips of the horns of the cattle
could be seen above it.   Rivers alive with fish intersected this
new Canaan in every direction, and the forests that lined their
banks were rich with every sort of game and fruit, and literally
flowed with wild honey.  Nor was the element of adventure,
so dear to the true Slav, wanting to complete the happiness of
the first settlers.   Obliged, for fear of the Tatars, to go about
constantly with arms in their hands, they gradually grew strong
enough to raid their raiders, selling the rich booty thus acquired
to the merchants of Moscovy and Poland.   Moreover, the Turks
and Tatars being the natural enemies of Christendom, a war
of extermination against them was a sacred duty, so that the
Cossacks had the rare satisfaction of obeying their consciences
and satisfying their natural inclinations at the same time.
Curiously enough, these champions of orthodoxy borrowed the
name, which has stuck to them ever since, from their "dog-
headed" adversaries.   The rank and file of the Tatar soldiery
were known as *Kazaki*, or Cossacks, and this came to be applied
indiscriminately to all the free dwellers in the Ukrain, though
the Polish Cossacks, in contradistinction to their Moscovite
brethren, were generally known as Cherkasses.*   As time went
on the Cossacks multiplied exceedingly.   Their daring grew
with their numbers, and at last they came to be a constant
annoyance to all their neighbours, both Christian and Mussulman, frequently involving both Poland and Moscovy in dangerous
and unnecessary wars with the Ottoman Empire.   Every river
of any importance had its own Cossack settlement.   Thus,
beginning from the extreme east of Europe, we find the Yaitsie

* From one of their chief establishments, the fortress of Cherkassui.

Cossacks on the Yaitsa, which separates European from Asiatic Russia. Then came the Volgan Cossacks. South of the Volga, on the Terek, were settled the Terskie Cossacks. Further west-wards were the Cossacks of the Don. The Cossacks of the Yaitsa, the Volga, the Terek, and the Don, were under the nominal dominion of Moscovy ; but the most important of all the Cossacks, the Cherkasses, or Cossacks of the Dnieper, were the vassals of the Crown of Poland.

The origin of the *Syech,* or Community of the Dnieperian Cossacks, is still somewhat obscure, but it was of importance as a military outpost as early as the beginning of the sixteenth century. In 1533, the *starosta* of Kaniew, Eustasy Daszkowicz, first proposed to construct in the lower reaches of the Dnieper, beyond the waterfalls, a permanent entrenched camp, garrisoned by 2,000 light troops ; but it was not till 1556 that the pro-ject was accomplished by Prince Dmitry Wisniewiecki, and a fortress, to serve as a barrier against the incursions of the Tatar Khan, arose on the island of Hortica on the Dnieper, only to be abandoned in 1558. Twelve years later, however, we find the Cossacks permanently entrenched among the islands of the Lower Dnieper, but the bulk of them only appeared *na niz,* "down below,"* in the summer, preferring, during the winter, to dwell in the various towns of the Ukrain, principally Kiev and Cherkassui. The Union of Lublin (1569) which united Lithuania with Poland, and led to the Polanisation of the former country, was the immediate occasion of a considerable exodus to the lowlands of the Dnieper, of those peasants who desired to escape from the taxes of the Polish Government, and the tyranny of the Polish Pans, or landlords. This greatly increased the number of the Cossacks, and the Polish Government gladly seized the opportunity of converting them into a strong military colony for the defence of the border. The great Hungarian, Stephen Bathory,† who sat on the Polish throne from 1575 to 1586, enrolled the pick of them into six registered regiments of 1,000 men each, with allotted districts where they could live with their

---

* I.e., in the lowlands of the Dnieper.
† See Nisbet Bain : "The Valois and Bathory Election," Cambridge Modern History, vol. III.

wives and families, and fixed the town of Trachtimirow as their headquarters, which was ultimately re-transferred to the island of Hortica, just below the falls of the Dnieper; and thus on the numerous islands of that broad river there gradually grew up the famous Cossack community known as the *Zaporozhskaya Syech.** For the more prudent of the Polish rulers judged it expedient to leave the Cossacks as free as possible, so long as they fulfilled their chief obligation of guarding the frontiers of the republic from Tatar raids. The Cossack *Kosh*, or community, had the privilege of electing its *Koshevoi Ataman*, or chief of the *Kosh*, and his chief officers the *starshins*, which election took place annually, in the midst of the *maidan*, or great square, in front of the church of the *Syech*. The *koshevoi* received from the King of Poland direct the insignia of his office, namely, the *bulawa*, or bâton, the *bauschuk*, or horse-tail standard, and his official seal; but he was responsible for his actions to the *Kosh* alone, and an inquiry into his conduct during his year of office was held at the expiration of that term in the *Obshchaya Shkodka*, or general assembly, where complaints against him were invited and considered. In times of peace his power was little more than that of the responsible minister of a limited monarchy; but in time of warfare he was a dictator, and disobedience to his orders in the field was punished with death.

The Cossacks prided themselves on being the frontier guardians of both Eastern and Western Russia, and occasionally they rendered notable service both to the Pans and the Tsars. But on the whole they were a disturbing element; even their finest exploits, as, for instance, the capture of Azov, were very embarrassing to the Governments which employed them. Poland, with the Porte as her next-door neighbour, was bound, in her own interests, to keep the Cossacks within due bounds, and this she endeavoured to do by limiting their numbers and setting over them Polish officers. The Cossacks, on the other hand, resented the slightest curtailment of the liberty to " go in search of 'zhupans,'" as they phrased it,† and only after three bloody

---

* *I.e.*, "The settlement behind the falls." Hence the Dnieperian Cossacks were known as " Zaporozhians," or " Backfallsmen," similar to the American "Backwoodsmen."

† *I.e.*, go a-raiding. The *zhupan* was a warm upper garment.

rebellions, during the years 1592/96, did they submit to Polish dictation, and their registered number was reduced to the original 6,000. Matters were made far worse than they need have been by the incredibly stupid niggardliness of the *Sejm*, which, while forbidding the Cossacks to live upon their neighbours, nevertheless withheld from them their covenanted allowance of money and cloth. Another cause of irritation was the insolent tyranny of the Pans of the Ukrain, who treated their peasantry like the dirt beneath their feet, and savagely chastised every attempt of the serfs to run away and become "free," that is to say, "unregistered" Cossacks. Moreover, since 1557 the Pans were empowered by statute to punish their disobedient serfs with death, and they frequently left the execution of this iniquitous privilege to their generally detested Jewish factors. And presently the spark of religious fanaticism set this mass of combustible material in a blaze. The "Disunited" orthodox Church of Lithuania, in her extremity, sometimes appealed to her co-religionists the Cossacks for assistance, and in 1601, 1603, and 1625, bands of desperadoes from the Ukrain ravaged the environs of Mogilew and Witebsk, inflicted nameless outrages on women and children, and returned *na nis* laden with booty and captives. The *Sejm*, revolted by these and similar excesses, frequently debated the question whether it would not be better to extirpate the Cossacks, but the idea was always rejected as undesirable, as, but for the Cossacks the Ukrain would be unceasingly exposed to the attacks of the Turks and Tatars. The Zaporozhians were ordered, however, to burn their boats, forbidden to engage in piracy, and cautioned against receiving foreign ambassadors, or making separate alliances with foreign Powers, the latter prohibitions demonstrating eloquently enough to what heights of ambition the Cossacks had already ascended. Their audacity increased year by year. In 1627 they demanded that their number should be raised to 10,000. In 1630 they murdered Gregory Czerny, whom the *Sejm* had appointed their Ataman. In 1631 they again raided the Black Sea. In 1635 they destroyed the fort of Kodak which the Poles had built below Samara to hold them in check. Early in 1637 there were fresh disturbances, and the Polish commissioners, *na nis*, in

their reports to the *Sejm*, expressed the opinion that a wilderness
of wild beasts on the Dnieper was preferable to this *bellua sine
capite.* Late the same year the Cossacks rose against Poland
*en masse* under Kizimenko, who captured the town of Lyubno,
cut to pieces all the priests and Pans, and flung their carcases to
the dogs. Kizimenko was defeated and impaled alive by the
Crown Hetman Potocki; but in the following year there was a
still more dangerous rising, as the registered Cossacks this time
fought, along with the free Cossacks, against the Polish Government. Once more, however, Polish valour prevailed, and the
Zaporozhians were humiliated as they had never been humiliated
before, being deprived of the right of electing their officers and
forced to swear a new oath of fealty to the republic, and lay
all the insignia of their independence at the feet of the Crown
Hetman. Yet the very completeness of their triumph was
regretted by the Poles themselves two years later. In 1640 a
countless horde of Tatars devastated the whole Ukraine and
carried off immense booty in cattle and captives—unopposed
and unpursued, because the Cossack guardians of the frontier
were no longer at their posts. Eight years before, when King
Sigismund III. lay on his parade bier with a Moscovite diadem
round his temples, while, by his side, Uniate prelates from Kiev
were singing masses in the Slavonic language for the repose of
his soul, delegates from the Cossacks of the Dnieper arrived at
Warsaw to present a petition to the Polish Senate. They
claimed to have a voice in future in the election of the Polish
Kings, and they based their claim on the fact that they too
formed part of the republic. "Yes," replied the Polish senators,
"ye do form part of the republic, just as hair and nails form part
of the human body, and when hair and nails grow too long they
are clipped short." Only sixteen years after this haughty rebuke
was uttered, the unclipped nails of the Zaporozhian Cossacks
had lacerated the gallant Polish Republic out of all recognition,
and a Polish King was not ashamed to submit to the dictation of
a Cossack Ataman.

In the later years of Wladislaus IV. there dwelt in the
*starosty* of Korsun, in the Polish Ukrain, a certain Cossack,
Bogdan Chmielnicki, whose father Michael, after serving Poland

all his life, had died for her on the field of Cecora, leaving to his son Bogdan the village of Subotow, with which the Polish King had rewarded his valour and fidelity. Bogdan, after learning to read and write, a rare accomplishment in those days, entered the Cossack ranks, was dangerously wounded and taken prisoner in his first battle, and found leisure during his two years' captivity in Stambul to acquire the rudiments of Turkish and French. On returning to the Ukrain, he settled quietly down on his paternal estate at Subotow, and, in all probability, history would never have known his name if the intolerable persecution of a neighbouring Polish squire, Daniel Czaplinski, had not converted the thrifty and acquisitive Cossack husbandman into one of the most striking and sinister figures of modern times— a Joshua or an Attila, according to the point of view. Czaplinski was a typical representative of that exclusive, narrow-minded squirearchy, which, recognising no authority above and no privileges below it, was primarily responsible for the ruin of the Polish Republic. To an aristocratic bigot of this type, every low-born orthodox Cossack was an abomination, and Czaplinski's official position as sub-starosta of Chigorin, the nearest fortress-town, enabled him to persecute Chmielnicki with impunity. With no provocation, apparently, Czaplinski raided the Cossack's village, stole four hundred of his hayricks, murdered his servants, put him in chains, and, when he complained to the local courts (naturally, in vain, the oppressor being a gentleman), Czaplinski proceeded to the crowning outrage of seizing one of Chmielnicki's sons, and flogging him through the bazaars of Chigorin, so effectually, that the child (he was but ten) died at his father's house a few days later. On being released at the intercession of his tyrant's wife, Chmielnicki found himself practically a ruined man. Failing to get redress nearer home, he determined to seek justice at Warsaw, whither he had been summoned, with other Cossack delegates, to assist King Wladislaus IV. in his long-projected campaign against the Turks. The King, perceiving him to be a man of some education and intelligence, appointed him *pisarz*, or secretary, of the registered Cossacks, and chief recruiting officer; and Chmielnicki, encouraged by these marks of favour, complained to the King of the outrages inflicted upon him at Subotow, and of the seizure of his property. Wladislaus at once ordered the matter to be investigated by the law officers of the crown, but, inasmuch as Chmielnicki could produce no " privilege " entitling him to a property actually given to his father for military services, the Polish jurists decided that he had no redress. Then Wladislaus, revolted at this fresh instance of aristocratic chicanery, from which he himself had suffered so frequently, fastened a sword to the Cossack's side, and said to him significantly : " You are a soldier now, remember ! and can defend yourself."

Chmielnicki returned to the Ukraine another man. Wladislaus hint was not lost upon him. There can be little doubt that from henceforth he meant to be his own master. It is just possible, however, that the opportunity of winning fame and booty in the impending Turkish war might have reconciled him to his lot, and kept him faithful to the republic, and he actually served under the Grand Hetman Koniecpolski in the raid against the Tatars of the Ukrain in 1646. His hopes of distinction were, however, cut short by a sudden decree of the Polish Diet, which, in order to vex the King, refused to sanction the Turkish war, and forbade the levying of troops. Chmielnicki, who was now doubly hateful to the Pans as being a royalist as well as a Cossack, was deprived of his fair share of booty, accused of meditating rebellion, and, after an attempt upon his life had failed, he was thrown into jail, from which he escaped by bribing his jailers. Feeling that neither his life nor his liberty was any longer secure among the Pans, Chmielnicki, in December, 1647, fled for refuge *na niz*, and from the rocky islet of Bucka, in the Dnieper, sent messages to the Khan of the Crimea, proposing a simultaneous invasion of Poland by the Tatars and the Cossacks. To mask his designs, which continued throughout the winter months of 1648, Chmielnicki overwhelmed the dignitaries of the crown with humble epistles, imploring redress, even sending a supplication to the King at Warsaw ; and, in the meantime, his agents were busy throughout the Ukrain stirring up the peasantry and inviting them to assemble among the islands of the Dnieper. Islam Gerai, the Khan of the Crimea, at first saw only a Polish ruse in Chmielnicki's advances. Not till the

Cossack had professed himself a convert to Islam, and had sent his son Timothy to the Crimea as a hostage, did the Khan despatch Tugai Bey to the Dnieper with 4,000 Tatar auxiliaries. By this time all Chmielnicki's preparations were complete. On April 18, 1648, at an assembly of the Zaporozhians on the Lower Dnieper, he openly declared his intention of proceeding against the Poles, and was elected Ataman by acclamation; immediately afterwards he marched rapidly northwards. Unfortunately for Poland at this critical moment, the grand bâton of the crown* was in the tremulous, incapable hands of the drunken and dissipated Nicholas Potocki, who had all a Polish magnate's sovereign contempt for every opinion but his own. Though warned betimes of the approaching danger, and expressly commanded by the King to await reinforcements, Potocki, relying on the fidelity of the registered Cossacks who were with him, imagined it would be an easy task to crush the rebellion, and accordingly sent his son Stephen with a portion of his army and 4,000 registered Cossacks into the steppe. On May 9 the elder Potocki received word that the registered Cossacks, who, unpaid for months by the Diet, were ready enough to listen to Chmielnicki's emissaries, had murdered their officers and gone over to the enemy, and yet, in spite of this, he halted obstinately at Borowica, and sent not a single trooper to the assistance of his hard-pressed son, though the sound of heavy firing in the steppe was audible for three days. Meanwhile, Stephen Potocki had encountered the Cossack host on the banks of the river *Zheltuiya Vodui*, "Yellow Waters." Deserted by his dragoons and overwhelmed by the countless hordes of Cossacks and Tatars, the younger Potocki, nevertheless, offered an heroic resistance, but finally, after fighting hard during May 16, 18/19, he was slain and his army annihilated. At the news of this disaster, old Potocki lost his head altogether. Instead of falling back on the fortress of Korsun, as advised by Kalinowski, his second in command, he fled precipitately towards Bohuslaw, ran straight into an ambush prepared for him by Chmielnicki in the marshy valley of *Kruta Balka*, "Hard Plank,"

* The official title of the Polish commander-in-chief was the "Grand Hetman of the Crown."

near Korsun, and there 8,500 of his 10,000 men were massacred
or taken prisoners; he himself, Kalinowski, and a few other
superior officers, being sent in chains to the Crimea to be held
at ransom (May 26). To complete the misfortunes of Poland,
she now lost the one man capable of repairing other men's
blunders. On May 20, a week before the battle of "Hard Plank,"
Wladislaus IV., just as he was on the point of marching against
the rebels, died of a chill caused by over-exerting himself at hunting, and the republic was overwhelmed at the same time by the
miseries of an interregnum and the horrors of a jacquerie.*

The immediate consequence of the victories of "Yellow
Waters" and "Hard Plank" was the outbreak of a *khlopskaya
sloba*, or "serfs' fury," the like of which is, fortunately, unknown in
Western Europe. Throughout the Ukrain the gentry were
hunted down, flayed, burnt, blinded, and sawn asunder. Every
manor-house and castle was reduced to ashes. Every Uniate or
Catholic priest who could be caught was hung up before his own
high altar, along with a Jew and a hog. Everyone who shaved
his head after the Polish fashion, or wore Polish costume, was
instantly cut down by the *haidamaki*, as Chmielnicki's bands
were called. The panic-stricken inhabitants fled to the nearest
strongholds, and soon the rebels were swarming all over the
palatinates of Volhynia and Podolia. Chmielnicki must be held
responsible for the worst of these atrocities. He had a long
score to settle with his enemies the Pans, and with him vengeance
meant extirpation. Affecting to believe a wild rumour that the
envoys sent by him to Warsaw had been impaled, he let loose
the vilest of his satellites, Krzywonos and Gandza, upon the
defenceless inhabitants of the Ukrain. At Polonny the Jews
were cut up into joints and sold as meat by the butchers, and at
Bar the Cossacks roasted and ate little children in the presence
of their mothers.† But the Ataman was as crafty as he was
cruel. Disagreeably awakened to the insecurity of his position
by the refusal of the Tsar and the Sultan to accept him as a
vassal, he magnanimously opened negotiations with the Pans,

---

* Compare Sokolowski: " Dzieje Polski," 909—911 ; Solovev : " Istoria
Rossy," X., 1.
† See Kulish : "Ot padenie Malorossy ot Polshi," II., 219.

and addressed a letter, half apologetic, half submissive, to Wladislaus IV., whom he knew to be dead. At Warsaw these hypocritical overtures were regarded as a sign of weakness, instead of what they really were, an attempt to gain time, and commissioners, the chief of whom was the orthodox Castellan of Braclaw, Kisiel, were sent to the Ukrain to negotiate with Chmielnicki. The Ataman detained the commissioners during the summer of 1648, and then dismissed them with impossible conditions. Meanwhile the Polish army, 40,000 strong, with 100 guns, had assembled on the frontier. It was composed entirely of gentlemen, and resembled a bridal procession rather than a battle array. These splendid cavaliers dressed themselves in magnificent ermine-trimmed mantles ; heron plumes waved from their jewelled caps ; their spurs were of gold and silver, and their saddles and shabracks ablaze with precious stones. For Chmielnicki and his host they expressed the utmost contempt. " This rabble must be chased with whips, not smitten with swords," they cried. On September 23, 1648, the two armies encountered each other near Pilyawa, and after a stubborn three days' contest, the gallant Polish pageant was scattered to the winds. The steppe for miles around was strewn with corpses, and the Cossacks are said to have reaped 10,000,000 guldens worth of booty when the fight was over. All Poland now lay at Chmielnicki's feet, and the road to the defenceless capital was open before him, but after capturing Konstantinow and Zbarzh, and blackmailing Lemberg, he wasted two precious months in vain before the fortress of Zamosc, and then the newly-elected King of Poland, John Casimir, Wladislaus IV.'s brother, privately opened negotiations with the rebel, officially recognised him by sending to him the *bulawa* and the other insignia of the Ataman's office, and promised his " faithful Zaporozhians " the confirmation of all their ancient liberties if they would retire from Zamosc, break off their alliance with the Tatars, and await peace commissioners at Pereyaslavl. The Pans were furious with the King for thus making friends with the worst enemy of the republic ; yet it is hard to say what else could have been done under the circumstances, and Chmielnicki recognised his obligations to the royal House of Vasa by retiring from Zamosc to distant Kiev. In June, 1649, arrayed in cloth of gold, mounted on a white horse, and surrounded by his officers, he made his triumphal entry into the orthodox metropolis of Poland. At the gates of the cathedral of St. Sophia the metropolitan and clergy hailed him as the new Macchabæus of orthodoxy, and the rector and pupils of the academy eulogised his exploits in Latin and Slavonic orations, whereupon the conqueror richly endowed the Church with Polish spoils, and made the whole city drunk night after night at an endless round of banquets. And now in the hour of prosperity the true character of Bogdan came to light. A capable savage raised suddenly by fortune to unheard-of eminence, this child of the steppe at once betrayed his Cossack origin. Like other superior savages, of whom history tells us, he was the creature of every passing mood or whim, incapable of cool and steady judgment, or of the slightest self-control—an incalculable weathercock, blindly obsequious to every wind that blew. Chmielnicki was never the same two days, or even two hours, together. In the morning he might be found kneeling in fervent prayer before the high altar of an orthodox church, the same evening he would be consulting wizards and "wise women." On Monday his house would be open to all the world; on Tuesday he would be inaccessible to his trustiest comrades. In the morning he might welcome you with embraces and professions of eternal friendship, but approach him in the evening you would run the risk of a broken pate. The Polish commissioners who met him at Peryaslavl to arrange the preliminaries of peace and invest him as Ataman, had a taste of all his qualities. On the first day appointed for the conference he excused himself from attendance on the plea that he had been drinking all the previous night with his soothsayers. When Kisiel, the chief commissioner, tearfully implored him to remain faithful to the republic, the Cossack fiercely replied that he would not lay down his arms till he had released the whole orthodox population of the Ukrain from Polish tyranny. Then, in a paroxysm of maudlin fury, he exclaimed: "First I made war on my own account to avenge insults; now I will fight for our orthodox faith. I won't give up the people to be made into serfs. I will have a horde of 300,000 men all to myself, and by my side shall ride Tugai Bey, my brother, my darling, my bright falcon, the only true falcon in the world. We will drive all the Poles behind the Vistula, and there they shall sit as quiet as mice."* Then he proceeded to insult the commis-sioners by upbraiding them with their degeneracy. "The Poles are not what they used to be," he said. "They are faint hare-hearts, children in armour, who die of fright when they see the Cossacks at a distance." He meant, he said, to hang all the *Lyakhs*† up by the heels, carry off their belongings in their own waggons, and hand over all that remained of their realm to the Turkish or the Moscovite Tsar. When Kisiel reminded him that if Fortune were as bright she was also as brittle as glass, and that to seek the protection of the Turk was to condemn the orthodox to extirpation, he stamped and swore, tore his hair, and fingered his sword. His conditions of peace, when he did condescend to offer them, were so extravagant that the commis-sioners durst not accept them. On their return they reported that the whole Ukrain was terrorised by the Cossacks and strewn with Polish spoils. In the public square in Kiev old silver-plate was sold at a shilling a piece and even cheaper. A single merchant of Kiev bought from a Cossack, for a mere song, a sack of damaged silver-plate which a strong farm labourer could scarce carry. Chmielnicki himself had appropriated twenty-four chests of silver which he buried at Chigorin in huge vats, and his stable held 130 of the best Turkish thoroughbreds. They also reported that nearly the whole agricultural population had joined the Cossacks and made no secret of their intention of rooting out the gentry. At Kiev unspeakable atrocities were committed in broad daylight. The Catholic and Uniate monas-teries and churches were pillaged and the clergy dragged out by the hair and massacred, or drowned, while the gentry were coursed and hunted down with dogs like so many hares or stags amidst shouts of laughter. The citizens of Kiev were forbidden, under pain of death, to harbour the fugitives, and they turned from their thresholds scores of women and children to torments worse than death. The very corpses of the gentry were taken

* Solovev: "Istoria Rossy." X., 1.
† The name given to the Poles by the Cossacks.

out of their coffins and thrown to the dogs ; the bodies of dead
priests and professors were propped up in the corners of the
streets with large books in their stiff hands.  Chmielnicki was
obviously preparing for war, and in June, 1649, he again invaded
Poland with a countless host of Tatars, Zaporozhians, and Don
Cossacks.  Fortunately for the republic she found a champion
in Prince Jeremiah Wisniowiecki, a fanatical Catholic convert of
heroic valour and no mean military capacity, who kept the
Cossack host at bay in his entrenched camp at Zbaraz for a
month, till the King relieved him at the head of 25,000 men.
A bloody battle ensued near Zborow, on the banks of the Strypa,
when only the personal valour of John Casimir, the superiority of
the Polish artillery, and the skilful diplomacy of the Polish
chancellor, Ossolinski, who succeeded in buying off the Tatars
at the critical moment, enabled the royal forces to hold their own.
Chmielnicki, checked in his career of victory, though still
unconquered, now dictated peace on his own terms.  By the
compact of Zborow (August 21, 1649) he was recognised as
Ataman of the Zaporozhians, the whole *starosty* of Chigorin
was ceded to him as an appanage, and the number of the
registered Cossacks was fixed at 40,000 ; the garrison of Zbaraz
was ransomed for 400,000 guldens,* an amnesty was granted to
the Cossacks ; Jews, Pans, and Jesuits were excluded from their
domains, and all official dignities in the orthodox palatinates of
Kiev, Chernigov, and Braclaw were henceforth to be held solely
by the orthodox gentry.  In return for these humiliating con-
cessions Chmielnicki did homage to the King of Poland on
bended knee in the presence of both armies, kissed the King's
hand, and the Chancellor of Lithuania recited his pardon.

For the next eighteen months Chmielnicki ruled the Ukrain
like a sovereign prince.  He divided the country into sixteen
provinces, made his native place, Chigorin, the Cossack capital,
levied taxes and entered into direct relations with foreign
powers.  Poland and Moscovy competed for his alliance, and in
his more exalted moods he meditated an orthodox crusade
against the Turk at the head of the Southern Slavs.  But he
was no statesman, and his difficulties proved overwhelming.

* Sokolowski : "Dzieje Polski," 916.

Instinct told him that his old ally the Khan of the Crimea was unreliable, and that the Tsar of Moscovy was his natural protector, yet he could not make up his mind to abandon the one or turn to the other. With the Pans he could never be friendly, and his attempt to carve a principality for his son Timothy out of Moldavia, which Poland regarded as her vassal, led to the outbreak, in February, 1651, of a third war between suzerain and subject which speedily assumed the dignity and dimensions of a crusade. Chmielnicki was now regarded not merely as a Cossack rebel, but as the arch-enemy of Catholicism in Eastern Europe. The Pope granted a plenary absolution to all who took up arms against him, and sent John Casimir his benediction and a consecrated banner. But Bogdan also was not without ecclesiastical sanction. The Archbishop of Corinth girded him with a sword that had lain upon the Holy Sepulchre, and the Metropolitan of Kiev absolved him from all his sins without the usual preliminary of confession, and solemnly blessed the snow-white standard under which the Cossack Hetman rode forth to battle, dressed in purple and ermine. This standard bore upon it, in letters of gold, the inscription : "Peace to Christendom!" But Fortune, so long Bogdan's friend, now deserted him, and at Bereszteczko, on the banks of the Stuiva (July 1, 1651), the Cossack chieftain was utterly routed. All hope of an independent Cossackdom was now at an end, but it was not till three years later that Chmielnicki recognised that he was not strong enough to contend single-handed with the Polish Republic, and became the un- willing vassal of the Tsar. Thus, as we shall see in the following chapter, not Poland, but her rival Moscovy, reaped the fruits of Poland's hard-won victory over her rebel Cossacks.

# CHAPTER IV.

## The Reign of Tsar Alexius to the Peace of Andrussowo. 1645—1667.

Administration of Boris Morozov—Misery of the People—Dokhturov's Mission to England—Exclusion of the English Merchants from Moscovy—Marriage of the Tsar and the Rise of the Miloslavskies—The Moscow Riots of 1648 and the Fall of Morozov—Disturbances on the Dwina—Rebellions of Novgorod and Pskov—The cautious Foreign Policy of Moscovy—Attempts to pick a Quarrel with Poland—Chmielnicki, defeated by the Poles, does Homage to Moscow—Beginning of the Thirteen Years War—Campaigns of 1654 and 1655—Conquests of the Moscovites—Intervention of Charles X. of Sweden—War between Sweden and Moscovy—Athanasy Orduin Nash-chokin—His Negotiations with Sweden—Peace of Kardis—Progress of the Polish War—Disasters of Konotop, Czudnow and Yeromsk—Division of the Cossacks into Two Sections—Peace Negotiations—Doroshensko's Raid—Peace of Andrussowo—Its Importance to Moscovy—Orduin Nashchokin appointed Guardian of the Great Seal.

WE remember how, with his dying breath, Tsar Michael recommended his surviving son and successor, Alexius, then a youth of sixteen, to the care of the boyarin Boris Ivanovich Morozov. Hardly could he have chosen, under the circumstances, a more suitable guardian. Shrewd and sensible, sufficiently enlightened to recognise the needs of his country, and by no means inaccessible to Western ideas, Morozov stood high above his fellows. He possessed besides the entire confidence of his new master, a singularly gentle and affectionate young prince, whose tutor he had been from his earliest years. Morozov's principal colleague was the *dumny dyak* Nazar Chestoi, formerly a merchant at Yaroslavl, a clever but greedy financial expert. Moreover the death of the Tsaritsa Eudoxia on August 18, 1645, a month after her husband's decease, left Morozov a free hand, for the patriarch Joasaf was, politically, a nonentity.

The first acts of the new Government showed that vigorous

people able to act with wisdom and dignity were at the head of affairs.   Prince Waldemar of Denmark was honourably restored to his father, King Christian IV., and a punitive expedition against the predatory Tatar Khan was prepared despite the violence of Sultan Ibrahim, who killed Telepnev, one of the two Moscovite envoys at Stambul, by ill-treatment, and threatened to roast his colleague Kuzovlev on a spit if the Don Cossacks were let loose against the Khan.   A confirmation of the truce of Polyankova was also obtained from Poland, and the republic was invited to co-operate with Moscovy against "the Hagarens" of the Crimea.   King Wladislaus IV. received the Tsar's ambassadors courteously, and his own envoy to Moscovy, Kisiel, expressed the hope that Poland and Moscovy, " like two cedars of Lebanon planted by the same almighty hand," might for ever stand side by side ; but the negotiations came to nothing owing to Poland's fear of provoking the Porte, Turkey, as the next-door neighbour of the republic, being always far more dangerous to her than more distant Moscovy.

Morozov's domestic policy was severe but equitable.   The economical condition of Moscovy at this period was anything but satisfactory.   The native traders, overburdened as they were with taxes, and hampered by all manner of disabilities, found it very difficult to compete with the privileged foreign merchants.   In 1646 they petitioned the Tsar against the " English Germans," who, being in the possession of unlimited capital, and having at their disposal a whole army of well-paid middlemen, were able absolutely to control the Moscovite market and undersell the native traders.   They were also accused of exporting corn and provisions without paying any tolls.   " Merciful Gosudar," conclude the petitioners, " look on thy slaves and orphans and let us not be brought to eternal wretchedness by them of another faith ! "   The ordinary trading classes were impoverished still further by the unfair competition of the *stryeltsui*, the Cossacks and the serfs of the monasteries, metropolitans, boyars, and other powerful people, all of whom were free of taxation ; hence the number of the taxable traders tended steadily to diminish, till the Government, alarmed at the falling off of the revenue, summoned delegates from all the commercial

R.                                                                                    H classes to deliberate with the Tsar upon the subject, when it was decreed that henceforth nobody engaging in trade should remain outside the usual assessment lists or categories (1648). The same year, after previously consulting the patriarch, the Tsar held a council of prelates and magnates for the purpose of codifying the laws and thus making the course of justice more expeditious and inexpensive. In this wise reform Morozov also took a leading part. It was more difficult to deal with the privileged foreign merchants, especially with the English, to whom, since Merrick's days, Moscovy had been under some obligations. But the course of events presently enabled the Tsar to help his subjects in this matter also. In 1645 Gerazim Dokhturov was sent to London by Tsar Alexius to inform Charles I. of his accession. He refused to present his credentials to the Parliament and demanded a free passage to the King, but the Parliament would neither send him to Charles nor allow him to return to Moscovy. In May, 1646, hearing that the King had surrendered to the Parliament, Dokhturov again demanded an audience of his Majesty. " Now that he is in your hands let me see him ! " he said ; to which it was replied that this could not be, as the King had now no authority. Ultimately Dokhturov was presented to both Houses, and Manchester and Lenthal took off their hats at the mention of the Tsar's name, but Dokhturov still refused to deliver his credentials to anyone but the King, and complained that England was the only country in which the Tsar's envoys were not allowed full liberty. In consequence of his report the English merchants in Moscovy were deprived of their privileges, and when the news of the execution of Charles I. reached Alexius he issued an *ukaz* excluding them from his dominions. "At the request of your Sovereign King Charles, and because of our brotherly love and friendship towards him," ran the *ukaz*, "you were allowed to trade with us by virtue of letters of commerce, but it has been made known to us that you English have done a great wickedness by killing your Sovereign King Charles, for which evil deed you cannot be suffered to remain in the realm of Moscovy." They were permitted, however to call and trade at Archangel. Encouraged by Tsar Alexius's loyalty to his cousin of England, several royalist envoys

appeared at Moscow between 1647 and 1650 to ask for assistance. Culpepper, who came in 1647, was permitted to purchase
30,000 quarters of wheat to sell abroad, and in 1650 the same
envoy received from Alexius 15,000 rubles' worth of furs and
5,000 rubles' worth of rye in return for a promise to repay the
Tsar 40,000 Lübeck thalers in three years. The Government
also made some money out of tobacco. The fluctuations in the
tobacco trade were curious. Under Tsar Michael the use of
" the vile, godless grass imported by foreigners " was prohibited,
and all smokers had their noses slit. In 1646 the sale of the
weed was again permitted, but now it was made a Government
monopoly. In 1648 it was prohibited altogether. Morozov also
endeavoured to replenish the exchequer by a rigid system of
economy, such as abolishing a great many useless and expensive
Court offices and reducing salaries wholesale, measures which,
together with his supposed partiality for the detested foreigner,
contributed to make him exceedingly unpopular. Yet the
powerful favourite had seemed unassailable when on January 27,
1648, he married the Tsar's sister-in-law, an event which led to
the elevation of the clever, unscrupulous Miloslavskies, branded
at a later day by the unappeasable hatred of Peter the Great.
When it was deemed necessary for Tsar Alexius to marry, two
hundred of the prettiest girls in the Tsardom were sent to Moscow according to ancient custom. Out of these, the six most
beautiful were presented to the Tsar himself, and his choice fell
upon the daughter of Theodore Vsevolozhky. The favoured
damsel was so excited by her good luck that she swooned on the
spot, whereupon it was assumed that she was liable to the falling
sickness, and the unfortunate beauty and her family were forthwith transported to Siberia. Her removal has sometimes been
attributed to the intrigues of Morozov, but on very insufficient
evidence. The fact remains, however, that, ten days after the
Tsar had married Maria, daughter of Ilya Miloslavsky, Morozov
married her sister Anna. Ilya, the head of the Miloslavsky
family, owed his advancement in life to his connection with the
unscrupulous but eminently capable *dumny dyak* Ivan Taras-
vich Gramotin,* the leading diplomatist of Moscovy between 1621

* See Putsillo : "Dumny Dyak I. T. Gramotin."

and 1638.  Miloslavsky seems to have been a typically self-
seeking seventeenth century boyarin, and he gave shelter to
parasites like Leonty Pleshchev and Trakhaniotov, intriguers
even more eager than himself to get rich quickly.  Morozov's
reputation was bound to suffer from his connection with such
men, and he was hated more than ever when it was found that
the numerous petitions against the extortions of the Tsar's new
ministers remained unheeded.  At last the people took the law
into their own hands.  In May, 1648, as the Tsar was returning
with his suite to Moscow from the Troitskaya Monastery, he was
stopped by a large crowd, whose ringleader seized his horse's
bridle, rehearsed the grievances of the people, and begged the
Tsar to substitute good counsellors for bad.  The bearing of the
crowd was respectful enough and Alexius patiently listened to
them and promised to grant their requests.  They were about to
disperse when some of the younger courtiers, impatient at the
meddling of the mob, had the folly to curse the people and flip
them with their *nagaikas* or Cossack whips.  A dangerous riot
immediately ensued.  The infuriated mob stoned their assailants,
dispersed them, murdered Pleshchev and the *dumny dyak*
Chertoi in the streets, and fell to plundering the houses of
Morozov and the other wealthy boyars.  Morozov hid from their
violence, but his wife was caught and stripped of her clothes and
jewels, which the mob threw to their comrades outside.  Yet,
even now, the rioters showed some moderation, and spared the
life of Anna Miloslavskaya because she was the sister of the
Tsaritsa.  On the following day the rioting was renewed.  Conflagrations burst forth in all quarters of the town, and the mob,
intent on further mischief, proceeded to the *kreml*, but found the
foreign troops drawn up before it with drums beating and colours
flying.  Alexius sent out to them his cousin Nikita Romanov,
one of the most mysterious personages in Russian history, of
whom we know only that he enjoyed throughout his lifetime an
extraordinary and unaccountable popularity.  Doffing his hat to
the mob, Nikita declared that the Tsar was ready to comply
with their demands, but that they must first disperse.  The
people shouted that they had no complaint against the Tsar
himself, but only against those who plundered the people in his

name, and they demanded that Morozov and Trakhaniotov should be delivered over to them. Nikita urged them to leave the fate of the two ministers in the hands of the Tsar, but the people were not so easily persuaded, and went away still murmuring. For the next three days it was thought necessary to regale the *stryeltsui*, who were at the head of the riot, with mead and vodka, and then the Tsar personally appealed to the people on his return from church. He thanked them for revealing to him the villainy of Pleshchev and Trakhaniotov; he promised to put in their places " honest and pleasant people; " he guaranteed that there should be no more oppression by engaging henceforth to look after things himself, and, finally, he made a touching appeal to them on behalf of Morozov. "I must confess," said the young Tsar, "that I cannot altogether justify him, yet will I not judge him. He is a man dear to me, the husband of my wife's sister, and to give him up to death would be most grievous to me." At these words his voice was choked with tears, and the people, grateful at being admitted to the confidence of their Gosudar, exclaimed : " May the Tsar live many years, and may the will of God and the Gosudar be done." Ultimately Peter Trakhaniotov, who certainly seems to have deserved Olearius's* description of him as "the flayer of the people," was duly executed. Morozov was banished to the Kirillov-Byelozersky Monastery till the storm had blown over, but within two months' time was brought back privily, and to the day of his death (in 1661) remained one of the Tsar's chief, if secret, counsellors, even when his increasing infirmities withdrew him from all active participation in affairs.

The successful issue of the Moscow riots was the occasion of disquieting disturbances all over the Tsardom. In Solvuichegodsk, on the northern Dwina, the trappers and traders had already compounded with the tax collector for the modest sum of 20 rubles, instead of 535, the amount originally claimed, when the news reached them that the mob at Moscow had proved stronger than the Government, and procured the banishment of Morozov. The temptation to recover the 20 rubles by similar methods proved irresistible. The tax collector was seized by a

* Olearius: " Voyages and Travels." etc.

furious mob, hustled and beaten, his papers were torn up and flung in his face, he was plundered to his very shirt, and was only saved from a terrible death by the intervention of a rich and powerful lady, Theodora Stroganova, who hid him in the parish church, which her family had built, and smuggled him away by night in a canoe down the river Vuichegoda. This was at the end of July, 1648. In the beginning of August another riot of the same sort broke out at the manufacturing centre of Ustyug, on the Sukhona. Here also the mob repented them of having paid 260 rubles' worth of taxes to the *voivoda*, and, led by a blacksmith, murdered the *voivoda's* secretary and plundered the Government stores. An investigation ensued, with the usual accompaniment of hanging and torturing. In the midst of this savagery we come across a curious piece of folk-lore, which, like a rushlight flickering feebly in deep darkness, faintly illuminates the manners and customs of the period. One of the rioters, "Jacky* the Soldier," while under torture, had a stone drawn out of the sole of his foot, and confessed to learning enough magic from a highwayman named "Kettledrum"† to make him insensible to pain. The process was to put a stone into the sole of his foot and repeat the following formula: "Heaven is tree-bark and earth is tree-bark, and as the dead under the earth feel nothing, so may I never feel cruelty and torture." It was also characteristic of the times that the investigator Ivan Romodanovsky, who was sent down to restore order with 200 *stryeltsui*, abused his authority shamefully by torturing innocent and guilty indiscriminately in order to extort as much money as possible out of them, till he was summoned back to Moscow to answer for his misdeeds.

Much more serious were the rebellions of Novgorod and Pskov, the chief commercial cities of the realm, and far too powerful to be overawed by a few companies of *stryeltsui*. Here however, the outbreaks were due not to oppression but to ignorance and intolerance. The immediate occasion of the disturbances at Pskov was an *ukas* permitting a Swedish agent, one Nummers, to take away with him 11,000 quarters of wheat for which the Swedish Government had paid beforehand. The

---

* Ivashka                                    † Buben.

Pskovians, always jealous and suspicious of their " German "*
neighbours, implored their *voivoda* Sobakin and their archbishop Makary not to let so much corn go out of the country
till they had petitioned the Tsar about it. As, however, the
Tsar's *ukas* was stringent and the corn had been paid for, the
*voivoda* let Nummers depart, but the mob seized him and his
escort as they were passing through the gates, robbed them of
everything and then hoisted them on to the top of two huge vats,
in the sight of all the people. The ringleaders then proceeded
to cross-examine the unfortunate foreigners as to the details of
a purely imaginary conspiracy against the city—executioners,
armed with knouts, unmercifully flogging them at intervals, in
order to loosen their tongues. The news of this outrage profoundly excited the neighbouring city of Novgorod, and when,
a few days later (March 26, 1649) the Danish ambassador Grab
arrived there from Moscow on his way home, there was a general
outcry that the Germans were taking treasure out of the country,
and the unfortunate Dane was set upon, severely mauled, and
robbed of everything. This was followed by an attack upon the
warehouses of the rich merchants both native and foreign, which
were plundered with impunity, the *voivoda* Prince Theodore
Khilkhov having no adequate police force at his disposal. And
now was heard the ominous tolling of the great *sploshny kolokol*,
or alarm bell, which from time immemorial had ever been the
signal for the assembling of the mob of Novgorod in the great
square. From every quarter resounded the cry, " The Gosudar
cares not for us! He feeds the German lands with our money
and corn." Then the stone *gorod*, or citadel, in the centre of the
city was stormed, the prisons were broken open, and the people
chose their leaders from among the most desperate of the
liberated convicts. The *voivoda*, in his utter helplessness,
implored the metropolitan Nikon, of whom we shall hear a
great deal presently,† to resort to spiritual weapons, and on
St. Alexius's day, March 29, in the cathedral of St. Sophia, the
archbishop solemnly excommunicated the insurgents. But this

---

* All foreigners, it will be remembered, were regarded as Germans (*Nyemtsui*)
by the Moscovites.

† For the early career of this remarkable man see next chapter.

extreme measure only increased the uproar.  Both the cathedral
and the archbishop's palace were attacked by the mob, and
Nikon scarce escaped from their hands alive.  Fortunately for the
Moscovite Government, a cold fit of panic at the enormity of their
latest misdeed now suddenly fell upon the insurgents, and they
deemed it prudent to send to Moscow their own account of the
affair, which differed materially from the report of Nikon, whom
they hastened to accuse of tyranny and violence.  But the archbishop himself, recognising that this was a case in which clemency
was expedient, exhorted the Tsar " to imitate the compassionate
and merciful God," and at the end of April, Novgorod, freely
pardoned, returned to her allegiance.  Only a few of the ringleaders of the mob were beheaded, the rest were more or less
severely knouted and expelled the city.

Pskov, so far from following the example of its "elder
brother," obstinately persisted in evil-doing and heaped outrage
upon outrage.  Her rebels, encouraged by the riots in Novgorod, now put the metropolitan Makary in chains, tortured
the wretched Swede Nummers for half an hour at a time, and
beat their own *voivodui* with clubs and axes.  Prince Khovansky,
with 2,000 men, was sent against them from Novgorod, but not
only did they sally forth and capture his waggons, but when he
weakly offered them terms, they flogged his messenger and
threatened to boil and eat the *voivoda* himself if ever they got
him into their hands.  Throughout May and June the Pskovians
successfully resisted all Khovansky's efforts to capture the town.
Their savagery increased daily, and they are said to have
worried the corpses of the soldiers they slew, "like wild beasts."
Instead of despatching fresh troops against them, the Government once more had recourse to the spiritual arm, and on
July 11, Rafael, Bishop of Kolomna, with a few attendant
archimandrites and priests, courageously ventured among the
Pskovians and promised them a full amnesty if only they would
lay down their arms.  They were not even required to surrender
their ringleaders.  Again it was Nikon who advised the Tsar
and his Council to show this extraordinary clemency to rebels
who had not the slightest justification to offer for what they were
doing and had done.  The astute prelate, perceiving that the

young and inexperienced Tsar was surrounded by feeble and
incompetent counsellors, rightly judged that extreme measures
were out of the question.   He represented that the four ringleaders of Pskov were omnipotent and indivisible, that the
people would never deliver them up, and that the rebel bands
were ravaging the whole country-side, killing and burning in
every direction, so that all the roads were covered with corpses.
" I beseech thee, O Gosudar," he concludes, " to give these men
their lives, arch-rogues though they be, lest the whole district be
utterly ruined."   The Tsar's Council was still further impressed
by the subsequent intelligence that on July 23 the rebels made a
sortie in force and captured Khovansky's whole camp, though
ultimately repulsed with the loss of 300 men and all their
cannons and banners.   Nikon's advice was therefore followed.
On August 31, in the cathedral of the Trinity, Bishop Rafael,
at the peril of his life and amidst an indescribable uproar,
induced the Pskovians to kiss the cross to the Gosudar, and
granted the whole city a free pardon.   None was punished at
the time, but long afterwards, when the better people had
regained their former influence in the city, they searched out
and punished the former ringleaders of the rebellion quietly and
at their leisure.

A Government afraid to punish its own rebels would naturally
be anxious to avoid complications abroad, and thus, during the
earlier years of Tsar Alexius, the foreign policy of Moscovy
was necessarily cautious and expectant.   Weak as she was, and
surrounded by powerful enemies, she had grown accustomed
to insinuate her way to power and greatness warily, gradually,
and by the most devious ways, which are generally the most
dirty ones.   Yet never for a moment did Moscovy leave out of
sight the goal of her ambition—the recovery of the lost Slavonic
lands—and Chmielnicki, by suddenly laying bare the nakedness of the Polish Republic, outwardly so splendid and imposing,
had opened the eyes of Moscovy to the fact that her secular
enemy was no longer the mother of warriors equal to those
whom King Stephen Bathory, and the great Hetmans Chodkiewicz and Zolkiewski, had led impetuously against innumerable
odds to certain victory.   In the autumn of 1649, as we have

already seen,* the redoubtable Satrap seemed to have carved a *tertium quid* for himself out of Polish territory, and the Moscovite Government, foreseeing the inevitability of yet another war between Poland and the Cossacks, was thereby encouraged to send to Warsaw (January, 1650) an embassy, which can only be described as a blackmailing speculation of the most impudent description. The envoys complained that in many books recently printed in Poland, shameful and sinful allusions had been made to the late and the present Tsars. One Latin work published at Dantzic in 1643, recording the exploits of Wladislaus IV., had that monarch's portrait as a frontispiece, with the subscription : " He subdued Moscovy." Moreover the said book insinuated that the Moscovites were Christians only in name, while their habits were barbarous and bestial. It was also alleged that another book, printed in 1649, described Moscovy as " poor Moscovy," and contained other offensive things impossible to repeat. The envoys then announced that, in consequence of these insults, war would be declared unless the King surrendered all the towns ceded by his late Tsarish Majesty to King Wladislaus, and paid 500,000 guldens by way of compensation for the damage done to the Tsar's honour. The Pans, with Chmielnicki already on their hands, were more alarmed than amused by this novel and *naïve* way of picking a quarrel. Besides it was no easy matter to deal with people so childish, proud, and stupid. They tried to explain (what was strictly true) that the King had nothing to do with the publication of books, good, bad, or indifferent. " If fools choose to print coarse, silly stuff, we only laugh at it," said the Pans. " You may print what you like about us. We should not be offended at all, let alone make it a pretext for breaking a solemn treaty." The Moscovites doggedly insisted that the Tsar meant to take back the towns ceded by his father because of the dishonour done to his name. " What," cried the indignant Poles, " you come into Poland, you buy books written by some drunken parson or other, and for tomfoolery like that you have the assurance to ask us to give up Smolensk and other fortresses purchased with our best blood! Why you will be asking for Warsaw next!" They also sarcastically

* See preceding chapter.

ALEXEI — MICHAÉLOVITS
Czaar et Grand Duc de Moscouie Conseruateur de toutles Russes
et Dominateur de Plus.res terres et Seigneuries. & Fils de Michael
Foederovits Czaar et Grand Duc de Moscouie Auquel Il a
Succede en L'annee 1645. le 12.e Juillet estant Aga pour lors de 15
Ans Il a Espousse en L'annee 1647 la fille d'Ilia Danilovits Miloslauskj, &

TSAR ALEXIUS

AS COMMANDER-IN-CHIEF.

expressed their astonishment that no one in the Moscovite realm seemed to know Latin or Polish well enough to understand the plain meaning of the most ordinary words. Mutual recriminations ensued, and at last the Moscovite envoys declared they would be satisfied if the offensive volumes were burnt in public by the common hangman. "That is impossible," replied the Pans; "it would put us to shame before all Europe, but we will burn them privily." At last a compromise was arrived at. The pages containing the objectionable matter were to be torn out of the volumes and burnt in public, and this was actually done, though the people murmured loudly at seeing the chapters recording the glorious deeds of Kings Sigismund III. and Wladislaus IV. ignominiously burnt in the market place. It would have been better, they said, to have surrendered the towns to the Tsar, or even to have fought for them, rather than have submitted to this dishonour. The victory of the Poles over Chmielnicki at Bereszteczko, in July, 1651, somewhat cooled the martial ardour of the Moscovites, and for the next three years both Poland and Moscovy watched with some apprehension the windings and doublings of the crafty and unstable Ataman, who openly interfered in the affairs of Wallachia, Moldavia, and Transylvania, assumed the high-sounding and ominous title of "Guardian of the Ottoman Porte,"* and in 1652 inflicted a severe defeat on the Polish chivalry at Batoka, on the Moldavian frontier. In 1653 Poland made a supreme effort, the *Sejm* voted seventeen millions in subsidies,† and the Polish King, John Casimir, led an army of 60,000 men into the Ukrain. In the course of the same year the republic commanded Chmielnicki to break off all relations with the Tatars, and send his son as a hostage to Warsaw. The Ataman haughtily refused to obey, and declared that henceforth he would serve "the Lord's Anointed, the Tsar of Moscovy." On August 24 he issued "universals" from Pere-yaslavl, ordering the whole population to rise against the *Lyakhs*,‡ and soon gathered 600,000 men around him, but

* Szajnocha: "Szkice," I., 3.
† In Polish guldens. Sokolowski: "Dzieji Polski," p. 933.
‡ The Poles.

the Poles defeated him at Zranto, and in January, 1654, he welcomed the Moscovite envoys at Pereyaslavl. Long negotiations ensued, but on February 19 the Ataman took the oath of allegiance to the Tsar. The Cossacks were confirmed in all the privileges they had enjoyed under the Polish crown, including judicial and administrative autonomy, and their registered number was fixed at 60,000. The Moscovite commissioners refused, however, to bind the Tsar by oath to keep his promises, as Chmielnicki required. It was an unheard-of, impossible thing, they said, for an absolute sovereign like the Tsar to swear to be faithful to his own subjects, as if he were the sort of king they had in Poland. The Zaporozhians must be content to trust their new master, and this the drunken Chmielnicki, after being solemnly invested with all the insignia of the Atamanship, agreed to do. Thus was accomplished the transference of the free Cossacks from Poland to Moscovy. It was an important political event, and the first step towards the ultimate subjection of both " Russia "[*] and Poland by the Tsars. But, as yet, it was only a first step, and its inevitable corollary was the outbreak of the long deferred struggle between the Tsardom and the republic. As early as March 25, 1653, Alexius's Council had determined upon war with Poland, and in July the Moscovite envoys informed John Casimir at Lemberg that the Tsar had decided to take the Zaporozhians under his high protection unless the King of Poland redressed all their grievances forthwith. The Poles refused even to treat with "a thief and a traitor who had already sold himself to the Sultan," but promised to forgive him if he resigned the Atamanship. On October 1, 1653, a national assembly met at Moscow to sanction the war, and find means for carrying it on. The diminution of the Tsar's title by the Pans, and their refusal to put to death the authors of the books offensive to his Tsarish Majesty, were the alleged *gravamina*, but the assembly went to the real root of the matter by declaring that hostilities were necessary because John Casimir had broken his oath to the Cossacks, and it was to be feared the Zaporozhians would turn Mussulmans if Moscovy did not help them against Poland. Muskets and

---

[*] *I.e.*, the Russian provinces lying between Poland and Moscovy.

powder had already been purchased in large quantities from Sweden and Holland, and embassies had been sent to the Kaiser and to the youthful Louis XIV. to justify the war, and obtain, if possible, the neutrality of the two great Catholic Powers. In April, 1654, the army was blessed and asperged by the patriarch, and exhorted to go forth to victory, "hoping in God, the Father of Lights, in whom is no variableness or shadow of turning, the Most Blessed Virgin, and all the holy Thauma-turges of Moscow." In May Tsar Alexius, after weeks of solemn preparation and humble supplication, himself set out for the front.

The most holy and righteous of crusades could not have been consecrated by a more imposing display of august ceremonial, a more edifying out-pouring of pious unction, and yet the Thirteen Years War, as it is generally called, far exceeded even the Thirty Years War in grossness and brutality. No other war of modern times can show so little of the glories, so much of the horrors, of warfare. The Thirty Years War, anyhow, confirmed the principle of religious toleration and brought to light a goodly array of heroes and great captains whom the world will never cease to admire. The Thirteen Years War produced nothing, taught nothing, guaranteed nothing. It resembled nothing so much as a hideous scramble of ravening beasts and obscene fowls for the dismembered limbs of a dying giant, and it was fought out with a ferocity which places the combatants, with very few exceptions, beyond the bounds of our common humanity.

Meanwhile the war had opened favourably for the Moscovites. In Lithuania Prince Alexander Nikitich Trubetskoi, aided by 20,000 of Chmielnicki's Cossacks, easily prevailed over the weak and scattered forces of the Poles, though much hampered by a terrible outbreak of the plague which depopulated the whole Tsardom and made Moscow a desert during the summer and autumn months of 1654. In the course of June and July the towns of Dorogobuzh, Byelaya, Polock and Mstislavl fell into Trubetskoi's hands; in August he defeated Prince Radzivill at Szepielwica, and Mogilev surrendered to Poklonsky, who hesi-tated to accept the allegiance of the Catholic inhabitants

"because they were not Christians!" The ill-provided fortress
of Smolensk, whose feeble garrison of 2,000 men found it
impossible to defend the immense circuit of its walls, flanked
as they were by no fewer than thirty-four towers, for more than
a couple of months, opened its gates on October 4. Towards
the end of the year Witebsk also accepted a Moscovite garrison.
In the Ukrain Theodor Buturlin, sent thither to co-operate
with Chmielnicki against the Khan of the Crimea, who had
definitely broken with the Cossacks after their surrender to
Moscovy, could do little owing to the friction between his troops
and the Zaporozhians. And there were other symptoms of a
rupture between the orthodox of Moscovy and the orthodox of
Poland. The barbarities of the Moscovite soldiers so revolted
the Lithuanians that many of the surrendered towns returned
to their former allegiance. This was especially the case at the
city of Mogilev, where the Tsar's soldiers outraged the women,
desecrated the altars and plundered the churches wholesale.
Even the Metropolitan of Kiev looked askance upon these
strange deliverers of enslaved orthodoxy and drew nearer to
Poland. In January, 1655, occurred the first Moscovite disaster,
when a combined Polish and Tatar host almost annihilated
Shermetev's division at Ochmatow, whereupon the pious Tsar,
who had done his utmost to preserve the discipline and punish
the excesses of his troops, deemed it expedient to return to
Moscow to pray before the ikon of the Holy Mother of God,
visit the relics of the saints and comfort the boyars and the
people by his presence. By the time he returned to Smolensk,
the Poles were no longer dangerous. In the summer of 1655
Charles X. of Sweden, on the flimsiest of pretexts, forced a
war upon reluctant and inoffensive Poland, and before the year
was out his forces, very largely recruited from the veteran
mercenaries and desperadoes who had learnt their trade in the
Thirty Years War, had occupied the capital, the coronation city
and the best half of the land, and King John Casimir, abandoned
by his subjects, fled to Silesia. Profiting by the cataclysm
which, for the moment, had swept the Polish state out of existence, the Moscovites, unopposed, quickly appropriated nearly
everything which was not already occupied by the Swedes. In

July Wilna, the capital of Lithuania, was taken, in August fell Lublin and Kowno, in September Grodno, while Chmielnicki devastated Galicia and blackmailed Lemberg, and Prince Volkonsky ravaged all that remained to be ravaged in central Poland, burning the towns of Dawuidow, Stolin, and Pinsk on his way, and leisurely returning to Moscovy, at the beginning of October, encumbered with booty, without losing a man. By this time the sublime self-confidence of the Moscovites had transported them far beyond the limits of reality. When the Poles offered to negotiate, the whole Grand Duchy of Lithuania was the least of the demands of Alexius. The patriarch Nikon went still further. On August 9, 1655, he exhorted the Tsar not to be content with Lithuania, but to take all Poland likewise. But the end of Poland was not yet. In the midst of Moscovy's triumphant career a dangerous competitor suddenly appeared in the field in the person of the Swedish King, Charles X.

Charles's object in attacking Poland was to secure her rich Baltic provinces, the acquisition of which was regarded by the Swedish statesmen of the seventeenth century as necessary for the maintenance of Sweden's hegemony in the North.* Religious motives had little weight with him, but he was statesman enough to use the Polish Protestants and schismatics for his own purposes, and Magnus De la Gardie was no doubt acting under his master's instructions when, by the compact of Kejdani, October 10, 1655, he formally took the Estates of Lithuania under the protection of the Swedish crown. Tsar Alexius was warned at the same time to keep his hands off Courland, as the Courlanders were now the allies of the King of Sweden.† It is easy to imagine the indignation in the Moscovite camp when another royal freebooter claimed a share in the booty which the Tsar had already seized upon. Still more incensed was Alexius when Charles X.'s Calvinist friend Prince Radziwill proclaimed himself "Grand Hetman of the Swedish Crown and of the Grand Duchy of Lithuania and Palatine of Wilna." On August 29 the Tsar sent Likharev to Radziwill to protest warmly against the assumption of such titles, as

* Veibull: "Sveriges Storhedstid," pp. 372 et seq.
† Solovev: "Istoria Rossy," XI., 1.

" Lithuania had never belonged to Sweden." But Charles, with characteristic nonchalance, ignored the very existence of the Tsar. Not only did he take away Lithuanian towns from the Moscovites, but he entered into direct negotiations with their vassals Chmielnicki and the Cossacks. These high-handed proceedings were a great diplomatic blunder. They excited equal apprehension at Vienna, Moscow, and Stambul, a partition of Poland, as projected by the Swedish King, being equally opposed to the interests of the Kaiser, the Tsar and the Ottoman Porte. Moreover, Austria regarded Charles as the natural ally of her rival France, and the triumph of Sweden in Poland meant the triumph of Mazarin.* The treaty of alliance, therefore, ultimately concluded between the new Kaiser Leopold I. and John Casimir, on May 27, 1657, on hard enough conditions for Poland, may be regarded as the first step in a general league against Sweden. During the previous October two imperial commissioners, Allegretti and Lorbach, appeared at Moscow and used all their efforts to reconcile Moscovy and Poland and unite them both against Sweden. They were followed by the Polish envoy Galinsky, and the result of their negotiations was the suspension of hostilities between Moscovy and Poland to enable the plenipotentiaries of both Powers to meet on the frontier. Previously to this the Swedish envoys, who had reached Moscow in December, 1655, were treated harshly and detained as prisoners; a Moscovite embassy under Muishetsky set out for Copenhagen to persuade Frederick III. to make common cause with the Moscovites against the King of Sweden, " who was known to be aiming at the sole dominion of the Varangian Sea" ;† war with Sweden was resolved upon at Moscow at the end of May, 1656; and on July 26, Tsar Alexius at the head of an enormous army invaded Livonia.

Great things were expected from the Swedish War. It was well known at Moscow that the Swedes, occupied elsewhere, had no armies to oppose to the invaders of their Baltic provinces, and Nikon, on blessing the departing Cossacks, expressed the pious hope that " these famous devastators of the

---

* Sokolowski: " Dzieje Polski," p. 944, 945.          † The Baltic.

Black Sea shores may repeat their exploits on the shores of the Baltic and go by sea to Stockholm," as they had so often gone to Stambul. These anticipations were scarcely realised. Duna-burg indeed was taken on August 10 and re-christened Boriso-glyebov* by the pious Tsar, who could not, however, prevent all the people in the upper town from being massacred. Koken-hausen was also taken, and its name changed to Tsarev-Dmitriev-Gorod,† but this was the limit of the Moscovite successes. Riga, heroically defended by Simon Helmfelt, resisted all the efforts of Alexius's huge but incompetent army, from August to October, when the siege was raised. The subsequent capture of Dorpat was a small compensation for the thousands lost before Riga.

Simultaneously the Polish and Moscovite plenipotentiaries met at Wilna under the mediation of the imperial commissioners, but as Moscovy demanded Lithuania and war expenses while the Poles could only offer Alexius the succession to the Polish throne and the possible surrender of Smolensk, the negotiations came to nothing. The firmness of the Polish plenipotentiaries was due to the sudden recovery of the republic beneath the stimulus of a popular outburst of religious enthusiasm. Just as Moscovy had been saved from destruction half a century before by the heroic resistance to the invader of the Troitskaya Monastery, so now the whole religious and patriotic life of Poland was focussed in the monastic stronghold of Czechstochowa, where the valiant abbot, Kordecki, first demonstrated that the Swedes were not invincible, a triumph speedily followed by the return of the Polish King from exile and the recovery of the lost provinces from the Swedes, who were driven back headlong to the sea, where with difficulty they held their own. The mar-vellous resurrection of Poland necessarily changed the whole policy of Moscovy. Poland had suddenly become a much more dangerous foe than Sweden, and it was impossible to wage war with both at the same time. The Tsar resolved to rid himself of the Swedes first, and the negotiations were entrusted to a man who now comes pre-eminently forward for the first time—a

---

* In commemoration of the Russian saints Boris and Glyeb.
† Tsar Demetrius's Town.

man worthy of some attention as being one of the most remarkable of the forerunners of Peter the Great.

Athanasy Lavrent'evich Orduin Nashchokin* was the son of a poor official of Pskov, of whom we only know that he was greatly in advance of his times, for he saw to it that his son was taught German, Latin, and mathematics, so many abominations to the ordinary Moscovite of the seventeenth century. Athanasy began his brilliant diplomatic and administrative career under Tsar Michael as one of the delineators of the new Russo-Swedish frontier after the Peace of Stolbowa in 1642. Even then he had a great reputation at Moscow as one who thoroughly understood "German things and ways." He was one of the first Moscovites who diligently collected foreign books, and we hear of as many as sixty-nine Latin works being sent to him at one time from abroad. In the beginning of the reign of Alexius he attracted the young Tsar's attention by his resourcefulness during the Pskov rebellion of 1650, which he succeeded in localising as much as possible by sheer personal influence, for he had little or no force at his disposal. A deeply religious and thoroughly honest man, he soon became a close friend of Alexius, whose own sincere and upright nature had a natural affinity with every variety of worth and goodness. At the beginning of the Swedish war Orduin was appointed to a high command, in which he displayed striking ability, and as Governor of Drui and Tsarevichev-Dmitriev, qualified himself for the office of minister and plenipotentiary, to which he was appointed in 1657. His letters† to the Tsar during this period are illuminating, and do equal honour to himself and his master. With perfect frankness Orduin warns the Tsar that the atrocities of the Cossacks in Ingria and Livonia were driving even the orthodox inhabitants into the arms of the Protestant Swedes. "Now that the Lord God has given His Anointed these lands without bloodshed," he adds, "the Lord God demands mercy for all those who submit to us," and he urges repeatedly that all such orthodox desperadoes as the Cossacks should be summarily punished. When the negotiations with Sweden were seriously resumed on the river

* See biography, by V. Ikonnikov, in "Russkaya Starina," 1883, Nos. 11, 12.
† Solovev, "Istoria Rossy," XI., 1.

THE FIRST RUSSIAN CHANCELLOR.
ANASTASY ORDUIN-NASHCHOKIN.

Narova, in 1658, he was the only Moscovite statesman with sufficient foresight to grasp the fact that the Baltic seaboard, or even a portion of it, was worth much more to Moscovy than ten times the same amount of territory in Lithuania, and, despite the ignorant opposition of his jealous colleagues, he succeeded, at the end of December, in concluding a three years' truce whereby the Moscovites were left in possession of all their conquests in Livonia. In 1660 he was again sent as the chief Moscovite plenipotentiary to another congress in order to convert the truce of 1658 into a perpetual peace. By this time Sweden had composed her differences with Poland by the Peace of Oliva, an event which modified the political situation very much to the disadvantage of Moscovy, and now the Tsar was nervously anxious to conclude peace with the Swedish regency on any terms, hoping to compensate himself at the expense of Poland. Again Orduin, with true statesmanlike instinct, deprecated the sacrifice of the Baltic provinces. He advised his master that a peace with Poland was far preferable to a peace with Sweden. "If any towns be ceded," writes he, "let them be Polish towns. I stand for Livonia." In his opinion the truce with Sweden should be prolonged and Charles II. of England invited to mediate a Northern peace, "which he would very willingly do as we had no dealings with Cromwell." Finally, he lays stress upon the immense importance of Livonia for the development of the trade of Novgorod and Pskov. Finding that at Moscovy they were blind to his arguments and deaf to his entreaties, he craved permission to withdraw from the embassy, "lest the intrigues of those who hate me make my efforts to serve the Gosudar of no avail." His request was complied with, and in the beginning of 1661 other envoys were sent in his place to Kardis, a little town between Dorpat and Reval, where, on July 2, 1661, a treaty confirming the Peace of Stolbowa was signed, whereby Moscovy ceded all her conquests. For half a century longer Sweden was to dominate the Baltic.

All this while the Polish War, which was to pay for the Peace of Kardis, dragged wearily along, interrupted by fruitless negotiations and punctuated, from time to time, by bloody disasters.

There is no need to describe it in detail.  I will merely indicate its salient events.

Simultaneously with the recovery of Poland, died (August 7, 1657) the once terrible Ataman of the Cossacks, Bogdan Chmielnicki ; and the Tsar (September 6) gave the *bulawa* to his chief secretary, Vuigovsky, a gentleman by birth, and therefore secretly well disposed towards Poland.  In September, 1658, alarmed at the disciplinary measures of the Moscovites in the Ukrain, and enticed by the dignified and comfortable prospect of a senatorial armchair at Warsaw, Vuigovsky went over to the republic on very advantageous terms to himself, and, acting in conjunction with the Tatars, annihilated a large Moscovite army under Alexander Trubetskoi at Konotop, in the Ukrain (July 8, 1659), where the flower of the Moscovite cavalry perished, and 5,000 wretched captives were led forth after the battle and slaughtered like sheep.  This unexpected disaster caused an unreasonable panic at Moscow.  The Tsar appeared in mourning before the people, and the city was hastily fortified and provisioned against a siege of which there was never any danger. The Cossacks, with whom Vuigovsky was very unpopular, were divided among themselves, and in 1660 Bogdan Chmielnicki's son, Yury, was elected Ataman by the Russophil Zaporozhians, and the choice was confirmed by Moscovy, but subsequently Yury also deserted to Poland.  After this we cannot be much surprised to find a very poor opinion of Cossack stability prevailing at Moscow.  " Though they profess the orthodox faith," it was naïvely said, " they have bestial habits due to a single political heresy which makes them regard the rule of the Tsardom of Moscovy as a sort of bondage."  Young Chmielnicki, a boy of eighteen, who looked, we are told, more like a sacristan than an Ataman, ultimately retired into a monastery (end of 1662), but not before he had taken part in the siege of the Moscovite general, Sheremetev, in his entrenched camp at Czudnow, which resulted in the surrender of the whole Moscovite army, and the subsequent abandonment of Kiev, Pereyaslavl, Czernigow, and other towns, so that it was an even greater disaster than Konotop.  On the withdrawal of Yury Chmielnicki, both Poland and Moscovy selected their own Cossack Atamans, known henceforth respectively as the Koshevoi of the western* and the Koshevoi of the eastern† side of the Dnieper, except on the rare occasions of the union of all the Zaporozhians under a single chief, when his official title was Dux, or Ataman Koshevoi, of both sides of the Dnieper.‡ And while Moscovites and Poles were thus ruining each other in the Ukrain, in the central provinces the republic was painfully recovering lost ground, thanks to her superior armaments and strategy. In the autumn of 1661, Orduin Nashchokin and Khovansky were utterly defeated at Zeromsk with the loss of 19,000 men, ten cannons, all their standards, and a miraculous ikon of the Mother of God, especially lamented by Tsar Alexius. Before the year was out Grodno, Mogilev, and Wilna were recaptured by the Poles, and Lithuania was almost swept clean of the invader. The Moscovite Government was now in great distress. Its soldiers, paid in debased copper money, began to desert by companies and fly to Siberia and the Ukraine, and when Orduin Nashchokin, in the course of 1662, was sent to Warsaw to sue for peace, his offers were curtly rejected. But both Powers were becoming exhausted by the interminable strife, and the failure of Poland to subdue, even with the aid of the Tatars, the Cossacks of the eastern side of the Dnieper in the course of 1663, induced her to reopen negotiations with Moscovy. Early in 1664 a peace congress met at Durovicha, Orduin Naschokin being once more the chief Russian plenipotentiary. Before his departure, Naschokin tried to impress upon the Tsar the necessity of a close alliance with Poland, as in no other way could orthodoxy be protected there, especially as Sweden was always so near and so dangerous a foe. He also advised the surrender of the Cherkasses, or Zaporozhian Cossacks, to Poland, evidently over-estimating the strength of Poland. But the pious Tsar did not agree with him on this point. "It is indecent," he replied, "to feed dogs with a single piece of orthodox bread."§ The congress opened on June 12, 1664, and the first three weeks were wasted in mutual recriminations and the usual ceremonial squabbles. The Poles

---

* Polish.   † Moscovite.   ‡ Mazepa was the last to bear this title.

§ *I e.* "It is unbecoming for the Poles to rule over even the western bank of the Dnieper."

demanded the restitution of all the conquered provinces and
10,000,000 gulden for war expenses, and, as no agreement could
be come to, the negotiations were broken off at the end of
August.  But the rebellion of Prince Lubomirsky, which involved
Poland in a dangerous civil war at the very moment when she
needed all her armed strength to sustain her diplomacy abroad,
and furnishes another memorable instance of the utter inability
of the Poles to take care of themselves, compelled the republic
to treat once more with Moscovy, and another peace congress
assembled at the village of Andrussowo, between Smolensk and
Mstislavl.  The negotiations were protracted.  Not till the end
of the year could Nashchokin report to the Tsar that, "contrary
to all human expectations," the city of Kiev had been ceded for
two years, and the whole of the eastern side of the Dnieper
definitively.  The causes of this surrender were the raid of the
new Cossack Ataman Doroshenko, the nominee of the Turks
and Tatars, who in 1665 ravaged Poland as far as Lublin and
Lemberg with bestial ferocity,* carrying off more than 100,000
captives, and the simultaneous warlike preparations of the Grand
Vizier Kuprili against the helpless republic, which was driven,
in its extremity, to solicit help from all the Christian Powers of
the West.† Finally, at the thirteenth session of the congress, February 11, 1667, a truce for thirteen years was agreed to.  Witebsk,
Polock, and Polish Livonia were restored by Moscovy, who
was to retain Smolensk, Siewerz, Chernigov, Kiev for two years,
and the whole of the eastern bank of the Dnieper, the territory
thus acquired including not only the land lost by the Treaty of
Deulino, but a large tract south of Chernigov, between the
Dnieper and the affluents of the Don, containing the towns of
Konotop, Gadyach, Pereyaslavl, Mirgorod, Poltava, and Izyum.‡
The Cossacks of the Dnieper were to be under the joint dominion
of the Tsar and the King of Poland, whose territories they were
to defend.  The two Powers also covenanted to restrain the
Cossacks from rebelling against either of them, or engaging in

* His Cossacks cut off the breasts of the women, and flogged the children to
death.
† Sokolowski : "Dzieje Polski," p. 960.
‡ See Dobryakovich : "Uchebny Atlas Russkoi Istory." Map 3.  The territory
thus ceded to Moscovy added ten millions of rubles to her annual revenue.

piracy on the Black Sea, and jointly to repel any invasion of the Ukrain by the Khan of the Crimea.

Thus, in 1667, the secular struggle between Poland and Moscovy came to an end. It was also to be the last open struggle between the two Powers. Henceforth the influence of Russia over Poland was to increase steadily without any struggle at all, the republic being already stricken by that creeping paralysis which ultimately left her a prey to her neighbours. Moscovy had done with Poland as an adversary, and had no longer any cause to fear her ancient enemy. She was now free to devote herself to other and more important matters, upon which depended her historical continuity and existence, such as the subjection of the Cossacks, whose utter incapacity for self-government had been one of the chief lessons of the war; the colonisation and the extension of the vast southern Ukrain; internal reforms in church and state; the recovery of the Baltic seaboard.

The nominal Truce of Andrussovo proved to be one of the most permanent peaces in history, and Kiev, though only pledged for two years, was never again to be separated from the orthodox Slavonic state to which it rightly belonged. But for the terrible and persistent ill-luck of Poland, it is doubtful whether the Treaty of Andrussovo would ever have been signed, yet its accomplishment was due in no small measure to the superior ability and tenacity of Orduin Nashchokin. It was, undoubtedly, his greatest diplomatic achievement, and the reward of the capable minister was commensurate with his success. On his return to Moscow he was created a *blizhnui boyarin*,* and put at the head of the *Posalsky Prikaz*, or Foreign Office, with the extraordinary title of " Guardian of the Great Tsarish Seal and Director of the Great Imperial Embassies," while half a dozen of the chief public offices were placed under his control. The Russian chancellor, for that is what the new dignity really amounted to, was now in his proper place. He was the first Moscovite statesman who gave due importance to foreign affairs, and thus helped to break down the barrier which for centuries had separated Russia from the rest of Europe. Of his domestic reforms and subsequent career I shall speak elsewhere.†

* One of the boyars nearest to the Tsar's person.    † See Chapter VI.

# CHAPTER V.

## NIKON AND AVVAKUM, OR THE RELIGIOUS LIFE OF OLD MOSCOVY. 1652—1681.

Necessity of Reform recognised in Moscovy—Influx of Foreign Artisans—The Learned Monks from Kiev—Native Reformers—Theodore Rtishchev—Obstruction of the Majority—Causes of Moscovite Conservatism—Rooted Objections to Changes in Religion—Rtishchev's Efforts to introduce Oral Preaching — The Anonymous Author of "Statir" — Nikita Minin — His Early Career and Character—Nikita becomes Nikon—Nikon Metropolitan of Novgorod—The Translation of the Relics of St. Philip—Correspondence of Tsar Alexius with Nikon—Nikon Patriarch of Moscow—Other Reformers —Vonafitev—Neronov—Avvakum—His Early Career, Courage and Genius—Nikon and the *Protopops* as Reformers—Superior Liberality of Nikon—His Attitude towards the Greeks—The Revision Synods of 1654 and 1656—The Nikonian Reforms—Resistance and Dispersion of the *Protopops*—Condemnation of Avvakum—Incidents and Horrors of his First Siberian Exile—Defects of Nikon as Patriarch—Breach between Nikon and the Tsar —Nikon Resigns the Patriarchate—The Abortive Synod of 1660—Paisios Ligorides and the Œcumenical Patriarchs—Violence of Nikon—His Sudden Return to the *Kreml*—His Deposition by the Synod of 1666—Last Years of Nikon—Enthusiastic Reception of Avvakum on his Return to Moscow—The Boyaruinya Morozova—Avvakum's Second Banishment—Degradation and Third Banishment of Avvakum—Persecution, Sufferings and Death of Morozova—Avvakum at Pustozersk—His Martyrdom.

THE Peace of Andrussovo was beneficial to Moscovy in three ways. It gave her the profit and the *prestige* of victory; it relieved her from all fear of Poland for the future, thus permanently safeguarding her western frontier; and, above all, it enabled her to move forward more rapidly along the path of reform.

The recognition of the superiority of foreigners, accompanied by the natural desire to imitate them within safe limits, is discernible as early as the reign of Ivan III. (1462/1505), becomes very apparent in the reign of Ivan IV. (1533/84), and dominates the reigns of Boris (1598/1605), and the false Demetrius (1605/6). Unfortunately the movement was discredited by the Polonising tendencies of the last-named sovereigns, and, when the Poles were finally driven from Moscovy, a strong reactionary current set in. With the establishment of the new dynasty, however, the necessity of Western discipline again grew urgent, and resulted in a steady influx of foreigners into Moscovy, who were allowed special privileges in return for teaching the Moscovites their arts and mysteries. We have already seen how, to begin with, the army was remodelled on European lines, and the foreign soldiers were quickly followed by foreign artificers and manufacturers, the Moscovite Government taking the initiative. Thus, in 1634, emissaries were sent abroad to hire competent coppersmiths. Three years earlier, ten goldsmiths were sought for in Holland, because, in the words of the *ukaz*, "this business is costly and yields small profit to our treasury, because there are no good masters of it in our realms." In 1643 Falck the bellmaker arrived at Moscow, the forerunner of many of his trade. In the same year the Swedish mason, Kristler, began to build a stone bridge over the Moskva. In 1634 the German, Fimhand, obtained a ten years' monopoly for the preparation of elk leather, while the Dutchman, Coet, was granted a similar privilege for the manufacture of potash and glass. Clockmakers were also imported to teach the Moscovites *their* mystery. So great, indeed, was the influx of foreigners into Moscow at this time, that the clergy grew anxious and petitioned the Tsar to prevent "the Germans" from building houses and churches, as they always got the best sites by overbidding the poorer native merchants. This produced an *ukas* forbidding the sale to the Germans of any building within the White town or the China town,* and ordering the demolition of the churches already built there. But land was given to the foreigners to settle down upon between the Frolovsky and Petrovsky gates, where they enjoyed full liberty of worship,† together with extraordinary trading privileges. This was the origin of the subsequently famous German settlement where Peter the Great completed his education. As early as 1638, we know, from Olearius, that at least 1,000 families were settled here. And now, too, we find foreign scholars at Court as well as foreign artisans at

* See p. 20.  † Rinhuber. " Relation du Voyage en Russie," etc

the capital. But these scholars were not *nyemtsui.** From German heretics the Moscovite was content to learn the profane mechanical sciences, which had to do with the safety of the realm, and the business and comfort of everyday life, because he could not help himself. But when it came to spiritual sustenance, philosophy, theology, he would listen to no teachers who did not come to him in the cassocks of orthodox monks. Fortunately Kiev, the centre of orthodox learning, was soon to be a Moscovite possession, and from about the middle of the eighteenth century, the flower of Kievlyan scholarship was transplanted to the Court of a young prince whose favourite study was theology, and who was reputed to have read every book already published in the Slavonic language. Thus, in 1650, the learned ecclesiastics, Epifany Slavenitsky, and Arsenius Satanovsky, were summoned from Kiev to Moscow, to teach rhetoric and help translate the Greek Bible into Slavonic, and they were followed, a few years later, by the most learned of all the West Russian scholars, Simeon Petrovsky Sitianovich, better known as Polotsky, from Polotsk or Polock, the place of his birth. Something, indeed, had already been done for learning in the reign of Tsar Michael. We remember that the patriarch Philaret established a Greek-Latin school at the Chudnov Monastery, and, at a later day, the still more enlightened boyar Theodore Mikhailovich Rtishchev, one of Tsar Alexius's chamberlains, built, at his own expense, the Andrevsky Monastery, on the Kiev road, not far from Moscow, where he lodged and fed thirty learned monks from Kiev, on the sole condition that they should teach Greek and Slavonic to all students who presented themselves for the purpose. He himself was engaged at Court all day, but so eager was his thirst for knowledge that he would spend whole nights in his monastery, discoursing with the learned men he had gathered round him. Equally full of reforming zeal were Orduin Nashchokin and Artamon Matvyeev, the latter of whom we shall learn to know presently.† These men and their fellows were the pioneers of Peter the Great. They succeeded in passing the

---

* "Germans," in the Moscovite sense, that is to say, roughly speaking, all Protestant foreigners.                              † See next Chapter.

torch of enlightenment on to that great regenerator, but there were moments when its feeble light seemed about to be extinguished by the all-encircling, mephitic gloom through which they painfully bore it. For it must never be forgotten that, while Tsar Alexius and the wiser of the boyars and prelates were groping their way, in much doubt and hesitation, towards the dawn of a new and better civilisation, they encountered on the way the most determined obstruction and opposition from the mass of the people of all classes. This obstruction was mainly owing to the long intellectual stagnation of Moscovy, due, again, to her isolation from the rest of Europe. The mental horizon of the ordinary Moscovite of the seventeenth century was extraordinarily limited. For centuries he had lived in a world of phenomena which he regarded as unchangeable, because they had never changed. The secular immobility of his surroundings gave to them, in his eyes, a religious character, and therefore a religious inviolability. Any alteration of his ancient ancestral customs was to him a sinful surrender. It has well been said that existence in old Moscovy, as compared with existence in Western Europe, was as the dull stagnant life of an agricultural district compared with the mobile, inquisitive, enterprising, life of a great city. And at this period Moscovy was actually an empire of villages. Hence the violent opposition to reforms of every sort, for the rustic mind is everywhere essentially, doggedly, conservative. Now, if in seventeenth century Moscovy, in consequence of a long protracted stagnation, all the ordinary externals of life had acquired a sort of religious sanction, it is easy to understand how pious ignorance would regard the slightest attempt to meddle with the externals of religion. In the absence of enlightenment, the ordinary Moscovite was unable to distinguish between things essential and things unessential, and thus any, even the most necessary, rectification of the externalities of religion would be looked upon by him as a blow directed at the very foundations of religion itself. In fact, the majority of even educated people was quite incapable of grasping the fact that an alteration could be a rectification at all. " Did not our holy forefathers pray thus ?" they would say. " Surely they, who were so much better than we are, could not have been wrong." The first thought of a religious and conservative Moscovite was to stand firm for the faith once delivered to the saints, but unfortunately in his eyes the minutest point of ritual observance was of equal importance with the central dogmas of the Christian faith, and a man who crossed himself with three fingers instead of with two was as much Anti-christ as a man who denied the divinity of the second Person of the Trinity. For this state of things the clergy were largely responsible. Had the Moscovite clergy been sufficiently enlightened to explain to their flocks that the reforms introduced into the Moscovite Church were necessary rectifications, the orthodox Church of Moscovy would never have been divided. But even amongst the better class of the Russian clergy, amongst the holiest monks and the most conscientious prelates, were to be found woefully ignorant men who regarded every sort of religious reform, even if sanctioned by the highest antiquity, as a visible token of the Beast of the Apocalypse. To men of this type (and unfortunately they outnumbered the reformers ten to one) to look at a Latin grammar was to stray from the right path ; and the monks of Kiev were "wicked old fellows" for introducing a knowledge of the official language of the Roman heresy. But the utter unreasonableness of their intolerance is perhaps best shown by their loud indignation when, through the efforts of Rtishchev, oral preaching was introduced into the Moscovite Church. The preachers were branded as "hypocrites," "heretics," and "possessed by devils" ; yet, when hard pressed, the only objection these censors could oppose to such a salutary ordinance was that it was a departure from the practice of their forefathers, who had been wont to teach the people privately, not "publicly in church." Those who attempted to brave this bigotry often fared badly enough. Take, for instance, the case of the pious boyar Gregory Dmitrievich Stroganov and his preacher. This nobleman, renowned among his fellows for his liberality, hospitality, and his "love for the beauty of holiness," built a church at Orel in honour of the Blessed Virgin, and placed in it one of the new preachers, whom, after long searching, he had unearthed in the little Arctic town of Solikamsk. This worthy priest, rejecting written sermons like those of St. Chrysostom and the Court preacher Polotsky,* then in vogue, as beyond the capacity of his hearers, took upon himself to preach to the people extempore in a simple, direct way. The sermons of this anonymous preacher, subsequently collected by him into a MS. volume which he called "Statir,"† have come down to us, and as pictures of contemporary manners are inferior only to the autobiography of Avvakum. The following extract presents us with a drastic enough picture of the parish priests of the period.

"Our pastors care not for the flock of Christ, but for gold and silver, for transitory serfs, carts and horses, . . . for much wine, for showy garments. . . You will find such blind guides, thinking themselves to be wise, but really most coarse and ignorant, who say : What have we to do with learned books? The Horologion and the Psalter are good enough for us. Ye say truly. They are good enough if ye know the power that is in them, but such knowledge is far beyond you. Ye fools! Sitting behind full glasses at a pothouse, ye are great orators, but in church ye are bound up in speechlessness and full of stupidity. Ye say it is sufficient if the priest read a book before the people in church, and ye blame them that teach by word of mouth and call it heretical. Fools! whom do ye account to be heretics? The patriarchs, the prophets, the apostles? But now the bishops and clergy are all for drunkenness and men-pleasing, desiring to rule, but despising the vineyard of Christ . . . Therefore it is that the poor pastor receives shame and blame, evil report, ill treatment, blows, bonds and death, not from Tsars and boyars, but from them that are the vilest, from as it were mangy sheep and fœtid goats. Of the rest I am silent. I can but weep. How shall I explain the operation of the crafty demon?"

Had the author of the "Statir" come twenty years later, when the eloquent Avvakum had made extempore preaching popular, he would have obtained a hearing, but now the people, egged on by the local clergy, rose and drove away the denouncer of their sins. But no amount of clamour could permanently stay the course of reform, the necessity for which was becoming more

* See next Chapter.    † The " penny " in our version of St. Matthew xvii. 27.

and more patent every day. The best men of the younger
generation were taking up the cry, and in the new patriarch,
Nikon, they seemed at last to have got an archpastor after their
own hearts. But first a few words as to the early career of this
impressive but disappointing ecclesiastic.

In May, 1605, in the village of Valmanovo, 90 versts from
Nizhny Novgorod, was born Nikita, the son of the peasant-farmer
Mina. Misery pursued the child from his very cradle, and
prematurely hardened a character not naturally prone to the
softer virtues. His mother dying in his infancy, his father
immediately provided him with a stepmother, and the grim
Russian proverb : " *machika v domu kako medvyed v lyesu*,"*
indicates pretty plainly what the general run of stepmothers was
in old Moscovy. Nikita's stepmother was no exception to the
rule, and she treated the lad so inhumanly that he had to run
away from home to save his life. And it was a life well worth
the saving. From a very early age Nikita gave promise of the
energy and application which were to distinguish him throughout
his career. Under the most discouraging circumstances he contrived to teach himself reading and writing, sure means of advancement in those days of general ignorance, and speedily devoured
every book he could lay his hands upon. All the books of that
period were of a severely religious character. Their favourite
theme was the exploits of old-time saints and anchorites, and
they enkindled in the heart of the young enthusiast an over-
powering desire to tread in the footsteps of these heroes of the
spirit, which ultimately led him within the walls of the monastery
of St. Makarius of Zheltovodsk. Moreover, his ambition was
stimulated by the admiration which his precocity excited in the
neighbourhood. Both Christian priests and Mordvinian soothsayers prophesied that he would one day be both patriarch and
Gosudar, predictions singularly to be verified. But the entreaties
of his family, which began at last to be proud of their prodigy,
summoned Nikita back to the world. He was persuaded to
marry, and his learning and talents obtained for him a cure of
souls when he was but twenty. The eloquence of his preaching
soon attracted attention, and, through the efforts of some Moscow

* " A stepmother in the house is as a bear in the forest."

merchants, he was transferred to a populous parish in the capital. For a time all went well, but seeing in the loss of his three little children, almost simultaneously, a providential warning to seek the higher life, the stern young priest first persuaded his wife to take the veil, and then withdrew himself to the desolate hermitage on the island of Anzersky,* in the White Sea, where he received the tonsure under the name of Nikon. Yet Nikon found anything but peace among the eternal ice and snow of this Arctic wilderness. The high ideals of the extravagant neophyte brought him into collision with the laxer time-honoured principles of the easy-going brethren of Anzersky, and, unable to have his own way, he shook the dust off his feet as a testimony against them, and transferred himself to the Kozhuzersky Monastery in the diocese of Novgorod, where his superior merits were appreciated and ultimately rewarded by his election to the dignity of *igumen*, or abbot, of the monastery in 1643. In his official capacity as *igumen*, Nikon had frequently to visit Moscow, whither his fame had already preceded him, and in 1646 he made the acquaintance of the pious and impressionable young Tsar, who at once and entirely fell under the influence of the famous zealot, twenty-four years his senior. Alexius appointed Nikon archimandrite, or prior, of the wealthy and aristocratic Novospassky Monastery at Moscow, which, as an imperial foundation, was under the direct control of the Tsars. It was now a part of Nikon's duty to be present at mass in the principal church of the monastery every Friday morning, in order to confer with the Tsar afterwards. Such conferences were by no means confined to things spiritual, and Alexius, more and more impressed by the gravity and the judgment of the new archimandrite, made him, first, Receiver of Petitions, a post of great authority and influence, and, two years later, procured his election to the metropolitan see of Great Novgorod. In this capacity Nikon, as we have already seen, displayed both courage and statesmanship in the most critical period of the rebellion of Novgorod, but, at the same time, we catch ugly glimpses of less pleasing features of his character—a very bad temper and a disposition to play unscrupulously on the

* The largest island of the Solovetsk Archipelago.

superstition of the young Tsar.   For instance, irritated once at the
charge of cruelty brought against him by the rioters, he wrote to
his master as follows : " You are vexed with me because of their
lies, and to this day you have sent no answer to what I wrote to
you.    This seems to me very suspicious, and henceforth I will
neither speak nor write to you concerning your affairs at
Novgorod."*    But he knew right well that the effect of this
petulant outburst would be more than counterbalanced by the
effect produced by the following account of a vision previously
sent to the Tsar : " I was praying before the image of the Saviour,
known as the *Zlataya Riza*,† when, suddenly, I beheld a golden
kingly crown suspended in the air over the Saviour's head.
Gradually this crown drew nearer and nearer to me, and from
great fear I had almost fainted when the crown upon which I
was gazing intently came and sat on my sinful head.   With both
my uplifted hands I felt it there upon my head, and no sooner
had I felt it than it vanished."    There is no reason to suppose
that this vision was simulated.    Ascetics like Nikon who practise
habitually a discipline, which despises hunger and almost dis-
penses with sleep, are very apt to pass unconsciously into that
curious state of ecstasy which may or may not be the medium
for supernatural suggestion, divine or diabolic, but is certainly
the nursery of hallucinations.   The vision was genuine enough,
no doubt, but Nikon applied it as a parable, insinuating that him
whom the Tsar now despised, the Tsar of Tsars might one day
reward with the martyr's crown.   Be that as it may, when Nikon,
in 1651, returned to Moscow, his influence at Court was paramount.   How completely he dominated the will of the young
Tsar at this period is plain from the curious episode of the
translation of the relics of Philip (the saintly archbishop whom
Ivan the Terrible, more than fifty years before, in a fit of passion,
had foully murdered for courageously protesting against his
cruelties) from the remote Solovetsky Monastery to the Uspensky
Cathedral at Moscow.   The proposal came from Nikon, who cited
the precedent of the Emperor Theodosius and the relics of St.

---

* Quoted by Solovev : " Istoria Rossy," X., 2.
† *I.e.*, "The Golden Setting or Frame." The ikon in question was said to
have wrought miracles for the Emperor Manuel Comnenus, and had been
presented to the cathedral of Novgorod by Ivan the Terrible.

John Chrysostom. His obvious intention was to demonstrate, in the sight of all men, the supremacy of the spiritual power by imposing on the civil power a retrospective act of public penance. It must also be admitted that Nikon, when once he put his hand to the plough, did not look back, for he took with him to Solovetsk a deprecatory letter from the Tsar to the saint, which was to be laid on Philip's tomb, and contained these words: " I supplicate and desire thy presence here to absolve the sin of my predecessor, Tsar John. Wherefore I abase my Tsarish dignity before thee because of my predecessor who sinned so grievously against thee, that thou mayest free him from sin by coming to us, and wipe away the disgrace which cleaveth to him for driving thee away, so that we may believe and know that thou art reconciled to him." The pilgrimage to the tomb of the martyred archbishop was not an altogether pleasant expedition. Nikon plagued Prince Khovansky and his other noble associates with such severities, that their proud flesh revolted, and they complained bitterly to the Tsar, by letter, that they would rather perish miserably in Siberia than live in fellowship with the Metropolitan of Novgorod. Much as he venerated Nikon, Alexius felt it to be his duty to interfere, and his tactful if timid correspondence with the domineering prelate is very curious and illuminating. He begins as follows: " Elect and immovable Pastor and Guardian of our souls and bodies, gracious, kind, benevolent, guileless, and well-beloved child of Christ, and cherisher of the sheep of His Word! O strong champion and confessor of the Heavenly Father, my own beloved familiar friend and yoke-fellow, pray for me a sinner, that by reason of thy holy supplications the heavy burden of my sins may not overwhelm me!" After this preamble, the Tsar proceeds to inform "the Great Shining Sun, the most holy Nikon," that "it hath pleased the Creator to take unto Himself from the false and treacherous world, and place in Abraham's bosom" the patriarch Joasaf, whereby "our Mother the holy Apostolic Church hath become a widow, and as it were a dove in the wilderness." Having thus communicated his most important piece of news, Alexius gently takes his own familiar friend to task for his severity to his fellow pilgrims, imploring him not to

R.                                                             K

extort too much from them in the way of religious discipline.
"It is good, O Gosudar," pleads the royal peace-maker, "it is
good to reprove the wise, as thereby they become wiser, but
reproof to the foolish is like treading on their corns." "They
tell me," he adds, "that you would force them to fast, but alas!
O Gosudar, none can be made religious by force." And then he
is suddenly overcome at the thought of his over-boldness, for he
adds : "Keep this letter secret, be not vexed by our aimless and
incoherent scribble." This letter, which carries us back to papal
times when the rulers of this world humbled themselves before
the Vicar of Christ, makes many things clear. It explains, to
begin with, how Nikon came to occupy his unique position in
Moscovy. Evidently his own masterfulness and energy were
not the only factors which contributed to his elevation. He
owed quite as much to the sincere admiration and entire affection of the Tsar, and Tsar Alexius was one of those amiable
persons who will endure a great deal rather than quarrel with
their bosom friends. But the letter also shows that Alexius was
no fool, that he had a considerable knowledge of human nature,
and, above all, that he possessed, in an eminent degree, the
qualities of tact and prudence in which the masterful archbishop
was so lamentably deficient.

On July 13 the relics of St. Philip were brought into Moscow
and laid with great pomp in the Uspensky Cathedral. Towards
the end of the same month, at a synod assembled at Moscow
for the election of a new patriarch, Nikon, who was known to be
the Tsar's candidate, was duly chosen. When all the necessary
ceremonies had been accomplished, the Tsar summoned to his
presence the newly elected patriarch, but Nikon obstinately
refused to occupy the patriarchal throne. This was not affectation, but the wise determination of a would-be reformer,
conscious of the difficulty of the task before him, to secure a
free hand by being elected on his own terms. Again and again
the Tsar sent prelates and patricians to persuade Nikon, but he
remained immovable. At last the Tsar ordered him to be
brought to the cathedral by force, and they brought him. Then
the Gosudar, the boyars, and the prelates implored Nikon to
accept the patriarchate. He persisted in his refusal till the

Tsar, and all who were present in the cathedral, fell at his feet and besought him, with tears, to yield to the prayers of the whole community. Nikon, deeply moved, himself began to weep, and, turning to the Tsar and the congregation, uttered these memorable words : "Ye know that in the beginning we received the Holy Gospels, the traditions of the Holy Apostles, the canons of the Holy Fathers, and the imperial laws from orthodox Greece, and thereafter were called Christians. But of a truth we have followed neither the evangelic precepts nor the canons of the Holy Apostles and the Holy Fathers, nor the laws as to religion of the Greek Tsars. . . . If it seem good to you that I should be your patriarch, give me your word, and make a vow in this cathedral church before God our Saviour and His Most Pure Mother, and before the angels and all the saints, that ye will keep the evangelic dogmas and observe the canons of the Holy Apostles and the Holy Fathers, and the laws of the pious Emperors. And if ye promise to obey me also as your chief archpastor and father in everything which I shall teach you concerning the divine dogmas and the canons—then will I, according to your wish and supplication, no longer reject this great archpastorate."* The Tsar, the boyars, and all the members of the synod, thereupon swore unanimously upon the holy Gospels, and before the holy thaumaturgical ikons, that they would do all that Nikon commanded them, "honour him as their archpastor and father, and assist him to edify the Church." Thus, on August 1, 1652, was Nikon elected. Three days later he was solemnly consecrated and enthroned as the sixth Patriarch of Moscow.

Even before Nikon appeared upon the scene, the necessity of ecclesiastical reform had been admitted in the highest circles, and had found advocates in the immediate *entourage* of the young Tsar, who was keenly interested in all theological questions, and very willing to learn. Among the Tsar's chief advisers at this time was his confessor, Stephen Vonafitev, a relatively learned man, generally beloved for his mild and gentle disposition which made him averse to all harsh measures, though, personally, he led a life of extreme austerity, and was largely responsible for the

* Sipovsky: "Rodnaya Starina," III., 211, 212.

**K 2**

puritanism of the Court. Vonafitev was a friend of the excellent Rtishchev, and approved of the introduction of oral preaching and the reform of church music, two questions largely occupying the ecclesiastics of those days. Another leading man at Court was Ivan Neronov, a stern zealot, who regarded even Christmas festivities as "devilish," and who, as a parish priest, had often been nearly beaten to death by his flock for interfering with their juggling, dancing bears, and other pastimes. In his youth Neronov had suffered much from a singularly sluggish brain. His teachers had wept over him in despair, and frequently took his alphabet away from him lest he should read himself blind.* But he doggedly persevered, "praying God the while for wisdom," and the famous archimandrite Dionysy,† finally took him in hand and made a scholar of him. As the pastor of the church of the Resurrection at Nizhny Novgorod, Neronov became very famous as a street preacher, and his reputation for holiness finally procured him, at the suggestion of Vonafitev, the dignity of *protopop*, or dean, of the Kazan Cathedral at Moscow. To the same group belonged the protopop Daniel of Kostroma, and the protopop Login of Murom, both of them men of burning zeal and austere virtue. Presently the Party of the Protopops, the name generally given to this reforming group, was reinforced and overshadowed by a new ally, the priest Avvakum. This perversely heroic creature, the proto-martyr of Russian dissent, and one of the most striking personalities of his age, was born at the village of Gregorovo, near Nizhny Novgorod, fifteen miles from the place where Nikon was born fifteen years before, in 1619 or 1620. The son of a drunken priest, he owed everything to the care of a pious and devoted mother, who educated him, found him an excellent wife, Nastasia Markovna, the orphan daughter of a poor blacksmith, and started him in life as a parish priest (1643). Absolute fearlessness, sublime austerity, and a perfect fidelity to his religious convictions, were to characterise the young priest through life. In his first cure he had the courage, unheard of in those days, to denounce the governor of the place for abducting a poor widow's daughter, and insist on instant and complete restitution.

* Borozdin: "Protopop Avvakum."        † See Chapter II.

The high-placed ruffian, infuriated at the boldness of a common priest, broke in upon him during divine service with an armed band, dragged him about the church in his vestments, and, after horrible ill-usage, left him for dead on the floor. This is only a specimen of what Avvakum had to endure for endeavouring to do his duty as he understood it. Nothing in the world would ever make him condone wickedness or truckle to the mighty. The following anecdote, recorded in his autobiography, illustrates the moral heroism of the man : On one occasion a woman, who was a grievous sinner, came to confess to him, and, during the narration of her abominable misdeeds, says Avvakum, " the burning of an unchaste desire suddenly gat hold upon me. Now, at that same hour, three lights were burning beside me, and, leaning back against the reading desk, I placed my hand in the flame and held it there till the evil prompting within me died away."* Naturally, those who did not regard such a man as a nuisance to be suppressed at any cost, venerated him as a confessor, but saints and sinners were alike subdued by his rare gift of oratory. No other Moscovite ecclesiastic of the seventeenth century could compare with Avvakum as a preacher. He was no imitator of classical models like the Court preacher Polotsky. He spoke to the people in the language of the people, straight from the heart, in a way which made the rudest feel and tremble. His style is always simple, lucid, vigorous, garnished with racy proverbs, full of quaint and vivid touches, and rising at times to flights of irresistible eloquence. For there was as much of the poet as of the preacher in Avvakum ; he had imagination as well as humour. His autobiography, one of the most engrossing and pathetic histories ever penned, is, in point of composition, not so much superior to as centuries ahead of what passed for style in his days, an unconscious literary masterpiece as well as a historical document of the highest value. Unfortunately, this great and heroic nature was also one of the most narrow-minded of men, standing far below the intellectual level of a Rtishchev, an Orduin, or even a Nikon. Still more unfortunately, his narrowness was so absolutely conscientious as to be quite incurable, and, as we shall see, it involved him in endless controversies, to his own

* Borozdin . " Protopop Avvakum."

undoing and to the infinite damage of the Russian Church. Such a champion of orthodoxy was gladly welcomed by the party of Vonafitev, and in 1648 we find Avvakum established in the capital as protopop in one of the Moscow churches.

Before his elevation to the patriarchate, Nikon and the proto-pops had been induced to co-operate for the good of the Church. Anyhow, there had been no hostility between them, and even Avvakum, in his correspondence, frequently alludes to the archbishop as "our friend." But it is plain that the protopops were apprehensive of what so independent and ener-getic an archpastor as Nikon might do, for, on the death of the old patriarch Joasaf, after fasting and praying for a whole week, "that God might give his Church a pastor for the salvation of souls," they presented the name of their leader, the gentle and pliant Stephen Vonafitev to the Tsar as a candidate for the vacant patriarchal throne. But Vonafitev, being neither a prelate nor a monk, had little chance against a competitor who was at the same time the highest of the Moscovite metropolitans and the favourite of the Tsar. But in any case the protopops were not the sort of men to undertake even such modest ecclesiastical reforms as were possible in Moscovy in the seventeenth century. Their point of view was erroneous, because they were not sufficiently enlightened to be able to pierce to the root of matters themselves, and nevertheless shrank from the assistance of their natural teachers, the clergy of Kiev and Constantinople, because they suspected the former of being crypto-Catholics, and knew many of the latter to be scoundrels and impostors. They were therefore, thrown back upon Moscovite tradition, as represented by the *Stoglav*,\* or Reforming Council of Moscow of 1551, a council unrecognised outside of Moscovy, and of questionable authority, inasmuch as its members, while professing to follow Greek precedents, had been notoriously ignorant of the Greek language, the very key of orthodox interpretation. Thus the antiquity to which the protopops were never tired of appealing, was barely a century old, and the canonicity of the *Stoglav*, their ultimate court of appeal, was, at the best, highly problematical Yet they had pinned their faith implicitly to this purely national

---

\* So called because its canons were 100 in number.

synod, and cut off all possibility of a dignified retreat from an impossible position by accepting the responsibility for the revision of the Church service-books inaugurated by the late patriarch Joasaf. This was really no revision at all, but a clumsy attempt to apply the hitherto unexecuted canons of the *Stoglav* to the bettering of the liturgies, which resulted in the interpolation of various schismatical prescriptions into five or six of the thirty-eight books so revised; such, for instance, as the *dvuperstia*, or making the sign of the cross with two fingers, and the *sugubaya alleluya*, or two-fold alleluia, to which the Moscovite Church was consequently committed.*

Nikon, as a reformer, was much more liberal. He shared the protopops' distrust of the Greek priests and prelates. He was well aware that the bishops without sees, and the archimandrites without monasteries, who appeared, from time to time, at Moscow with forged letters of recommendation from the Eastern patriarchs, were at best place-seekers and relic-mongers, who, in the words of Krijanic, "sell us Christ a thousand times over, whereas Judas only sold Him once." But he also recognised the fact that if the morals of these vagabond pastors were detestable, their scholarship was far superior to what passed for learning in Moscovy, and he did not see why he should not sift the gold from the dross.

A typical instance of these problematical prelates was Paisios, Patriarch of Jerusalem, who visited Moscow in 1649, with an imposing suite, which included "a number of lewd fellows whom he called archimandrites and archons, so as to obtain a larger alms, inasmuch as all the gratifications received by the members of the patriarchal suite were from first to last appropriated by the patriarch himself." Amongst the patriarch's followers was a Greek monk, Arsenios by name, whose orthodoxy was of so elastic and accommodating a description that the patriarch himself had his doubts about it. Educated at Rome by the Jesuits, Arsenios is next heard of at Stambul, where he professed alternately the orthodox and the Mussulman faith, ultimately

---

* Borozdin ("Protopop Avvakum") has established the fact that the protopops were not the actual revisers, as hitherto supposed, but only the responsible editors of these service-books.

resuming orthodoxy in Moldavia, and turning Uniate when adverse circumstances drove him into Lithuania. In Moscovy, on the other hand, he made friends by praising the *Stoglav.* Both Paisios and Arsenios were learned men, however, and their visit to Moscow profoundly affected the fortunes of the Russian Church, inasmuch as they convinced Nikon, then Metropolitan of Novgorod, that many of the ceremonial observances of the Moscovite Church were contrary to the usage of the œcumenical churches of the East. Finally Nikon felt bound to submit in all things ecclesiastical to the authority of the Greeks, and it was largely due to his initiative that the eminent Kievlyans, Arseny Satanovsky, Damaskin Pitsky, and the still more famous Epifany Slavenitsky, were invited to Moscow, to instruct the Moscovite clergy, and translate Greek and Latin books, both religious and secular, into Slavonic for the use of the schools.

Thus the scholars of Constantinople and Kiev opened the eyes of Nikon to the fact that the Moscovite service-books were unorthodox, and subsequent, independent, investigations of his own, conducted with the assistance of the learned Slavenitsky, in the patriarchal archives, convinced him that the sooner these liturgies were rectified the better. With characteristic energy he at once (1654) summoned a properly qualified synod of experts to re-examine the service-books revised by order of the late patriarch Joasaf, and the majority of the synod decided that "the Greeks should be followed rather than our own ancients." But the minority included Paul, Bishop of Kolomna, and several of the old revisers, most of them members of the party of the protopops, who protested energetically against the decision of the council. Nikon thereupon addressed six-and-twenty interrogatories to Paisios, Patriarch of Constantinople, inquiring at the same time how he should deal with the dissentients. Paisios recommended excommunication, and authorised the holding of a second council to settle matters, to which Makarios, Patriarch of Antioch, and the metropolitans of Servia, Nicea and Moldavia, all of whom happened to be at Moscow, were invited. This second council, which assembled in the Uspensky Cathedral, in Orthodox Week, the first week of the great fast, 1656, sanctioned the revision of the service-books as

NIKON REVISES THE SERVICE BOOKS.   137

suggested by the first council, and anathematised all who still persisted in crossing themselves with two fingers instead of three.*   The revision of the service-books was then entrusted to the learned Epifany Slavenitsky and the Greek monk Arsenios, and carried out in accordance with the wishes of Nikon and the suggestions of the council.

Heavily weighted with the fullest œcumenical authority, Nikon's patriarchal staff, never very gentle, now descended with crushing force upon those of his opponents who still refused to obey the precepts of the Church, as interpreted by himself.   He was no rigorist indeed, and to those who repented and submitted, even at the eleventh hour, he could be generous enough.   Thus when Neronov, whom he had imprisoned in chains for outrageously abusing him at the council and appealing to the Tsar against him afterwards, when Neronov found it expedient to agree with his adversary quickly, remarking at the same time that, after all, the Greek authorities had not formally condemned the Moscovite service-books, Nikon assented.   "Both are good," said he, "it is a matter of indifference, follow whichever you will."†   To those, however, who obstinately resisted his divine authority, the most holy patriarch could be as "a ravening bear of the forest."   But among his opponents he was now to find men as rugged and as unbending as himself, men who, if they could not succeed in dominating the Church below, were quite prepared to join the army of martyrs in Heaven.   Foremost among these irreconcilables, who were neither to be convinced by the testimony of Greek archbishops, nor silenced by the decrees of œcumenical councils, stood the protopop Avvakum.   Not only pride and obstinacy, but conviction and conscience, moved the intrepid protopop to withstand, for the sake of what he believed to be the truth, the omnipotent and triumphant patriarch. He never realised that his position was absurd and untenable, and it is this which makes his heroic steadfastness so pathetic.

For, indeed, Nikon was so entirely in the right, that it requires a mental effort to imagine how anyone could ever have seriously

---

* The Greek prelates solemnly declared on this occasion that such a practice had never obtained in the Eastern Church.

† Nikon at the same time voluntarily returned to him a packet of very compromising letters.

believed him to be in the wrong. The patriarch stood firm for antiquity, a real antiquity, pruned of all the parasitical excrescences, the outcome of ignorance and misunderstanding, which had overgrown the Moscovite Church in the course of ages. His opponents, blinded by prejudice and suspicion, failed to see that his reforms were but a return to primitive antiquity, and denounced them as the inventions of Antichrist. Agreement was impossible. The question at issue had to be fought out till the bitter end. So long as there were men in Moscovy ready to be tortured to death rather than cross themselves with three fingers instead of two, or spell the name of our Lord with two iotas instead of with one iota, there could be no peace in the Church, especially as the martyrs of to-day might very easily have become the persecutors of to-morrow, toleration being accounted a mortal sin by both parties.

The patriarch certainly showed the schismatics no mercy. It was a rough age when gentle methods did not recommend themselves even to the mildest of men. Nikon was naturally hard if not cruel, and above all things he was thorough. His scheme of reform included not only the service-books and the Church ceremonies, but the ikons actually in use, which had widely departed from the ancient Byzantine models, being, for the most part, imitations of Polish and Frankish* originals. The patriarch ordered a search from house to house to be made for these "new-fangled" ikons, and we are told by an eye-witness that his soldiers and servants were charged first to gouge out the eyes of these " heretical counterfeits," and then carry them through the town in derision.† He also issued an *ukaz* threatening with the severest penalties all who dared to make or use such ikons in the future. Hundreds of pious Moscovites, who had grown up to venerate these holy images, naturally regarded such acts of violence as sacrilege and iconoclasticism. The plague which visited Moscow about this time was popularly supposed to be a divine judgment on the impiety of the patriarch. There was a loud murmuring, and for a time Nikon went in danger of his life.

Nevertheless he departed not a hair's-breadth from the narrow

* West-European.  † Sipovsky : " Rodnaya Starina," III., 221.

path. The utmost concession he would make to the timid remonstrances of the pious Tsar, whose sense of propriety had been shocked by the anathematising and trampling under foot of scores of offending ikons in the Uspensky Cathedral itself, in the presence of an immense and horror-stricken congregation, was that the degraded images should be privately and decently buried instead of being burnt publicly by the common hangman.

This ruthlessness goes far to explain the unappeasable hatred with which Avvakum and his followers ever afterwards regarded Nikon and all his works. The protopop was not the man to keep silence under the persecutions of Antichrist, and the virulence of his denunciations speedily led to his seizure. He was dragged, in full canonicals, from a loft which he used as a chapel,* after being expelled from his church, and was sent in chains to the dungeons of the Andronev Monastery. During his detention the party of the protopops was broken up, Vonafitev and the weaker members submitting to the patriarch, while the stronger spirits were flogged, tortured and exiled in all directions. On September 15, 1657, Avvakum's fate was also decided. He escaped the tonsure through the personal intercession of the Tsar, but was banished to Tobolsk with his wife and family. His adventures and sufferings are recorded in his autobiography. The journey to Tobolsk lasted thirteen weeks, and on the way thither his wife bore him another child. His fame had preceded him. Simeon, Archbishop of Tobolsk, received him kindly, and appointed him protopop of the cathedral, with very extensive powers. He soon came to be regarded as a specialist in spiritual cases, and the most desperate and abandoned sinners were sent to him for discipline. His dealings with his flock were drastic indeed. On one occasion he completely converted a drunken monk, who was the terror of the city, by dressing him in a winding-sheet and getting the sexton to flog him till he could not keep his feet, while Avvakum himself, standing before the holy ikons, recited a requiem over him. But these methods were not always efficacious. Thus, amongst his penitents was a young prostitute whom he locked up in an underground cellar, where he kept her in mid-winter without food

* Borozdin. "Protopop Avvakum."

and water, till her continuous howling disturbed his devotions, whereupon he had the wretched creature hauled up, placed a rosary in her hands, and bade her do obeisance to the ikons till she fell to the ground from exhaustion. The sexton was then summoned to complete the cure with a tough rope's end. "And I wept over her before God," continues Avvakum, "and I plagued her continually, mindful of what is written in the canons: an adulteress plague without mercy even at Eastertide. Yet this vessel of Satan sinned more than ever when I let her go."

Avvakum naturally raised up against him the lukewarm and the backsliders who form the majority of every congregation. During the absence of the archbishop his enemies banded together, and nearly succeeded in drowning him in the river. For a whole month he had to hide for his life. But never for an instant did he cease his anti-Nikonian propaganda, till, at the end of 1655, orders came from Moscow to transport him still further north, to Eniseisk, where he arrived in the course of 1656. But here Avvakum found fresh orders awaiting him ; he was to accompany, as chaplain, the punitive expedition of Athanasy Pashkov to the far distant regions of the Amur, where " the Daurians " were in rebellion. Pashkov was a rough soldier with an extraordinarily difficult task before him. His ill-fed, ill-clothed and worse-paid troops were the scum of the earth, who could only be kept within bounds by an iron discipline. Pashkov himself is described by the Archbishop of Tobolsk as " a great ruffian " ; but he seems to have been no worse than previous military explorers in these regions, and he was certainly a man of unusual energy and administrative capacity. Pashkov and Avvakum took a dislike to each other from the first. Perpetual collisions between two such masterful natures were indeed inevitable, and for the unfortunate protopop the whole expedition was a prolonged agony heroically endured. Pashkov's revolting brutality to his troopers frequently made Avvakum denounce him as " a savage beast " to his face. Pashkov retaliated by flogging the protopop till he was half dead, and flinging him in chains to the bottom of one of the prahms in which they sailed down the rivers. No inconsiderable part of the protopop's time was spent in dungeons foul with vermin, often without food for hours, where he had to lie on his stomach because his back was still raw from flogging. A winter residence in a warm hut crowded with dogs and dog-like savages was comparatively comfortable. But his most poignant anguish was separation from his family, who were placed at the other end of the caravan. Once his little son Ivan tried to find out his father, but Pashkov speedily cured the child of any such inclination by shutting him up in an ice-cold prison till his feet and hands got frost-bitten, when he sent the lad back to his mother. This was at Christmas-tide. On crossing Lake Baikal during the following spring the whole party suffered terribly. Many of the soldiers died of fatigue while dragging the boats along, and Avvakum, who had to take his turn at the tow-rope, was thrice nearly drowned, and his clothes rotted from off him. The further the expedition advanced the more horrible grew its torments. Pashkov often imposed impossible tasks on his men, with the knout and the bludgeon as motive powers, till the worn-out wretches literally died in harness. This was notably the case when he sent them to haul timber down the river Ingoda. For days together they had nothing to eat but grass, roots, pine-bark and the remains of carcases already torn by the wolves. The one piece of finery possessed by Nastasia, Avvakum's wife, was an *odnaryadka*,* worth fifteen rubles, for which Pashkov gave her two sacks of rye, on which the whole family subsisted for twelve months, helped out with horse-flesh and "other abominations." Two of the children now died beneath these straits. Only Nastasia's unquestioning faith in her husband sustained her during this long martyrdom, but there were moments when even she began to despair. "Tell me protopop!" she cried in the bitterness of her heart on one occasion; "tell me, will our torments last for long?" "Yea, Markovna, till death itself," was the sublime reply.

Yet Avvakum was not altogether without friends. The wife and daughter-in-law of his tyrant became his spiritual children, and brought him gifts in secret, "scraps of meat, an egg or two, and grain, the scrapings of the hen-coop." Yet, for conscience

* A long, collarless outer garment.

sake, the inflexible protopop was ready to sacrifice even these little comforts. Once, during his temporary absence, the lady's little son, Avvakum's godchild, fell sick, and she had recourse to the drugs of a pagan magician without effect. On hearing of this the protopop washed his hands of her altogether, because she had broken the canons of the Church. Only with the greatest difficulty could the penitent and deeply humiliated mother persuade him to heal the child, for he had some skill in medicine. Then Pashkov himself, full of gratitude, did obeisance to the man he had so long tormented, "and henceforth he was soft-hearted towards me, and supplied me with abundance of food."

Avvakum's first Siberian captivity, which lasted for eight years, came to an end in May, 1662, when, through the influence of powerful friends at Court, he was invited to return to Moscow. At the same time the joyful intelligence reached him that his arch-enemy. the patriarch Nikon, had fallen.

From 1652 to 1658 Nikon was not so much the minister as the colleague of the Tsar. The whole internal administration, especially during the unlucky Swedish War, when Alexius was absent from the capital, remained in the strong hands of this spiritual Gosudar.* So vast was his power, and such a free use did he make of it, that some Russian historians † have suspected him of the intention of establishing "a particular national papacy." Certainly he himself consistently maintained that the spiritual was superior to the temporal power. It would be grossly unfair to Nikon not to admit that in many respects he was no unworthy predecessor of Peter the Great. He loved many branches of learning, especially history and archæology, and all those arts which minister to religion found in him an intelligent and munificent patron. He enriched the numerous and splendid monasteries which he built with libraries of considerable importance for those days. His emissaries scoured Moscovy and the Orient, to search out and bring together precious Greek and Slavonic MSS. Many of these MSS. contain illuminating notes from the patriarch's own hand. Nor did he confine his

---

* Both in public documents, and in private letters from the Tsar to the patriarch, Nikon is allowed this sovereign title.

† Y. T. Samarin, for instance.

attention to ecclesiastical documents. Some of these hardly-won treasures are the works of profane classical authors, Homer, Hesiod. Æschylus, Plutarch, Thucydides, Demosthenes, to say nothing of numerous Byzantine Chronicles, and grammatical treatises.

As an administrator Nikon was indefatigable in purging the Church of abuses. His standard of excellence was high. Sloth, immorality, slackness of any kind, found little mercy with him. Unfortunately he was one of those persons who never know when to stop, and his rapid and extraordinary elevation speedily brought to light the less amiable aspects of his character. To begin with, this archpastor of the Moscovite Church lacked the first principles of the Christian life, meekness and humility. He thought far more of his patriarchal rights than of his patriarchal duties. As the highest interpreter of the divine law in Moscovy, he judged all things to be lawful to him ; he never paused to consider whether they were also expedient. Hence the charges of cruelty brought against him, magnified no doubt by his enemies, but true enough in substance. His magnificence and exclusiveness were equally offensive to those, and they were many, who simply envied him because he "held his head high and walked spaciously." Finally there was the multitude of conscientious adversaries who detested him as a troubler of the Church, and the criminous clerks whose misdeeds he had punished. Against the rising flood of hatred Nikon possessed but one efficacious barrier, the favour of the Tsar, nor was it an easy matter to shake the belief of the most pious of princes in the impeccability of the bosom friend whom he generally addressed as "Great Shining Sun," and before whom he figuratively abased himself in the dust. " Be not vexed, O Gosudar, at our aimless and incoherent words," he writes to Nikon on one occasion, and in another letter he exclaims : "So vile are my deeds that I am not fit to be a dog, let alone a Tsar !" But there are limits to everything. No sooner was the Tsar made to understand that the sovereign patriarch was eclipsing the sovereign Tsar. than Alexius suddenly awoke to a sense of his personal dignity and began to think less of the shining virtues of his own " familiar friend." How the change was brought about is not quite clear, but it was first made manifest to Nikon when, in the summer of 1658, he received no invitation to the banquet given on the occasion of the arrival of the Georgian Prince Teimuraz at Moscow.  He immediately sent one of his boyars to the palace to discover the cause of this neglect, and the messenger came back with a broken pate.  Nikon thereupon wrote to the Tsar for instant satisfaction.  Alexius, much too timid to face the irate prelate, sent word that the matter should be investigated, but Nikon's enemies took good care that it was not.  But there was more to come.  On July 8/19, the feast of Our Lady of Kazan, the Tsar, contrary to the practice of years, absented himself from divine service in the Uspensky Cathedral. Two days later he sent Prince Yury Romodanovsky to tell the patriarch that he was not to expect him at the still more ancient festival in honour of the translation of the Sacred Coat of the Saviour.  "The Tsar's Highness is wroth with you," added the prince.  "You write yourself Great Gosudar, and we have only one Great Gosudar, the Tsar. . . . The Tsar's Highness bids me say you are not to write yourself so in future."

The same day, after the solemn celebration, Nikon bade the sacristan close the doors of the cathedral, as he would address the congregation.  The people crowded round the pulpit to hear the sermon, and a very strange sermon they heard.  Nikon informed them, at some length, that he was no longer patriarch, and whosoever henceforth called him by that name was anathema. Then, divesting himself publicly of his patriarchal vestments, he retired into the sacristy, and wrote a letter to the Tsar containing these words : " I depart because of thy wrath, for the Scripture saith : ' Give place to wrath,' and again it is written : ' If they reject thee in one city go to another, and if they receive thee not, shake the dust from off thy feet as a testimony against them.' "*  Then, enveloped in the hood and mantle of a simple monk, and with a staff in his hand instead of a crozier, Nikon departed, despite an urgent message from the Tsar commanding him not to vacate his office.  For three days, however, he lingered at Moscow eagerly awaiting overtures of reconciliation which never came, whereupon he shut himself up in the Voskresensky

* Solovev : "Istoria Rossy," vol. XI.

Monastery, the richest of his foundations which he and his Tsarish friend, in happier days, impressed by its beauty, as they strolled together through its gardens, had called "The new Jerusalem."

The consternation at Court was indescribable. More than once Alexius sent friendly boyars to attempt to turn Nikon from his resolution. But Nikon was immovable. Yet he apologised for his hasty departure, which he excused on the plea of ill-health ; he sent his blessing to his *locum tenens*, the Metropolitan of Krutisk ; and he made tender inquiries respecting the Tsar's bodily and spiritual welfare. His enemies grew alarmed, especially when they perceived that the Tsar was in no hurry to appoint a new patriarch, and, well aware of Alexius' tenderness for his old friend, they did their utmost to widen the breach between them. Their efforts would have been unavailing had not Nikon's mood suddenly changed. As a matter of fact, his abdication had not produced quite the effect he had anticipated. He was treated with indulgence, with respect even ; but there was no repetition of the scenes which had occurred at his election. The Tsar had not begged his pardon. He had not even come to see him. The disappointed prelate grew irritable, and in his irritation he said and did things which his best friends could not approve of.

In February, 1660, a synod was held at Moscow to terminate "the widowhood" of the Moscovite Church, which had now been without a chief pastor for nearly two years. The synod decided not only that a new patriarch should be appointed, but that Nikon had forfeited both his archiepiscopal rank and his priest's orders. Against the second part of this decision, however, the great ecclesiastical expert, Epifany Slavenitsky, protested energetically. He demonstrated that, according to the canons of the orthodox Church, archbishops voluntarily resigning their offices could not, unless guilty of canonical offences, be deprived of their sacerdotal character, or be forbidden to exercise their archiepiscopal functions. Thus the whole inquiry collapsed. The scrupulous Tsar shrank from enforcing the decrees of the synod for fear of committing mortal sin, and Nikon was escorted back to the monastery of the Resurrection with something like

R.					L

a half triumph, comparing himself now to the woman in the wilderness who was persecuted by the dragon, and now to St. John at Patmos.

For six years longer the Church of Moscovy remained without a patriarch. Every year the question of Nikon's deposition became more complicated and confusing. Almost every contemporary orthodox scholar was consulted on the subject, and no two authorities agreed. Amongst these experts must be mentioned the Greek adventurer, Paisios Ligorides, calling himself Archbishop of Gaza, though as he had been excommunicated and deprived of his see (which, by the way, he never visited)* by the Patriarchs of Constantinople and Jerusalem, he seems to have had no right to the title. Paisios, who was educated at the Greek college at Rome, and is said to have taken orders there and received a pension from the Pope, professed orthodoxy in orthodox lands, but was most probably a crypto-Jesuit of illimitably broad views on all moral and religious subjects. While intriguing at the Court of Wallachia in 1657, he was invited by Nikon to come to Moscow to assist in the reformation of the Church. Paisios did not think it worth while to obey the summons till five years later, by which time his patron was in disgrace. The shrewd Greek at once attached himself to the winning side, and, to help the matter on, addressed five-and-twenty interrogatories to the œcumenical patriarchs, bearing upon Nikon's case but without mentioning Nikon's name. Replies were received to the interrogatories in 1664. They were to the effect that the patriarch and clergy of Moscow were bound to obey the Tsar; that they ought not to meddle with temporal affairs; that the local bishops could sit in judgment on the patriarch; and that the objections of Epifany Slavenitsky against the decrees of the synod of 1660 were untenable. Unfortunately, close upon the heels of this decision came independent letters from the Patriarchs of Constantinople and Jerusalem expressing doubts as to the accusations brought against the Patriarch of Moscow, and advising the Tsar to be reconciled with Nikon. Nectarius, Patriarch of Jerusalem, went still further. He strongly urged Alexius to reinstate Nikon; reminded him that there were innumerable instances of

* See Gorsky : "P. Ligarid do priyezda ego do Rossy."

archbishops who had been restored to their sees after abdication;
adjured him not to be the first Tsar to introduce schism into the
Russian Church, "which the captive churches regard as the one
ark of Noah"; and warned him, above all things, to beware of
the impostor Ligorides.*

The Tsar, in desperation, now resorted to the expedient of an
œcumenical council, or the nearest approach to it attainable under
the circumstances.   Letters of invitation were accordingly sent
to the Eastern patriarchs to come to Moscow.   At the end of
1666, Paisios, Patriarch of Alexandria, and Makarios, Patriarch
of Antioch, travelling by way of Astrakhan and the Volga, set
out for Moscow, where they arrived in May, 1667.†   Meanwhile the council had already opened its sessions on November
18, 1666, in the presence of the Tsar, who produced and
expounded the accusations.

All this time Nikon, so far from improving his position, had,
to the delight of his enemies, been entangling himself inextricably
in fresh difficulties.   He insinuated that the Tsar was guilty of
cruelty, sacrilege, and mortal sin.   He openly declared that
while the spiritual power was the greater light that ruled the
day, the temporal power was only the lesser light that ruled the
night.   He claimed the exclusive right to lay hands upon his
successor, and sarcastically inquired whether the Holy Ghost
required the aid of an imperial *ukaz* to consecrate the bishops
and pastors of Christ's Church?   When Ligorides, attempting
to pour oil upon the troubled waters, addressed a friendly letter
of remonstrance to his former patron, counselling submission
and urging him to render tribute to Cæsar—"Ah, and what a
Cæsar!"—Nikon retorted with anathemas, not even excepting
the Tsar; whereupon poor Alexius remarked piteously: "I know
I am a great sinner, but what have my wife and children done
to be cursed?"

Yet, for all his bad temper and arrogance, it is impossible not
to feel some sympathy with Nikon.   It is quite plain that his
numerous enemies exhausted every means of goading him into

* It would seem from this, either that Nikon's friends had got hold of Nectarius,
or that Nectarius suspected Paisios of forging replies to his own interrogatories.

† The two other patriarchs were represented by proxy

fresh indiscretions, and many of the accusations drawn up against him by Ligorides were frivolous enough. Take, for instance, Stryeshnev's case. The boyarin Rodion Stryeshnev, a near relation of the Tsar's, was one of Nikon's bitterest foes who lost no opportunity of ridiculing him. Amongst other things, he called his pet dog the "patriarch Nikon," and taught the creature to stand on its hind legs and stretch out its front paw as if in the act of blessing. When this witticism was reported to Nikon, he solemnly cursed Stryeshnev for sacrilege, and this was one of the charges subsequently brought against him.

But if Nikon had many foes, his few remaining friends were the most enlightened people in Moscovy, including Rtishchev, Orduin Nashchokin, and Artamon Matvyeev. The sympathy of such men at such a time speaks well for the character and reputation of Nikon. They evidently regarded him as one of themselves, as one of the little band of enlightened reformers of whom Moscovy stood in great need, and they were very anxious to bring about a reconciliation between the Tsar and the patriarch. The means they took to this end was to get a common friend, the boyar Zyuzin, to write to Nikon, advising him to come in secret to Moscow and pay the Tsar a surprise visit. The old affection still subsisting between the two men would then, they hoped, do the rest. But again Nikon's masterful temper spoiled everything. He did come to the *Kreml'*, as his friends advised, but he came not as a suppliant seeking for forgiveness, but as a conqueror dictating his own terms.

At midnight, on December 17/18, 1664, a long line of sledges halted before the outer barrier of the city of Moscow. "Who goes there?" challenged the sentries. "Prelates from the Savin Monastery," was the reply. The procession was immediately admitted and made straight for the *kreml'*. At that moment early mass was being celebrated in the Uspensky Cathedral. John, Metropolitan of Rostov, was officiating, and the second *kathisma** had been reached, when a loud knocking was heard outside; the doors of the cathedral opened wide, and

---

* The name of each of the twenty parts into which the liturgical psalter is divided.

a procession of monks entered bearing aloft a cross. Behind the cross, in full canonicals, walked the patriarch Nikon. He at once ascended into the patriarch's place, and the well-known voice, which for six years had not been heard within those walls, exclaimed, "Cease reading." He was instantly obeyed, and the presbyters of the monastery of the Resurrection, who had accompanied him, then began singing "Honour hast Thou, Lord," and "Thou art worthy." This done, Nikon ordered a deacon to recite the *Ekteniya,** and, after doing obeisance to the ikons and relics, he sent the metropolitan John to tell the Gosudar that the patriarch was there. The Tsar, whom they found at mass in the church of St. Eudoxia, was amazed at the audacity of this public summons from a prelate in disgrace, who had been forbidden to appear within the walls of Moscow. The whole *kreml'*, dark and silent a moment before, was instantly ablaze with candles and lanterns, and alive with *streltsui* and *zhiltsui* hastening in every direction to summon a council of prelates and boyars to the Tsar's staircase. There was as much uproar and confusion as if the Poles and Tatars had suddenly attacked the capital. Half an hour later a deputation of boyars, all more or less hostile to Nikon, headed by his arch-enemy, Rodion Stryeshnev, was sent to the Uspensky Cathedral to order the patriarch to return at once to his monastery. Nikon refused to budge till they had brought back to him an answer to a letter he had written to the Tsar which he now offered to them.† The deputation refused to accept the letter, and roughly insisted on his immediate departure. It was still an hour before dawn when at last Nikon consented to go. On stepping into his sledge, he ostentatiously shook the dust off his feet, and, at the same time, raised his eyes to heaven, where the flaming tail of a huge comet filled the darkened sky. The superstitious *stryeltsui* escort began sweeping up the dust of condemnation shaken off against them by Nikon; but he, pointing to the celestial portent, exclaimed, "You may sweep and sweep, but God shall sweep you all away with His divine besom before many days be passed."

---

\* A prayer to which the choir responds, "Lord have mercy upon us "
† This document was full of apocalyptic visions and warnings of which Nikon professed to be the recipient.

This senseless attempt to terrorise the Tsar did great harm to Nikon, and largely contributed to his ultimate condemnation.

That condemnation was pronounced on December 12 (O.S.), 1666, before the arrival of the patriarchs. The œcumenical council pronounced Nikon guilty of reviling the Tsar and the whole Moscovite Church ; of deposing Paul, Bishop of Kolomna, contrary to the canons, and of beating and torturing his dependants. His sentence was deprivation of all his sacerdotal functions ; henceforth he was to be known simply as the monk Nikon. Nikon questioned the jurisdiction of the synod because the Patriarchs of Constantinople and Jerusalem were not personally present. So far from being cowed by the sentence, he was defiant to the last, and overwhelmed the Greek prelates with abuse. " You have taken from me my mantle and *panagia*,"* he cried, "that you may make a few guldens by picking out the jewels and selling them. You are the Sultan's slaves and vagabonds, begging everywhere for alms that you may pay tribute to your master." The same day he was put in a sledge and sent as a prisoner to the Therapontov Byelozersky Monastery.

Yet it was not Nikon but Alexius who suffered the most from this catastrophe. Face to face with the angry and offensive prelate, the Tsar, supported by the whole weight of the council's authority, had stood his ground with commendable firmness. But when all was over, and the former Gosudar and patriarch was nothing but a simple monk, imprisoned in a distant and dreary monastery, the gentle breast of Alexius relented, and he began to ask himself whether he had acted in a Christian spirit. He was the first to make advances to his old friend, by sending for his blessing ; but Nikon, who always found it difficult to forgive, let five years pass before he so far humbled himself as to write to the long-suffering Tsar for forgiveness (Christmas Day, 1671). Something of the old intimacy was immediately resumed. Scarce a week passed without the Tsar sending rich gifts to "the holy and great presbyter Nikon," who, as if on purpose, did his utmost to show how little he deserved either epithet. From 1672 onwards we find him wrangling perpetually with his hosts, the monks of the Therapontov Monastery, and

* A sacred image in a pectoral ring worn by prelates of the orthodox Church.

complaining to the Tsar of the quantity and the quality of his food. With inexhaustible patience Alexius carefully investigated every complaint, however petty, and replenished Nikon's table from his own. We hear of "rare and toothsome fishes" and other delicacies passing from the palace in the *kreml'* to the distant cloister, and even then the querulous old man was not satisfied. Apples, plums, and grapes were still unsupplied. "I suppose," he writes, "that the Lord God has not told you that I never see such blessings here? If such things ripen before your Highness's eyes, for the Lord's sake send thereof to your poor elder." It is interesting to note that once a splendid sable cloak was sent to him in the name of the little Tsarevich Peter, afterwards Peter the Great. Yet the last days of this fallen greatness were not altogether abject. We have a more pleasing picture of the ex-patriarch praying over multitudes of sick pilgrims who came to him from every quarter that he might lay his hands upon them and cure them with the simples of which he had a great store. In his joy he even wrote to the Tsar to tell him of how a voice from heaven had said to him: "The patriarchate hath been taken from thee, but the cup of healing hath been given to thee; heal the sick." He survived his old friend five years, expiring on August 17, 1681, aged seventy-six.

Avvakum returned to Moscow, when Nikon, though not yet dethroned, was in disgrace and powerless. Everyone who had any reason to hate the patriarch hailed the fiery arch-enemy of "Nikonism" as "an angel of God," whilst the more religious section of the community naturally regarded the man who had endured such sufferings for the faith that was in him as a holy confessor. At Court, also, he was received with effusion. The Tsar set him over one of the chief churches of the *kreml'*, and came frequently to discuss spiritual things with him, at every visit doffing his hat and begging for Avvakum's blessing.* The *blizhnuie* boyars, equally obsequious, were proud to be reckoned amongst his friends; but the house where he was most honoured and which he frequented the most was the dwelling of the wealthy and pious boyaruinya Morozova, whose strange and pathetic tale forms such an important and

* Borozdin : "Protopop Avvakum."

illuminating episode in the history of the religious life of old Moscovy.

Theodosia Prokopievna Morozova* was the wife of the *okolnichy* Glyeb Ivanovich Morozov, whose brother Boris, it will be remembered, was the tutor and famous minister of Tsar Alexius in his younger years. She had been one of the chief ladies-in-waiting at Court, and had held the fifth place in the ceremony of the christening of Alexius. Her father, moreover, was a kinsman of Tsar Michael's consort. Theodosia was married at the age of seventeen to a boyar, thirty-three years her senior, of such austere piety that his household must have been the nearest attainable approximation to the monastic ideal of the *Domostroi*.† But Theodosia was every whit as religiously disposed as her husband, and both she and her sister had been among the earliest of the spiritual children of the uncompromising Avvakum. Left a widow at the age of thirty, with immense wealth,‡ and the charge of a young family, she occupied the privileged position of a widow-mother, and her whole life was henceforth divided between the care of her children and household, good works, and the practice of the most rigid spiritual discipline. To quote her friend and confessor, Avvakum, she was as fair of countenance as Judith, and "as famous in Moscow as Deborah was in Jewry." The only recreation she allowed herself was religious argument, and as her talented brother-in-law, Boris, the ex-minister of state, used to discourse with her for hours at a time, and declare afterwards that her words were "more satisfying than mead and honeycomb," she must certainly have stood far above the intellectual level of the Moscovite women of her day.

Morozova's house was an asylum open night and day to the needy and the suffering. She entertained five poor nuns at her own table. Aged pilgrims she waited upon herself, washing their festering wounds, and putting food into their mouths when they were too feeble to feed themselves. The whole establishment was full of poor little orphans, who wandered all over it at

---

* The best of the many accounts of Morozova will be found in Zabyelin: "Domashny buit russkikh tsarits." † See Chapter I.

‡ She had thirty domestics, eight thousand serfs, and landed property worth half a million.

will, and fed together, at stated times, out of the same huge dish.
Free admission was also granted to those curious products of the
extravagant asceticism of the Greek Moscovite Church, the
*yurodui*, enthusiasts enamoured of holy humility and poverty,
who, for Christ's sake, voluntarily exposed themselves to the
ridicule of the world by affecting to be witless, and going about
in rags or half naked.    Among them were two disciples and
*protégés* of Avvakum, Theodore and Cyprian.    The former, who
was one of the sights of Moscow, and ultimately died a martyr's
death, used to roam the city in the daytime, barefooted and
frost-bitten (wearing nothing, even in the depths of winter, but
a little shirt), and pass the night in tears and prayer.*    The
other *yurod*, Cyprian, was known personally to the Tsar.    He
was one of the "upstairs pilgrims."†    He used to go about
the streets publicly denouncing "the Nikonian novelties," and
frequently implored Alexius to restore the ancient order of
things.

As the obedient spiritual child and pupil of Avvakum,
Theodosia naturally committed herself unreservedly to the reactionary views of the great protopop, and being as courageous
as she was dutiful—Avvakum called her a "lioness among
foxes"—she was speedily involved in the ruin which overwhelmed her master.

In Moscow, after the resignation and retirement, but before
the condemnation of Nikon, a more moderate spirit seems to
have prevailed.    The best men of both parties desired a
compromise, and met together for discussion in the house of
the enlightened boyarin Theodore Rtishchev, who, though an
advocate of the reforms, was a determined peace-maker, and
tolerant on principle.    Into the midst of this tranquillising
medium, Avvakum, on his return from exile, plunged like a
bombshell.    For a short time the earnest exhortations of the
Tsar, and the generous sympathy of Rtishchev, prevailed with
him so far as to induce him at least to listen to the arguments of

---

* Avvakum said he had never known such a hero.  He would make a thousand
obeisances at one time, and pray on his knees for three hours without ceasing.
At last, however, he became too much even for Morozova, and Avvakum inter-
ceded for him in vain.                    † See Chapter I.

the other side, most fairly and ably presented by the archimandrite Pleshchev, who affectionately urged him not to be obstinate as no novelties had really been introduced, and the revision of the service-books was the work of sound scholars of unimpeachable orthodoxy. To these incontrovertible arguments Avvakum could only oppose denunciation of the Greek as opposed to the national standpoint, skilfully evading the charge of ignorance by repudiating mere learning altogether. God, he said, had declared He would hide His wisdom from the wise and prudent and reveal it unto babes,* the babes in this case being, of course, himself and his followers. Presently he began openly to preach schism and sedition, and then the firebrand had to be quenched.† The Tsar had already been alienated by Avvakum's anti-Nikonian petition, and his savage diatribe against the archimandrite Dionisy for teaching Ilarius, Archbishop of Ryazan, Greek. Thus, a little more than twelve months after his return to Moscow, the protopop's fanatical violence resulted in his second banishment—this time to Mezen, a little town near the White Sea.

Two years later, by order of the Tsar, all the principal schismatics in exile, including Avvakum, were summoned to Moscow, to make their peace with the Church. The council, which had deposed Nikon had, at the same time, confirmed all the Nikonian reforms, and anathematised all who should refuse to accept the revised liturgies, the *troeperstie*,‡ etc. It had also condemned the *Stoglav* and the " Life of St. Efrosin," the chief authorities to which the anti-Nikonians appealed. Every conceivable effort was made by the council to win over its most formidable opponent, for, by this time, Avvakum was regarded by a large minority of his countrymen as a " confessor for Christ's sake." For ten weeks deputations passed between the council and the protopop, but he answered all their arguments with ridicule and invective. When brought before the council itself, he refused to recognise its authority, and finally, May 13, 1666, was pronounced a heretic, and deprived of his orders.

* Borozdin : " Protopop Avvakum."
† He even insisted on the re-baptism of the Nikonians.
‡ Making the sign of the cross with three fingers.

BANISHMENT OF AVVAKUM. 155

His further sentence was postponed till the arrival of the œcumenical patriarchs, a year later, and then, for six weeks, all the resources of argument and persuasion were once more employed to convince Avvakum of the reasonableness of the Nikonian reforms. Never was ignorance so proudly invincible. When asked why he held out so obstinately against the whole orthodox world he could only taunt the Eastern patriarchs with their political subjection to "the Turkish Mahomet," and thank God that "we Moscovites are independent." Nevertheless, for three months longer, the Court and the council temporised. Finally, the great reforming boyarin Artamon Matvyeev, and the learned Polotsky, the tutor of the Tsar's children, were sent to make another effort. The debate was fierce but futile. "I can have as little fellowship with you as light can have with darkness, or Christ with Belial," were Avvakum's parting words. "Alas! we have nought in common," was the sorrowful rejoinder of Matvyeev. A few days later Avvakum and his three chief associates were handed over to the secular arm, and condemned to lose their tongues, and be banished to Pustozersk on the Pechora, the northernmost town of European Russia. The mutilation, in Avvakum's case, owing to the intercession of the Tsaritsa, was remitted.

Morozova, the most powerful of all Avvakum's disciples, was the last to suffer. In 1664 she had been in great danger, and her property was confiscated as a preliminary measure. But in October, 1666, it was restored to her by the intercession of the Tsaritsa Maria, and she was left in peace for a time. She now gave herself up still more to religion, took the veil privately under the name of Theodora, and submitted herself absolutely to an old nun, Melania by name, who had long been one of her pensioners. On the death of her protectress, the Tsaritsa Maria, in 1669, which was a great blow to the anti-Nikonians, Morozova withdrew altogether from the world, living in her own house in cloistral seclusion. Two years later, on the plea of infirmity, she refused to take her proper place at the marriage ceremony of Alexius with Natalia Naruishkina, the liberal-minded pupil of Matvyeev, whom Morozova regarded as a heretic. Her motives were perfectly well understood, and bitterly resented at Court. "Would she pit herself against us?" cried Alexius angrily. "She will find out that one of us must give way." Her brother-in-law, Prince Urusov, was first sent to admonish her privately to accept the new doctrines, and when this friendly effort failed, her house was broken open at midnight, and she and her devoted sister, the Princess Eudoxia Urusova, were put in chains and thrown into a cellar. Two days later they were brought before a synod held in the Granovitaya Palata in the *kreml'*, presided over by Peterim, Metropolitan of Krutitsk. The examination lasted from the second to the tenth hour of the night. The tribunal had evidently been instructed to deal gently with the accused; but her provocative defiance soon exhausted its patience. First she was asked whether she would communicate according to the new service-books, like the Tsar and the Tsaritsa. She refused on the ground that the new service-books were corrupt. "Then thou dost believe us all to be heretics?" inquired Peterim. "It is plain ye are the followers of Nikon, the enemy of God, who hath spewed forth his heresies like vomit, which filth of his ye now lick up," was her fierce reply. Then they cursed her as a child of the devil. "Nay," she said, "I am a child of Christ, though an unworthy one." As she was reconducted through the *kreml'* to her dungeon she passed by the gallery of the corridor of the Chudov Monastery, from which Tsar Alexius was inquisitively peeping down. On perceiving the Gosudar the impenitent boyaruinya could not resist committing an overt act of defiance. Ostentatiously crossing herself *with two fingers*, she raised her fettered hands and kissed her chains with rapture. For the next few weeks she and her sister steadfastly refused to listen to or even look upon Nikonian presbyters sent to convert them. The fame of their constancy soon spread throughout Moscovy, and stimulated everywhere the zeal of the schismatics. Avvakum, from his distant dungeon, contrived to convey messages of encouragement to "God's witnesses on earth. . . . Incorruptible vessels filled with sweet-smelling unguents," as he proudly called them. Words failed him for adequate epithets. In the capital itself the endurance of the sisters excited respect and sympathy even in the most orthodox

Court circles. The humane and enlightened Rtishchev stopped one day outside the prison of the sisters at the Aleksyeevsky Convent, and said to them: " Your constancy amazes me. But one thing puzzles me: I don't understand for what you are suffering." Crowds of people flocked daily to the convent to see the two confessors dragged out to their sledges for their daily involuntary exercise. At last the abbess and nuns of the convent grew alarmed, and implored Peterim, now patriarch,* to relieve them of their troublesome charge. A fresh examination before Peterim and a mixed council was thereupon held. The patriarch did everything he could to make submission easy. When the sisters refused to allow any orthodox priest in Moscow to confess or communicate them, he offered to do so himself. " I am an old man," said he, " and distressed concerning you." Morozova replied she had no need of his services. She then reproached him for changing his principles: " You serve an earthly Tsar," said she, " and despise your heavenly Tsar and Creator." Such obstinacy pointed so clearly to mental disturbance that Peterim prepared to anoint her as one who was sick, but she forcibly resisted his " unhallowed anointing," and was dragged back to her dungeon. Her sister also approved herself " thrice valiant." When they attempted to anoint her likewise, she abashed the bishops by suddenly letting down her long and beautiful hair before them, exclaiming, " Shameless and senseless ones, what do ye! Will ye look upon my nakedness!" Whereupon the prelates withdrew, baffled and ashamed.† Argument and entreaty proving fruitless, the women were next taken to the torture-chamber. But first, as a deterrent against further obstinacy, sundry of their devoted female servants were horribly tormented before their eyes. The sight of the awful sufferings of her beloved Maria Danilovna, who was scourged savagely on the stomach when her back could not safely bear further laceration, almost broke Morozova down. Bursting into tears, she exclaimed: " Are ye Christians, to torment a poor faithful wench

---

* Peterim, one of the most virulent opponents of Nikon at the council, had, in June, 1672, succeeded Nikon's immediate successor, Joasaf II. He died in April, 1673. See M. G. Popov: " Materialui dlya istoriu Piterima."

† Such an uncovering was deemed the last degree of shamelessness in a Moscovite lady.

so ?" But not flogging, nor burning, nor freezing,* not even the bitter shame of being stripped half naked in a room full of curious spectators, could extort one word of surrender from either of the noble ladies.†

On the following morning the Tsar held a council to decide what was to be done with the impenitent schismatics. Some of the ecclesiastics proposed that they should be burnt alive, but the boyars of the council refused to permit one of their own order to be so punished. As a last resource, Alexius, in a letter beginning : " Righteous mother Theodosia, thou second St. Catherine !" implored Morozova to give way, and at least forego the heretical practice of crossing herself with two fingers. " Righteous mother," he concluded, " for the people's sake do me this honour!  I, the Tsar, render thee homage ! "  But even this appeal was fruitless, and the sisters were ultimately banished to Borovsk, in the province of Kaluga. Their treatment was inhumanely rigorous, even for eighteenth century Moscovy. After ten weeks the Princess Urusova died of starvation. Morozova lingered on a little while longer. Infinitely pathetic is the account of her last moments. Tormented by the pangs of hunger, when near her end, she sent for the *stryelets*, or musketeer, who mounted guard over her, and said to him : " I am weak from hunger ; for Christ's sake pity me, and bring me a roll of bread."  " I dare not," answered the soldier.‡  " A piece of biscuit, then !"  " I dare not."  " Then bring me an apple, or some gherkins."  " I dare not."  Last of all she begged him, at least, to wash her dirty shift for her.  " Look now," said she, " it pleases God to take me away from this life.  But it is unseemly that this body of mine, which He hath created, should lie in the bowels of its mother earth in a filthy garment."  Then the soldier took it and washed it for her in the stream hard by, weeping all the time at the thought of her former greatness, and of how a single word, which she would not speak, might have restored her to more than her ancient splendour.§

* Their flogged and naked backs were plunged into snow for three hours, and then exposed to a blazing fire.          † Zabyelin : "Domashnui Buit," etc.

‡ No doubt he recollected that a poor monk who had tried to help her a few weeks before, had been burnt alive for his act of mercy.

§ Zabyelin : " Domashnui Buit."

Avvakum long survived his spiritual daughter. For fourteen years the great protopop remained at Pustozersk. At first his imprisonment was light, and he was allowed to communicate with the outer world. But when he abused this liberty by assailing the Tsar with violent letters (in one of them he threatened him with the pains of hell unless he repented and restored the exiled schismatics) he was treated with a savage rigour only intelligible on the assumption of a deliberate intention of shortening his life. "I was a living corpse," he tells us, and there is no exaggeration in the description. But the unconquerable spirit of the man sustained him. He redoubled his religious exercises. He added self-inflicted torments to the cruelties of his persecutors. He fasted for ten days at a time, till power of speech forsook him. He even discarded his clothing and lay for hours in an ecstatic trance. At last his very gaolers became his disciples, and not only connived at but assisted in the propagation of his doctrines. The starved and naked anchorite in the clay dungeon at Pustozersk became the leader of a vast popular movement, and devoted the whole of his ample leisure to polemical literature. From 1673 to his death in 1681, he composed his autobiography, seven commentaries on the Psalms, nine dogmatic treatises, and forty-three epistles to various persons. All these works were jotted down on old pieces of rag, which were then secretly conveyed out of the prison ; carefully transcribed by the pilgrims and other visitors who came to him for advice and comfort from all parts of Moscovy ; circulated in hundreds of copies bound in costly velvet ; and revered like so many divine revelations.*

Avvakum's success as a controversialist is not surprising. Although his name will be found in very few histories of Russian literature, he was indubitably the first Russian who knew how to write his own language. His style is admirable. Whilst his literary contemporaries are still struggling in the meshes of an obscure and pedantic jargon, Avvakum's diction is a model of lucidity, abounding, moreover, with bold and original metaphor, and expressing every mood and feeling

---

* Notably his epistles to the deacon Theodore, which were kept in the schismatical churches close to the sacred ikons.

with a simple directness which was bound to catch and hold the
popular taste.

But when we pass from the form to the substance of the
great schismatic's teaching, we are amazed to find that literally
there is nothing in it.   The whole dispute turns upon the
*minutiæ* of ceremonial, the true history and bearing of which
Avvakum, obviously, is either too ignorant to understand, or
too obstinate to wish to understand.   There is no question of
dogma, no question even of discipline.   On all essentials the
Avvakumites were really at one with the Nikonians.   Only the
most microscopical differences, the veriest mint and cummin of
ecclesiastical observance, divide them, and these bagatelles are
magnified by Avvakum into articles of faith, the slightest departure from which is denounced as heresy and branded with
anathemas.   We gather, for instance, that tetragonal crosses are
permissible on certain vestments, but those persons who presume
to stamp them on the *prosforui*, or sacramental wafers, instead of
the old-fashioned octagonal crosses, will infallibly be turned into
fire unquenchable along with those other backsliders who say
" alleluia " thrice instead of four times consecutively.

All Avvakum's earlier writings breathe this fierce intolerance.
" 'Twere better for a man never to have been born than to cross
himself with three fingers instead of two," is their constant
refrain.   His followers are to hold no intercourse with the
Nikonians, who are " blood-suckers," " soul-destroyers," " viler
than the ancient heretics."   He rejoices that the " land of Russia
is sanctified by martyr-blood "—nay, he approves of wholesale
suicide if there be no other way of avoiding conformity with
Nikonian practices.   Beneath the stress of persecution we find,
from time to time, faint glimpses of a better spirit in his later
works ; but nothing is more certain than that, if Avvakum had
had the power, he would have been far less forbearing to his
adversaries than they were to him.

Yet, after all, to come to the root of the matter, Avvakum's
objections to the Nikonian reforms are political rather than
theological.   He objects to them not so much because they are
anti-Christian as because they are anti-Russian.   They are heterodox because they run counter to the national tradition, and the

national tradition is orthodox because it is the historical develop-ment of the belief of the independent Russian people. Thus the whole argument springs from a bigoted patriotism.

Signs are not wanting that, during the latter years of his imprisonment, Avvakum's powers were on the wane. His coun-sels to the faithful grow more and more uncertain, and he commits himself to glaring heresies on the authority of his faulty old Russian texts.* Moreover his communications with the outer world reveal a very intelligible want of self-control, and it was to one of these epistolary indiscretions that he owed his martyrdom. In 1681 he wrote to the new Tsar, Theodore III., declaring that the Saviour had revealed to him, Avvakum, that the late Tsar Alexius was now in torments. For this he was condemned to be burnt in the market-place at Pustozersk, the Government, no doubt, eagerly embracing the first oppor-tunity of ridding itself of such a persistent troubler of the peace. His three comrades in exile, Lazar, Epifany and Nikiphor, who had already lost their tongues and right arms, were to suffer with him. On April 1, 1681, the aged protopop, inflexible to the last, met his death with joyful composure. He had long yearned after the crowning martyrdom of "the fiery oven," and, with piercing eloquence, had again and again held his terrifying ideal up to his shrinking followers. "There is terror in the stake till thou art bound to it," he wrote, "but once embrace it and all will be forgotten. Thou wilt behold Christ ere yet the heat hath laid hold upon thee, and thy soul, released from the dungeon of the body, will fly up to heaven, like a happy little bird, along with the angelic choirs." When the faggots were being lit Avvakum turned to the crowd which stood by uncovered, in respectful and mournful silence; crossed himself, for the last time, with two fingers; and exhorted his hearers never, when they prayed, to depart from that ancient Russian practice, for doing so their house would be founded upon a rock. When the faggots were in full blaze, the youngest of Avvakum's fellow-sufferers, unable to endure the torture, shrieked aloud. Avvakum

---

* In one of these the Blessed Trinity is described as *trisushchnoi*, or tri-substantial. Avvakum accordingly adopted this teaching, but his followers repudiated it after his death.

R.                                                                                     M

thereupon bent over him, as a father bends over his ailing child, with soothing words of comfort, till the ascending flames engulfed and consumed both the sufferer and his sublime consoler. An ancient local tradition tells us that at the moment when the proto-pop's towering form collapsed and disappeared, a snow-white dove, which had long been hovering over the fire, straightway spread her wings and ascended up to heaven. A rude monument at Pustozersk, known as the Cross of Avvakum, still marks the spot where the heroic protopop cheerfully gave up his soul to God.

ARTAMON MATVYEEV.

THE GREAT REFORMING BOYAR.

# CHAPTER VI.

## The Latter Years of Tsar Alexius. 1667—1676.

THE principal event of the latter years of Tsar Alexius was the
terrible rebellion of the Cossacks of the Volga and the Don,
under Stenka Razin, a rebellion which might have been as
damaging to Moscovy as Chmielnicki's rebellion had been to
Poland but for the lucky accident that the catastrophe devastated
her eastern instead of her western borders. Here, fortunately,
unlike Poland she had no powerful neighbours to make capital
out of her distress.

The Cossacks, as we have seen, were a perpetual trouble both
to the Polish Republic and the Moscovite Tsardom, principally
because of their proximity to Mussulman territory, which these
orthodox Vikings, despite the warnings and prohibitions of King
and Tsar, regarded as their natural prey. The usual mode of
procedure of the Moscovite Cossacks was to sail down the Don
into the Sea of Azov, and thence into the Black Sea, but when,
in the middle of the seventeenth century, the Khan of the
Crimea closed this outlet by building forts on the Lower Don,
the Cossacks took to sailing down the Volga into the Caspian

Sea instead. When the Moscovite Government attempted to put a stop to these raids by guarding the mouth of the Volga, the freebooters dispersed inland, established themselves in a fastness amidst the marshes of the Upper Don, inaccessible except in winter, which they called Riga, and plundered all the vessels sailing down the Volga, along 170 miles of its course from Tsaritsuin to Saratov. This went on from 1659 to 1665, but ultimately the local *voivodui* prevailed over the robbers, and the new Riga, which had become a vast depository for stolen property, was attacked and destroyed.

But in the summer of 1667 a much more formidable male-factor suddenly appeared on the scene. This was the Cossack Stephen Timofeeich Razin,* whom we first hear of in 1661, on a diplomatic mission to the Calmuck Tatars. He is described as a sturdy, thick set man of middle height, about fifty years of age, full of the restless adventurous energy which cannot stay quietly at home. The immeasurable steppe, or "the broad bosom of Mother Volga," were his natural haunts. Atrociously cruel and utterly unscrupulous, yet, as a son of the orthodox Church, he owned to a conscience, and, in moments of remorse and weariness, would think seriously of the salvation of his soul. Thus, in the autumn of 1661 we meet him on a pilgrimage, of a thousand miles, to the great Solovetsky Monastery on the White Sea, and soon afterwards we find the penitent cut-throat founding a hermitage as an asylum for aged and wounded Cossacks. After that all trace of him is lost for six years; but in 1667, the *voivodui* of Astrakhan received a warning from the Tsar that a multitude of Cossacks and fugitive peasants, well provided with arms and ammunition, had settled in the district. The leader of this robber community was the ex-pilgrim Stenka or Steeny Razin. Fixing his headquarters at the village of Panshinskoe, between the rivers Tishina and Ilovla, amidst an inaccessible waste of waters, he deliberately set himself to levy blackmail on all the vessels passing up and down the Volga. His first exploit was to attack the "Water Caravan," consisting of the Government treasury barge, the barge of the patriarch, and the corn barges of the rich Moscovy merchant Svorin, which were sailing down

* See Kostomarov: "Bunt S. Razina," and Solovev: "Istoria Rossy," t. II.

the river to Astrakhan. Razin fell suddenly upon them, over-whelmed and dispersed their *stryeltsui* escort, and, next day, the scene of the encounter was strewn with the charred and mutilated corpses of his horribly tortured victims. Stenka next sailed down the Volga himself with a flotilla of thirty-five *strugi* and 150 men, levying blackmail as he passed on the fortress of Tsaritsuin, and devastating the open country far and wide. He captured the fortress of Yaitsk by a stratagem. Presenting himself at the gates with forty of his comrades in the garb of pilgrims, he craved permission to pray in the church, and on being admitted, massacred 170 of the garrison in cold blood ; the rest submitted. In November the same year Stenka scornfully rejected an offer of a free pardon from the Tsar, if he would lay down his arms. At the beginning of 1668 he defeated the *voivoda*, Jakov Bezobrazov, sent against him from Astrakhan, and in the spring of the same year embarked on an enterprise which relieved Moscovy of his presence for eighteen months. Sailing into the Caspian, he ravaged the Persian coasts from Derbend to Baku, leaving nothing but smoking ruins behind him. On reaching Resht he offered his services to the Shah, and began measuring out the land for a permanent settlement, but while the negotiations were proceeding, the inhabitants of Resht rose against him and slew 400 of his followers. Stenka there-upon took a horrible and treacherous vengeance on the wealthy town of Farabat. For five days the Cossacks traded peaceably with the inhabitants. On the sixth day Stenka readjusted his cap. This was the preconcerted signal. The Cossacks flung themselves on the defenceless and unsuspecting inhabitants, massacring half of them and exchanging the remainder with the Persian authorities at the rate of one Mussulman for four Christian captives.

In the spring of 1669, the Cossack Ataman established his headquarters in the isle of Suina, whence he could conveniently raid the mainland. Here, in July, a Persian fleet, with 4,000 men, attacked Razin, but was utterly annihilated, only three ships escaping. Among the captives was the daughter of the Khan Menedi, who saved her life by becoming the concubine of the victorious Cossack.

Stenka was now a potentate with whom monarchs need not disdain to treat. In August, 1669, he reappeared at Astrakhan, and magnanimously accepted a fresh order of pardon from the Tsar. The conditions were easy enough. He had only to lay down his *bunchuk*, or horse-tail standard, relinquish his captives and his guns, and send a deputation to Moscow to acknowledge his submission. From Aug. 25/Sept. 4, Stenka remained at Astrakhan, and speedily became the hero and the marvel of the city. The common people, whose dull, monotonous life was one ceaseless round of bitter toil, were fascinated by the sight of the Cossack Ataman and his comrades, fresh from their romantic oriental adventures, swaggering about the bazaars arrayed in atlas caftans and jewelled caps, scattering their sequins broadcast and selling priceless oriental silks at 9*d.* a pound. Stephen Timofeeich was something like a *batyushka*,* they cried. He was very different from the *voivodui* and the officials of the *prikaz*, who lived on the sweat and blood of the people and treated them like dirt. He had a good word for everyone, gave you your heart's desire ere yet it had quitted your lips, and feasted you like a prince day and night. No wonder, then, if the common people regarded this fairy-tale paladin as greater even than the far distant Gosudar. And was he not also a master-magician? Did not everyone say that darts and bullets were powerless to hurt him? No wonder, then, if they willingly bowed the knee before him. Even his extraordinary outbursts of violence were admiringly looked upon as something elemental and superhuman, something in the nature of a volcanic eruption or a thunderstorm. His most famous extravagance has often been recorded. One day Stenka was sailing down the Volga in his state barge, which had satin sails and ropes of silk, with his concubine, the beautiful Persian princess, by his side, in gorgeous apparel. Suddenly the half drunken Ataman, starting up from a profound reverie, lifted the Khan's daughter on high, and apostrophised the broad stream flowing beneath him : " Take her, Mother Volga ! take her ! " he roared. " Much silver and gold hast thou given me, and all manner of good things, and

---

* The " Little Father." the affectionate epithet bestowed by the common people on great protectors, especially the Tsar.

what have I ever given thee in return? Take, then, my greatest treasure!"—and with that he hurled the unfortunate woman into the swift current, which speedily engulfed her.* And his exploits appealed as much to the popular greed as to the popular wonder. What booty might not be won at next to no risk under such a *batyushka*? If, as we are told, prosperous merchants on the Don frequently cast their ordinary pursuits to the winds to join in the more lucrative speculation of an ordinary Cossack raid, how much greater must have been the fascination of an expedition under a chieftain who levied blackmail on Shah and Tsar alike with perfect impunity? Such an adventurer could always count not only upon the peasantry, who were of the same stock as himself, but also upon the *stryeltsui*, or musketeers, who were demi-Cossacks by profession. Finally, we must remember that the semi-Asiatic "kingdom of Astrakhan,"† in the heart of the eastern Ukrain, where the whole atmosphere was predatory, and nine-tenths of the population were nomadic, was the natural *milieu* for such a rebellion as Stenka Razin's.

Under these circumstances, the Moscovite Government, in common prudence, should have rid itself of Stenka while it had the chance. Instead of that, on September 4, 1668, it sent him from Astrakhan to the Don, with provision for the journey, to report himself to the official Cossack Hetman there, at the same time forbidding the governors of the Volgan cities to admit him within their walls. This, however, was easier said than done. Enraged at the refusal of the *voivoda* of Tsaritsuin to sell wine to the Cossacks, Razin burst into the town, half murdered the *voivoda*, and broke open all the prisons and pothouses. Hearing of the anarchy at Tsaritsuin, Prince Prozorovsky, governor of Astrakhan, sent the Swede Vaderos to Razin, commanding him to dismiss his followers and abstain from harbouring fugitive peasants. "How dare you come to me with such disrespectful words?" roared the Ataman. "What! am I to give up my friends who have come to me out of pure love and affection? And you dare to threaten me with

---

* This incident is much embellished by local tradition, but its truth is vouched for by Strause, an eye-witness.

† Tsar of Astrakhan is, to this day, one of the Emperor of Russia's many titles.

punishment? Very well! Tell your governor from me that I fear neither him nor those who are higher than he. Just wait a bit, and I'll settle accounts with him, fool and coward that he is!"

Nevertheless, Razin quitted Tsaritsuin, but, feeling that he had burnt his boats, he now proceeded to commit one act of rebellion after another. First he established the fortress of Kagalnik on an island of the Don, in defiance of the fortress of the official Cossack Ataman, Kornilo Yakorlev, at Cherkask. Then, in 1670, he audaciously presented himself at Cherkask, and murdered the Tsar's special envoy, Evdokimov, whom he found there with a friendly message from the Gosudar to himself. He next proceeded higher up the Don to Papshina, where he was joined by another freebooter, Vas'ka Us, who had distinguished himself by the wholesale massacre and plunder of the gentry of the districts of Tula and Voronezh. The peasantry flocked to him now from every quarter, and in the course of 1670 he was strong enough, aided by treachery in the city itself, to capture both the town and citadel of Tsaritsuin, and to defeat the Government troops in two engagements. A council of war was then held by the Cossacks at Tsaritsuin to decide whether they should march against the boyars at Moscow or against Prozorovsky at Astrakhan, and the latter course was finally adopted, the deserting *stryeltsui* having assured him that the Volgan capital would declare for him if only he marched against it boldly forthwith.

Prozorovsky, well aware that Astrakhan was seething with discontent, and that most of his own *stryeltsui* were half-hearted relied, nevertheless, on the assistance of two foreign officers, an Irishman named Butler, who was the captain of the *Orel*, the first Russian warship ever built, then actually at anchor in Astrakhan harbour, and an English colonel, Thomas Boyle, who undertook to man the ramparts on the land side, and was determined to defend the place to the best of his ability. But the loyal portion of the garrison was full of a panic fear of the magician Stenka, and they were still further depressed by the sight of a thick shower of meteorites descending from a clear sky. Full of fear, they hastened to the cathedral to inquire of the metropolitan Joseph the meaning of this portent. The metropolitan tearfully declared that God was about to pour the vials of His wrath upon the doomed city. The old man had had bitter experience of Cossack cruelty. Years before, in the time of his predecessor, Theodosius, he had fallen into their hands, and ever since his head had shaken with palsy.

On the 22nd June the Cossacks came in sight, on the 23rd they occupied the vineyards surrounding the city, and burnt the Tatar suburb; on the 24th they swarmed over the ramparts, encountering no serious opposition. The only resistance offered was by Prince Kaspulat Metralovich Cherkasky, who, with eight comrades, defended the tower of the official torture-chamber, firing silver buttons and coins when their bullets failed them, till the evening, when they tried to escape, and were bludgeoned to death or hacked to pieces. The Cossacks were received as friends and deliverers. Butler and Boyle fled ; Prozorovsky, mortally wounded, was conveyed to the cathedral, the last refuge of the well-to-do classes, who filled it to overflowing, and shut the huge oaken doors. But the Cossacks burst the doors open ; massacred all the fugitives, and cast 441 corpses into a huge pit, dug for the purpose near the Troitskaya Monastery, a Cossack priest standing by to count the slain as they were flung in. The city was then given over to pillage. All the wares of the Russian, Persian, Indian and Bokharan bazaars were piled up into a huge heap for future division.

Master of Astrakhan, Razin at once proceeded to convert it into a Cossack republic, dividing the inhabitants into thousands, hundreds and tens, with their proper officers, all of whom were appointed by a *vyecha*, or general assembly, whose first act was to proclaim Stephen Timofeeich their Gosudar. The remainder of the better classes were then hunted out and massacred, and their widows and daughters given in marriage to the Cossack rabble, Razin's official seal serving in lieu of the archbishop's blessing to legalise these unions. The terror-stricken metropolitan hid himself in his palace, and, on the name-day of the Tsarevich Theodore, attempted weakly to conciliate Razin and his *starshins* by inviting them to a banquet. Very different was the behaviour of the two sons of the dead governor Prozorovsky, and of the *podyachy*, or recorder, Aleksei, who were examined

by Razin at the same time. " Where has your father hidden all
the treasures ? " stormed the Cossack. " There are no treasures
left," boldly replied the youngest lad, a child of eight. " You
and your people have taken good care of that." The recorder
confirmed the lad's words, whereupon Razin ordered him to be
hoisted up on the ramparts at the end of a huge hook thrust
through his ribs. The two lads were suspended by his side on
a gallows, head downwards. On the following day the elder lad
was hurled from the battlements on to the rocks below, and the
younger was sent back to his mother with a flogging. The
recorder had already expired.

After a three weeks' carnival of blood and debauchery, during
every day of which the new Gosudar and his starshins were
drunk from morn till eve, Stenka turned his attention to affairs
of state, and leaving the ferocious Vas'ka Us behind him at
Astrakhan as Ataman with half the *stryeltsui* and volunteers
at his disposal, set out, with 200 barges escorted by 2,000
horsemen, to establish the Cossack republic along the whole
length of the Volga, as a preliminary step towards advancing
against Moscow itself. Saratov and Samara were captured, and
the Cossack rule inaugurated with the usual ceremonies, but at
Simbirsk the two *okolnichie* Prince Yury Nikitich Baryatinsky
and the boyarin Ivan Bogdanovich Miloslavsky, held him at
bay for twenty-four hours ; and though he ultimately took the
town, Miloslavsky for a whole month defied all his efforts to
capture the citadel. This respite enabled the Government to
rally its forces, and, on the banks of the Sviyaga, on October 1,
after two bloody encounters (October 1 and 4), Baryatinsky, now
strongly reinforced, routed Razin, who fled away down the Volga,
leaving the bulk of his followers to be extirpated by the victor.

But the rebellion was by no means over. The emissaries of
Razin, armed with inflammatory proclamations, had stirred up the
inhabitants of the modern governments of Nizhny Novgorod,
Tambov and Penza, and had penetrated to Moscow, Great
Novgorod, and even to the Solovetsky Monastery on the
White Sea. It was not difficult to revolt the sorely oppressed
population by the promise of instant deliverance from their heavy
yoke. Razin proclaimed that his object was to root out the

boyars, the Court nobles, and the *prikaznui* people, level all ranks and dignities, and establish Cossackdom, with its corollary of absolute equality, throughout Moscovy. "I do not want to be your Tsar," he wrote. "I would live among you as a brother." Yet, knowing the veneration of the Russian nation for the Gosudar, he affected a similar reverence himself; at the same time artfully endeavouring to discredit the Tsar's authority by declaring that the Tsarevich Alexius, who had died on January 17 that same year, and the patriarch Nikon, already a disgraced exile in the distant Byelozersky Monastery, were to accompany him. By his orders, a Cossack of Cherkask, Makum Osipov by name, even posed as the Tsarevich, and sailed down the Volga in a state barge covered with purple cloth.

Presently over the whole of the vast region extending between the Volga, the Oka and the Dwina, a *jacquerie* was raging, and the unspeakable horrors of the interregnum of 1611/13 and of Chmielnicki's rising in the northern Ukrain were repeated and exceeded. In all the villages the peasants rose in bands, butchered the landowners, and joined the Cossacks. In the towns the common people, at the first appearance of the horsetail standard, murdered their *voivodui*, and threw open the gates to the Cossacks. The surrounding semi-pagan Finnish tribes, the Mordvinians, the Chuvasses and the Cheremisses, speedily made common cause with the native Moscovites in such numbers that, in one band of 15,000 rebels, only 100 were Don Cossacks.

Nizhny Novgorod, which had sent an invitation to the Cossack leader Osipov, was saved for the Government only by the promptitude of Yury Aleksyeivich Dolgoruki. From Sept. 28/Oct. 14 this capable boyarin had at least held his own at Arzamasa against a countless host of rebels, who for a long time prevented him from taking the offensive. On October 22 his lieutenants succeeded in defeating one large band at Murahkina, and he himself terrorised the mutinous city of Nizhny Novgorod into obedience by quartering captured insurgents inside and gibbeting them outside the walls. He also drove them out of the strong entrenchments which, with infinite labour, they had thrown across the Kurmuishkaya road, from forest to forest, when 4,500 captives were taken and executed.

After pacifying the North, Dolgoruki moved southwards, everywhere encountering the most furious resistance, mostly from behind enormous barricades, one of them three miles in length and one mile in breadth. The effusion of blood was horrible. Driven gradually from lair to lair, the desperate wretches fought like ravening beasts, and the slow but steady progress of the merciless Tsarish generals was marked by hundreds of burning villages and long lines of wheels and gibbets.* Occasionally odd bits of human flotsam came to light. Thus at Tenenikov, on December 4, an amazon of Armenian origin, who, under more favourable circumstances, might have developed into a national heroine, was caught plundering and massacring at the head of a robber band. She confessed to sorcery as well as sedition, and was burnt along with her magic roots and books of spells.

Meanwhile Prince Daniel Baryatinski was slowly subduing the extreme eastern districts. All through November and December, 1670, the work of " pacification " went on, but till the beginning of 1671 the issue was very doubtful. No fewer than eight pitched battles had to be fought before the insurrection showed the slightest sign of weakening, the people repeatedly breaking their promises, and resuming their depredations as soon as the Government troops had departed. Razin's fate had already been decided. At Simbirsk his *prestige* had been irreparably shattered. Even his own settlements at Samara and Saratov had refused to open their gates to the fugitive. At Cherkask the Don Cossacks, impressed by the tidings that the patriarch Joseph had solemnly anathematised Stenka in the Uspensky Cathedral at Moscow, also declared against him. His last acts were those of a maniac. Amongst other atrocities he fed his stoves with the bodies of his captives, but his fortress of Kagalnik was now his last refuge, and in April, 1671, Stenka was captured and carried to Moscow. On June 6, after enduring unspeakable tortures with dogged bravado, he was quartered alive.

Astrakhan alone remained unsubdued. The first intelligence of the collapse of the rebellion elsewhere was brought to the city

---

* One hundred thousand peasants and Cossacks are said to have perished in these parts.

by a Tatar courier from Moscow, with a letter from the Tsar to
the archbishop. Fortified by the intelligence, the metropolitan
atoned for his former weakness by boldly reading the letter to
the people in the cathedral, and urging them to seize and
imprison the Cossack leaders, whom he excommunicated forthwith. The Cossacks shouted that the letter was a forgery. Had
it not been Holy Week they would have murdered the metropolitan on the spot for contradicting them. But the crime was
only postponed. On May 11 the Cossacks burst into the
cathedral while the archbishop was at the altar, and summoned
him to their general assembly. He appeared in full canonicals
with all his clergy in attendance. After tearing off his vestments they laid him on burning embers, to extort from him
a confession that the Tsar's letter was a forgery. But the
constancy of the metropolitan tired out all the efforts of his
tormentors, who finally flung the dying old man down from the
battlements. This outrage was the act of the extreme desperadoes. Most of the townsfolk, and even the majority of the
Cossacks, were horrified by such an act of sacrilege. But there
was still no thought of surrender. When, at the end of August,
the armada of Miloslavsky appeared before the city, the
Cossacks howled at all his offers of mercy "like savage dogs."
For three months, ably led by Fedka Shelyudak (Vas'ka Us's
loathsome life having meanwhile been fitly terminated by a
loathsome death)* the Cossacks beat off the besiegers and, in
frequent sorties, damaged or destroyed the tall wooden towers
from which Miloslavsky attempted to scale the walls. At last,
on November 27, they obtained their own terms, an absolute
amnesty, and the troops of the Gosudar, preceded by the clergy
bearing the sacred ikon of Our Lady, entered the city. Not till
the following year did the Moscow Government feel strong
enough to order an inquiry, when Shelyudak and four other
ringleaders were hanged.

Apart from the obvious reflections suggested by the rebellion
of Razin, a speculative historian must inevitably be struck by its
shocking waste of excellent human working material. Ruffian
and freebooter as he undoubtedly was, Stenka nevertheless had

---

* He is said to have been eaten alive by worms.

within him something of the stuff of which enterprising colonists and heroic adventurers are made. The Caspian expeditions may not unfairly be compared with some of the exploits of Drake and other buccaneers of whom we are so justly proud. Indeed, the Cossack element of the Russian nation, with its pioneering audacity and its restless *abandon*, when adequately controlled and directed, was to be largely instrumental in extending the empire of Moscovy over the barbarians of the central Asiatic steppes. Even under the first Romanovs this great movement eastwards had already begun, and to us, at the present time especially, its rudiments are of peculiar interest.

From the dawn of her history Moscovy had to deal with savage nomadic neighbours, who were far more frequently her conquerors than her subjects. Of these neighbours, the three principal, the Pechenegs,* the Polovtsui, or Cumanians, and the Tatars, had either disappeared altogether, or were becoming subordinate ; but at the commencement of the seventh century the Calmucks still remained. The Moscovite Calmucks formed the western branch of the great Mongol family who first penetrated into Siberia in the reign of Vasily Shuisky (1606/10), and ultimately (1630/32) settled on the shores of the Volga and the Yaika (though their chief *yust*, or encampment, lay beyond the Urals), where their depredations speedily brought them into collision with the Moscovite Government. In 1657 they nominally became Russian subjects ; were permitted to trade freely with Astrakhan ; and alternately fought with and against the Crimean Tatars. In Siberia proper, during the reign of Michael Romanov, the Moscovites, with the assistance of firearms, easily subdued the aborigines, who had only bows and arrows, and compelled them to pay *yasak*.† But the authority of the Russians in those remote regions was by no means established, and from 1634 to nearly the end of the century, scarcely a year passed without an attack of the eastern Calmucks upon the thinly garrisoned Russian settlements. In 1662 there was a dangerous rebellion on the river Iseta, when the combined Tatars, Mordvinians, Cheremisses and Bashkirs, took the town of Kangur. In 1663 the Ostiaks of Berezov

---

* From late Greek, πατζινακῖται.                    ʼ Tribute of pelts.

attempted to take Tobolsk and drive the Moscovites out of Western Siberia. Further eastward, Kuznetsk was constantly exposed to the attacks of the Telentai, or White Kalmucks, while the inhabitants of Krasnoyarsk suffered even more from the Kirghiz, and vainly petitioned for leave to abandon the colony altogether. The subsequent measures of the Moscow Government to suppress the Telentai brought it into collision with the great Altuim Khan, who aimed at the subjection of all these *yasak*-paying tribes. The fear of him extended as far as Tomsk, till, in 1674, Daniel Baryatinsky, uniting the forces of the four chief Siberian cities, severely punished the surrounding tribes.

At the very time when the Moscovite trans-Uralian settlements were thus fighting for their very existence with the Kalmucks and the Bashkirs, Moscovite pioneers were making fresh conquests in the remotest districts of Northern Asia, conquests which ultimately brought the ambassadors of the Great Gosudar into the presence of the "Son of Heaven" in the Middle Kingdom. In 1655, after a bloody struggle, the Buriates were subdued by the Cossack Ataman Kolesnikov, who had previously operated successfully against the Tunguses. In 1661 Irkutsk was founded. From the Yenesei the exploring Russian bands proceeded along the Angora, the Shilka and the Selenga, and round Baikal, conquering and colonising in every direction. One band went northwards to the Arctic Ocean. Others proceeded eastwards to Ochotsk, and southwards to the Amur. In 1648 Semen Dezhnev, sailing from the mouth of the Koluimna, in search of new lands, was the first successfully to navigate the extreme north-eastern coast of Asia and sail through the narrow strait separating the Chucotch Peninsula from the island of St. Lawrence, into the North Pacific, thus anticipating the navigator Bering by sixty years. In 1652 the same explorer rowed down the Anaduir to the ocean in search of walruses, getting as far as Cape Nazaruin, where he levied tribute on the Koriaks. In 1647 another band of Cossacks, under Semen Shelkovnik, appeared at the mouth of the river Ulia where it falls into the Sea of Ochotsk, and sailed to the mouth of the Okhota. Rumours of silver and gold mines, and

of corn in abundance, attracted the Moscovites to the Amur.
The first explorer of these regions was Vasily Poyarkov, sent
from Yakutsk, in 1643, by the *voivoda* Golovin, in search of
fresh *yasak*. Sailing down the rivers Shilka, Ziya, Lena, Aldan,
and their tributaries, he entered the Amur unwittingly, taking it
to be a continuation of the Shilka. After wintering at the
mouth of the Amur, he returned to Yakutsk by way of the
Aldan and the Lena, bringing rich stores of sables with him,
and recommending the occupation of the Amur district, which
he reported to be rich and populous, abounding with corn, pelts
and fat rivers, "so that the Gosudar's fighting men will lack
nothing." Strange and horrible tales of Poyarkov's barbarity
had preceded him. It was not merely unavoidable hardships
which had reduced his little band from 133 to 80 men. He is
said, on excellent authority, to have flogged many of his Cossacks
to death, exclaiming: "They're cheap enough!" and to have
burnt all the cornfields *en route*, that his followers might be
compelled to buy grain from him at his own price. Some of
them preferred to devour the corpses of savages and the
carcases of wild beasts. Another pioneer, Erothei Pavlovich
Khabarov, explored the Amur by way of the rivers Olekma,
Tagir and Ukra. He discovered three or four vast deserted
cities, and reported to Yakutsk that the Amur was even richer
in fish than the Volga, while round about it lay rich cornfields,
lush meadows, and "large dark forests full of sables." "If the
Daurian province be subdued," he added, "it will be of great
profit to the Gosudar. There will also be no need to send corn
to Yakutsk from Russia, as it takes only a fortnight to sail from
the Amur to Yakutsk." In 1650 Khabarov was sent back with
twenty Cossacks, seventy heretics, and three guns, and occupied
the fort of Albazin. But the aborigines, who were already the
tributaries of China, refused to give *yasak* to the Tsar, and
Khabarov went into winter quarters at Ashansk, where, in 1652,
he was attacked by a large Manchurian army led by a Chinese
viceroy. The guns of the Moscovites proved better than the
guns of the Manchurians, yet Khabarov, unequal to a prolonged
contest with the innumerable Mongolian hordes, was obliged
ultimately to fight his way back into Moscovite territory. The

Moscow Government was not disposed, however, to abandon this El Dorado, and, in 1653, Onufry Stepanov was appointed " Governor of the river Amur, and of the new Daurian lands." In 1654 he undertook an expedition down the Amur, but was defeated by the Chinese, and entrenched himself on the Kamara, a southern confluent of the Amur, where, in March, 1655, 10,000 Chinese attacked him. The besiegers had firearms, and advanced to the attack in waggons covered by wooden hide-bound shields. They were also provided with long ladders with wheels at one end and long grappling-irons at the other. After a struggle, lasting the whole day, the Chinese were defeated, and all their poliorcetic devices captured, but the Chinese Emperor soon made Stepanov's position untenable by ordering an exodus from Manchuria of the entire corn-growing population. The Russian governor was at last reduced to living upon grass and roots, and pathetically petitioned to Moscow to be recalled. The Tsar was now driven to employ diplomatic methods. In 1654, Theodore Baikov set out from Tobolsk to Kanbalnik, as the Moscovites called Pekin, which he reached in March, 1656. Half a mile from the city, envoys from the Chinese Emperor met him with tea, sweetmeats, butter and milk, of which good things the conscientious Moscovite refused to partake, because it was a fast-day. Baikov's mission was wholly abortive, as the Russian envoy refused to deliver his credentials except in person, while the Chinese refused him access to the imperial presence. Two years later the Amurian governor, Stepanov, was defeated and slain, but the Moscovites still retained their hold upon the district, and founded the forts of Albazin and Nerchinsk (1658). In 1670 four Cossacks, sent from Nerchinsk to Pekin for the purposes of trade, having been well received, the Moscow authorities were encouraged to send a fresh embassy to the Chinese Court, and in 1675 the interpreter of the *Posolsky prikaz*, Nikola Gavril Spafari, a Moldavian Greek to whom we owe the earliest Moscovite account of China, Japan and Korea,* was despatched to Pekin. Spafari reached his destination on May 16, 1676, and was at once encountered by the old difficulty.

* "Opisanie Kitaya," edited by Arsen'ev. See also Mikhaelovsky: " Ocherk Zhizni N. Spafariya v Rossy."

It was explained to him that the Bogduikhan, or Chinese Emperor, never accepted letters from foreign potentates unless they had been examined beforehand, that it might be seen whether they were sufficiently respectful. The envoy was much perplexed, but a friendly old Dutch Jesuit came to his assistance and persuaded him to dictate a Latin translation of his credentials, which was submitted to the Chinese authorities. Finally Spafari was admitted to a preliminary audience with the Bogduikhan, when tea boiled with butter and milk was handed round, and there was an extraordinary musical entertainment, both vocal and instrumental, which being finished, the Son of Heaven withdrew to his own apartments, without deigning to take any notice of the Tsar's ambassador. At a second interview Spafari was more fortunate. After doing obeisance to the ground ten times, he and his suite were comfortably disposed on silk cushions facing the Bogduikhan, who sat on a high octagonal gilded seat, and is described as a mild-faced young man about twenty-three years old. Two Jesuits interpreted, first kneeling to receive the Emperor's messages, and then conveying them to the envoy. The Bogduikhan in a soft voice first inquired concerning the health, the age, and the personal appearance of " the Great Gosudar, the White Tsar, autocrat of all Russia." Then he asked the ambassador how old *he* was, and whether he was acquainted with philosophy, mathematics and trigonometry, in which sciences, as the envoy learned subsequently, the Khan had been instructed by the Jesuit fathers. Sweets were then brought in, together with Rhenish wine, the latter a fabrication of the Jesuits ; but these delicacies were tasted only by the ambassador and his suite, the Chinese in attendance drinking tea. Nevertheless, Spafari's mission proved to be as fruitless as Baikov's. Try as he would, he could not obtain a reply from the Bogduikhan to the Tsar. His presents were accepted as "tribute," and he was told not to be surprised thereat, as this was the ancient and immutable custom of the Chinese Court. " For just as there is only one Sun in the Heavens, so likewise there is but one God upon earth, to wit the Bogduikhan, who is set in the centre of the world, in the midst of all other potentates." After this we cannot wonder if Spafari took away with him the most unfavourable impression of the Chinese generally. " In all the world," he writes, "you will find no such rogues and robbers in matters of trade. Unless you keep a sharp look out upon them, they will filch the very buttons from your jacket." But the Jesuits were both candid and courteous, and, at their earnest request, Spafari gave them an ikon of St. Michael in a silver frame, the fathers explaining to him that Moscovite travellers in China, who visited their churches, frequently took them for idolaters instead of Catholics, because they saw no ikons on the walls. Henceforth this gross error would be impossible.

While Moscovy's policy in the far East was, even now, a policy of progress and aggrandisement, her occidental policy was mainly determined by her perennial fear of the Ottoman Porte.

In the spring of 1672 the long deferred Turko-Polish War burst forth. The victories of Sobieski over the Cossacks and their allies the Tatars roused Sultan Muhammad IV. from his lethargy, and, quitting his harem for his charger, he crossed the Danube with a host " like the sands of the sea for number, and like the stars of heaven for splendour "—in plain prose, with 300,000 men. The advance-guard of 40,000 was defeated, indeed, by Luzeczky, near Batoga, but the great fortress of Kamieniec, the key of Podolia, which, with criminal negligence, the Poles, well aware of the approaching tempest, had left utterly unable to resist it,* surrendered to the Sultan (August 27, 1672), who attended thanksgiving service in the cathedral, now converted into a mosque, while eight Christian lads were solemnly circum-cised in his presence. Six weeks later (October 17, 1672) the republic, by the shameful Treaty of Budziak, ceded the Polish Ukrain and Podolia, with Kamieniec, and engaged to pay an annual tribute to the Porte. The fall of Kamieniec greatly alarmed the Tsar. The Russian Ukrain was now immediately threatened, and Kiev, Chernigov and Pereyaslavl were in immi-nent danger. A council of notables was summoned to take pre-liminary measures; a new general tax was imposed on the already over-taxed people ; and Vasily Mikhailovich Tyapkin was sent

---

* It had a garrison of only one thousand five hundred men, and four gunners to serve four hundred guns.

to Warsaw to conclude an offensive and defensive alliance with the republic. On his way thither the news reached him of the not unwelcome death (November 10. 1673) of the King of Poland, Michael Wisniowiecki, whose weak and futile character had been one of the most dangerous elements of a well-nigh desperate situation. At Warsaw he found the Lithuanians, represented by their chancellor, Michael Pac' and his friends, inclined to adopt the Tsarevich Theodore as their candidate for the vacant throne, partly from a distrustfulness of Poland's ability to defend them permanently against the Turks, but principally because of Pac''s jealousy of the Crown Hetman John Sobieski, who, refusing to accept the conditions of the Peace of Budziak, had renewed the war against the Turks, routed Hussein Pasha beneath the walls of Chocim (November 11, 1673) and driven him across the Dnieper. Pac' was for an Austro-Polish-Muscovite league, which he proposed to consolidate by a matrimonial alliance between Theodore and the widowed Queen of Poland, herself an Austrian archduchess. But as two of the conditions precedent were the adoption of Catholicism by Theodore and the surrender by Moscovy of all her Polish conquests, the whole project was visionary, and, on May 21, 1674, Sobieski, who supported his own candidature with an army of 6,000 veterans, was unanimously elected King of Poland under the name of John III.

But though Moscovy would never have surrendered her ortho-doxy for the sake of a heretic throne, she was willing enough to co-operate with the hero of Chocim against the common enemy, and the Tsar's forces united with the army of the Polish Hetman on the Dnieper. The burden of the war fell indeed upon Poland, but Sobieski's fresh victories enabled him to make peace with the Porte at Zoraw (October 16, 1675), whereby two-thirds of the Ukrain, minus Kamieniec, were recovered by the republic.

With the rest of Europe Moscovy had still but little to do. During the stress of the Turko-Polish struggle, Tsar Alexius sent Andrei Vinius to England, France and Spain, to solicit help against "the enemies of the Cross of Christ." This ambassador did infinite credit to the piety of the Gosudar, but we can imagine the amused astonishment of the maturer diplomatists of the West at the *naïve* simplicity of such overtures.

From London Vinius sent a curious account of the working of the English Constitution, as he understood it, in which he describes the members of the House of Commons as the "elders of the country folk." Louis XIV. he found in his camp in Flanders, but *Le Grand Monarque* politely declined to commit himself to anything. From France Vinius proceeded to Spain. Six years previously (1667) the boyarin Potemkin had conducted the first Russian embassy to that country, on which occasion the Tsar had apologised for the remissness of his predecessors. "Distance and the will of the Almighty," wrote Alexius, had hitherto prevented diplomatic intercourse between the two states. At Madrid, also, Vinius got nothing but compliments and excuses.

The Moscovite Government had greater hopes of the Venetian Republic, which was equally menaced by the aggressiveness of the Ottoman Porte, especially after the recent loss of Candia. Venice had already had diplomatic relations with Moscovy. In 1656 a Venetian embassy had desired that the Don Cossacks might be let loose upon the Turks, to divert their attention from the Morea. They had also petitioned for leave to trade with Archangel. In 1668 the German merchant Kellermann presented to the Doge and the Senate a letter from the Tsar expatiating on the advantages of the overland trade to Persia through Moscovy; and, during Muhammad IV.'s attack on Poland, Menezius was sent from Vienna to Venice to propose a league against the Turk. From Venice Menezius proceeded to Rome with a letter for Clement X. The Tsar urged the Holy Father, as the chief pastor of the West, not only to assist Poland directly, but to write to Louis of France and Charles of England, urging them to cease fighting against the Dutch states, and turn their arms against the common foe of Christendom. At first it was doubtful whether Menezius would be received in audience, as he raised difficulties about kissing the Pope's toe. He was finally admitted on undertaking to do obeisance after the Roman fashion. At the parting interview the Pope objected to addressing the ruler of Moscovy as Tsar, on the ground that it was the same word as Kaiser,* a title belonging to the Emperor alone, who would be seriously

* As a matter of fact, it means King, not Emperor.

offended if it were bestowed upon any other potentate. Menezius persisting, the Pope fell back upon philological difficulties. It was impossible, he said, to translate the word into Latin. "Then don't translate it at all," replied Menezius. "Do you not write such titles as the 'Roman Emperor,' the 'Sultan of Turkey,' the 'Shah of Persia,' the 'Great Mogul,' just as they are? Treat the Tsar of Moscovy in the same way." Finally the Pope declared that he could not bestow the title of "Tsar of Moscovy," as none of his predecessors had done so, nor would the cardinals permit such an innovation. "If your Holiness is rude in any way to his Tsarish Majesty," retorted Menezius, "the Gosudar will write about it to all the other Christian gosudars."

From our point of view, all this diplomatic groping and fumbling is, no doubt, ludicrous enough. Evidently, seventeenth century Moscovy was painfully ignorant of the very rudiments of international intercourse, and thus exposed herself unwittingly to the barely veiled derision of her more experienced and civilised neighbours. And yet these embassies point to a real awakening, to the beginning of a new order of things. There had been a time when Moscovy prided herself on her rigid exclusiveness, and deliberately shut herself up within a Chinese wall of national and religious self-satisfaction. That time had for ever gone. As already indicated, she had begun to recognise the material superiority of the West, and endeavour to imitate her masters. This was especially the case as regards trade and navigation, the main sources of the national wealth she so greatly envied. As early as 1663, the necessity of acquiring a sea-board—ultimately the pivot of Peter the Great's whole policy—was generally recognised by the authorities at Moscow. In that year Zhelyabushky was sent to Courland, whose duke was under many obligations to the Tsar, to induce him to permit the construction of Russian vessels in his ports, for trading to the Indies. Three years previously to this, Moscow's business relations with Holland had been so important that she found it necessary to have an agent there, the Englishman John Hebden. Equally significant is the history of the construction of the first Moscovite ship, the *Orel* or *Eagle*. In May, 1667, a contract was signed for the building of a large vessel for the Caspian trade, at Dyedinovo, on the river Oka, under the supervision of Orduin Nashchokin and three *dumny dyaks*, assisted by two foreigners, Lambert Holt and Cornelius Bockhoeven. The work was actually begun on October 1, 1668, but at the end of 1669 the vessel was still unfinished, owing to the difficulty in procuring a sufficient number of capable workmen, and the perpetual quarrelling of all concerned in the enterprise. Finally, with the additional help of David Butler, a ship's captain from Amsterdam, who drafted shipping regulations for the instruction of future Moscovite skippers, and a Dutchman, Van Swieten, the *Orel*, with one golden eagle on her prow, another on her stern, and seven more eagles on her flag, was got under way, and sailed from Dyedinovo to Nizhny Novgorod, and thence to Astrakhan, where, as already related, she was burnt by Stenka Razin, after costing the Moscovite Government 9,021 rubles.

Here, as in every other matter promoting the welfare of his country, we observe the guiding hand of Athanasius Orduin Nashchokin. We have already seen something of his superior statesmanship,* and in Alexius he found, for a time, an appreciative master. It was Orduin who, as *voevoda* of Pskov, first abolished the excessive system of tolls on exports and imports, and established a combination of native merchants for promoting direct commercial relations between Sweden and Russia, and did his best to introduce free trade generally. These reforms did not long survive him, but they eloquently testify to the foresight of their originator. Orduin also set on foot a postal system between Moscovy, Courland, and Poland; made the Moscow road safe for foreign merchants, and introduced bills of exchange and gazettes. With his name, too, is associated the building of ships on the upper Dwina and Volga, and the extension of market-gardening in Russia on a scale vast enough to make it remunerative. But, despite the friendship and the protection of the Tsar, Orduin's whole official career was a constant struggle with the narrow routine of the *prikazui* and the jealous enmity of the boyars and the dyaks of the council, who bitterly resented his indisputable superiority, and pretended to regard him as a second Malyuta Skaratov, the infamous low-born minister of

* Chapter IV.

lvan the Terrible, and the murderer of St. Philip of Moscow.
But Orduin also had his defects. He rather presumed sometimes on his indispensability, and at last the Tsar grew weary of
his constant complaining, and was not always prepared to admit
that the minister's personal enemies were necessarily the enemies
of the state. Athanasius was last employed officially in the negotiations for confirming the Peace of Andrussowo (Sept., 1669/
Mar., 1670). In January, 1671, we hear of him as one of the
boyars in attendance on the Tsar at his second marriage ; but
in February, the same year, he was dismissed and withdrew to
the Kruipetsky Monastery, near Kiev, where he took the tonsure
under the name of Antony, and occupied himself with good
works till his death in 1680. He was certainly one of the most
enlightened and progressive Moscovites of his age, preaching in
season, and out of season perhaps, the absolute necessity of
reform. In many respects he anticipated Peter the Great. He
was also absolutely incorruptible, thus standing morally, as well
as intellectually, far above the level of his age.

The responsibility of Alexius in dismissing so capable and
conscientious a minister as Orduin was minimised by the fact
that he found an even abler substitute in Artamon Sergyievich
Matvyeev.

The earlier career of this remarkable man, unquestionably the
greatest predecessor of Peter the Great, is wrapped in impene-
trable mystery. His very parentage and the year of his birth
are uncertain. If, as is generally supposed, the son of a dyak
or scribe, his origin was humble, yet his parents must have been
singularly enlightened people ; for, when the obscure figure of
young Artamon first emerges into the light of history, we find
him equipped at all points with the newest ideas, absolutely free
from the worst prejudices of his age, a ripe scholar, and even an
author of some distinction.* How the humble, unobtrusive
dyak's son became the personal friend of the Tsar, his "little
Sergy," is equally unknown. We can only say that in 1671
Alexius and Artamon were already on the most intimate terms,

---

* Unfortunately nothing but the titles of his works have come down to us,
among which may be mentioned: " The History of the Russian Tsars distinguished
in Warfare," and " The History of the Election and Coronation of Tsar Michael."

and that, on the retirement of Athanasius Orduin, Artamon Sergyievich was entrusted with the administration of the Malorussian and the Posolsky *prikazui*,* both of which important charges he attended to at his modest little house in Moscow. In striking contrast to Orduin Nashchokin, Matvyeev was not in too great a hurry to get on, and, though courageous enough to sacrifice his life for his principles, as we shall see in the sequel, he tactfully avoided riding rough-shod over other people's prejudices, especially when those other people were both powerful and stupid. His promotion had been very gradual. Previously to 1672 he seems to have been no more than a *dumny dvoryanin* and colonel of *stryeltsui* (he had won some military experience in the Ukrain and at the siege of Riga); but at the end of 1672 foreigners already regarded him as the Tsar's chief counsellor, and all petitions were presented through him.† Matvyeev's house was a source of never-ending delight to the receptive and inquisitive Tsar. It was like a bit of seventeenth century Western civilisation transported bodily into another age and another country. Within its walls could be seen all the wondrous half-forbidden novelties of the West, painted ceilings, rich pile carpets, ingenious clocks, pictures by French and German artists. Matvyeev's wife, who is said to have been a Scotchwoman, moved freely among her male guests on equal terms, and drove out boldly in a carriage and pair instead of in a closely-curtained litter. But there was yet another and still greater attraction for the Tsar in the house of Artamon. It was here that Alexius, after the death of his first consort Maria, in 1669, first encountered the beautiful Natalia Kirillevna Naruishkina, Matvyeev's intelligent and carefully-educated pupil. The elderly but susceptible Tsar fell in love with the beautiful girl of seventeen at first sight. "Little pigeon," said he, " I will find thee a suitable mate"; and on his next visit he put his own ring on her hand. Matvyeev, foreseeing the

---

* A combination of the Foreign Office and the Irish Secretaryship would be the modern equivalent.

† Thus he is called: "Præcipuus Tzaris Russorum Consiliarium," and "Czarischer vornehmster Minister." See Rinhuber. "Relation," etc. Compare Solovev: "Istoria Rossy, XII., 326, XIII., 309, 310; Pogodin, "17 pervnikh lyet v zhizni Petra Vel."

jealousy of the boyar families, besought the Tsar, on his knees.
rather to take his life than his pupil.   But Alexius assuring him
that he had nothing to fear from calumny, Natalia consented to
" go upstairs."*   The usual ceremony of selection from sixty
virgins was kept up, as a matter of form, but the choice of
Alexius had already been made, and he wedded Natalia on
January 21, 1672.   The friends of the new Tsaritsa naturally
shared in her good fortune.   At the end of 1672, on the occasion
of the birth of the Tsarevich Peter, Matvyeev was raised to the
dignity of *okolnichy* along with the Tsaritsa's father, Kirill
Poleukhtovich Naruishkin.   On September 1, 1674, he attained
the still higher dignity of *boyarin*.

The influence of Matvyeev remained paramount to the end of
the reign, and Tsar Alexius, stimulated by his handsome young
wife and his wise mentor, advanced along the path of Western
civilisation at an accelerated pace which amazed himself.   He
who had sternly banished jugglers from his Court while still but
a youth, now gave himself up, in his old age, to such heterodox
diversions as the drama—first of all, however, obtaining the
consent of his confessor, the protopop Savinov, to the introduction of this perilous pastime.   The scene of these innocent orgies
was the Tsar's old-fashioned wooden country-house at Preobrazhenskoe,† or Transfiguration, a village two miles beyond the
German settlement at Moscow, beautifully situated on the banks
of the Yaïtsa, amongst dense forests peopled by elks and other
royal game.   There, too, Alexius stored away his exotic curiosities and over-sea wonders, including the two European carriages
which Matvyeev had given him.

Despite the prohibitions of the *Domostroi,* which anathematised
all games as sinful, the presence of jugglers and fools in the
houses of the boyars, to say nothing of the multitude and popularity of the strolling conjurers, puppet-showmen, and bear-actors,
sufficiently indicated that the Russian people had a natural
bent towards spectacular art, and possessed adequate materials
for its cultivation and development.   A free scope and full

---

* *I.s.,* to go to Court.
† For a description of the place and the festivities, see Sinitsuin : " Pre-
brazhenskoe "; Zabyelin : " Domashnui Buit."

liberty to pursue it might have anticipated by two centuries the glories of the modern Russian drama. But natural impulse proved stronger than all artificial restraints, and, at last, the very men who shrunk from altering a single letter of the old Slavonic Bible were content complacently to look on while foreigners and heretics put the Bible itself on the stage before their very eyes.

It was the Moscovite envoy, Likachev, who first astonished his countrymen by bringing back from Florence, in 1660, tidings of what he had been privileged to behold in that sunny city. He had a great deal to say about the splendid palaces and the aromatic gardens of the Tuscan grand dukes; but what seems to have impressed him most was the theatre, which he describes as " a palace wherein there were six transformations, and seas tossing with real waves, and fish in the waves, and people catching the fish. And at the top of this palace there was the sky with clouds, and in this sky and on these clouds people sitting. And I saw these clouds, and the people sitting on them, descend earthwards and lift other people up and ascend again, and many other marvels."* Tsar Alexius was keenly interested by the report of Likachev. He at once had gardens laid out for himself on the European models round his country-houses at Kolmenskoe and Izmailovo. But further than that he durst not go. His first consort, Maria, was an austere rigorist. Gardens and palaces, in her opinion, might be well enough, but spectacles were damnable. But Natalia Naruishkina was of a joyous and more liberal disposition, and the good Tsar did his utmost to gratify his young consort, especially as his own inclinations ran in the same direction. So plays were introduced at Court. Yet Alexius still had his scruples. At first he would have excluded all instrumental music as savouring of paganism ; but when it was explained to him that the actors could not dance properly without it, he left the matter entirely to their discretion. During the representation the Tsar sat on a chair in front of the stage, the boyars sat at the wings, while the Tsaritsa and the Tsar's children looked through the chinks of a boarded upper box. " Esther and Ahasuerus " was the first play acted. It was preceded by a *divertissement*, in which Orpheus, dancing between

* Zabyelin: " Domashnui Buit," etc.

two marble pyramids, delivered himself of a panegyric on the Tsar. It should be observed that this play was acted in the *Maslenitsa*, or "Fat Week," just before the great fast, the one week in the orthodox year when a little extra relaxation was conceded to the faithful. The Tsar's joy at the birth of the Tsarevich, Peter, afterwards Peter the Great, encouraged him to go still further. On the very eve of the festival of St. Peter, he invited his friends to a private, informal entertainment in the golden hall of the Tsaritsa, to witness the acting of a new play especially composed for the occasion. This play, the subject of which was also taken from the Book of Esther, was full of topical allusions, which the privileged spectators fully understood. Thus Esther represented Natalia; Mordecai, Matvyeev; and Haman, the reactionary arch-conservative boyarin Khitrovo. The same piece, with variations, was frequently acted, with every scenic accessory, in the new *Komidyeinnaya Khoromna*, or Hall of Comedy, the name given to the Court theatre built, under the direction of Matvyeev, in the Tsar's mansion at Preobrazhenskoe. The erection of this playhouse was a very important step forward on the path of progress. It was, as a Russian historian has well observed, "the foundation-stone of the regeneration of our social life."* In 1673 another hall of comedy was actually built within the sacred precincts of the *kreml'*, as the theatre of Preobrazhenskoe was difficult of access in the winter-time. At this new theatre there was a ballet of sixty children and a troupe of German actors directed by Timothy Hasenkrug. Two of the most popular pieces in Hasenkrug's *repertoire* were entitled " Judith and Holofernes ; or, how the Tsaritsa Judith cut off the Tsar's head ;" and " How Artaxerxes commanded Haman to be hanged at the petition of the Tsaritsa, and at the suggestion of Mordecai." The performances generally lasted seven hours, from 10 a.m. to 5 p.m., the Tsar always being present, and following them from beginning to end with unflagging interest.

But the days of the Tsar Alexius were drawing to a close On the night between the 29th and 30th January, 1676, he calmly expired after bestowing his benediction on his eldest surviving son, Theodore, and solemnly declaring him his successor.

* Zabyelin.

Alexius was indubitably one of the most amiable and attractive princes who ever sat on the Russian throne.   Even foreigners found it difficult to resist the charm of his gentle, humane, and essentially courteous disposition, and by his numerous friends and dependants he was most tenderly loved.   Naturally, indeed, Alexius was excitable and passionate, and, like his illustrious son Peter, was liable to paroxysms of rage in which he would violently abuse and even assault those about him in a manner not conducive to his own personal dignity.   On one occasion he even plucked his foolish old uncle, Ivan Miloslavsky, by his long white beard, and drove him out of the council-chamber with a cudgel.   But the sun never went down upon the wrath of the pious Gosudar, and he freely applied a golden salve to every sort of wound.   No man was ever a kinder master or a more affectionate friend.   As a ruler he was equally remarkable for his conscientiousness and his diligence.   And he was not without enterprise, as he showed conclusively when he voluntarily quitted the comfortable and sacrosanct seclusion of the *kreml'* for the tumult and hardships of a camp, a thing his father never ventured to do.   His education, conducted as it was on exclusively ecclesiastical lines, was necessarily narrow ; yet he was learned in his way, read everything written in the Slavonic language, including translations of the Greek fathers, wrote verses himself, and even began a history of his own times.   His extreme sociability made him, perhaps, over-anxious to please those about him, in order that he might see nothing but smiling faces.   But he was no fool, and, for all his complacency, had as high an idea of his great calling as ever Ivan the Terrible had.   Alexius possessed, in an eminent degree, the truly royal gift of recognising and selecting great men.   Nikon, Rtishchev, Orduin Nashchokin, and Matvyeev, the best of Peter's precursors, were discovered and employed by Peter's father.

Yet, reviewing the reign of Alexius, it is quite obvious that the good Tsar, whose whole reign was an uninterrupted series of wars and rebellions, owed much to fortune.   His contemporaries frequently wondered how Moscovy contrived to survive such catastrophes as Konotop, Chudnov, Kamieniec and Astrakhan. The answer is that these disasters, close as they came upon each other's heels, nevertheless occurred successively instead of simultaneously, and so the impoverished, distracted, ill-served, and only half-obeyed Tsardom was able, but only just able, to right itself, and pursue its destined course. And all this time Western ideas were slowly filtering through and pervading the seemingly inert. unpromising mass of national and religious prejudice. and the successors of Alexius were to benefit by the transformation which had already begun, though few suspected it.

TSAR THEODORE III.

# CHAPTER VII.

## THE REIGN OF THEODORE III. AND THE REGENCY OF SOPHIA. 1676—1689.

Accession of Theodore III.—Fall of Matvyeev—Peace with Poland and the Porte
—The Reforms of Theodore—His Death—Elevation of Peter—Opposition of
the Miloslavskies—The Tsarevna Sophia—First Rebellion of the Stryeltsui—
Murder of Matvyeev—Elevation of Ivan and Peter as Joint Tsars—Regency
of Sophia—Khovansky and the Stryeltsui—The Dissenters in the Tesselated
Chamber—Courage of Sophia—Flight of the Court from Moscow—Repres-
sion of the rebellious Stryeltsui—Execution of Khovansky—Revolution in
European Politics—Moscovy joins the Holy League against the Turks—
Acquisition of Kiev—The Crimean Campaigns of 1687—1689—The Conspiracy
of Sophia and Shaklovity—Childhood and Early Youth of Peter the Great—
His Character and Tastes—Life at Preobrazenskoe, and Marriage—The Third
Revolt of the Stryeltsui, and the Struggle with Sophia—Triumph of the
Petrine Faction.

TSAR ALEXIUS had thirteen children by his first consort, Maria
Miloslavskaya, five sickly sons, three of whom, Demetrius,
Alexius, and Simeon, predeceased him, and eight healthy
daughters, all of them still living, all of them women of intelligence and character. His successor, Theodore III., a lad of
fourteen, was greatly to be pitied. Providence had endowed
this young prince with a fine intellect and a noble disposition.
He had received an excellent education under the care of Simeon
Polotsky, the most learned Slavonic scholar of his age; knew
Polish, then the chief civilising medium of the east Slavonic lands,
as well as his mother-tongue, and even possessed the unusual
accomplishment of Latin. But horribly disfigured, and half
paralysed by a mysterious disease supposed to be scurvy, he had
been a hopeless invalid from the day of his birth.

The deplorable condition of this unhappy prince suggested to
Artamon Matvyeev the desirability of elevating to the throne
the sturdy little Tsarevich Peter, the son of Alexius by Natalia
Naruishkina, then in his fourth year. Artamon at once took

measures to secure his object.   First he purchased the allegiance
of the stryeltsui for his *protégé* and then summoning the boyars
of the Council, he earnestly represented to them that Theodore.
scarce able to live, was surely unable to rule ; that his younger
brother, Ivan, was an idiot ; but that in Peter Aleksyeevich
Moscovy possessed the promise of a healthy and vigorous propa-
pagator of the dynasty.   But the reactionary boyars, among
whom were the Stryeshnevs and the Miloslavskies, the uncles,
and cousins of Theodore, all of them more or less hostile to
the progressive Matvyeev and his disciples, the upstart Naruishkins, refused to entertain the proposal.   They had already been
informed by the patriarch that Alexius, on his death-bed, had
consecrated Theodore his successor.   His right to the throne was
therefore indisputable, and they proclaimed him Tsar, though his
legs at that moment were so swollen that he could not use them.
The triumph of the Miloslavskies naturally meant the fall of the
opposite party.   Matvyeev was banished to Puztozersk, on an
easily established charge of witchcraft, and his property was
confiscated.   Natalia Naruishkina and her children* were, at the
same time, banished from Court.

The chief foreign event of the new reign was the termination
of the Turkish War.   Disappointed in his expectations of
Moscovite assistance, Sobieski had been obliged to come to
terms with the Porte, and the Court of Moscow was not slow in
following his example.   A peace was mediated by the Hospodar
of Moldavia, and the negotiations took place (1680) on the
Alma in the Crimea, when the Russian envoys were lodged in
quarters "colder and filthier than dog-kennels."   The Turks,
humbled by their disasters in the Polish War (they had lost
40,000 men before Chigorin alone), swore on the Koran to
observe strictly a truce for twenty years, in exchange for which
the Moscovites joyfully ceded the trans-Dnieperian steppes.   The
Tsar's relations with Poland were settled by the Treaty of
Moscow (July, 1678), which extended the nominal truce, already
existing between the two countries, for thirty years from 1680.

But it is the domestic policy of Theodore III. which makes
his brief reign so epoch-making.   In 1679 the young Tsar

---

* Peter had a younger sister, Natalia, now two years old.

married his first cousin, Agatha, and assumed the sceptre. His native energy, though crippled, was not crushed by his terrible disabilities, and he soon showed that he was as thorough and devoted a reformer as a man incompetent to lead armies or direct councils, and obliged to issue his orders from his litter or his bedchamber, can possibly be. The atmosphere of the Court ceased to be oppressive ; the light of a new liberalism shone forth in the highest places ; petitioners were forbidden to address the Gosudar with the old servility, and the severity of the penal laws was considerably mitigated. When the all-engulfing Turkish war was at last over, Theodore, anxious, " like a new Solomon, to honour wisdom as the mother of all royal virtues, and the distributress of all benefits," founded the Academy of Sciences in the Zaikonnospasky Monastery, where everything not expressly forbidden by the orthodox Church, including Slavonic Greek, Polish, and Latin, was to be taught by competent professors. This academy was, no doubt, partly intended as an additional bulwark of orthodoxy, and was, in some respects, as much an inquisitorial tribunal* as a university ; but, anyhow, it introduced into Moscovy the cultivation of the sciences with a practical aim, the chief difference between the Theodorian and the Petrine reforms being that the former were primarily for the benefit of the Church, the latter for the benefit of the State.

But the most notable reform of Theodore III. was the abolition of the *Myestnichestvo*, or "place priority," which, as already explained,† had paralysed the whole civil and military administration of Moscovy during the two preceding reigns. The initiator of this salutary measure was Prince Vasily Vasilevich Golitsuin, sometimes called "the great Golitsuin," who now comes prominently forward for the first time.‡ Golitsuin, who belonged to one of the most ancient families in Moscovy, was unusually well educated. He understood German and Greek as well as his mother-tongue, and could express himself fluently in Latin. Born in 1643, he entered the service of Alexius at an

---

* Thus no Romanist, Lutheran, or Calvinist, was suffered within its walls ; it was to take cognisance of all lapses from orthodoxy ; and all the renegades it detected were to be burnt to death. † Chapter I.

‡ Compare De la Neuville: "Relation curieuse et nouvelle de Moscovie"; Gordon "Diary"; "Arkhiv Knyaz Kurakina."

early age, and, in 1676, was created a boyarin. Sent to the Ukrain to provide for its defence against the incursions of the Turks and Tatars, he served with distinction during the famous Chigorin campaign, and returned to Moscow with the conviction that the *Myestnichestvo* was at the root of Moscovy's deplorable military inefficiency. The young Tsar was readily convinced by his arguments, and a special *ukaz* forthwith removed, at one stroke, an abuse which had so long appeared unassailable. The *razryadnuiya knigi*, or records of rank, to which the boyars had been wont to appeal as infallible authorities in all their claims for precedence, were at the same time destroyed. Henceforth all appointments to the civil and military services were to be determined by merit and the will of the Gosudar. The fact that the dying Theodore could so easily remove so deep-lying and far-reaching an abuse. is a striking testimony to the steady, if silent, advance of liberal ideas in Moscovite society, even since the death of Alexius. It is often too much taken for granted that Peter created modern Russia. The foundations of modern Russia were laid while he was still in his nursery.

To the last Theodore continued to fight resolutely against the inveterate prejudices of his people. It almost seemed as if the fast-failing Gosudar, conscious of his approaching end, endeavoured to crowd into a few months reforms which it would have taken a long life to accomplish. He surrounded himself with enlightened counsellors, and his consort, Agatha, seems to have shared his progressive views. It is said that she was the first to induce the Moscovites to crop their hair, shave off their beards, and wear more becoming costumes. This lady died on July 14, 1681, and her son, the Tsarevich Ilya, followed her to the grave six days later. On February 24, 1682, Theodore married his second wife, Martha Apraksina; on April 16, he was able to take part in the solemn Easter Day procession in the Uspensky Cathedral, but a few weeks later (April 27) he was no more. As he had died without issue, and appointed no successor, the throne was left vacant.

No sooner were the eyes of Theodore closed, than the great bell *Vyestnik*, or "The Announcer," began to toll, and the people assembled in crowds before the *Chertog Tsarsky*, or elevated platform of the Uspensky Cathedral, to take leave of the dead and to greet the new Tsar. The boyars, previously counselled by the patriarch as to which of the two Tsareviches should be chosen, were of the opinion that the people should be consulted. Joachim went out accordingly into the great Red Square, and inquired which of the two Tsareviches, Ivan and Peter, they would have for their Gosudar. " Peter Aleksyeevich !" was the unanimous response, whereupon the patriarch blessed Peter, now ten years old, and proclaimed him Tsar. His mother, Natalia, was to act as Regent, and the first *ukaz* issued in Peter's name summoned the exiled Artamon Matvyeev to return to the capital and occupy the post of chief counsellor to the new Government.

But the elder branch of Tsar Alexius' family, the Miloslavskies, were by no means disposed to submit to the upstart Naruishkins, the younger branch of the same family, as represented by the Tsaritsa Natalia and her son Peter. The Miloslavskies had the advantage in numbers, seniority, and actual possession of the principal offices of State. The Naruishkins, on the other hand, though new to power, had the support of the people and the patriarch, and could rule in the name of the little Gosudar. If they could only gain time, they might gain everything else. Fear played a large part in the calculations of the Miloslavskies. Under Theodore, in their day of triumph, they had mercilessly persecuted the Naruishkins. But now the Naruishkins were in the ascendant, and might persecute the Miloslavskies, in the name of Peter, by the hand of Matvyeev.

It was a portentous sign of the times that the malcontents involuntarily and unhesitatingly looked for guidance neither to Prince Vasily Golitsuin nor to Prince Ivan Andreevich Khovansky, the two leading *voevodui* of the day, but to a girl of five-and-twenty, who had been educated in the seclusion of the *terem,* and, a generation earlier, would never have dared to leave it. This product of the new enlightenment was the Tsarevna Sophia, the third daughter of Tsar Alexius. Russian historians are still divided in their opinion, concerning this extraordinary woman. While some of them paint her in the darkest colours as an unprincipled adventuress, the representative of a new Byzantinism, a Megæra as ambitious as Pulcheria, and as licentious as

Theodora,* others regard her simply as the victim of circumstances. Others, more indulgent still, acquit her of all blame,† and a few, impressed by her indisputable ability and courage, evade a decision altogether by simply describing her as a prodigy.‡   Perhaps, on the whole, the latest opinion is also the most reasonable one.§ According to this view, Natalia and Sophia were rivals aiming at the same thing in much the same way.   Both wanted the crown.   The only difference was that the former wished to see it on the head of her son, while the latter was content that her brother should wear the diadem so long as she herself wielded the sceptre.   But even so, the comparison is unfavourable to Sophia, for while the mother sacrificed everything for her son, the sister was prepared to sacrifice everyone, her brother included, to her own ambition.   Both women had had a relatively superior education.   But while, as the pupil of Matvyeev, Natalia belonged to the practical school of the West, Sophia's training, under the guidance of the learned monk, Polotsky, had been on more ecclesiastical lines.   But her orthodoxy sat pretty lightly upon her.   In emancipating herself from the restrictions of the *terem*, she had at the same time emancipated herself from its austere morality, and her overwhelming passion for Prince Vasily Golitsuin was already notorious.

Sophia, in defiance of Court etiquette, had nursed her sick brother Theodore during the closing years of his long illness,‖ and even ministered to him in the presence of the attendant boyars.   She had also publicly appeared at his obsequies, though it was usual only for the widow of the deceased and his successor to the throne to attend that ceremony.   When the indignant Natalia thereupon withdrew abruptly from the cathedral, on the plea that the long fast would be too injurious to the little Gosudar, Sophia cleverly took advantage of the opportunity to appeal to the people for protection.   Fortune, too, was on her side.   Three days after the proclamation of Peter, sixteen regiments of the stryeltsui proceeded to the *kreml'* and demanded

* Zabyelin: "Domashnui Buit," etc.; Ustryalov: "Istoriya tsartsovanya Petra Velekago."

† Aristov: " Moskovskiya smutui vo vremya pravlenya Sofii."

‡ Solovev.                         § Shmurlo: "Padenie tsarevnui Sofii.

‖ Zabyelin: " Domashnui Buit."

arrears of pay, and Natalia, helpless and perplexed, acceded at last to their demands. This incipient revolt was, to use the quaint language of a contemporary, as welcome to Sophia as the dove's olive branch was to Noah in the ark. It showed the weakness of the Government and the impunity with which it could be insulted.

During the next few days, the friends of Sophia succeeded by bribes, promises, and the circulation of rumours that the life of the Tsarevich Ivan was in danger, in winning the majority of the stryeltsui, but they postponed an outbreak till Artamon Matvyeev, the one strong man on the side of Natalia, was within their reach. Artamon had already been warned by seven of the stryeltsui of the dangers awaiting him. "I'll put down the rebellion or lay down my life for the Tsar," was his only reply. He reached Moscow on May 15, and at once proceeded to the head of the Red Staircase, accompanied by the Tsar, the Tsaritsa, the patriarch, and Prince Ivan, to meet and argue with the assembled stryeltsui. The rebels were disarmed by the unexpected appearance of Ivan, who stammered forth a few sentences assuring them that he was well, and Matvyeev had already succeeded in persuading them to disperse quietly, when one of their colonels, Prince Michael Dolgoruki, who had been invisible while the issue was doubtful, now suddenly came forward and began roundly to abuse the stryeltsui. Such hectoring from an officer they despised infuriated the still hesitating and half-suspicious musketeers. Laying hold of Dolgoruki, they flung him on to the pikes of their comrades below. Matvyeev clutched desperately at the sleeve of little Peter for protection, but the stryeltsui tore him away and literally hacked him to pieces. Catching up her son in her arms Natalia fled to the Tessellated Hall. All the courtiers followed her. The stryeltsui, full of bestial fury, then invaded the defence-less *kreml'*, massacring everyone they met. In the evening they departed to their quarters, leaving guards before the gates of the palace. The horrors of May 15 were repeated on the two following days. On the 17th the stryeltsui demanded that the Tsaritsa's brother, Ivan Naruishkin, should be delivered up to them. The helpless Natalia burst into tears. "Come, come," cried Sophia brutally, "the stryeltsui must have your brother. We cannot all perish because of him." Then his sister revealed his hiding-place, and, after confessing and communicating, Naruishkin was handed over to the mutineers, who tortured him to death. Their last victim was a Dr. von Haden, in whose study they had discovered preserved snakes and other specimens. They at once decided that a dealer in venom, as he needs must be, had had a hand in the death of Tsar Theodore, and murdered the unfortunate naturalist with unspeakable barbarity.

The stryeltsui now declared themselves satisfied, and willing to leave the punishment of any other traitors to the Tsar. But though the rebellion was over, there was still no Government. Everyone was panic-stricken and in hiding, except the Tsarevna Sophia, and to her, as the only visible representative of authority, the Court naturally turned for orders. She took it upon herself to pay the stryeltsui ten rubles a head, and reward them with the honourable title of "Court Infantry," and when, on May 23, she was informed that it was the wish of the people that Peter should share the throne with his elder brother, Ivan, so that there might always be one Tsar to rule at home, while the other went to war, she submitted the question to a council of magnates and prelates summoned expressly for the purpose. The council, anxious to save themselves and please the Tsarevna, hastened to approve of the project. The precedents of Pharaoh and Joseph, of Honorius and Arcadius, were cited, and Ivan and Peter were forthwith proclaimed joint Tsars. Still, Sophia was not satisfied. Again the stryeltsui were secretly worked upon, and on May 29 they presented a fresh petition to the council, to the effect that Ivan should be declared the senior, and Peter the junior Tsar, and that the Tsarevna Sophia should be appointed Regent during their minority. As Ivan was hopelessly infirm, half blind, and more than half idiotic,* it is plain that the absurd duumvirate aimed solely at the depression and humilia-tion of the Tsaritsa Natalia ; but the obsequious council hailed the impudent suggestion as " a divine inspiration," and Sophia thus became the actual ruler of Moscovy.†  The stryeltsui were

* Rinhuber: " Relation du voyage en Russie."

† Compare Solovev: "Istoria Rossy"; Pogodin: " Semnadtsat pervuikh lyet v zhizni Petra Vel."

not only pardoned for their atrocities, but petted. A general amnesty, in the most absolute terms, was granted to them, and, at their special request, a triumphal column was erected in the Red Square of the *kreml'*, to commemorate their cowardly massacre of Matvyeev and the Naruishkins.

But even now they were not satisfied, and presently the Regent had to reckon with the soldiery who had placed her on the throne, and with the self-appointed leader of that soldiery, Prince Ivan Andreevich Khovansky.

It is possible that Khovansky himself may have aimed at the throne. As a lineal descendant of Gedemin, Grand Duke of Lithuania, he belonged to one of the most ancient and illustrious families in the Tsardom. He was also a soldier of some distinction, and, as an arch-conservative, averse to every reform, he could always depend on the support of the reactionary elements of the population, especially on the Raskolniks, or Dissenters, of whom at least half the stryeltsui was composed. How he contrived to gain the confidence of these mutinous bands is not quite clear, but he emerged from the horrors of May 15/17 their acknowledged ringleader.

The agitation of the stryeltsui was the more dangerous, as it now assumed a distinctly religious character. Having got a government to their liking, they began to busy themselves with Church affairs. They wanted to know, they said, why the patriarch and the boyars hated the old books and loved the Latin-Roman faith? Khovansky's attachment to everything ancient embraced the so-called ancient faith likewise. He professed to be convinced by the arguments of the anti-Nikonian monks, Sergius and Savaty, and their colleague, the priest Nikita, and, with his approbation, Nikita drew up a petition, the signatures to which covered twenty huge sheets of parchment, setting forth the views of the stryeltsui and their dissenting friends. The patriarch Joachim was persuaded to receive this petition in the great reception hall of the *kreml*, the *Granovitaya Palata*, or Tessellated Chamber, and thither, on July 5, the stryeltsui and Raskolniki marched in solemn procession, with lights, orthodox crosses, open copies of the Gospels, and ikons of the old style. After some scuffling with the orthodox, the petitioners, assisted by their patron Khovansky, who expelled some of their opponents to make room for them, forced their way into the Tessellated Chamber. They had come to protest against all novelties, but they failed to recognise the greatest novelty of all although it confronted them directly they entered the hall. Upon the throne in front of them sat the Tsarevna Sophia with her aunt Tatiana Mikhailovna; a little below them sat the Tsaritsa Natalia, the Tsarevna Maria, and the patriarch, and, lower still, on the right hand and the left hand side of the throne respectively, were ranged the spiritual and the temporal dignitaries. The chief women of Moscovy had boldly quitted the claustral seclusion of the *terem*, to preside, for the first time, over a public assembly. It was a portentous sign plainly indicating, little as the spectators realised it, the dawn of a new era. Nor was this all. The women had taken the initiative and been valiant while the men trembled. The patriarch had gone tearfully to an assembly which he never thought to quit alive, but when Khovansky strongly urged the Regent to absent herself, Sophia replied: "God's will be done! I will not desert Holy Church!" Khovansky was unaware that she had previously been in communication with the orthodox half of the stryeltsui, and was assured of their support.

The patriarch, encouraged by the presence of the Regent, took heart and quitted himself manfully. He began by rebuking the petitioners for their disobedience and presumption. The books they called new, he said, had been amended by learned men by the light of ancient and authoritative documents. "We have not come hither about grammar but about dogma," screamed Nikita in reply. He proceeded to show what he understood by dogma, by demanding why the patriarch, in the act of blessing, held the cross in his left hand and the candle in his right? Athanasius, Bishop of Kholmogory, was about to reply, when Nikita turned furiously upon him with uplifted hand, and shouted: "Dost thou, the foot, exalt thyself above the head? I spake not to thee but to the patriarch." At this Sophia could not restrain her indignation. "What!" she cried, "wouldst thou strike a holy bishop before our very eyes? Thou art not fit to stand or speak in our presence! Take away his petition, and

let another read it !"    The petition was then read till a passage
was reached which reviled Nikon as a heretic.    Sophia instantly
sprang to her feet.   " Stop the reading," she commanded.   " I
will hear no more !    If the patriarch Nikon was a heretic, then
my father, Tsar Alexius, and my brother, Tsar Theodore, were
also heretics, and the reigning Tsars are no Tsars, and the reigning patriarch is no patriarch, and we have no right to rule this
realm."   She then turned towards the stryeltsui, and bitterly
reproached them for calling themselves faithful servants of the
Tsars, and yet admitting ignorant *muzhiks* into the palace to
mock at them.   " If we are going to be exposed to these insults,"
she continued, "'twere better for the Tsars to quit Moscow, and
go to some other town and say there how they have been treated
here."   There was policy as well as resentment in this outburst.
Uncertain of their own position in the country, there was nothing
the stryeltsui feared so much as the departure of the Court from
the capital.   Their leaders at once submitted, and professed their
readiness to lay down their heads for the Tsars.   Sophia thereupon resumed her seat, and the reading of the petition proceeded.
The proceedings terminated in a wrangle, during which the
Dissenters, after shouting down their opponents, marched out of
the hall, again loudly proclaiming to the expectant crowd outside
that they had gained the day.   And there the matter ended.

    For a moment the firmness of the Regent had prevailed, and
when subsequently the Dissenters reproached the stryeltsui for
" selling the old faith for thirty pieces of silver," the stryeltsui
broke openly with them, and cut off the head of the monk
Nikita.    But such unstable and capricious supporters as the
stryeltsui were not to be depended on.   All through the summer
they continued to be a source of uneasiness.   Every day their
pretensions grew more intolerable, and Khovansky, who was
the usual medium of their extravagant demands, frequently
harangued his hirelings in language tantamount to sedition.   In
a word, Khovansky hoped that the stryeltsui would prefer the
rule of a man to that of a woman, and that ruler was to be himself.   In August the Court fulfilled its threat, and removed to
the village of Kolmenskoe, where it remained till September 1,
the Russian new year.   By this time Sophia and Khovansky

were at open war, the former refusing to allow the little Tsars to visit Moscow for the usual ceremonies at the *kreml'*, the latter ignoring the Regent's summons to come and give an account of himself at Kolmenskoe. Sinister rumours now began to circulate. The people of Moscow trembled in anticipation of another outbreak of the stryeltsui, while the stryeltsui were apprehensive of a combination of the boyars against them, and Khovansky never took a drive without an escort of fifty guards. For another fortnight things remained in suspense, but, while Khovansky had been idle, Sophia was concentrating her forces. At a council held at Vozdrozhenskoe, on September 17, she felt strong enough to strike, and she struck fiercely. Sentence of death was pronounced against Khovansky and his two sons Andrei and Ivan, for conspiring against the Tsars, and they were seized at their country houses, and brought into Vozdrozhenskoe. Ivan Khovansky, the elder, and Andrei were executed the same day, protesting their innocence. The younger son, Ivan, escaped to Moscow, and persuaded the stryeltsui to seize and fortify the *kreml'*. But when the news reached them that the Court was assembling an army at the great Troitskaya Monastery, under the command of Prince Vasily Golitsuin, and when, shortly afterwards, Michael Petrovich Golovin arrived to take over the government of the capital, the stryeltsui lost heart altogether, wept like children, and sent a deputation to Sophia, begging forgiveness, and promising absolute submission in the future. They were forgiven, but only after a public confession of their crimes and a solemn renunciation of all their usurped privileges, in the Uspensky Cathedral, in the presence of the patriarch and a large congregation. They relinquished, at the same time, their honorific title of Court Infantry, and volunteered to demolish, with their own hands, the column erected as a memorial of their exploits, in the Red Square. On November 6 the Court, satisfied with the fulness of its triumph, returned to Moscow.

At the very time when Moscovy, beneath the guidance of the most progressive government she had yet possessed, was turning more and more from the barbaric East to the civilised West, a revolution had occurred in European politics, which attracted her, for the first time, within the orbit of international diplomacy.

The cardinal political result of the Thirty Years' War was the depression of the Hapsburg Empire, and the elevation of the French monarchy. The beginning of that war saw France maintaining a struggle for existence against neighbours seemingly stronger than herself; at the end of it we find her surrounded by comparatively feeble, and, therefore, more or less dependent states. The House of Hapsburg, distracted by her Hungarian rebels, and directly threatened by the Ottoman Porte, was henceforth to fight more for self-preservation than for dominion, while Turkey, singularly favoured by circumstances, and ably administered by the great Kuprili family, had, on the very eve of her own collapse, become once more a terror to Europe. The danger grew acute when Emerich Tököli, the *protégé* of the Porte, made his triumphal entry into Buda as King of Hungary, and an immense Turkish army sat down before Vienna. If the fatal blow were struck, and the capital of the King of the Romans passed beneath the dominion of the Crescent, Poland and Moscovy had good reason to tremble on their own account. Perhaps nothing in modern history is so eloquent of the depravity of politics as the attitude of "the most Christian King" at this crisis, when the fate of continental Christendom hung in the balance. Louis XIV. exhausted all the resources of diplomacy to prevent Sobieski from succouring the distressed Emperor. John III. thereupon very pertinently inquired of Louis XIV. whether, in case Poland did not help Austria, France would engage to come to the assistance of Poland " when the Turks, after taking Vienna, sit down before Cracow." It is only fair to add that in Poland itself politicians were by no means agreed as to the expediency of relieving Vienna. At the *Sejm* of 1683 many deputies protested against fighting the battles of Austria. "What is it to us," they cried, " if the Turks *do* extend their dominions to the Danube ? Two years ago, did the Emperor move a step to help us when the Turks threatened the Vistula ? Our real enemies are Brandenburg and Austria. There is nothing in Poland to tempt the Turks." This was true enough. But Sobieski, well aware that the danger was pressing, and that his Polish critics had, as usual, no alternative policy, wisely resolved to minimise his risks. In May, 1683, he concluded an alliance

with the Court of Vienna, in September he drove the Turks from
Vienna, in October he pursued their retreating forces through
Hungary, and severely defeated them at Párkány.  Still there
was no sign of surrender at Stambul, and in September, 1684,
a Holy League was formed by Poland, Austria, Venice, and the
Pope, to which "the most serene Tsars of Moscovy" were to be
invited to accede.  In the spring of 1685 the Polish and Imperial
plenipotentiaries appeared at Moscovy.

Prince Vasily Golitsuin, who, in 1683, had been appointed
"Guardian of the Great Seal" (a dignity which had remained
vacant since the retirement of Orduin Nashchokin), and consequently directed the foreign affairs of Moscovy at this time,
clearly recognised that, in regard to the Eastern question, the
interests of Moscovy and Poland were identical.  Moreover,
Moscovy possessed an excellent pretext for a rupture with the
Porte in the prevalence of the Tatar raids into the Ukrain.
Every year thousands of captives, and tens of thousands of
cattle, were carried off and sold at Kaffa, despite the fact that
a regular tribute was paid to the Khan of the Crimea as a sort
of insurance against such depredations.  The shame and reproach
of this humiliating yoke became intolerable when Moscovy
began to have intimate relations with the civilised Western
powers  She could not claim to be their equal so long as she
submitted to such blackmailing from barbarians.

But Golitsuin was much too good a diplomatist to sell the
Moscovite alliance cheaply.  The negotiations with Poland were
protracted till the growing distress of the republic constrained
her to sacrifice everything for the co-operation of the Moscovites.  The negotiations dragged on from the spring of 1685
to the spring of 1686, the main obstacle to their conclusion
being the refusal of the Poles to cede Kiev definitely to the
Moscovites.  At last, on April 21, 1686, a "perpetual peace"
was signed at Moscow, by the terms of which Kiev was surrendered to Moscovy in exchange for 146,000 rubles.  But
Poland lost much more than Kiev by this treaty, for it contained
a provision binding her to maintain the liberties of the Dissidents, thus opening the door to the interference of Russia in the
domestic affairs of the republic.  Later in the same year, Sobieski,

who, after capturing Jassy, had been obliged to lead his sick and starving army back to Poland, tearfully ratified at Lemberg a treaty from which the eclipse of Poland may be definitely dated.

The Porte had done its utmost to prevent the conclusion of the Russo-Polish league.   The Patriarch of Constantinople had even been employed by the Divan to dissuade the Tsars from embarking on a war which would, he warned them, call down the vengeance of the Sultan on the orthodox population of his domains.   The patriarch had also consented to surrender his jurisdiction over the metropolitan see of Kiev to the Patriarch of Moscow.   But neither blandishments nor menaces could avail.   Russia had gone too far to retreat, and in the autumn of 1687 100,000 Moscovites, under Prince Vasily Golitsuin, set out to conquer the Crimea.   At Samara Golitsuin was joined by the Cossack Hetman Samoilovich, with 50,000 men, and the army then plunged into the steppe.   There was no sign of the Tatars, but Golitsuin soon encountered a far more terrible enemy in the steppe fires, which destroyed all the grass, and made further progress impossible.   After traversing eight miles in forty-eight hours he decided to turn back, and, leaving 30,000 men on the Lower Dnieper, retired with the rest of the army across the Kolomak, not far from Poltava.   According to Patrick Gordon, who accompanied the expedition, Samoilovich was strongly suspected of firing the steppe to compel a retreat, foreseeing that the subjection of the Crimea must inevitably lead to the suppression of the free Cossacks.   The Moscow Government shared this suspicion, and, on July 25, Samoilovich, whose pride and pretentiousness had made him very offensive to the Cossack community, was deprived of his hetmanship.   Ivan Mazepa was then elected unanimously in his stead, and Golitsuin solemnly invested him with the usual insignia of office: the bâton, the mace, and the horsetail standard, for which the new Hetman privately paid him 10,000 rubles.

At the very time when Golitsuin was ingloriously retreating from the wasted steppe, the other members of the Holy League were everywhere triumphant.   Defeated in Hungary, Dalmatia, and the Morea, the Turks could with difficulty defend themselves; Sultan Muhammad IV. fell a victim to an outburst of

popular fury which placed Selim II. on the throne; and so great
was the confusion that the collapse of the Ottoman Empire was
confidently anticipated. The same orthodox prelates, who, twelve
months before, had warned the Tsars against provoking the
Porte, now urged them to administer the *coup-de-grâce*. Thus,
in 1688, a special envoy from Dositheos, Patriarch of Constantinople, arrived at Moscow with the intelligence that all the
Balkan states were ready to shake off the Turkish yoke, and
only awaited a promise of help to fly to arms. Similar letters
were received from the Servian patriarch, Arsenios, and from
Sherban Cantacuzene, Hospodar of Wallachia. These reports
stimulated still further the martial ardour of the Moscovite
Government, and, taught by experience, Golitsuin resolved to
begin his second campaign in the spring, when there was plenty
of water, and little possibility of steppe fires. Victory at any
cost had now become a personal matter with Golitsuin. He
had to conquer the Tatars in the steppe in order to conquer
his far more dangerous enemies at home, who were every day
becoming more vexatious. Shortly before his departure for the
front an assassin attacked him in his sledge, and a grave was
dug in front of his house, with the inscription: "For the
commander-in-chief, if the second campaign fails!"

In February, 1689, Golitsuin, for the second time, led more
than 100,000 Moscovites into the steppe; but the march was
delayed by snowstorms and lack of provisions, and it was not till
the middle of May that he encountered the Khan near Perekop.
The lightly armed Tatars were easily beaten off, indeed they
gave very little trouble during the whole campaign; but, with
the Crimea open before him, Golitsuin suddenly realised that
there were waterless steppes beyond as well as before Perekop,
and as he had done nothing to provide against such a contin-
gency, and his beasts of burden began to die off at such a rate
that he feared he would soon not have enough of them to carry
the baggage, there was nothing for it but to turn back a
second time. Thus Moscovy's contribution to the work of the
Holy League had been very trifling, ludicrous indeed in propor-
tion to the forces actually employed. Yet her intervention had
not been altogether useless, for she had prevented the Tatars

from co-operating with the Turks, and the very appearance of the Russian army at the gates of the Crimea was a significant sign that the steppe was no longer a barrier to Russia's progress southwards.

The Regent had followed the adventures of her lover with intense anxiety, and her correspondence reveals both the depth and the blindness of her passion. On hearing from the discomfited hero that he was safe again on Russian soil, she fervently thanks Jehovah for saving "the light of her eyes" from the Tatars, as of old He saved Israel from the Egyptians. Her foolish fondness magnified into a brilliant triumph a retreat which had only just stopped short of disaster, while the rewards she heaped upon her "little Vassy" disgusted everyone who had the honour of the nation at heart. Most of the malcontents rested their hopes for the future on the young Tsar Peter, who was the first to benefit by the growing unpopularity of his sister. Sophia was shrewd enough to recognise that her position was very insecure. When Peter reached man's estate, she would only be in the way, and she was not the sort of woman who is lightly pushed aside. To use Solovev's quaint but apt analogy, like those who have sold themselves to the devil, she might, for a time, enjoy all the good things of this world, her lover included, but hell, in the shape of a monastery, awaited her at the end of her pleasant course. She had crowned her brothers in order that she might reign in their name. She had added her name to theirs in state documents, boldly subscribing herself " Sovereign Princess of all Russia." She had officially informed the Doge of Venice that she was the co-Regent of the Tsars. And meanwhile the terrible term of her usurped authority was approaching. Peter was growing up, and Peter's mother, the long-despised Tsarevna Natalia, was beginning to criticise and even censure the doings of the Regent. Nay, more, she had protested openly against Sophia's assumption of the title of Sovereign. Something had to be done speedily, and Sophia turned for counsel to her chief ministers, Vasily Golitsuin and Shaklovity. But Golitsuin's *liaison* with the Regent made his position very difficult, and he lacked, besides, the nerve for practical villainy, just when villainy seemed the only saving expedient. Murder he did not object to, but he would not be the murderer. His colleague, Theodore Shaklovity, a far stronger man, had no such scruples; by sheer ability he had risen from the humble office of a *podyachy*, or scribe, to the high dignity of *okolnichy*, and, from first to last, he was the heart and soul of Sophia's Government. When Golitsuin, the professional soldier, had failed in his first Crimean expedition, Shaklovity, the penman, had been sent to the Ukrain to erect fortresses, levy troops, and set things right generally. It was Shaklovity who had incited the stryeltsui to revolt, and suppressed them again when they became dangerous, and he now proposed to employ them once more in order to dethrone Peter, and place Sophia on the throne. But, before proceeding to the history of this conspiracy, we must first make the acquaintance of the intended victim.

Peter Aleksyeevich was born on May 30, 1672. The numerous accounts of his extraordinary precocity are fabulous. In all respects little Peter was a singularly backward child. He was two and a half before he was weaned, and in his eleventh year we find him still playing with wooden horses, and struggling with the difficulties of Russian etymology. His earliest teacher (omitting the legendary Scotchman, Menzies) was the dyak Nikita Zotov, warmly recommended for the post by the learned Polotsky, who taught his pupil to spell out the liturgical and devotional books on which the children of the Tsar were generally brought up. After Zotov's departure on a diplomatic expedition to the Crimea in 1680, the lad, now eight years old, had no regular tutor. But books could never have taught him what he was to learn in the school of life. From the day of his father's death, when he was only three, to his tenth year, when he was raised to the throne, Peter shared the miseries and the perils of the rest of his family. The stories of innocent orphans remorselessly persecuted by wicked relatives, which other children learn from their nurses with comfortable tremours, were, in Peter's case, terrible experiences. His very election was the signal for a rebellion. Scenes of bloodshed were enacted daily before his eyes. He saw one of his uncles dragged from the palace, and butchered by a savage mob. He saw his mother's beloved mentor, and his own best friend, Artamon Matvyeev, torn, bruised

THE TSAREVNA SOPHIA ALEKSYEEVNA.

and bleeding, from his detaining grasp, and hacked to pieces. The haunting memories of these horrors played havoc with the nerves of a super-sensitive child. We have it, on excellent authority, that for long afterwards he could not sleep at night without clinging hard for safety to one of his attendants. In after years he said to a friend : " When I was a boy the thought of the rebellious stryeltsui made me quake, and kept me from sleeping." The convulsions from which he suffered so much in later years must be partly attributed to this violent shock.

Dunce though he was, from the ordinary pedagogue's point of view, the child was, nevertheless, of an amazingly alert and inquisitive intelligence, with eyes and ears wide open for everything that was going on around him. From his very cradle he must have been made acquainted with Western ideas, even if, at the first, they only took the shape of mechanical toys from abroad, for his mother had been the favourite pupil of Matvyeev, and must have been full of her master's ideas, even if she only half understood them. She does not seem to have been very intelligent; indeed we have it on the authority of a friendly contemporary, Prince Kurakin, that she was "rather stupid,"* and she certainly did very little for her son. After the triumphs of Sophia, Natalia was altogether excluded from the conduct of affairs, and lived for nine months out of the twelve at Preobrazenskoe, on the outskirts of the capital. During this period Peter was rarely to be seen at Moscow, except when he and his semi-imbecile brother had to undergo the ceremony of receiving foreign ambassadors at the *kreml'*. Fortunately the Saxon envoys, who came to Moscow to conclude a commercial treaty, have left us a vivid glimpse of one of these public audiences when Peter was twelve years old.† The young Tsars sat on two thrones, side by side, surrounded by the boyars, and, in front of them were twelve *palashes*, "big fellows with flaming battle-axes raised aloft as if about to strike," dressed in ancient Roman costumes invented by the late Tsar Theodore. When the envoys presented their credentials, Peter examined the seals with the

* " Uma malago."
† " Wahrhafte relation von der moscovischen Reise, 1684." In Rinhuber : "Relation." etc.

R.                                                                    P

attention of a connoisseur, and admired the workmanship. When the envoys came forward to kiss hands, Ivan V. had to be held up by his uncle, Ivan Miloslavsky, because he was so short-sighted; but at Peter's turn, he gave the envoys his hand of his own accord, with a friendly and gracious smile. The envoys were greatly impressed by his unusual beauty* and intelligence, and opined that Peter's royal birth was an advantage far inferior to his natural gifts.

It is quite plain that little Peter very soon felt cramped and stifled in the dim and close semi-religious atmosphere of old Moscovite family life. Like the fabulous heroes of old Russian folk-lore, he would fain run before he could walk, and go forth to shake his mighty shoulders in free and boundless spaces. He escaped from the boredom and the melancholy of Natalia's *terem* by rushing out into the streets, and the streets of Moscow in the seventeenth century, as Solovev shrewdly observes, were very dirty streets. Already we notice what was to become a leading trait of his character, that rollicking joyousness—an exaggeration, no doubt, of his gentle father's sociability—which clutched at life with both hands, and squeezed out of it, recklessly, all the pleasure it could yield. He surrounded himself with bands of lads of his own age, preferably of the lower rougher classes, and with these "blackguards,"† as his sister, Sophia, dubbed them, the nucleus of the famous "merry company" of later days, he scoured the country, indulging in all sorts of riotous and scandalous pranks. It is hard to say how it could have been otherwise under the peculiar circumstances. There was nobody near him of sufficient character and authority to keep the passionate fiery nature within due bounds. His mother was incapable of controlling him. The old religious Moscovite families were averse to and avoided Natalia and her family, while the semi-emancipated portion of Russian society had unfortunately emancipated itself not only from the narrowness but also from the strictness of "the old religion." Take, for instance, the *kravchy*, or Cup-Bearer, Prince Boris Golitsuin, Vasily's cousin, the most intelligent and courageous friend of the young Court. This eminent

* " Ein überaus schones Her an welchem die Natur son pouvoir wol erweisen."
† *Ozarniki.*

boyar was, in many respects, far in advance of his age. He was highly educated ; spoke Latin with graceful fluency ; frequented the society of scholars ; and had his children carefully educated according to the best European methods. He was honestly devoted and unshakably loyal to Peter, he looked after Peter's interests, and he rendered Peter inestimable services. Yet this eminent, this superior personage was an habitual drunkard, an uncouth savage who intruded upon the hospitality of wealthy foreigners, and was not ashamed to seize upon any dish he liked at the table of his hosts, and send it home to his wife. In a word, Muscovite society was in a transitional state, and it was Peter's misfortune to be brought up in the midst of it.

From his tenth to his seventeenth year, Peter amused himself in his own way at Preobrazenskoe, with his "blackguards." But it was not all amusement. Instinct was already teaching him his business. From the first the lad took an extraordinary interest in the technical and mechanical arts, and especially in their application to military science. Mimic warfare was his favourite sport. In his twelfth year he built, not far from his father's palace at Preobrazenskoe, a wooden "toy fortress" on an earth foundation, with walls, bastions and ditches, which he called "Preshpur."* The little Gosudar, who had provided himself with all the necessary tools, worked alongside the labourers who constructed this fortress, even helping to dig the trenches and place the guns in position.† On his twelfth birthday, half of his band of lads defended Pressburg against the assault of the other half, headed by Peter himself, who finally prevailed, and made his triumphal entry into the conquered fortress.

Peter's tastes were, by this time, pretty well known, and Prince Yakov Dolgoruki, who was about to conduct a special embassy to France, shrewdly calculated on pleasing the young Tsar when he told him that there was an instrument by means of which one could measure distances accurately without moving from the spot. Peter, then fourteen, was deeply interested. "Get me one at Paris," he cried. Dolgoruki brought back with him the first astrolabe ever seen in Moscovy, and Peter was instructed how to use it by a Dutchman, Franz Timmerman, who also taught him

* *I.s.*, Pressburg.    † See Sinitsuin : "Preobrazhenskoe."

the rudiments of geometry and fortification. The same year he began to take that absorbing interest in boats and boating, the final result of which was to be the creation of the Russian navy. Rummaging one day among the rubbish left by his cousin, Nikita Romanov, in his house at Preobrazenskoe, Peter came upon a boat of peculiar shape and foreign make. Timmerman explained that it was of English workmanship, and superior to the ordinary boats. " Why is it superior ? " asked Peter. " Because it can sail against as well as with the wind," replied the Dutchman. This Peter could not believe till he had experimented with the boat on the river Yanza, which ran through Preobrazenskoe, and was the nearest way to the German settlement at Moscow, already the favourite resort of the young Tsar. But the Yanza soon grew too narrow for Peter, and he transferred his boats to a pond at Izmailovo close by, and finally to a large lake at Pereyaslavl, eighty miles away, where the German shipmaster, Brandt, began to build larger boats for the indefatigable young navigator. His mother regarded these dangerous pastimes with increasing dissatisfaction, and to wean him from them, resolved to provide him with a home of his own. It was the first time she had interfered with him, and her interference was disastrous, for on January 27, 1689, she compelled him to marry Eudoxia Lopukhina. This unfortunate match was largely due to political considerations. Sophia, a few years before, had wedded the imbecile Ivan V. to Praskovia Saltuikova. This union had produced only daughters, but Peter's friends hoped that his would be blessed with a son. They had tried at first to choose him a fitting spouse from one of the princely families, but this design was frustrated by the Sophian faction, and Natalia had to fall back upon the Lopukhinas, a family of poor squires, no fewer than thirty of whom appeared at Preobrazenskoe immediately after the marriage, in search of preferment, disgusting everybody by their rapacity. Natalia herself now conceived such a hatred of her daughter-in-law, that she rather preferred to see the young people at variance than living harmoniously together, nor had the bride herself, a nun-like virgin of the strict old school, any charm for the young groom of seventeen. Three months after his wedding, Peter was back again at Pereyaslavl, whence, four months later, he returned to Preobrazenskoe.

While Peter was thus amusing himself at Preobrazenskoe and Pereyaslavl, the authorities at the *kreml'* were compassing his ruin. As early as 1687, Shaklovity had invited the leaders of the stryeltsui to present a petition that Sophia should be proclaimed Tsaritsa. " But to whom," asked the stryeltsui, " is the petition to be presented? The elder Tsar would not understand, and the younger would not consent." " Make him consent by going up and seizing his uncle, Lev Naruishkin, and the cup-bearer, Boris Golitsuin," replied Shaklovity. " But the patriarch and the boyars are with him," objected the stryeltsui. " The patriarch can be removed, and the boyars are rotten wood," was the answer. But the proposal was so coldly received that the Regent herself abandoned it. Nor was she more successful when she summoned the stryeltsui to the *kreml'* and hinted at the existence of a conspiracy against her and Tsar Ivan on the part of Natalia and Natalia's friends,; her vague complaints only elicited still vaguer assurances. After every means of persuasion, corruption and terrorising had been freely used, only five officers of the stryeltsui could be found willing to remove " the old she-bear and her cub," as they called Natalia and Peter. Even when Shaklovity, as a last expedient, suborned an armed band to proceed to the quarters of the stryeltsui, and murder one of their *desyatniks*, or sergeants, at the same time circulating the rumour that this outrage was the work of Lev Naruishkin, Natalia's brother, even then the bulk of the stryeltsui remained quiet and indifferent. Meanwhile Peter and Sophia had twice come into actual collision. On the first occasion the young Tsar had protested against his sister's participation in a solemn procession in the Kazan Cathedral, which was, indeed, an unheard-of breach of ancient usage. Sophia, openly flouting him, had snatched up an ikon and joined the procession, and Peter had retired discomfited. On the second occasion he had openly protested against the rewards bestowed upon Vasily Golitsuin, and refused to receive the prince in audience when he came to thank Peter for his undeserved promotion. Shortly afterwards Peter went so far as to arrest Shaklovity, but immediately let him go again as if afraid of what he had done. This was feeble, but the fact remained that Peter had struck first, and the opposite faction speedily countered. On August 7 an anonymous letter was received "upstairs" at the *kreml'*, to the effect that Peter, at the head of his "jolly ostlers,"* was marching on Moscow to extirpate Tsar Ivan and all his friends. Shaklovity seized the opportunity to assemble, at the *kreml'*, 400 of the stryeltsui, whom he provided with artillery. But even now they were very divided in opinion. Many of them regarded Peter as the rightful Tsar, and it was by some of these friendly stryeltsui that warning of the conspiracy against him was brought to Preobrazenskoe. Suddenly aroused at midnight, on August 12, 1689, Peter leaped from his bed, flung himself on a horse, and galloped to the nearest forest, whither a suit of clothes was brought to him. Continuing his flight with a handful of adherents, he never stopped till he reached the fortress-monastery of Troitsa at six o'clock in the morning of August 13. Two hours later his mother and sister Natalia joined him. Presently he was fortified by the arrival of " the jolly ostlers," and the stryeltsui of the Sukharev regiment, and placed the supreme command in the energetic hands of Prince Boris Golitsuin.

Great was the consternation of the conspirators at the *kreml'* when they learnt that Peter had taken refuge in the great and famous bulwark of Moscovite orthodoxy and patriotism. Only Shaklovity affected to make light of the incident. "Let him run ! He's mad," cried he. Sophia gauged the situation more accurately, and endeavoured to hedge while there was still time. But the responses from Troitsa to her overtures were not encouraging, and when, on August 13, Ivan Troekurov appeared at the *kreml'* and demanded, in Peter's name, that ten deputies from each regiment of the stryeltsui should proceed to Troitsa on the following day, she forbade them to go under pain of death. Then she grew afraid again, and sent the patriarch Joachim to Troitsa to mediate. This was a false step, for, by so doing, she converted a valuable hostage into a formidable opponent. The patriarch had long desired to escape from the treason-able atmosphere of the *kreml'*, and his presence at the Troitsa

---

* A company of like-minded youths.

Monastery immensely strengthened the position of Peter. On August 27 came a fresh summons from Troitsa to the stryeltsui, of so peremptory a character that they durst no longer disobey it. Sophia, at this fresh desertion, set out for Troitsa herself to make peace with her brother ; but, at the halfway village of Vozdrozhenskoe, the scene of her triumph over Khovansky seven years before, she was turned back by a special messenger from the Tsar, who overcame her obstinacy only by assuring her that if she persisted in going she "would not be treated honourably." Hastening back to the *kreml'* the desperate woman summoned "the old stryeltsui" to her presence, and, in a stirring oration, set forth her past services and present perils, and passionately appealed to their loyalty for help. The stryeltsui promised to stand by her, and when, on September 1, New Year's Day, Colonel Nechaev arrived from Troitsa to demand the surrender of Shaklovity, Sophia asked him how he dared to deliver such a message, and ordered his head to be struck off. He was saved only because a sword could not be found at once, and, in the meantime, the Tsarevna's wrath had subsided. She then harangued the people from the top of the Red Staircase, and assured them that the demand for the head of the faithful Shaklovity was a mere pretext, her own head and the head of Tsar Ivan were really what the rebels at Preobrazenskoe wanted. Finally, the semi-imbecile Ivan V. was brought forward to distribute glasses of vodka to the stryeltsui with his own Tsarish hand.

This was Sophia's last demonstration. Even her strong hand could not wield for long a weapon which crumbled away in her grasp. Her lover, Prince Vasily Golitsuin, on whom she relied the most, was visibly weakening. He had already begun to correspond privately with his cousin, Prince Boris, urging him to reconcile the brother and sister, as the best way out of the difficulty. But Prince Boris opined that it would be better still if Prince Vasily himself proceeded to Troitsa, where he might count on an indulgent reception. Sophia's last hope vanished when, on September 4, the foreign legion in the German settlement, obeying an urgent summons from Troitsa, quitted Moscow the same afternoon, despite all the efforts of its colonel,

Vasily Golitsuin, to keep it back. Two days later (September 6) Sophia's own stryeltsui compelled her, at last, to deliver up Shaklovity, in order to save their own heads. Then all the boyars of her party went over to Peter, and Vasily Golitsuin hid himself in his country-house at Medvyedkovo. On the night of September 7, Shaklovity, after undergoing the question extraordinary, demanded pen, ink and paper, and filled nine sheets with a statement in which he confessed to a plot against the life of Peter and his mother, but refused to betray his accomplices. Those about Peter would have extracted fuller information out of him by further torture; but to this Peter would not consent. On September 11, Shaklovity and his chief accomplices among the stryeltsui, whose confessions, also wrung out of them by torture, corroborated his statement, were publicly executed. Vasily Golitsuin's life was spared owing to the intercession of his cousin Boris, but his estates were confiscated and he was banished to Kirgopol for tolerating Sophia's usurpations, and for gross misconduct during the Crimean campaign. Sophia was compelled to retire within the Novodyevechy Monastery, but without taking the veil.

PETER THE GREAT
IN HIS SIXTEENTH YEAR.

# CHAPTER VIII.

## THE APPRENTICESHIP OF PETER. 1689—1699.

François Lefort—Peter's Pastimes—The Sham Fights—First Visits to Archangel
—Death of the Tsaritsa Natalia—Peter's "Jolly Company," and Revels—
The Azov Campaigns—Truikler's Conspiracy—The Grand Embassy to the
West—Riga—Königsberg— Zaardam — Amsterdam — Deptford — Vienna—
Rebellion of the Stryeltsui—Abolition of the Beards—The Reign of Terror
at Freobrazenskoe—Disappearance of Eudoxia and Sophia—Alexander
Menshikov—Alexei Kurbatov—The Reforms of the Year 1699.

THE new administration was reactionary in character. It was
composed entirely of the friends and relations of Natalia and
Eudoxia, and its most conspicuous members were the patriarch
Joachim and Lev Kirillovich Naruishkin, Peter's maternal uncle,
who, for the next few years, controlled foreign affairs. Boris
Golitsuin, the most capable member of the Government, was
relegated to a very subordinate position by colleagues who had
far keener eyes for his excesses than for his talents. Peter kept
altogether aloof from affairs. So long as he could indulge freely
in his favourite pastimes, he was quite content that others should
rule in his name. He had found a new friend in the Swiss
adventurer, François Lefort,* who, in 1675, when only nineteen,
had entered Tsar Theodore's service, and, after waiting for some
years for employment, flitted from Archangel to Moscow, where
he made the acquaintance of Patrick Gordon, whose cousin he
married. Gordon took him to the Ukrain to fight against the
Tatars. Lefort also participated in the Crimean expedition, and
ultimately settled down in the German settlement at Moscow,
where, most probably at the beginning of 1690,† he first became

---

* See Basseville: "Pieces historiques sur la vie de Lefort," and Posselt: "Der
General Franz Lefort," both valuable if uncritical works. Best Russian work:
"Golikov: "Istorichy izobrazhenie zhizni Leforta."

† According to Ustryalov, "Istoria tsarstv. Petra Velikago" II. iv. 1, Lefort
first offered his service to Peter at Troitsa in August, 1689. Compare Gordon:
"Diary."

acquainted with the young Tsar Peter. Lefort was a reckless, devil-may-care soldier of fortune, full of the joy of life, and infinitely good-natured and amusing. Peter, who was nothing if not jovial, took to the lively Swiss at once, and their friendship was severed only by Lefort's sudden death in 1699. Lefort was not, perhaps, the sort of mentor that a young man's parents and guardians would choose for him. We cannot wonder if both Peter's mother and Peter's wife looked askance at the merry Swiss toper. We are told that "things impossible to describe"* went on in the large hall, added at Peter's expense, to Lefort's house in the German settlement. It was here that Peter seems to have been initiated into all the mysteries of profligacy. Not infrequently the whole company drank hard, for three days together, behind locked doors ; occasionally some of the guests died during the debauch. It was here, too, that Peter learnt dancing, and made the acquaintance of his first mistress, Anna Mons, a German vintner's daughter. The forming of such a friend-ship was no doubt a mistake on Peter's part; but, in fairness, it should be remembered that the Peter of 1690 was not Peter the Great. Moreover Lefort was a shrewd as well as a pleasant rascal. He very soon divined that Peter was a genius who needed guiding to his goal, and that no one who had not previously gained Peter's affection could hope to influence him permanently—two cardinal facts which had escaped the attention of everyone else. It was the drunken, disreputable Lefort who persuaded Peter first to undertake the expedition against Azov, and then to go abroad to complete his education—in a word it was Lefort who put Peter the bombardier in the way of becoming Peter the Great.

But in 1690 young Peter had no thought save for dangerous or disreputable pastimes. Of the former the much miscalled "sham fights" largely occupied him. The most famous of these encounters was the "Kozhukovsky campaign," in 1694, when one division of Peter's troops, under Prince Theodore Romodanovsky, whom Peter habitually addressed as "Theodore, King of Press-burg,"† attacked Ivan,‡ King of Seminovskoe, in entrenchments,

* "Arkhiv Kn. Th. V. Kurakina."
† Pressburg, it will be remembered, was Peter's toy fortress.
‡ *I.e.*, Ivan Buturlin.

near the village of Kozhukova, on which occasion twenty-four men were killed and fifty wounded. Peter, who had now learnt fencing and riding from the Dane Butenant, held the modest rank of bombardier on this occasion, and greatly distinguished himself by capturing, in the *mellé*, a colonel of the stryeltsui. But boats and boating in the lake of Pereyaslavl claimed him quite as much as marching and manœuvring. At last even the lake at Pereyaslavl grew too small for him, and, wearied by his importunity, his mother, in July, 1693, at last allowed " my life and my hope," as she called him, to go to see the great ocean at Archangel, but not before he had solemnly promised only to look at the foreign ships from the shore. But the sight of the great vessels afloat was too much for Peter, and when Natalia sorrowfully reproached him for his breach of faith, and warned him against misadventure, he only expressed pious surprise at her anxiety.. Had she not committed him to the protection of the Mother of God? How could he have a better protectress? Besides, was not God over all? After this Natalia could only sigh. At Archangel, Peter helped to build a ship, fraternised with the foreign seamen, who told him "many strange and interesting things," and added the naval title of "skipper" to his military title of bombardier. During his stay at Archangel he was the guest of the archbishop Athanasius, who must have been much bored by his ceaseless talk of ships and shipping. Much more welcome to the old man was the sound of Peter's fine loud voice in the cathedral choir. The death of his mother, on January 25, 1694, in her forty-second year, recalled him to Moscow. Peter wept bitterly at the sad tidings, and wrote to a friend that his pen could not describe his grief and woe. Natalia was buried on January 26, and, on the 28/29, Peter drowned his sorrow in a wild debauch at Lefort's house, to the infinite disgust of his relations. On May 1 he was back again at Archangel. He now launched the ship built by him the year before, and christened *St. Paul*. A cruise to the Solovetsky Monastery at the mouth of the White Sea was interrupted by a violent storm. So great was the danger that Peter received the sacrament from the archbishop, but a skilful pilot steered them safely into the Gulf of Unska, and Peter, by way of thanksgiving, carved a

large wooden cross, which he planted on a hill overlooking the
sea, with the inscription in Dutch: "Skipper Peter made this
cross in the year of Christ, 1694." On his return to Archangel,
he found that the forty-four gun frigate, *Sancta Perfectie*,
built by his orders in Holland, had at length arrived, and he
celebrated the joyful occasion by a banquet with his "jolly
company."

This "jolly company," or "the company," as it was generally
called, though a characteristically Petrine institution, could trace
its descent from the ancient *druzhina* of the semi-barbaric
Russian princes of the eleventh and twelfth centuries, which
accompanied the prince wherever he went, and shared all his
exploits, labours and pastimes. Peter's *druzhina* was composed of all his personal friends and casual acquaintances whom
he had picked up in the course of his wanderings. They were
of all sorts and conditions, selected for purely personal qualities,
including not only jesters and mountebanks, whose first duty it
was to amuse the Tsar, but some of the best talent in the land.
Thus, in "the company," we find men like Andrei Vinius, an
orthodox Russian of Dutch* origin, who could turn his hand to
anything, from writing geographies to casting cannon ; Krevet,
or Gravat, the English translator in the *Posolsky Prikaz*, and
Prince Yury Romodonovsky, the terror and extirpator of robbers
and freebooters, whose ghastly functions were mostly performed
in the torture-chamber ; there were also Lefort, Shafirov, the
future vice-chancellor, Nikita Zotov, Peter's old tutor, and, at a
later day, Menshikov and the other "fledglings" of the Tsar.
With this motley band Peter took his pleasure. The "company"
was graduated into a sort of mock hierarchy, political and
ecclesiastical. It had its Tsar and its patriarch, and their
subordinate officials. There was no intentional profanity in all
this buffoonery, as has been sometimes supposed. Peter and his
"jolly company" in their frolics were really little more than
rough rollicking children, and the humour of such *gamin* is
always crude and very often cruel. We must never forget, too,
that Peter, for all his progressive ideas, had many of the old
Moscovite humours in his blood. Brought up in the *terem*,

* It was he who taught Peter Dutch.

amongst dwarfs and fools, to the end of his life he delighted in
these strange playthings. But while his father and his grandfather had been content to amuse themselves with such freaks of
nature in the seclusion of their "pleasure halls," Peter admitted
the whole world to these fantastic entertainments, to which he
added gross and extravagant touches of his own. As a specimen,
we may take the ceremonies attending the marriage of the jester,
Yakov Turgenev, with a sexton's daughter, in January, 1694.
The bride and bridegroom rode to church in the Tsar's best
velvet coach, and behind them, in solemn procession, came
the highest dignitaries and the most eminent patricians in the
land, mounted on oxen, asses, swine and big dogs, some arrayed
in the most splendid costumes, others dressed in sacking or
glazed linen, or cat-skin kaftans, with straw boots, mouse-skin
gloves, and bast mantles. The proceedings terminated, as usual,
with a three days' drinking bout.

But, after all, such entertainments were very exceptional.
Lefort, for the sake of his own interests, felt bound to divert
Peter from mere pleasure to serious enterprises, which would
place both the Tsar and "the company" in a more favourable
light. By this time the White Sea, frozen as it was nine months
out of the twelve, had become too narrow for Peter, and he was
looking about him for more hospitable waters. All sorts of
projects were forming in his head. At first he thought of
seeking a passage to India or China by way of the Arctic Ocean,
but this scheme he soon abandoned. Next he turned his eyes in
the direction of the Baltic, but the Baltic was a closed door to
Moscovy, and the key to it was held by Sweden, still the strongest
military monarchy in Europe. The Caspian remained, and it had
long been a common saying with foreign merchants that the best
way of tapping the riches of the Orient was to secure possession
of this vast inland lake. But so long as Turk, Tatar and
Cossack nomads made the Volgan steppe inhabitable, the Caspian
was a possession of but doubtful value, as Stenka Razin's
exploits had demonstrated. The first step making for security
was to build a fleet strong enough not only to overawe such
desperadoes as Stenka in the future, but also to provide against
the anarchical condition of these parts, for which the presence

of the hordes of the Khan of the Crimea was mainly responsible.
But the Khan, to whom Moscovy actually paid tribute, was himself the tributary of the Turks—it was, therefore, necessary for
the Moscovite authorities to attack the Turks direct.    They were
the more willing to do so as their European allies were constantly
reproaching them for their backwardness in the holy war still
proceeding against the enemy of Christendom, while the Cossack
Hetman Ivan Mazepa, the great authority on the politics of
the Ukrain, also declared that war was necessary, if only for the
purpose of keeping his unruly Cossacks in order.

War against the Ottoman Porte was therefore resolved upon,
and, the experience of Vasily Golitsuin having demonstrated the
unpromising character of a Crimean campaign, the Turkish
fortress of Azov, which could be approached by water from
Moscow, became the Russian objective.    Early in 1695 the old-
fashioned militia and the Cossacks under Boris Sheremetev
made a demonstration in the Ukrain, to distract the attention
of the enemy, while the army of the new order and the stryeltsui,
31,000 strong, under Golovin, Lefort and Gordon, proceeded
partly by land and partly by the rivers Moskva, Oka and
Volga, to the Cossack town of Panshino on Don, reaching
Azov by the beginning of July.    The bombardier regiment was
led by bombardier Peter Aleksyeevich.    The Russian batteries
were opened on July 8, bombardier Peter directing the guns
himself for the first fortnight, but no impression could be made
on the fortress.    In the beginning of August the Turks surprised
the Moscovite camp during its mid-day siesta, and, though
ultimately repulsed with great loss, captured five guns and
ruined all the Russian siege artillery.    After two subsequent
fruitless attempts to storm Azov, the siege was abandoned
(September 27), and on November 22, the Tsar re-entered
Moscow.

Peter's first military expedition had ended in unmitigated
disaster, yet from this disaster is to be dated the reign of
Peter *the Great*.    The young Tsar, fully accepting his failure,
determined to repair it by a second campaign.    On his return
from Azov, we hear no more of revels in the German suburb, or
of sham fights at Kozhukov or Preobrazenskoe.    Immediately

after his return, Peter sent to Austria and Prussia for as many engineers, sappers, miners and carpenters as money could get. He meant to build a fleet strong enough to prevent the Turkish fleet from relieving Azov. A model galley was ordered from Holland, and twenty-two copies were speedily made from it. The soldiers of the Semenovsky and Preobrazensky regiments, and all the workmen procurable, were driven together in bands to Voronezh, Dobro, Kozlov, Sokolsk, and other places among the forests of the Don, to fell timber, and in the course of the next few months 26,000 labourers, working night and day, turned out hundreds of barks and smaller vessels. Many of these boats, built hastily of damp and frozen timber, proved unserviceable; but the wonder was that they were built at all. Difficulties multiplied at every step. Thousands of the workmen deserted, thousands more dawdled on the road, many of them never appeared at all. Forest fires destroyed the shipping sheds, and severe frosts at the end of March, and heavy snowstorms in the beginning of April, were fresh impediments. Yet, by dint of working all through Lent and Holy Week, a fleet of two war-ships, twenty-three galleys, four fire-ships, and numerous smaller craft, were safely launched in the middle of April. "We have finished our task because, like our father, Adam, we ate our bread in the sweat of our brows," wrote Peter to his uncle, Peter Stryeshnev. His portion of this bread of labour had been eaten in a small two-roomed wooden house at Voronezh, where he lived among his workmen, himself the most strenuous of them all. "The company" was also with him, working hard and drinking hard at the same time. Lefort, who had been appointed Admiral-General, hearing that there was nothing to drink at Voronezh, brought down with him kegs of muscatel, and barrels of strong beer. Nine foreign doctors came with him, to serve as army surgeons, but, at Elets, the medical gentlemen quarrelled over their cups, and in the *fracas* which ensued, three of them were injured, though not seriously.

On May 3, the "sea-caravan" sailed from Voronezh, "Captain* Peter Aleksyeevich" commanding eight galleys of the flotilla from the galley *Principium*, built by his own hand. Nor was

* He had been promoted after the first Azov campaign.

all this labour in vain.  The new Russian fleet prevented the
Turks from relieving Azov by water; a general attack of the
Tatars on the Russian camp was repulsed; and in the daily
fighting the advantage was always with the besiegers.  Peter
was in excellent spirits.  In reply to a letter from his sister
Natalia, urging him to take greater care of himself, he replied :
" I don't get in the way of the bullets, it is the bullets that get
in my way.  You had better tell *them* to keep away, or come at
more convenient times."  On July 18 the fortress surrendered
on condition that the garrison was allowed to march out with
all the honours of war.  " My lord King,* I beg to report that
the Lord God hath blessed your Majesty's arms," wrote Captain
Peter to Yury Romadonovsky, " King of Pressburg."

The capture of Azov was one of those triumphs which
strongly appeal to the popular imagination.  It was the first
victory ever won by the Moscovites over the terrible Turks, who,
only a few years before, had destroyed the town of Chigorin
before the eyes of a helpless Moscovite army.  The new
patriarch, Adrian, wept when the good tidings reached him, and
ordered the big bell of Moscow to ring for a thanksgiving service
in the Uspensky Cathedral.  On September 30 the Moscovite
army made its triumphal entry into the capital.  The procession
was headed by Admiral Lefort and Generalissimo Alexei
Shein, and behind the gilded sledges walked Captain Peter
Aleksyeevich with a pike across his shoulder.  In the midst of
the façade of the principal triumphal arch sat a two-headed eagle
surrounded by trophies with the inscription : " If God be with us
who shall be against us ? "  The façade was supported by statues
of Hercules and Mars.  On a pedestal beneath the statue of
Mars was the effigy of a Turkish Mirza, who was represented as
saying : " Of yore we *fought* on the steppe, now scarce by flight
can we save ourselves from Moscow."

But the real significance of the victory of Azov lay in the
fact that it was a triumph of the new system, which had brought
in " the jolly company " and the foreign ship-builders.  Peter
now felt able to advance along the path of progress with a
quicker and a firmer step.  At two councils, held on October 20

* " Min Her Kenich."

and November 4, 1696, it was resolved to consolidate the victory by converting Azov into a fortress, by establishing a new naval station at the head of the Sea of Azov, to which the name of Taganrog was given, and by building a national fleet by special gangs of workmen, under the supervision of foreign ship-builders, at the national expense.* But it was necessary to guarantee the future as well as to provide for the present. A prolonged war with the formidable Ottoman Porte was a serious prospect for a poor and undeveloped country like Moscovy. It was, therefore, resolved to send a grand embassy to the prin-cipal Western Powers to solicit their co-operation against the Turk. At the same council it was decided that fifty young Moscovites of the best families should be sent to England, Holland, and Venice, to learn the arts and sciences of the West, especially ship-building, fortification, and foreign languages, so as to make Russia independent of foreigners in the future. The experiment had already been tried on a smaller scale by Tsar Boris Gudunov (1598/1605). It failed because the young Moscovites refused to return from civilisation to barbarism. Peter proposed to obviate this by being the pioneer as well as the ruler of his people. He would, first of all, be a learner himself, that he might be able to teach his people afterwards. But Peter's ideas, just because they were so much in advance of his age, scandalised the respectable classes of Moscovy. The old Moscovite sense of dignity was shocked at the humiliating spectacle of the Tsar of all Russia walking behind the sledge of a drunken Swiss adventurer. They also disliked the notion of sending their sons abroad to learn new-fangled practices from foreign heretics. Amongst the stryeltsui too, we notice the first symptoms of discontent which, a year later, was to burst forth in open rebellion. Effeminated by the ease of a comfortable domestic life at Moscow, these luxurious troopers were satisfied with the minimum of military service, while the digging of trenches and the building of boats seemed to them fit only for galley-slaves. Moreover, some of their leaders had put too high a price upon their service to Peter at Troitsa. All

---

* Unfortunately *this* fleet, which cost the country half a million in pounds sterling, proved quite useless.

R.                                                                      Q

these causes together led to a secret conspiracy against Peter's life, the ringleaders of which were a foreign officer of the stryeltsui named Truikler, and two *raskolnik* boyars, Aleksyei Sokovin and Theodore Pushkin. It was repressed with the ferocity of panic fear. Six of the ringleaders were executed, and their bleeding heads planted on pikes in the Red Square. Under torture they had confessed that the late Ivan Miloslavsky had counselled his niece Sophia to murder Peter. Ivan was beyond Peter's vengeance, but his corpse was dug up, dragged by swine to the foot of the block at Preobrazenskoe, and defiled by the warm blood of the decapitated traitors, which was made to trickle down upon it. This is the earliest instance of the would-be regenerator's frequent relapses into savagery, under the over-powering stress of terror or hatred.

On March 10, 1697, five days after this bloody vengeance, the grand embassy, under the leadership of Lefort, set out on its travels. Peter attached himself to it as a volunteer sailor-man, Peter Mikhailov, so as to have greater facility for learning ship-building and other technical sciences. Peter's first impression of foreign parts was, to use his own expression, " not very plea-sant." The way of the embassy lay through Swedish Livonia, and Eric Dalberg, the veteran commandant of Riga, observed Peter's incognito so literally as to refuse to allow him to inspect the fortress. Dalberg had had a lifelong experience of Moscovite hostility, and he was the more suspicious on this occasion as the embassy tried to make him believe that the Tsar was at Voronezh, inspecting his fleet. Peter, who was used to having his own way, everywhere and at all times, never forgave "the accursed hole," as he ever afterwards called Riga, for thus baffling his curiosity, and subsequently this trivial incident was magnified by him into a *casus belli*. At Libau Peter first beheld the Baltic. Thence he proceeded, by sea, to Königsberg, where he was hospitably entertained by the Elector Frederick of Bran-denburg. While waiting here for the arrival of the embassy, which travelled by land, Peter learned the practice of gunnery from the great engineer, Von Sternfeld, who gave Peter Mikhailov his master-gunner's certificate before his departure.[*]

---

[*] Solovev: "Istoria Rossy," XIV., 3.

Peter was detained in Prussia longer than he desired by the election in Poland consequent on the death of Sobieski (June 17, 1696). The two principal candidates were Frederick Augustus, Elector of Saxony, and the Prince of Conti, who was supported by Louis XIV. Moscovy's policy on this occasion was perfectly simple. It was a matter of indifference to her who sat on the Polish throne so long as he did not abandon the Holy League against the Turk. But France favoured the Turk, and Conti, as the French *protégé*, held out to the Polish electors the bait of a separate peace with the Porte, and the restitution of Kamieniec. Peter was bound to oppose "the nominee of the Turks and Tatars," as he not inaptly styled Conti, and he intimated to the Poles that the election of the French candidate would be regarded by Moscovy as a breach of the eternal peace between her and the republic. Both candidates were elected, and a brief civil war ensued, in which Frederick Augustus, proclaimed as Augustus II., ultimately prevailed. He ascribed his success in a great measure to a second minatory letter from Peter to the *Sejm*, and was profuse in his expressions of devotion and gratitude.*

The Polish difficulty adjusted, Peter was free to resume his travels. At Koppenburg, near Celle, he encountered Sophia, Electress of Hanover, and her daughter, the Electress Sophia Charlotte of Brandenburg. To both these princesses Peter was a far greater curiosity than any he himself had come to see. It was the duality of the extraordinary man-monster that impressed them the most. A handsome and noble presence marred by a twitching face and an unsteady hand ; a charming simplicity and natural-ness spoilt by gross and boorish habits, especially at table— elicited at first equal astonishment and disgust. Peter, pain-fully aware of his own shortcomings, had stipulated beforehand that his visit should be a perfectly private one. He entered the apartment of the Electresses like a big, shy child holding his hands before his face, and exclaiming, " I can't speak! I can't speak!" in reply to their compliments. But, the first bashful-ness overcome, he consented to go out into the courtyard and

* Compare Solovev : "Istoria Rossy," vol. XIV., chap. 3 ; Sokolowski. " Dzieji Polski," pp. 1,000, 1,001.

give the gentlemen-in-waiting large rummers of wine. He listened with pleasure to some Italian singers, though he admitted that he did not think very much of music. "What I like most," he said, "are ship-building and fireworks," and he proudly showed the ladies his horny hands. His mental vivacity and alertness they recognised immediately, and when he launched into a description of his plans and projects there was something magnetically attractive in his passionate enthusiasm.

From Celle Peter proceeded towards the Rhine, and leaving the embassy to follow by land, went with ten companions by water to Amsterdam, and from thence to Saardam, the famous ship-building town. Here Peter Mikhailov, the tall, handsome carpenter from Russia, dressed in a frieze jacket and white ducks, appeared as a workman in Rogge's ship-building yard. He rented a small room from an old carpenter, and mixed freely among those of the Dutch carpenters who had been to Russia, giving himself out as their comrade. His spare time was spent in visiting all the workshops. He always insisted on being shown how everything was done. At a paper factory, impatient at the slowness of the demonstrator, he snatched up the frame and turned out an excellent sheet of paper with his own hands. But his incognito could not be preserved for long. The old carpenter with whom he lodged received a letter from his son in Moscow, telling of wondrous things. A great Russian embassy was on its way to Amsterdam, and the Tsar was with it. They could tell him by his tall figure, twitching face, shaky hands, and the large wart on his cheek. But even after he was recognised, Peter refused to accept the handsome new quarters provided for him by the burgomaster. He and his comrades preferred, he said, to live in their rough cabins among simple folks. When addressed as "Your Majesty," he always turned his back on his interlocutor, but Peter, the carpenter of Saardam, readily conversed with everyone who addressed him as such.

On August 16 Lefort and the grand embassy arrived at Amsterdam, and Peter was obliged to take part in the festivities in honour of their arrival. He was introduced to the learned burgomaster, Niklas Wittsen, who had visited Moscovy in the reign of Alexius, and whose book, " Noord en Oost Tartarye," which told Peter more about his own Tsardom than he knew himself, is still one of our best authorities on eighteenth century Moscovy.  Wittsen placed at Peter's disposal a wharf in the East India Docks, where he set about building a frigate from a Dutch model, and took him to Utrecht to introduce him to William III.  The Tsar's curiosity was insatiable.  He soon tired out the most energetic and obliging of his cicerones.  He attended the surgical lectures of Professor Ruish, and was delighted with the demonstrations of Boerhave in the anatomical theatre at Leyden.  At Amsterdam he learnt the art of engraving, and engraved with his own hand an elaborate plate representing the triumph of the Christian religion over Mohammedanism, which he sent to the patriarch Adrian.  Occasionally, to the extreme consternation of his courteous entertainers, the cloven foot of the savage would emerge.  Thus, at Leyden, perceiving that his Moscovite comrades shrank back at the sight of the corpses exhibited in the anatomical theatre, he cured them once for all of such weakness by forcing them to tear the dead muscles with their teeth.

Peter spent four and a half months at Amsterdam, building his frigate, which was launched before his departure, and, in January, 1698, he went to England to learn naval construction on geometrical principles, working most of the time in the royal dockyards at Deptford, where he completed his education as a ship-builder, returning to Holland in April, only to find that his embassy had failed, as it was bound to fail, in its main object of obtaining the help of the Western Powers against the Turk.  All Europe, divided into two hostile camps, was anxiously awaiting the death of the childless and long-ailing Carlos II., and neither France nor the Grand Alliance, pitted againsther by William III., was willing to plunge into the distant Eastern war, with a war concerning the Spanish succession at their very doors.  So far, indeed, from interfering in the Turkish War, it was the earnest desire of the allies to bring about a peace between the Emperor and the Porte in order that the forces of the Empire might be employed exclusively against France.  For the same reason the prospect of the prolongation of the Russo-Turkish War was by no means disagreeable to England and Holland, as thereby the

Porte would be prevented from giving assistance to Louis XIV. Considerably depressed, Peter proceeded to Vienna. But the Emperor's ministers would give the Moscovite embassy no definite assurance of continued support, and it was obvious to Peter that Moscovy could not carry on the struggle with the Porte single-handed. He was about to go on to Venice to persuade the Signoria to cleave firmly to the fast dissolving Holy League, when he was suddenly recalled to Russia by tidings of the revolt of the stryeltsui.

We have already seen that the stryeltsui had long been dissatisfied with Peter's administration. Analysed to its ultimate elements, this dissatisfaction was the protest of indolent, incapable, and excessively privileged troops against a new system which demanded from them more work and greater efficiency. In the good old times, after sauntering somehow through as brief a campaign as procrastination could make it, the stryeltsui used to return to their wives and children at Moscow, and hang up their halberts and muskets, with the comfortable assurance that nothing more would be demanded of them till the next outbreak of hostilities. But Peter gave them no rest at all. When the fighting was over he set them to building fortresses on the Sea of Azov, and the last straw was added to their burden when he marched off four of their regiments from Azov to the distant Lithuanian frontier in view of a possible war with Poland, and sent six other regiments from Moscow to Azov to supply their places. This the stryeltsui regarded as little short of banishment, and 150 of them deserted *en route* and returned to Moscow, on the plea that their pay was in arrear. Driven out of Moscow, they rejoined their regiments at Toropets, and these regiments refused to obey a *ukaz*, subsequently issued by the boyars, demanding the surrender of the fugitives. Feeling that they had now gone too far to turn back safely, the ringleaders of the rebels proceeded to revolt the other regiments encamped on the Dwina. On June 6, 1698, a letter, supposed to have been written by the Tsarevna Sophia, urging the stryeltsui to join her in force at the Dyevichesky Monastery, was read to them, and the whole force, 2,200 strong, resolved to march against Moscow forthwith, and destroy the German settlement, as the source of the new heretical ideas, and the boyars, as the oppressors of the people in general and of the stryeltsui in particular. The Gosudar was to be killed, "because he goes with the Germans," and if Sophia refused to accept the vacant throne, it was to be offered to Prince Vasily Golitsuin "because he has always been merciful towards us."

There was great consternation at Moscow on the tidings of the approach of the stryeltsui. The wealthy families fled to the surrounding villages, and the boyars could not at first agree as to what precautionary measures should be adopted. But Boris Golitsuin put some heart into them, and, by his advice, the foreign soldiery, 4,000 strong, with twenty-five guns, under Shein, Koltsov-Masalsky, and Patrick Gordon, were sent against the rebels. On June 17 the Tsarish army came upon the stryeltsui at the ford of the river Istra near the Voskresensky Monastery. Shein, willing to avoid bloodshed, sent Gordon to them with the promise of a pardon, if they would obey orders and deliver up the fugitives ; but his rhetoric was met only with cries of " Death or Moscow." Koltsov then went to them, and to him they presented, under the modest form of a petition, what was really a fierce diatribe against the Tsar and his new counsellors. In this curious document the heretic Lefort was represented as the cause of all their hardships. Perceiving that further negotiations would only increase the insolence of the rebels, while an attack upon such a disorderly mob, without proper leaders or artillery, was certain of success, Shein gave the order to attack them. Three volleys sufficed to scatter them. In an hour's time all the rebels were in the hands of the Tsar's troops, of whom only one was mortally wounded, while the stryeltsui had lost fifteen killed and thirty-seven wounded. It was after the victory that the real carnage began. In reply to a report from Romodonovsky, Peter had ordered " the King of Pressburg " to deal very severely with the rebels, " as nothing but severity* can extinguish this fire." A strict investigation ensued. Many of the stryeltsui were done to death by torture in their own camp. Many more were

* Severity meant cruel severity. In old Moscovy, when "severe" capital punishment was pronounced against rebels, it meant breaking on the wheel or impalement.

mutilated and hanged on the roadside. The rest were imprisoned in the dungeons of the surrounding monasteries to await Peter's good pleasure. On August 26 it was reported that the Tsar had arrived the evening before, though nobody in the *kreml'*, no member even of his own family, had seen him. He had hastened to the arms of the vintner's daughter, Anna Mons, in the German settlement, and, after spending a riotous evening at Lefort's house, had slept in his little wooden hut at Preobrazenskoe. That very night, full of the fury of an ardent revolutionary against irreconcilable obstructionists whom fortune has delivered into his hands, he had determined to drown all contradiction in torrents of blood. The new era of enlightenment was to be inaugurated by a reign of terror.

Peter was well aware that behind the stryeltsui stood the sympathising mass of the Moscovite people, whom it was his mission to reform against their will. His foreign tour had more than ever convinced him of the inherent superiority of the foreigner, and, this superiority once admitted, imitation of the foreigner was, to his mind, inevitable. Any such imitation had necessarily to begin with externals, and Peter, with characteristic insight and thoroughness, at once fell foul of the long beards and oriental costumes which symbolised the arch-conservatism of old Russia. Other enlightened princes had already anticipated him. Tsar Boris had introduced the shaven poll, which was fashionable at the Polish Court. Peter's own brother, Theodore III., had ordered his *blizhnie boyare* to discard the *okhaben*\* and the *odnoryadka*,† while Theodore's first consort, Agatha, had declared war against the long beard. But all these more or less tentative efforts had foundered against the tyranny of ancient custom, and the strong opposition of the clergy. Avvakum had refused to bless the son of the boyar Sheremetev, because he presented himself in an indecent guise, in other words with a shorn head. Beardless officials had small chance of promotion. More than one patriarch had excommunicated those members of their flock who shaved. Such offenders were offered the choice between

---

\* A long upper garment with slits under the sleeves, and a four-cornered turn-up collar.

† A garment similar to the *okhaben*, but without the collar.

standing at the Judgment Day among the just with shining silvery beards, or among the heretics shaven into the semblance of cats and dogs.    Against this curious superstition Peter struck with all his might the day after his return to Moscow.    On August 26, 1698, the chief men of the Tsardom were assembled round his wooden hut at Preobrazenskoe, and Peter, emerging with a large pair of shears in his hand, deliberately clipped off the beards and moustaches of his boyars, beginning with Generalissimo Shein, and " his Majesty the King of Pressburg," Prince Yury Romodanovsky.    Only a few of the most venerable of the elders, like Prince Mikhail Cherkasky, and the Tsar's uncle, Tikhon Stryeshnev, were spared the indignity.    After thus vindicating the claims of common sense, Peter prudently consented to a compromise.    He decreed that after September 1,* 1698, beards might be worn, but a graduated tax was imposed upon their wearers.    Thus the beard ceased to be an object of worship in Moscovy ; but, at the same time, the people were not provoked too far, and a new source of revenue flowed into the treasury.

And now, without giving the reactionaries time to recover from this rude shock, the Tsar proceeded to horrify them by a strange and awful Bacchanalia, the like of which had never been known in Moscovy, even in the days of Ivan the Severe.† From the middle of September to the end of October, 1698, banquets and drinking bouts alternated with torturings and executions, in which the Tsar and his favourites played the parts of inquisitors and headsmen.‡ During those two months no fewer than a thousand of the captive stryeltsui were done to death with every refinement of cruelty.    The horrified patriarch, attended by his clergy, with the miraculous ikon of the Mother of God borne before him, appeared at Preobrazenskoe, to intercede for the sufferers.    Drunk as much with blood as with wine, Peter turned furiously upon him.    "Take that ikon to its proper place," he yelled.    "What is it doing here ? Perhaps I do greater honour than you do to God and His Most Holy Mother, by defending

---

* The old Russian New Year's Day.

† This, not "terrible," is the true translation of the word *grozny*, as applied to Ivan IV.        ‡ For details, see Koerb: "Diarium," a sickening record.

my people against evil-doers. Take it away, I say!" The
hideous tragedy reached its culmination on October 17, when
the Tsar, surveying the scene on horseback, compelled his
favourites and ministers to decapitate a number of the already
mangled wretches. Boris Golitsuin's tremulous hand bungling
over a single victim, he flung down his sword in disgust amidst
the curses and reproaches of his master. But the grim Romodanovsky decapitated five stryeltsui with the skill of a professional artist, while the Tsar's new favourite, "little Alec,"
gleefully disposed of no fewer than fifteen. Lefort and the
other foreign officers were also invited to try their hands at the
bloody work, but they excused themselves, on the plea that it
was not the custom of their countries for colonels to act as
provost-marshals. The ringleaders of the rebellion naturally
fared worst of all. Their arms and legs were first broken on
wheels at Preobrazenskoe. They were then conveyed in carts to
the Red Square at Moscow, where their backs were broken in the
same way, and they were left to die, some of them languishing
for twenty-four hours, unless shot, as an act of mercy, by Peter's
special command. The corpses were left on the place of execution for five months afterwards.

And now Peter seized his opportunity of breaking definitely
with the past. He began by removing from his path the last
remnants of "the seed of the Miloslavskies," his oldest and most
dangerous enemies, because they were of his own household.
The death of his half-brother, Ivan V., in 1696, had left him sole
Tsar, but Sophia, even in her monastery, had been a possible
source of danger. He determined she should be a danger no
longer. An intention, on Peter's part, to implicate her in the
conspiracy, is transparent from the first; but the utmost that the
most prolonged and exquisite torments could wring out of the
wretched stryeltsui was the admission that Sophia had sympathised with the movement, and would have helped it if she could.
The letter supposed to have been sent by her to the stryeltsui
turned out to have been written by her elder sister, Martha.
Both the Tsarevnas were shorn as nuns, and imprisoned for life
in nunneries under military supervision. Moreover, a score or so
of the stryeltsui were hanged in front of the window of Sophia's

cell, and allowed to remain there long after they had rotted on their gibbets.*

Peter's unhappy wife had been sent to a nunnery even before his half-sisters. This was, perhaps, his most cruel act of tyranny. Eudoxia was guilty of no offence; she had nothing to do with the rebellion; but Peter, profiting by the general consternation and imbecility of the reactionaries, gladly shook off an incumbrance whose very presence was a nuisance and a reproach to him. Long-suffering as she was, Eudoxia naturally resented the open and flagrant desertion of her husband, and hated the coarse and vulgar counter-attraction of the German settlement with all her heart. As he had married her in an orthodox way, Peter could only rid himself of her by the usual orthodox expedient of the cloister. At first, while still in London, he attempted to persuade Eudoxia voluntarily to embrace the religious life, but the gentle creature proving unexpectedly obstinate, she was on his return unceremoniously dispatched to the Pokrovsky Nunnery at Suzdal (September 23, 1698). So convinced were the ecclesiastical authorities of the uncanonicity of the whole proceeding that for nine months they hesitated to shear the Tsaritsa. Then Peter terrified them into compliance. The patriarch bowed before the first gust of fury, and a prolonged midnight interview with the terrible Romodanovsky in the torture-chamber at Preobrazenskoe convinced the most resolute of Eudoxia's friends among the clergy that the Tsar was in the right of it. In June, 1699, the Tsaritsa Eudoxia disappeared from the world under the hood of Sister Elena. Her son, the little Tsarevich Alexius, now in his eighth year, was confided to the care of Peter's sister, the Tsarevna Natalia, popularly supposed to be the worst enemy of his unfortunate mother.

The terrible events of September and October, 1698, were not without an injurious effect on Peter himself. The agitation caused thereby kept his excitable nature in a perpetual ferment, and more than once his nervous irritation exploded in tempests of frantic passion. Thus, at a banquet at Lefort's, on September 14, a dispute with General Shein about some trivial question of

* Henceforth Sophia was known as Sister Susannah. She gave no more trouble, and died in 1704.

military expenditure caused the Tsar to lose all control over himself. He rose from table, drew his sword, fell furiously upon Shein, Romodanovsky, Zotov, and Lefort, and would have murdered them all on the spot but for the soothing influence of his new favourite, Alexander Danilovich Menshikov. This extraordinary man, whom Peter literally plucked from the gutter to set among princes, was of so obscure an origin that it is doubtful whether his father was an ostler or a bargee. He first emerges into the light of history at twenty years of age, when we find him gaining his livelihood as a vendor of meat-pies in the streets of Moscow. The handsome looks and smart sallies of the young itinerant pie-man attracted the attention of Lefort, who took him into his service, and finally transferred him to Peter, who first saw him at Lefort's house, and took a great fancy to him. Young Menshikov now made himself indispensable, and on the death of Lefort in 1699 at once succeeded him as prime favourite, a position which, though frequently threatened, he contrived to hold to the end. Ignorant,* brutal, grasping, and corrupt as Menshikov was, he nevertheless deserved the confidence of his master. It is not too much to say that, after Peter, there was not a more alert, lucid, unprejudiced and versatile intellect than Menshikov's in all Moscovy, while his energy was boundless and inexhaustible. He could turn his hand to anything at a moment's notice. He could drill a regiment, build a frigate, administer a province, and decapitate a rebel with equal facility. During the Tsar's first foreign tour Menshikov worked by his side in the dockyard of Amsterdam, visited all the Dutch factories and workshops, and, at the same time, acquired a thorough knowledge of colloquial Dutch and German. Like Peter, Menshikov was a man of vehement passions, scarce restrainable except by the fist and stick of his master, from both of which he suffered frequently and terribly.† But in this respect he was no more fortunate than Lefort, whom Peter frequently knocked down and trampled upon. The employment of such expedients demonstrated, of course, the moral weakness of the society in which they were necessary.

* He could write his own name with difficulty, but could not read, though he often imposed on the foreign Ministers by pretending to do so.

† On one occasion Peter battered him about the face till he was covered with blood.

But we must bear in mind that eighteenth century Moscovy was a period of upheaval, and in all such periods, natural forces, too long repressed, burst forth with a volcanic violence which threatens to burst every barrier, so that every counteracting force, to be effective, must needs be despotic; the fiercer the licence, the more cruel the repression. Moreover, in Moscovy the contrast between old and new was the more glaring because the nation was forced to swallow in a generation what it could not properly assimilate for centuries. Anomalies abound everywhere. Besotted evangelists, barbarous regenerators, felonious administrators, meet us at every step. And the worst offenders were Peter's own fledglings. Their misdoings hampered him at every onward step. For instance, this very year the Tsar was at Voronezh impatiently awaiting the arrival of young Sklyaev from abroad, whither he had been sent to learn shipbuilding. Sklyaev was most capable, his help was indispensable, he had urgent orders to hasten to Voronezh, and still he delayed. Inquiries were made, and it was at last discovered that Sklyaev and his companion, Vereshchagin, after getting mad drunk in the pothouses of the suburbs of Moscow, had been flogged and imprisoned for a savage assault on some soldiers of the Preobrazenskoe regiment. It is not surprising if Peter sometimes wondered whether he had not undertaken a task beyond his strength, when he compared things at home with what they were abroad. Two days after the first punishment of the stryeltsui, he wrote to Vinius: " The shadow of a doubt crosses my mind. What if the fruit of my labour be delayed like the fruit of the date-palm, the sower whereof sees it not." Evidently the disquieting suspicion that the work of regeneration would remain undone unless he did it himself, spurred him on to fresh efforts. The remaining stryeltsui, some hundreds in number, were executed in January, 1699, and the same year several reforms were inaugurated. To save the people from the gross and notorious exactions of the *voevodui,** or governors, and, at the same time, to accustom them to self-government, burgomasters and town councils, on the Western model, were now introduced. But here, again, the inherent corruption of Moscovite officialdom

* See Chapter I.

at once asserted itself. The *starostas*, or elders, whose duty it was to see that "good and worthy men" were chosen, systematically excluded from voting those of the electors who refused to pay for the privilege. Peter attempted to extirpate these corrupt practices by flogging and banishment, and, to prevent their recurrence, appointed a new order of officials, the *pribuilshchiki*, whose duty it was to provide for the purity of public life and look after the interests of the Government. The first of these *pribuilshchiki* was Aleksyei Aleksandrovich Kurbatov, who had studied commercial and financial questions abroad in the suite of the boyar Boris Sheremetev, and was an intelligent man of many expedients. Shortly after his appointment he suggested to Peter a new source of revenue, by introducing stamped paper into Moscovy. Peter was so pleased with the idea that he straightway appointed Kurbatov his confidential adviser. At the same time Peter carried into effect Orduin Nashchokin's scheme of establishing trading companies in Moscovy for the better protection of the poorer class of merchants and tradesmen against foreign competition.

The last year of the seventeenth century saw another notable reform which drew a sharp line of demarcation between old and new. By the *ukas* of December 20, 1699, it was commanded that henceforth the new year should not be reckoned from September 1, supposed to be the date of the creation, as heretofore, but from the first of January, *Anno Domini.*

## CHAPTER IX.

### THE GREAT NORTHERN WAR FROM THE SECRET TREATY OF PREOBRAZHENSKOE TO THE BATTLE OF POLTAVA. 1700—1709.

The Rawa Conference—Theodore Golovin—Negotiations with the Porte—Truce of Constantinople—Patkul—The League against Sweden—Duplicity of Peter—Secret Treaty of Preobrazhenskoe—Battle of Narva—Charles's Polish Expedition Justifiable — Conference of Birse—The War in the Baltic Provinces, 1701/3 — Foundation of Petersburg — Capture of Dorpat and Narva—Anarchy in Poland—Charles XII. deposes Augustus—Alliance between Poland and Russia—Contempt for Russia on the Continent—Reports of the Russian Ambassadors from Vienna, The Hague, Paris and Stambul—Peter Tolstoi—The Campaigns of 1704, 1705, and 1706—Peace of Altranstadt — Execution of Patkul—Peter's New Ministers, Apraksin, Golovkin and Shafirov—Failure of Peter's Diplomatic Efforts to pacify Charles XII.—The Revolt of the Bashkirs and the Rebellion of Bulavin—Advance of Charles XII. to the Russian Frontier—Battle of Holowczyn—Charles marches Southwards to Unite with Mazepa—Causes of Mazepa's Treason—His Collapse—The Great Frost of 1708—Terrible Sufferings of the Swedes—The March to Poltava—Peter Subdues the Zaporozhians on the Dnieper—Battle of Poltava.

THE year 1700 is memorable as the starting-point of two momentous wars which were to change the whole face of the Continent of Europe—the War of the Spanish Succession in the West, and the Great Northern War in the East. The first of these wars was to substitute the predominance of Great Britain for the predominance of France, the second was to destroy the military empire of Sweden, and introduce a new great Power into the European concert. That new great Power was Russia.

Peter brought home with him in 1698 the conviction that he must conclude peace with the Porte. This conviction was accompanied by the melancholy reflection that such a peace would mean the relinquishment of the Black Sea, and the hope of a Russian navy along with it. But if the Black Sea were abandoned, why should he not compensate himself on the shores of the Baltic? The Baltic was nearer both to Russia and to Western Europe than the Euxine, and consequently a much more desirable possession. On the other hand, if it were impossible to continue the Turkish War without allies, allies were still more indispensable in a war with Sweden, the great Power from which the Baltic littoral was to be wrested. With these ideas already germinating in his mind, Peter on his homeward journey in 1698 encountered the lately elected King of Poland, August II., at the little town of Rawa. The inexperienced young Tsar was enchanted by the worldly wisdom and exuberant jollity of this facile and indulgent potentate, who gave him a handsome dress suit and a fine sword. Peter returned home wearing them both, and full of the praises of his incomparable friend. The Baltic question seems to have been discussed over their wine cups, and Peter was delighted to find that Augustus was willing enough to meet his ambitions half-way. Charles XI. of Sweden, whose creative genius had enabled Sweden to re-ascend to the rank of a great Power, had died the year before, and the Swedish Government was now in the hands of his son, an untried lad of sixteen. If the Baltic provinces were to be stolen at all, now was the time to steal them. But no definite agreement was come to on this occasion.* Augustus had not yet matured his plans, and Peter could not embark on a new war till he had terminated the old one.

On returning to Moscow the Tsar at once set about concluding peace with the Porte. It was his good fortune at this period to possess a foreign minister of the highest ability in Theodore Aleksyevich Golovin, whose superiority over all his contemporaries was due to the fact that he was already a statesman in the modern sense while they were still learning the elements of statesmanship. Golovin, like so many others of his countrymen in later times, learnt the business of a ruler in the Far East. During the regency of Sophia he had been sent to the Amur to defend the new Moscovite fortress of Albazin against the Chinese. In 1689 he concluded with the Celestial Empire the Treaty of Nerchinsk, by which the line of the Amur, as far as

* Solovev : " Istoria Rossy," vol. XIV., chap. 4.

its tributary the Gorbitsa, was retroceded to China because of the impossibility of seriously defending it.   In the grand embassy to the West in 1697 Golovin occupied the second place immediately after Lefort.   It was his chief duty to hire foreign sailors and artificers and obtain everything necessary for the construction and complete equipment of a fleet.   On Lefort's death in March, 1699, he succeeded him as Admiral-General.   The same year he was created the first Russian Count, and was also the first to be decorated with the newly-instituted Russian order of St. Andrew. The conduct of foreign affairs was, at the same time, entrusted to him, and from 1699 to his death in 1706, he was, in fact, what foreigners, from ignorance or courtesy, entitled him, "the premier minister of the Tsar."

Golovin's first diplomatic achievement was the conclusion of peace with the Porte.   The Turks, worsted by the Imperial troops in Hungary and on the Danube, were themselves anxious to come to terms with Moscovy.   A preliminary truce for two years was concluded in 1698, and in April, 1699, two Moscovite plenipotentiaries, Emelyan Ukraintsev and the *dumny dyak* Cheredeev, were sent to Stambul to convert the truce into a definitive peace.   Everything was done both to mollify and to impress the Turk.   The ambassadors were provided with 5,000 rubles worth of precious furs, and ten poods of walrus ivory for bribing purposes, and they were not to go by land, as usual, but by sea.   A man-of-war, commanded by a Dutch captain, awaited them at the new arsenal of Taganrog, and they were escorted into the Sea of Azov by a fleet of nine warships and two galleys, among which was the *Apostle Peter*, flying the flag of Skipper Peter Alekseyevich.   The Pasha of Kerch, much disturbed, wanted to know the meaning of this "vast sea-caravan," and a *ciaus* from Stambul attempted to turn back the ambassadors from their enterprise by representing that at that time of year the Black Sea was not called "black" in vain.   But Ukraintsev piously declared that he put his trust in God, and meant to obey the orders of the Gosudar.   On August 28 a Russian line-of-battle ship sailed for the first time into the Golden Horn, fired a salute, and cast anchor at the very gates of the Seraglio.   All the members of the foreign legations went forth to see the by no

R.                                                                              R

means welcome novelty, and they were followed first by the
Grand Vizier, and then by the Padishah himself. The negotiations were opened in November. The Russian plenipotentiaries
demanded peace on a *uti possidetis* basis, with cessation of the
tribute hitherto paid to the Khan of the Crimea, and absolute free
trade between the two Powers; and at the eleventh conference
(February 24, 1700) they agreed to demolish the newly-con-
structed Azovian border fortresses. The Turks were willing at
first to accept these terms, but that unhappy jealousy which
animated the Western Powers against Russia from the first
moment when her ships appeared in Turkish waters, and which
has ever since been the principal impediment to the solution of
the Eastern question, now arrayed against her all the Western
diplomatists at Galatz. Great Britain and Holland feared the
commercial competition of Russia in the Euxine and the
Levant, while France dreaded her political influence, and thus it
came about that the Divan, secretly encouraged by the foreign
ministers, grew more and more exacting and peremptory. Not
till July, 1700, was a truce for thirty years concluded between
Russia and the Porte. By the terms of this truce the Azov
district and all the land extending from thence to the Kuban
district for a ten hours' journey were ceded to Moscovy, who
undertook on her part to demolish Kazinkerman and other
extra-Azovian forts. The tribute to the Khan was waived. The
Porte further promised to lay waste the whole district between
the Zaporozhian Syech on the Dnieper, and the fortress of
Ochakov, so that the two realms might not be conterminous.
On August 8 Peter heard from Ukraintsev that peace had been
concluded. On the following day his army received orders to
invade Livonia. The Great Northern War had begun.

The person primarily responsible for this terrible conflagration,
which devastated half Europe for a whole generation, was a
Livonian squire, Johan Reinhold Patkul by name. Patkul was
born in 1660 in a dungeon at Stockholm, whither his mother
had accompanied his father, who lay there under suspicion of
treason. He entered the Swedish army at an early age, and was
already a captain, when, in 1689, at the head of a deputation of
Livonian gentry, he went to Stockholm to protest against the

rigour with which the land-recovery project of Charles XI. was
being carried out in his native province. His eloquence favourably impressed Charles XI. ; but his representations were
disregarded, and the violent and offensive language with which,
in another petition, addressed to the King three years later, he
renewed his complaints, involved him in what is known in
Swedish history as "the great Livonian process." To save
himself from the penalties of high treason, Patkul fled from
Stockholm to Switzerland, and was condemned *in contumaciam*
to lose his right hand and his head. His estates were, at the
same time, confiscated. For the next four years he led a
vagabond life, but in 1698, after vainly petitioning the new
King, Charles XII., for pardon, he entered the service of
Augustus II.

There can be no doubt that Patkul was harshly treated by
Charles XI. Ruin and banishment are excessive punishments
even for the most extreme freedom of speech. Moreover he could
not return to Livonia so long as that province belonged to the
crown of Sweden, and naturally enough he had no desire to live
in exile all his life. But we must be very cautious in speaking
about the patriotism of Patkul. Patkul acted exclusively from
personal motives. His point of view was that of the German
Junker. He had no thought for the liberties of the Livonian
people. To an aristocrat like him they were mere serfs. Nor
did he care much to whom Livonia belonged so long as it did
not belong to Sweden. But he had his political preferences.
The noble Republic of Poland was obviously the most convenient
suzerain for Livonian noblemen, and the present King of Poland
as being a German was equally acceptable to them. Accordingly,
in 1698, Patkul went to Dresden and bombarded Augustus with
proposals for the partition of Sweden. His first plan was a
combination against her of Saxony, Denmark, and Brandenburg,
but Brandenburg failing him, he was obliged to admit Russia
into the scheme instead. This he did very unwillingly, shrewdly
anticipating that the Tsar might prove to be the predominant
partner. "We must keep an eye on Russia," he said, "lest she
snatch the roast from our spit beneath our very noses." The
Tsar was to be content with Ingria and Esthonia, while Augustus

was to take Livonia nominally as a fief of Poland, but really as an hereditary possession of the Saxon house. Military operations against Sweden's Baltic provinces were to be begun simultaneously by the Saxons and the Russians. As to the latter, Patkul insisted that "they were not to practise their usual barbarities," a stipulation significant of the low opinion entertained of the Moscovite soldiery in the seventeenth century. Denmark, which had a real grievance against Sweden as the protector of the intrusive Dukes of Holstein-Gottorp, was to draw off Sweden's forces to her western provinces, while Peter and Augustus attacked her in the east. This nefarious conspiracy was carried out with the utmost secrecy and despatch. The allies, as Patkul said, were not to let their left hands know what their right hands were doing, and they certainly succeeded in hoodwinking the unsuspicious Swedes completely. As early as August 24, 1699, a convention between Denmark—Norway, and Russia had knit the first link in the chain of treaties which was to unite Sweden's three hostile neighbours against her. This convention was originally a league for mutual defence, but one of the earliest measures of the new King of Denmark, Frederick IV., was to conclude an offensive alliance with Augustus II. against Sweden (September 25, 1699). This treaty was, however, only to be binding if the Tsar acceded to it within three or four months.*

Patkul, accompanied by the Saxon general Karlowicz, arrived at Moscow in September, 1699. They found they had been preceded by a Swedish embassy sent by Charles XII. to confirm the Peace of Kardis. Peter on this occasion went far to justify the accusation of inveterate duplicity so often brought against him subsequently. The temptation to secure the Baltic seaboard with all its commercial and civilising possibilities was too strong for his easy morality, and he now showed that he possessed the low cunning as well as the wild fury of the semi-savage in an eminent degree. He assured the Swedish envoys that he would faithfully observe all his treaty obligations (though he was sufficiently superstitious to avoid kissing the cross on the renewal

* Compare "Danmarks Riges Historie," vol. V., p. 10; "Sveriges Historia," vol. IV., pp. 536—538; Solovev: "Istoria Rossy," vol. XIV., chap. 4.

of the old treaty made with Charles XI.), yet at a secret conference, held at Preobrazhenskoe, with the Saxon and Danish
envoys, he had already signed (November 11, 1699) a secret
treaty for the partition of Sweden.    By the Treaty of Preobrazhenskoe the Tsar undertook to invade the Swedish province or
Ingria as soon as he received confirmation of the peace with the
Porte.    Meanwhile Augustus, who had no cause of quarrel
whatever with Sweden, and was profuse in his expressions of
friendship to Charles XII., was to fall suddenly upon Livonia.
Everything was done by Peter to allay the growing suspicions
of the Swedish minister, Knipercrona.    When questioned point
blank as to the designs of Augustus, Peter professed incredulity
and indignation.    "If the King of Poland dares to take Riga,"
he said, "I'll take it away from him myself."    But it was
impossible to keep up the mystification for ever.    In the beginning of May the troops of Augustus, repulsed from Riga in
February, were defeated at Jungfernhof, and driven over the
Dwina ; the Livonian gentry showed not the slightest disposition to rise in arms at the appeal of Patkul ; and the discomfited
Elector of Saxony, already in difficulties, urged the Tsar to
fulfil his part of the compact by invading Ingria.    "If I hear
to-day of the conclusion of peace with the Turk," replied Peter,
"I will go against the Swedes to-morrow."    As we have seen,
he was as good as his word.    The arrival of Ukraintsev's
despatch from Stambul was the signal for the Moscovite forces
to cross the Swedish frontier.

Peter's objective was the fortress of Narva, the key of the
province of Ingria, at the mouth of the river Narova.    The
army, about 40,000 strong, which Peter sent against it, consisted,
with the exception of the Preobrazhenskoe and Semenovskoe regiments of the Guard, of three divisions of raw troops, levied so
late as November, 1699, the dispersion of the stryeltsui having
left Moscovy without any regular infantry.    Theodore Golovin,
now a field-marshal as well as a prime minister, commanded in
chief, Peter occupying, as usual, a subordinate position.    Narva
was reached by September 23, but the siege artillery, delayed by
the vile roads, could not open fire until the middle of October,
and the commandant Henning Rudolf Horn rejected every

summons to surrender.   In the middle of November the Russian
camp was astounded by the intelligence that the young King of
Sweden, who was supposed to be fighting desperately in Denmark, was approaching at the head of an innumerable army.   At
a hastily summoned council of war, Peter. without the slightest
hesitation, resolved to leave his useless army to its fate.   "Un-
reflecting courage, the tendency to expose himself to fruitless
danger, was completely foreign to his character. . . .   He was
the last man in the world to be influenced by any sentiment of
false shame."*   He knew that his wretched recruits could not
be pitted against veteran soldiers, indeed, it is highly probable
that he would never have brought them to Narva at all had he
conceived the appearance there of Charles XII. to be even a
remote possibility.   He could not help them if he stayed with
them, while any mishap to himself would inevitably bring about
the collapse of Russia, the new Russia which he was so painfully
uprearing.   His conduct on this unique occasion will be regarded
as prudent precaution or shameful cowardice, according to the
point of view.   Anyhow, he fled away to Novgorod, taking with
him Golovin, whom he also could not afford to lose, and leaving
his demoralised army in the charge of a mysterious adventurer of
presumably Hungarian origin, calling himself Prince Carl Eugene
de Croy, or de Croie, who had had some military experience in
the Austrian and Danish services.   The result was a foregone
conclusion.   On November 20 Charles XII. and his little army
of 8,000 veterans attacked the Russians behind their entrenchments in the midst of a snowstorm at two o'clock in the
afternoon.   In an hour the Moscovite left wing was scattered,
while their cavalry, under Sheremetev, which might easily have
turned the Swedish flank, fled in panic terror without waiting to
be attacked.   Only on the right wing did the Guards defend
themselves obstinately behind their waggons till the end of the
short winter's day.   The unfortunate De Croy, exclaiming, " The
devil himself could not fight with such soldiers," surrendered to
the Swedes to prevent himself from being murdered by his own
troops, and most of the foreign officers followed his example.
     The very ease of his victory was injurious to Charles XII.   His

     * Solovev.  This is not irony, but a justification.

best counsellors now urged him to turn all his forces against the terrified fugitives; establish his winter quarters in Moscovy; live upon the country till the spring, and then take advantage of the popular discontent against Peter to make him harmless for the future. But Charles declared that he would postpone the settlement of the Russian quarrel till he had summarily chastised Augustus. "There was no glory in winning victories over the Moscovites," he said, "they could be beaten at any time."

It is easy from the vantage-point of two centuries to criticise Charles XII. for neglecting the Moscovites to pursue the Saxons; but at the beginning of the eighteenth century his decision was apparently correct. The question was, which of the two foes was the more dangerous, and Charles had every reason to think the civilised and martial Saxons far more formidable than the imbecile Moscovites. He was also justified in hating Augustus more than his other enemies. The hostility of Denmark on account of Gottorp was perfectly intelligible. Equally intelligible was the hostility of Moscovy. How could Moscovy be anything but hostile so long as Sweden held old Moscovite territory and barred her from the sea? There was no excuse at all for the Elector of Saxony. Yet he had been the first to listen to Patkul; he had been the prime mover in the league of partition; he had deceived Sweden to the very last moment with lying assurances of amity. Charles could never trust Augustus to remain quiet even if he made peace with him. From this point of view Charles's whole Polish policy, which has been blamed so long and so loudly, the policy of placing a nominee of his own on the Polish throne in lieu of Augustus, takes quite another complexion: it was a policy not of overreaching ambition, but of prudential self-defence.

Nevertheless it saved Peter, who promptly took advantage of the departure of his great rival. He had cut a sorry figure enough at Narva; it is after Narva that his tenacity and resourcefulness once more extort our admiration. He himself summed up the situation in these words. " Necessity now drove away sloth and forced us to labour and devise night and day." Adversity always seemed to stimulate rather than depress him. He at once formed the nucleus of a new army out of the 23,000 fugitives who had escaped from Narva, and they were speedily reinforced by ten freshly recruited dragoon regiments of 1,000 men each. An *ukas* directed all the towns and monasteries in the Tsardom to send him their bells to be cast into cannon to supply the place of the artillery lost at Narva, and in less than twelve months afterwards, Vinius had converted them into 300 guns at a cost of 10,000 rubles. But Peter's chief anxiety was that Augustus should keep Charles occupied. He also endeavoured to draw the Polish Republic into the anti-Swedish league. In this he was unsuccessful, as the bitter recollection of the loss of Kiev was still too recent at Warsaw; but at a conference with Augustus at Birse in Samogetia, at which Patkul also was present, it was resolved that neither of the two allies should make a separate peace with Sweden. Peter further undertook to supply Augustus with 20,000 fresh troops, and 100,000 pounds of powder, and pay him 100,000 rubles annually for three years, a sum he was only able to raise by forced loans from the great monasteries and the rich merchants.

The troops which Charles XII. left behind him to defend Finland and the Baltic provinces, in the field amounted to only 15,000 men. Under the most favourable circumstances such inadequate forces could not seriously hope to defend against a tenfold odds a frontier extending from Lake Ladoga to Lake Peipus, from Lake Peipus to the Dwina, and from the Dwina to the Gulf of Riga, and unfortunately the circumstances were unusually unfavourable. Charles not only took his best men and his best officers away with him to Poland, but forbade the Swedish senate to send any reinforcements to the Baltic provinces so long as the more important Polish War was proceeding. Peter he regarded as a negligible quantity, who could easily be kept in check by a few scratch corps led by second-rate officers, till Augustus had been settled with. It was a terrible miscalculation, the fatal results of which were speedily apparent.

With Pskov as their starting-point, the Muscovites during 1701 and 1702 made frequent incursions into Ingria and Livonia. On December 29, 1701, the Swedish general Schlippenbach was overwhelmed by Sheremetev's superior forces at Errestfer, losing 3,000 killed and wounded and 350 prisoners. Peter was in ecstasies, "Narva is avenged," he cried. Bells were rung and salvoes were fired all day long at Moscow in honour of the first Russian victory over the Swedes ; the captured standards were solemnly exhibited in the *kreml*, and Sheremetev received his marshal's bâton, the order of St. Andrew, and the Tsar's portrait set in brilliants.   Urged on incessantly by Peter, the new field-marshal attacked Schlippenbach a second time, in July, 1702, at Hummelshof, and inflicted a still more terrible defeat upon him, the Swedes losing 5,500 men, or more than half their effective forces.* To intimidate the enemy still further and prevent him from drawing upon the country for supplies, Sheremetev, by the express command of Peter, now proceeded deliberately and methodically to reduce to a wilderness as much of Livonia as he could reach with his Cossacks and Calmucks.   The despatch in which he announced the accomplishment of his horrible commission is characteristic enough of the eighteenth century Muscovite. "I have to report," wrote Sheremetev, "that Almighty God and the Most Holy Virgin have fulfilled your Majesty's wishes.   It is impossible to ravage the land any more, the whole of it, without exception, has been wasted and destroyed.   Pernau and Reval alone remain whole.   Everything between them and from them round by the sea to Riga has been utterly obliterated."†

During the summer of 1702 Peter himself was at Archangel to defend the place against a rumoured descent of the enemy. In September he appeared at Ladoga to superintend the conquest of Ingria.   After obtaining the command of the lake with his galley fleet, he began the siege of the little fortress of Nöteberg, situated on the Neva at its junction with Ladoga.   The garrison numbered only 410 men, and Peter brought 10,000 against it, but the defence was stubborn, the final assault lasting from four in the morning till four in the afternoon.   "Truly a most evil nest," wrote Peter to Vinius, " but thank God, we have smashed it at last."   He called the place Schlüsselburg, instead of Oryeshek,‡ its old Slavonic name.

---

* Sheremetev had 30,000, Schlippenbach 8,000 men.

† Sheremetev's despatch cited by Solovev : "Istoria Rossy," XIV., 4.   Charles XII.'s commands to his generals in Poland were equally brutal, but while the humane Swedish generals frequently minimised their instructions, the Moscovite generals habitually exceeded theirs.

‡ "Little nut."   From the earliest times it had been a very hard nut to crack.

Early in the following spring, the Moscovites, under Sheremetev, proceeding from Schlüsselburg along the Neva to the
sea, captured Nyen, or Nyenskans,* another small fortress on
the Gulf of Finland at the mouth of the Neva (May 1, 1703).
Four days later, two Swedish vessels, unsuspectingly sailing up
the Neva, were captured by the Moscovite flotilla led by Captain
Peter Mikhailov and Lieutenant Menshikov.    And now the
woodman's axe was busy among the virgin forests in the
marshes of the Neva, and a little wooden village began to rise
up on the northern shore of the river.   This little village was
called Petersburg.   To-day it is the capital of the vast Russian
empire.   For the defence of the town on the seaside, the
fortress of Kronslot, subsequently called Kronstadt, was built
on the adjacent island of Retusaari, from plans drawn by Peter
himself.   A harbour large enough to hold the rapidly-increasing
Russian fleet, which Peter was already constructing on the river
Suiva, was also begun at Kronslot, and all the feeble and
ill-directed attempts of the Swedes during the next few years
to interrupt the work came to nothing.   Presently, to the great
joy of the Tsar, foreign merchantmen came to trade with the
new port.   The first of such vessels was boarded by Menshikov,
as Governor of Petersburg, who gave the skipper a present of
500 ducats, and each of the sailors 30 thalers.

In the spring of 1704 the Moscovites, after reducing all the
open towns of Ingria to cinder-heaps, sat down before the two
great fortresses of Dorpat and Narva.   Sheremetev with 20,000
men began the siege of the former place in the beginning of
June, and it surrendered on July 13.   Narva was besieged by
the Scotch general Ogilvie, whom Patkul had picked up at
Vienna and enlisted in Peter's service for three years.   On
August 9 the fortress was taken by assault, and a frightful
massacre ensued, in which not even the women and children
were spared.   Peter arrived with Ogilvie two hours after the
place had fallen, and stopped the carnage by cutting down half
a dozen of the plunderers with his own hand.   "Fear not," he
said to the people of Narva, who fled at the sight of his dripping
sword, "this is not Swedish, but Russian blood."

* It was renamed Slottburg.

Peter would now have made peace with Sweden if he had been allowed to retain Petersburg. He was in possession of all that he wanted, for, as yet, he had no intention of conquering Livonia, which was to have been Augustus's share of the spoil. But he required time to consolidate his position in the Baltic provinces, and for this purpose it was necessary to keep Charles "sticking in the Polish bog" a little longer, by actively assisting Augustus, who was again in difficulties. Moreover, a Western campaign would complete the discipline of the Russian soldiers, who were already beginning to develop superior martial qualities.

The condition of Poland was at this time deplorable. All her ancient valour and chivalry seemed to have descended into the grave with Sobieski. and she had become the natural prey of rebels and traitors. The cardinal-primate Radziejowski had been bought by the Swedes, and was openly intriguing against Augustus, whom Charles had determined to depose. Lithuania was lit up by the flames of a civil war between the Sapiehas and the Oginskis, the former of whom had placed themselves under Swedish protection. In the Polish Ukrain the attempt of the Pans to depose the Cossack Hetman had led to a fearful *iacquerie*, recalling the worst outrages of Bogdan Chmielnicki. The Moscovite ambassador at Warsaw, Prince Michael Dolgoruki, reported that the whole republic was going to wrack and ruin; that the Polish senators only regarded their personal interests, and lived like brutes; that the Saxon and Polish soldiers were losing heart because their commanders always ran away; and that Augustus squandered upon his mistresses and his opera-singers the money that ought to have gone into the pockets of his ill-fed and worse-clothed soldiers, who had not been paid for years.[*] Patkul himself at last recognised the unprofitableness of serving such a master as Augustus, and in 1702 he proceeded to Moscow and entered the Russian service. Peter was naturally glad to get a man so famous for his talents and energy, but Patkul speedily belied his reputation, indeed he never realised the expectations of his friends. His knowledge was too limited and local. He understood individuals, but he had none of the larger knowledge of nations and their history which goes to the making

---

[*] Dolgoruki's despatches cited by Solovev: "Istoria Rossy," XV., 1.

of a statesman. Then, too, he was impatient, obstinate and intractable, with a very high opinion of himself, and no opinion at all of anyone else. Thus his inexhaustible industry produced no permanent results, and he was never anything more than a wandering star in the political firmament.

Meanwhile in Poland events were occurring which would have been impossible anywhere else. At the Diet held at Lublin in June, 1703, the cardinal-primate was openly convicted of bringing in the Swedes. Having no defence, he played upon Polish sentimentality, and going down upon his knees in full senate before the King, swore on the Holy Cross that he would be faithful to the republic in future, whereupon the convicted traitor was actually reinstated in his position as the second highest dignitary in the state. The Diet was no sooner over than he joined Charles, who, at the end of the same year, commanded the Poles to elect James Sobieski King in lieu of Augustus. Great Britain, Holland, and Austria protested vehemently against such a high-handed interference in the internal affairs of a neutral state. The British minister Robinson even went so far as to represent to Charles how cruel and unjust it was to force any nation to reject its lawfully elected King. " It is strange," replied Charles drily, " to hear such remonstrances in favour of a King who well deserves to be punished from the minister of a nation which had the hardihood to cut off the head of its own lawful King."

But months of fruitless negotiation between the Swedes and their Polish partisans ensued before Augustus's successor could be fixed upon, Augustus complicating matters by seizing the Sobieskis, the most acceptable candidates, in Imperial territory, and locking them up in the fortress of Pleissenburg. Charles finally selected Stanislaus Leszczynski, Palatine of Posen, a young man of excellent character and good family, but so insignificant that, as Dolgoruki reported to Peter, his own friends did not think much of him. Nevertheless, with the assistance of a bribing fund and an army corps, Count Arvid Horn, Charles's minister at Warsaw, succeeded in procuring the election of Stanislaus on July 2, 1704, by a scratch assembly of half a dozen castellans and a few score of the lesser nobility.

Seven weeks later (August 19, 1704) the indefatigable Patkul
succeeded at last in bringing about a treaty of alliance between
Russia and the Polish Republic in order to strengthen the hands
of Augustus.  By this treaty Peter undertook to provide Augustus
with 12,000 Moscovite auxiliaries, to pay for the maintenance of
an additional Polish army corps of 26,000 infantry and 21,000
cavalry, and to pay him subsidies amounting to 200,000 rubles a
year till the war was over.  An attempt of Patkul to bring the
King of Prussia into the anti-Swedish league failed, because of
Frederick I.'s fear of Charles and his jealousy of Peter's progress
on the Baltic shores.

But in his struggle with the terrible King of Sweden, Peter
could not confine his attention to Poland.  He was also obliged
to follow the course of events in Western Europe, and endeavour
to find allies there in case of need.  But even when they were not
actually hostile, the Western Powers received the overtures of
the intrusive young Tsar with humiliating contempt.  Moscovy
was, in those days, regarded as outside the European family
altogether, and her efforts to force an entrance into it were
deeply resented.  Those were miserable and melancholy days
for the fathers of Russian diplomacy.  Peter's ambassadors,
without proper training, without any experience, often without
the means of maintaining themselves, or even paying their debts,
had to school themselves to endure all kinds of insults in their
endeavours to serve their country.  Thus, to take a few instances,
Prince Peter Aleksyeevich Golitsuin reported from Vienna, after
the battle of Narva, that the Swedes were greatly feared, and
the Russians were utterly despised.  The chancellor, Prince
Dominic Andreas von Kaunitz,* would not even see him, and the
ministers laughed at him.  "A victory, even if it be only a little
one, is absolutely necessary for our master,"† wrote the despond-
ing ambassador.  At the end of 1702 he was reinforced by
Patkul, who obtained a private interview with Kaunitz in his
garden.  But Kaunitz would not hear of an alliance between
Austria and Russia, and when Patkul declared that the Tsar,
if he were not properly supported, must throw over Augustus,

* Grandfather of the still more famous Anton
† Golitsuin's despatches cited by Solovev : "Istoria Rossy," XV., 1.

Kaunitz replied : " Let him do so then, in the devil's name, and we shall know where we are ! "

Still more piteous are the despatches of Andrei Artamonovich Matvyeev—the son of the great Matvyeev—from The Hague, which he describes as the dullest, the dearest, and the most unfriendly place in the world. He was obliged to spend two-fifths of his wretched pittance of 2,000 rubles* on house rent. and go on foot, to his great shame. "At least send thy orphan enough to keep a carriage and horses," he implores Peter. The hostility to Moscovy at The Hague was offensively patent. The defeat of Narva caused "unspeakable joy" there, while Peter's flight, the tidings of which, embellished with every insulting detail, were industriously circulated by the Swedish minister, diverted the coffee-houses immensely. "My hand cannot indite the calumnies he has spread about concerning your Majesty," adds Matvyeev. Commercial jealousy was at the root of this dislike of Russia, and Peter's manifest determination to build himself a fleet alienated the maritime Powers. After Narva, William III. went so far as to say that Peter was a barbarian who had been justly punished for trying to be more than a barbarian.† When Peter offered the allies an army corps free of charge to serve against the French, he was informed that such assistance was not required, though he knew that at that very time they were assiduously negotiating with Charles XII. for the use of a few thousands of his veterans, whom he refused to part with. Evidently the Moscovite troops were of very little account at The Hague. Matvyeev further represented that Great Britain and Holland now desired a continuance of the Russo-Swedish War, lest Charles should be tempted to help France. At the beginning of 1704, Matvyeev requested Golovin to supply him with a large sum of money, as diplomacy could not be carried on without it, especially as the omnipotent Marlborough, who had already been "dazzled by a pretty big purse from the Swedes," might otherwise "play us some trick."

In autumn, 1705, Matvyeev was sent, without any official character, to Paris, to feel his way. He had an audience of

---

* About £500 of the current English money of the day.
† Matvyeev's despatches cited by Solovev : "Istoria Rossy," XV., 1,

Louis XIV., and reported that the Swede was in high favour at Versailles, "but the people here don't think very much of us and our affairs." He returned to Holland in October, 1706, without having even succeeded in concluding a commercial treaty.

Peter the Great, like his rival, Charles XII.,* never liked France, or the French. There was as little affinity between him and Louis XIV. as between a perfumed and powdered *Marquis* of the *ancien régime* and a rough and horny-handed mechanic. He never felt comfortable at Paris. But if the friendship of France was impossible, her enmity might be very dangerous, particularly at Stambul, where her influence outweighed that of all the other Powers put together. In 1701, Prince Dmitry Mikhailovich Golitsuin was sent thither to obtain the confirmation of the truce signed by Ukraintsev in 1700. He was also to petition for the free navigation of the Black Sea by Russian ships. The Divan replied that the Sultan would as soon think of opening the doors of his seraglio as of opening the Black Sea. In November, 1701, the first permanent and regularly accredited Russian ambassador to the Porte arrived at Stambul in the person of Peter Andreecivich Tolstoi, who from henceforth plays a large part in Russian history. The early career of this sinister but eminently capable statesman was curious. The son of the *okolnichy* Andrei Ivanovich Tolstoi, he was brought up at Court, and had risen to the rank of *stolnik*, or chamberlain, when the first revolt of the stryeltsui broke out. Miscalculating the strength of Sophia, he became one of her most energetic supporters, but contrived to join the winning side just before the final catastrophe. For a long time, however, Peter kept his latest recruit at arm's length. Even Tolstoi's services in the second Azov campaign could not efface the Tsar's suspicions. But when, in 1697, Tolstoi volunteered to go to Venice to learn Italian and ship-building, Peter could not resist the subtle flattery implied in such a proposal from a middle-aged Moscovite nobleman, and freely forgave Tolstoi all his sins, though in moments of expansion he frequently reminded him of them, as when, on one

* Charles's dislike, inherited from his father, was mainly due to political reasons

occasion, he laid hold of Tolstoi's head, and exclaimed : "Oh, head, head, you would not have been on your shoulders now if you had not been so very, very clever ! "[*]

As Russian ambassador at the Porte, Tolstoi, by his extraordinary acuteness, more than fulfilled the confidence of his master, though his peculiar expedients savour more of the Italian than of the Russian renaissance. From Adrianople, the residence of the Turkish Court during the reign of Murad II., he kept the Russian Government well informed of all that was going on in the Turkish Empire. In 1702 he wrote that the Porte was much alarmed by Peter's ship-building operations at Azov and Taganrog, which were duly reported by the Crimean Khan, and that he himself was kept in constant surveillance and isolated as much as possible. In January, 1703, however, Tolstoi succeeded in bringing about the strangulation of a peculiarly virulent Russophobe Grand Vizier, and henceforth, till the middle of 1704, was left in peace and allowed a greater measure of freedom. But in the following September the new Grand Vizier (the eighth in four years) proved worse than all his predecessors, and Tolstoi began to fear that his own people, who had now learnt Turkish thoroughly, would go over to the Mussulman faith, "which," he observes quaintly, "is very tempting to the narrow-minded." Even his secretary, the Greek Timotheus, openly expressed his intention of apostatising, but Tolstoi locked him up in his bedroom till midnight and then sent him a cup of wine, "whereupon he soon died, so God preserved him from that calamity."[†] After this, things began to look better again. Tolstoi could now inform Golovin that the Turks were too poor to wage war. Reassured as to the Turk, Peter resolved to help Augustus by transferring the war to Poland. In May, 1705, he appeared at Polock, where 50,000 Russians were concentrated under Ogilvie and Sheremetev. Sheremetev was detached to conquer Courland, but at Gemauerhof (July 16, 1705) was so severely defeated by the Swedish general Levenhaupt that Peter was obliged to hasten to his assistance. Levenhaupt's superior

---

[*] Compare Popov : "Graf P. O. Tolstoi:" *ib.*, "Iz zhizni. P. A. T."; Solovev : "Istoria Rossy," XV., 1.

[†] Despatches of Tolstoi cited by Solovev : "Istoria Rossy," XV., 1.

strategy enabled him to fall back upon Riga unmolested, whereupon the Russians, after capturing Mittau and occupying Courland, went into winter quarters at Grodno.

During the winter Patkul made fresh efforts to gain the King
of Prussia, by holding out the bait of Polish Prussia;* but the
negotiations failed because Russia had yet to show, by conquering the unconquerable King of Sweden, that she was able to
fulfil her promises. Till then, the Prussian ministers prudently
resolved to remain neutral. From Berlin Patkul proceeded to
Dresden to conclude an agreement with the Imperial commissioners for the transfer of the Russian contingent of troops from
the Saxon to the Austrian service. The Saxon ministers, after
protesting in vain against the new arrangement, arrested Patkul,
and shut him up in the fortress of Sonnenstein (December 19,
1605), altogether disregarding the remonstrances of Peter against
such a gross violation of international law and courtesy.

But the fate of Patkul was speedily forgotten in the rush of
events which made the year 1706 so momentous. On Sept. 24/
Oct. 4, 1705, Charles XII. crowned Stanislaus Leszczynski
King of Poland; on Nov. 18/28 he concluded an alliance with
the Polish Republic, and in the beginning of January, 1706,
he suddenly appeared in Eastern Poland to clear the country of
the partisans of Augustus, and attacked the Russian army,
under Ogilvie, entrenched at Grodno. But Ogilvie could not
be tempted out of his entrenchments, and all that Charles could
do was to cut off his communications with Russia and destroy
his sources of supply in the surrounding country. Augustus
meanwhile had hastened from Grodno to Warsaw, and united his
Russian and Polish troops with the Saxon forces under Schulen-
burg, for the purpose of crushing the little Swedish army stationed
under Rehnskjöld, in the province of Posen, intending afterwards
to return and fall upon Charles at Grodno, while Ogilvie attacked
him in front. This plan was frustrated by Rehnskjöld's brilliant
victory over the combined Russians, Poles, and Saxons at Frau-
stadt (February 3, 1706), whom he almost annihilated, only
5,000 out of 20,000 succeeding in escaping. To Peter such a
rout was only intelligible on the assumption of treachery before

* Now West Prussia.

the battle and the wholesale massacre of Russian prisoners after it. Fearing for his forces at Grodno, he at once ordered Ogilvie to retreat into the heart of Russia, burying his heavy guns in ice-holes and breaking up his army into numerous detachments, so that at least some of them might escape. Ogilvie protested, whereupon he was superseded by Menshikov, with whom he had been at constant variance throughout the campaign, and the Russian army, favoured by the spring floods of the Niemen, which obstructed the pursuing Swedes, retreated so rapidly upon Kiev, that Charles was unable to overtake it, and abandoned the pursuit among the trackless morasses of Pinsk. Leaving his exhausted army to rest for a few weeks in Volhynia, he hastened off to Saxony to finish with Augustus, to the intense relief of Peter in his "Paradise" of Petersburg. In the autumn of the same year the combined forces of Augustus and Menshikov defeated the Swedish general Marderfeld at Kalisch (Oct. 19/29), but the victory came too late to repair the shattered fortunes of the Elector. On Sept. 14/24 his ministers at Dresden had already concluded with Charles XII. the Peace of Altranstadt, which was ratified by Augustus at Petrikow, in Poland, on Oct. 10/20, 1706. By this treaty Augustus recognised Stanis- laus as King of Poland, renounced all his anti-Swedish alliances, especially the alliance with Russia, and undertook to support the Swedish army during the winter in Saxony, and to deliver up Patkul. To the last he was tricky and treacherous. Thus, while imploring Charles to keep secret the Peace of Altranstadt, as otherwise he would fear for his personal security, he privately assured the Tsar of his unalterable devotion, and negotiated at Berlin and Copenhagen for a fresh anti-Swedish league. Charles rent asunder this web of falsehood by publishing the treaty, and compelling Augustus to re-ratify it (Jan. 9/19, 1707) and carry out all its stipulations. Patkul was now removed from his Saxon dungeon and delivered up to Charles. His fate was a foregone conclusion. Shortly after the departure of the Swedes from Saxony he was broken on the wheel and decapitated at Kazimir, Charles rejecting an appeal for mercy from his own sister, the Princess Ulrica, on the ground that "Patkul could not be par- doned for example's sake. He had chosen to be a traitor, as a

traitor he must die." The conduct of Charles in this matter
may have been somewhat harsh, but the conduct of Augustus
was wholly infamous. He had deliberately handed over, to a
horrible death, a man who, after faithfully serving him to the
utmost of his ability, had only committed the pardonable folly
of trusting in his honour.

Abandoned by Augustus, Peter, on December 28, 1706, held a
council of ministers at Zolkov, to discuss the affairs of headless
Poland. At this council we miss the familiar figure of Golovin,
who had died during the previous summer, to Peter's infinite
regret. His dignities were divided between Count Theodore
Matvyeevich Apraksin and Count Gabriel Ivanovich Golovkin,
both of them intimate friends of Peter, both of them men of
considerable ability. The new Admiral-General, Apraksin, born
in 1671, had been Peter's constant companion from his boyhood,
and had won the Tsar's undying friendship while Governor of
Astrakhan by building ships which could actually weather
storms. During the earlier years of the Great Northern War
he had been busy at Azov and Taganrog constructing fleets
harbours, dockyards and fortresses. Apraksin was the best
natured and most jovial of all Peter's "fledglings." His contemporaries describe the old sailor as full of a burning desire to
oblige everyone, especially when in his cups, and he could make
the unusual boast that even in the hour of disgrace he never had
a single personal enemy. Golovkin, eleven years Apraksin's
senior, was a cousin of the Tsaritsa Natalia, and had known
Peter from infancy. In the dangerous days of the Sophian
regency he had jealously guarded his young kinsman, and ever
afterwards enjoyed his complete confidence. He accompanied
him on his first foreign tour, worked by his side in the docks at
Saardam, and was now appointed minister of foreign affairs, an
office exalted to the dignity of Imperial chancellor in 1709, of
which he was the first and longest holder. Golovkin's ignorance
of French would have been a serious impediment to his intercourse with foreign ministers, but for the constant assistance of
his subordinate, Peter Pavlovich Shafirov, the translator of the
*Posolsky Prikas*, a most capable man, of Jewish origin, who
had long been Golovin's right hand. Shafirov was made

vice-chancellor at the same time that Golovkin was made chancellor.

The council held at Zolkov wasted a lot of precious time in negotiating with those of the Polish magnates who were discontented with Stanislaus Leszczynski. These gentlemen assessed the value of their problematical services at such an extravagant figure that Peter could only pay them a tenth part of their demands. But the difficulty of finding a suitable candidate for the Polish throne in place of Augustus proved insurmountable, and Peter was obliged at last to leave Poland to its fate, and endeavour to come to terms with his terrible opponent, the King of Sweden. This he could only do by soliciting the mediation of the Powers, as Charles steadily refused to have any direct communication with him. He began at London. At the end of 1706, Andrei Matvyeev was sent from Holland to England to promise Peter's adhesion to the Grand Alliance if Great Britain would bring about a peace between him and Sweden. If necessary, Matvyeev was to bribe Harley, Godolphin, Marlborough and the other ministers, but he was to proceed about it very cautiously. " I know not whether Marlborough would be inclined thereto, as he is already immensely rich," wrote Peter privately,* " but you may promise him £1,000 or so." After long procrastination, Harley informed Matvyeev that the Queen, under present conjunctures, could not afford to quarrel with the King of Sweden, especially as he had engaged not to attack the Emperor. The admittance of Russia into the Grand Alliance depended on the consent of the States General. Matvyeev complained that the English ministers gave him nothing but smooth and empty words. " In tricks and subterfuges they are more subtle even than the French," he wrote.

On the Continent Peter's Dutch agent, Huyssens, negotiated with Marlborough direct. The Duke promised to meet the Tsar's wishes if a principality in Russia were granted to him. Peter at once gave him the choice between Kiev, Vladimir and Siberia, besides promising him, in case peace with Sweden were concluded by his efforts, 50,000 thalers a year, "a rock ruby such as no European potentate possesses " and the order of St.

* Cited by Solovev: " Istoria Rossy," XV., 3.

Andrew in brilliants. But nothing came of it, although Peter now declared his willingness to surrender all his Baltic conquests except Petersburg.

In the spring of 1707 Peter negotiated for the mediation of France, through Desalliers, the French minister at the Court of George Rakoczy, Prince of Transylvania. Charles was approached on the subject of peace, but recognising that the line of the Neva was really vital to the existence of Sweden's Baltic Empire, he refused to cede Petersburg, and insisted on Peter's restitution of all his conquests and the payment of a war indemnity.

Meanwhile the Swedish ministers at Vienna and elsewhere insinuated perpetually that if Russia were allowed to increase, all Europe would be exposed to the peril of a second Scythian invasion, and all Europe was inclined to believe them. Prince Eugene, to whom Peter now offered the crown of Poland, refused the dangerous gift, and the Emperor hastened to recognise Stanislaus for fear of offending Charles. At Berlin, even a bribe of 100,000 thalers could not tempt the Prussian ministers to undertake the ungrateful task of mediation. Peter was clearly given up for lost.

At Stambul, the French ambassador, in league with the Crimean Khan, did his utmost to provoke a rupture between Russia and the Porte, as part of a larger plan of embroiling the Porte with the Emperor. In the spring of 1707 Tolstoi had need of all his astuteness to counteract the scheming of his French rival, who warned the Divan of the danger of allowing Russian war-ships in the Black Sea. But the apathy of the Turks was impervious to the most alarming arguments, and at the end of the year Tolstoi was able to report that his ermines, sables and blue fox skins had prevailed at last over the fuller purse of the active and malevolent French ambassador. The crisis again became acute when an envoy from King Stanislaus arrived at Stambul to urge the Porte to permit the Tatars to unite with the Poles in a combined attack on Russia. The war party, at Stambul, seemed about to triumph, when the Grand Vizier, worked upon by Tolstoi, procured the banishment of his two ablest and most martial colleagues, and peace was once more assured.

This was Peter's solitary success, and all diplomatic expedients for pacifying Charles having failed, he saw himself compelled to bear the whole brunt of a war *à outrance* with the invincible King-maker.   At a council of war, held at the village of Merech, in Lithuania, in 1707, he decided not to oppose the Swedes in the open field, but to retire before them, drawing them further and further from their base, devastating the country before them and harassing them as much as possible, especially at the passage of the principal rivers.   He had previously commanded that all the country folks should be warned beforehand of the approach of the enemy that they might have time to hide their stores of corn in pits or in the forests, and drive their cattle into the trackless swamps.   The Cossack Hetman Mazepa was entrusted with the defence of Little Russia and the Ukrain.   Kiev, with its congeries of monasteries, was strongly fortified and supplied with artillery.   All the light troops, including the Cossacks, were to fall back behind the Dnieper.

And now, at the very moment when the dreaded foe was approaching from the west, a long simmering rebellion suddenly broke out in the east and the south-east.

The conquest by Russia of the Volgan and Uralian districts had been too rapid and facile to be thorough.   From the first the subdued barbarians endured their yoke unwillingly.   Their discontent was increased by the extortions of the Russian officials, and as Mahommedans they looked upon the Turkish Sultan as their real head, and naturally bore their ever-increasing burdens more unwillingly than their Christian fellow-subjects.   In 1707 a Bashkir rebel gathered together all the surrounding tribes, besieged the fort of Terek, and was only with difficulty defeated by Apraksin on February 26th.   In November, the whole of the Bashkirs revolted ; defeated the troops sent against them ; burnt all the surrounding Russian villages and threatened the city of Kazan.   Peter, having no regular troops to spare at the time, employed barbarians against barbarians, and with the aid of 10,000 Calmucks the Russian general Bakhmatev succeeded, in June, 1708, in checking the Bashkirs, though it was not till April, 1709, that the complete submission of the rebels was extorted.   No sooner had the Bashkirs been put down, than a still more dangerous rebellion broke out among the Don Cossacks. It was the old story of the refusal of the Cossacks to give up the vagabond peasants, artificers and soldiers who had fled to their settlements to escape the burdens of a regular civilised life. Peter, always sorely in need of hard-working, tax-paying people, naturally could not permit these idle desperadoes to levy blackmail on their more industrious fellow-subjects, and in 1707, he sent Prince Yury Vladimirovich Dolgoruki to the Don to bring back the fugitives to their old homes. Most of the Cossack chiefs supported him, but Kondraty Afanasev Bulavin, the Ataman of the Trekhizbensky Cossacks, encouraged the malcontents to resist the authority of the Tsar, and completely wiped out Dolgoruki's little army on the banks of the river Aidara by a well-planned night attack (October 9, 1707). In the course of 1708, Bulavin's rebellion assumed such alarming dimensions that Peter had to send regular troops against him from the army of the West. On May 1 the rebellious Ataman capured Cherkask, the chief fortress of the Zaporozhians, and, for a time, Azov and Taganrog were in danger. Fortunately the capture of Cherkask was Bulavin's last triumph. Instead of proceeding up the Volga to the still disaffected Bashkir districts, where he might seriously have embarrassed the Government Bulavin opened negotiations with the Government which gave the monks of Kiev time to prevent the bulk of the Zaporozhians from joining him. On July 1 one of his divisions, 6,000 strong, was routed at Krivaya Luka, while another division of equal strength was repulsed from Azov. Bulavin thereupon committed suicide in his camp at Cherkask, and by the end of August the insurrection was completely suppressed.

Meanwhile the King of Sweden had already crossed the Russian frontier. Delayed during the autumn months in Poland by the tardy arrival of reinforcements from Pomerania, it was not till November, 1707, that Charles was able to take the field. On Christmas Day he reached the Vistula, which he crossed on New Year's Day, 1708, though the ice was in a dangerous condition. On January 26 he entered Grodno, only two hours after Peter's departure. "For God's sake," wrote Peter to Menshikov on this occasion, "entrust the command of the rearguard to faithful men of our own people, and not to foreign fools." The sneer is illuminating. It shows that even in the science of war the Moscovites were beginning to dispense with leading strings. Peter himself was suffering at this time (March) from malarial fever caught in Poland, and went to his "Paradise" to recruit.

On February 12 Charles encamped at Smorgonie on the Velya, one of the tributaries of the Niemen. Two courses now lay open to him. He might either recover the lost Baltic provinces before attacking the Tsar. or he might pursue Peter into the heart of his Tsardom, and dictate peace to him after destroying his army. His ablest officers strongly advised him to adopt the first course as being both "cheap and reasonable" ;* but the alternative appealed irresistibly to the young hero's love of adventure and tempted him by presenting difficulties to be conquered which were insuperable by anyone else. And, unfortunately for Sweden, he adopted it. Apparently, for it is largely a matter of guess-work, his plan was, first, after crossing the Dnieper. to unite with the army corps of Levenhaupt, which was advancing from Riga to join him, and then to winter in the fruitful and unspoilt Ukrain, whose fortresses were held at his disposal by the Cossack Hetman Mazepa, with whom he and Stanislaus had been in secret communication since the autumn of 1707. Simultaneously, the Finnish army under General Lybecker, with the help of the fleet, was to take Petersburg and recapture Ingria, while King Stanislaus, aided by a third Swedish army under General Krassov, was to quell all disaffection in Poland. In the summer of 1709 the three Swedish armies, reinforced by the Poles, the Cossacks and the Crimean Tatars, were to attack Moscovy from the north, south and east simultaneously, and crush Peter between them. It was a characteristically audacious scheme, but as it absolutely disregarded difficulties, and was built upon nothing but the most fantastic expectations, its realisation, even under the most favourable circumstances, lay far beyond the bounds of possibility.

After a brief rest at Smorgonie, Charles resumed his march eastwards. The superior strategy of the Swedes enabled them

* "Sveriges Historia," vol. IV., pp. 568, 569.

to cross the first two considerable rivers, the Berezina and the Drucz, without difficulty, but on reaching the Wabis, Charles found the enemy posted on the other side, near the little town of Holowczyn, in an apparently impregnable position, evidently bent upon barring his passage. But his experienced eye instantly detected the one vulnerable point in the six-mile-long Russian line; on July 4, 1708, he hurled all his forces against it; and after a fierce engagement, lasting from daybreak to sundown, the Russians retired with a loss of 3,000 men.

The victory of Holowczyn, memorable besides as the last pitched battle won by Charles XII., opened up the way to the Dnieper, and four days later Charles reached Mohilev where he stayed till August 6 waiting for Levenhaupt. The Swedish army now began to suffer severely, bread and fodder running short, and the soldiers subsisting almost entirely on captured bullocks. The Russians, under Menshikov and Sheremetev, would not risk another general engagement, but slowly retired before the invaders, burning and destroying everything in their path, till at last the Swedes had nothing but a charred wilderness beneath their feet and a horizon of burning villages before their eyes. Moreover the Moscovites now displayed a boldness which amazed the Swedes, attacking more and more frequently and obstinately every week, with ever-increasing numbers, as for instance at Chernaya Napa (August 29), where they fell upon a separate Swedish division which lost 3,000 men and was only saved from annihilation by the arrival of Charles himself. By the time the frontier of eighteenth century Russia was reached at Miczanowicz, September 20, it was plain to Charles that he could go no further in that direction. A council of war was then held at Tatarsk. Rehnskjöld prudently advised the King to wait for Levenhaupt whose reinforcements and caravan of provisions were becoming indispensable, and then to retire to Livonia, so that he might winter in his own lands. But Charles, partly from a horror of retreating, partly because of urgent messages of assistance from Mazepa,[*] and partly because he hoped to find a fruitful, untouched country in the Ukrain, and serviceable allies in the Cossacks and their neighbours, the

* "Svenska Historia," IV., pp. 569—571.

Crimean Tatars,* Charles, I say, resolved to proceed southwards instead of northwards, and to this resolution everything else was sacrificed.

And now began that last march of the devoted Swedish army from Mohilev through the forests and morasses of Severia, and the endless steppes of the Ukrain, which was to be a long-drawn-out agony punctuated by a constant succession of disasters. The first blow fell in the beginning of October, when the unhappy Levenhaupt joined Charles with the *débris* of the army he had saved from the not inglorious rout of Lesna, where the Russians, with vastly superior forces, had intercepted and overwhelmed him after a two days' battle (Sept. 29/30), in which the Swedes lost 8,000 killed and wounded, 16 guns, 42 standards, and 2,000 waggons of provisions, and the Russians, 4,000 killed and wounded.† And Levenhaupt had been sacrificed in vain, for when, on November 8, Mazepa at last joined Charles, at the little Severian town of Horki, he came not as the powerful *Dux militum Zaporowiensium*, but as a ruined man with little more than his horsetail standard and 1,300 personal adherents.

The unlooked-for collapse of Mazepa was a terrible blow to Charles XII. He had built his hope of ultimate victory on his alliance with the Cossack Hetman, and in justice to Charles it should be added that this alliance, so far from being a mere mirage luring him on to destruction, as Swedish historians have too often described it, was really the one solid and substantial element in his fantastic combinations. It must not be forgotten that in those days the Hetman of the Zaporozhian Cossacks was often the determining factor of Oriental politics. Chmielnicki had held the balance even between Poland and Moscovy for years. Doroshenko, as the ally of the Sultan, had for a time been more powerful than Tsar and King combined. Mazepa himself was not so much the subject as the semi-independent tributary of the Moscovite crown. He ruled on the Dnieper with more than princely power ; 100,000 Cossack horsemen were at his disposal ; the whole Ukrain obeyed him ; the Khan of the Crimea called him " my brother." If Charles X. of Sweden,

---

* Despatches of Matvyeev cited by Solovev : " Istoria Rossy," XV., 4.
† Peter's own account of it in Solovev

one of the astutest statesmen as well as the greatest warrior of
his age, in the plenitude of his power considered it not beneath
his dignity to seek the alliance of the Hetman Chmielnicki
against Poland, why should not his grandson, Charles XII., have
sought the alliance of the Hetman Mazepa against Moscovy now
that Poland also was with him?  The power and influence of
Mazepa were fully recognised by Peter the Great himself.  No
other Cossack Hetman had ever been treated with such deference
at Moscow.  He had been made one of the first cavaliers of the
newly established order of St. Andrew, and Augustus of Poland
had bestowed upon him, at Peter's earnest solicitation, the
universally coveted order of the White Eagle.  He ranked with
the highest dignitaries in the state.  He sat at the Tsar's own
table.  He flouted the Tsar's kinsmen with perfect impunity.
Mazepa had no temptation to be anything but loyal, and loyal
he would doubtless have remained, had not Charles XII. crossed
his path.  At the very beginning of the Great Northern War,
the crafty old Hetman began to have his doubts how this life-
and-death struggle going on before his very eyes would end.  At
first they were only doubts.  When in 1705 he was approached
by Frantisek Wolski, a secret agent of King Stanislaus, Mazepa
sent the would-be corrupter in chains to Peter, virtuously protesting that this was the fourth attempt that had been made on
his inviolable loyalty.  But as Charles continued to advance, and
Peter continued to retreat, Mazepa made up his mind that not
Peter but Charles was going to win, and that it was high time he
looked after his own interests.  Like all the Cossacks, a semi-
nomad, he recognised no abiding fatherland, and had changed
sides so often in the course of his adventurous career, that muta-
bility had become a law of his nature.  And he had his personal
grievances against Peter besides.  The Tsar was going along so
fast that the arch-conservative old Cossack could not follow him.
He did not like the new ways because they interfered with his
old ones.  He was very jealous of the omnipotent Menshikov,
whom he suspected of a design to supplant him.  More than
once his Cossack squadrons had been taken from him to be
converted into dragoons, and he resented it.  But he proceeded
very cautiously.  When in 1706 a fresh attempt was made upon

his virtue by his kinswoman, the Princess Dolska, who was in the pay of Stanislaus, Mazepa had her letter read aloud in the Cossack assembly, and exclaimed : " She is a damned old fool to try and snare a downy old bird like me." But King Stanislaus persevered, and on September 16, 1707, he wrote to Mazepa direct, offering him practically his own terms if he would take the anti-Moscovite side. Caught between two such mighty opponents as Charles and Peter, Mazepa would have preferred to remain neutral, but he was not strong enough to stand alone. The crisis came when Peter ordered him actively to co-operate with the Russian forces in the Ukrain. Mazepa thereupon took to his bed. He sent word to the Tsar that he was on the point of death, and about to be carried to Kiev to receive extreme unction from the archbishop. At this very time he was in com- munication with Charles's first minister, Count Piper, and had agreed to harbour the Swedes in the Ukrain, and close it against the Russians (October, 1708). Menshikov was sent by Peter to see "the dying Hetman," who hearing of the approach of his deadliest enemy, at once took horse and "sped away like a whirlwind" for three days and three nights, to the Swedish outposts at Horki.

Mazepa's treason took Peter completely by surprise. He had always refused to believe in the accusations brought from every quarter against the Hetman, and his indignation was now pro- portionate to his amazement. "To think that this old Judas, after serving me for one-and-twenty years, should betray his country at last, on the very verge of the grave," he wrote to Apraksin. He instantly commanded Menshikov to get a new Hetman elected, and raze Baturin, Mazepa's chief stronghold in the Ukrain, to the ground. A race for Baturin now ensued between Charles and Menshikov, but the Moscovites outmarching the exhausted Swedes got there first, and when Charles, a week later, passed it by, all that remained of the Cossack capital was "a heap of smouldering mills and ruined houses, with burnt, half-burnt, and bloody corpses,"* scattered all around. The total destruction of Baturin, almost within sight of the victorious

---

* " Historia ablegationis Danielis Krmann." Comp. Solovev : " Istoria Rossy," XV., 4.

Swedes, overawed the bulk of the Cossacks into obedience to the Tsar, and Mazepa's ancient *prestige* was ruined in a day when the Metropolitan of Kiev and two other archbishops solemnly excommunicated him from the high altar, and his effigy, after being dragged with contumely through the mud at Kiev, was publicly burnt by the common hangman.

For the next few weeks Charles and Peter fought each other with manifestoes, Charles promising the Malo Russians protection from the tyranny and oppression of " the godless Tsar," and Peter declaring that Charles intended to drag the orthodox population in chains to eternal servitude in Poland, and convert all the orthodox churches into Lutheran kirks. To quicken the exterminating zeal of his soldiers, moreover, Peter set a price upon every Swede brought into the Russian camp, alive or dead. Generals were to be paid for at the rate of 2,000 rubles a head, colonels at the rate of 1,000 rubles, and so on. The common Swedish soldiers were priced at five rubles, and their corpses at three rubles per head. Mazepa also issued "universals " to the Cossack inhabitants of the Ukrain, but only the Zaporozhians still clung to him.

And at the end of 1708 the Swedes had to encounter a new and terrible enemy in the great frost, the severest that Europe had known for a century. So early as the beginning of October the cold was intense ; by November 1 firewood would not ignite in the open air, and the soldiers warmed themselves over huge bonfires of straw ; but it was not till the vast open steppes of the Ukrain were reached that the unhappy Swedes experienced all the rigour of the icy Scythian blast. By the time the army arrived at the little Ukrainian fortress of Hadjach, which they took by assault (January, 1709), wine and spirits froze into solid masses of ice ; birds on the wing fell dead ; saliva congealed in its passage from the mouth to the ground. Hideous were the sufferings of the soldiers. " You could see," says an eye-witness,[*] " some without hands, some without feet, some without ears and noses, many creeping along after the manner of quadrupeds." " Nevertheless," says another narrator,[†] " though earth, sky, and

[*] Krmann: "Historia ablegationis," etc.
[†] Max Emmanuel von Wurtemburg: "Reise," etc.

air were against us, the King's orders had to be obeyed, and the daily march made." Never had Charles XII. seemed so super-human as during those awful days. His soldiers believed him to be divinely inspired, and divinely protected It is not too much to say that his imperturbable equanimity, his serene *bonhomie*, kept together the perishing but still unconquered host. His military exploits were prodigious. At Cerkova he defeated 7,000 Russians with 400, and at Opressa, 5,000 Russians with 300 men.*

The frost broke at the end of February, 1709, and then the spring floods put an end to all active operations for some months. The Tsar set off for Voronezh to inspect his Black Sea fleet, while Charles encamped at Rudiszcze, between the Orel and the Worskla, two tributaries of the Don. By this time the Swedish army had dwindled from 41,000 to about 20,000 able-bodied men, mostly cavalry. Supplies, furnished for a time by Mazepa, were again running short. All communications with Europe had long since been cut off. Charles was still full of confidence. He had given up none of his plans. He hoped, in the ensuing campaign, with the hope of the Tatars, the Zaporozhians and the Hospodar of Wallachia, to hold his own till Stanislaus, with Krassov's army corps, had joined him by way of Volhynia. On May 1 he began the siege of Poltava, a small fortress on the western bank of the Vorskla, and the staple of the Ukrain trade, so as to strengthen his positions till the arrival of Krassov. But the ordinary diffi-culties of a siege were materially increased by the lack of artillery and ammunition,† and the proximity of the Russian main army, which arrived a few days later, and entrenched itself on the opposite or eastern bank of the Vorskla.

Peter himself was still further delayed by the resistance offered to him by the rebellious Zaporozhian Cossacks on the Dnieper. At the beginning of the year Mazepa, perceiving that things were going badly with Charles, sent the Cossack Apostol to Peter offering to deliver Charles and all his generals into Peter's hands, if his former treason were forgiven. He received an assurance from Golovkin that if he succeeded in his latest

---

* Krmann.

† Nearly all the powder had been spoilt by the weather during 1708—9, and it is said that the report of the Swedish guns was no louder than the clapping of gloved hands.

design, he should be made far greater than before. But even now the old Hetman had two strings to his bow, and, while attempting to cajole Peter, was, at the same time, urging King Stanislaus to "extend his conquering hand over his ancestral domains, and trample the Moscovite dragon in the dust." It was also due to his secret assurances of forthcoming help from Poland that the Zaporozhians so stoutly withstood Peter in their *syech*, or great water fortress, among the islands of the Dnieper; but on May 17, 1709, "this root of all the evil and the main hope of the enemy," as Peter called it, was stormed by the dragoons of Volkovsky and Galaghan. A fortnight later, the Tsar set out for Poltava, arriving there on June 4.

At last Peter had resolved to make a firm stand. "With God's help, I hope this month to have a final bout with the enemy," he wrote to Apraksin. Only a narrow stream now separated him from the victors of Narva. Yet, even now, though the Swedes of 1709 were very different from the Swedes of 1700, or the Swedes of 1706; though they were a famished, exhausted, dispirited host, surrounded by a four-fold odds, Peter decided, at a council of war, held soon after his arrival, that a general attack was still too hazardous. Charles XII. had never yet been defeated in a pitched battle, and Peter was determined to run no risks. Only when the garrison of Poltava, by means of letters in empty barrels, informed the Tsar that their powder had run out, and the enemy's sappers were burrowing beneath their palisades, did he order his army to advance. On June 17, the Russians began to cross the Worskla, but took the precaution of entrenching themselves. On that very day a crowning calamity overtook the Swedes. While reconnoitring the Russian camp, Charles received a wound in the foot from the bullet of a Cossack patrol, which placed him *hors de combat*. On hearing of this accident, Peter resolved not to refuse battle if it were offered him. Charles was equally ready to fight, and at a council of war held on June 26, Marshal Rehnskjöld, whom he had appointed commander-in-chief in his stead, was ordered to attack the Russians in their entrenchments on the following day. The Swedes joyfully accepted the chances of battle to escape slow starvation and manifold misery, and, advancing with irresistible *élan*, were at first successful on both wings.   Then one or two tactical blunders were committed, and the Tsar, taking courage, drew all his troops from their trenches, and enveloped the little band of Swedes in a vast semicircle, bristling with the most modern guns, the invention of the French engineer Le Metre,* which fired five times to the Swedes' once, and literally swept away the Royal Guards, the heart and soul of the army, before they could grasp their swords.   After a brief struggle, the Swedish infantry was annihilated, while the 14,000 cavalry, exhausted and demoralised, surrendered two days later at Perewoloczna, on the Dnieper, which they had no means of crossing.   Charles XII., with Mazepa and 1,500 horsemen, took refuge in Turkish territory.

"The enemy's army," wrote Peter to Romodonovsky next morning, "has had the fate of Phaeton.   As for the King, we do not know whether he be with us, or with our fathers."   To Apraksin he wrote : " Now by God's help are the foundations of Petersburg securely laid for all time."   At the end of the year, on his return to "the Holy Land,"† he laid the foundation stone of a church dedicated to St. Samson, to commemorate the victory of the strong and patient man who had at last vanquished his masters in the art of war.

* Krmann: "Historia ablegationis," etc.   For an account of the battle com-pare Krmann ; Solovev: " Istoria Rossy," XV., 4, and "Sveriges Historia," IV., 572—575.                                                 † Petersburg.

# CHAPTER X.

## THE GREAT NORTHERN WAR, FROM THE BATTLE OF POLTAVA TO THE PEACE OF NYSTAD. 1709—1721.

Renewal of the Anti-Swedish League—Battle of Helsingborg—Peter conquers Livonia and captures Viborg—The Diplomatic Struggle at the Porte—Triumph of Charles XII.—Turkey declares War—Illness of Peter—His Advance to the Pruth—Desperate Situation of the Russian Army—Peace of the Pruth—Peter's despairing Letter to the Senate—Fresh Diplomatic Struggle with Charles XII.—Turkey declares War against Russia a Second and a Third Time—Peace of Adrianople—Condition of Poland—The War transferred to Northern Germany—Hostility of Great Britain to Russia—Outrage on the Russian Minister at London—The Battle of Gadebusch and the Capitulation of Tönning—Peter conquers Finland—The Stettin Sequestration—Return of Charles XII.—The Third Coalition against Sweden—The Mecklenburg Complication—The abortive Scanian Expedition—Discord between the Allies—The Jacobite Plot—Peter's Visit to Paris—Treaty of Amsterdam—The Congress of Åland—Görtz and Osterman—Death of Charles XII.—Rupture of the Negotiations—Sweden abandoned by the Western Powers—The Peace of Nystad and its Consequences.

THE immediate result of the Battle of Poltava was the revival of the old hostile league against Sweden. It was too hastily assumed by the enemies of Charles that "nothing was left of the lion but his roar," and the jackals accordingly emerged to divide the fallen quarry between them. Augustus, who had suffered the most from Charles, was naturally the first to raise his head. On hearing of Peter's victory he sent his chamberlain, Count Vizthum, to fix a conference, and the two monarchs met together on a bridge of boats in the Vistula, a mile from Thorn (September 26, 1709). A fortnight later a treaty was signed between them, cancelling all previous compacts. Peter undertook to assist Augustus to regain the throne of Poland, and Augustus undertook to assist Peter against all his enemies. By a secret article in this treaty it was agreed that Livonia should be surrendered to Augustus in his capacity of Elector of Saxony and should henceforth form part of his hereditary domain.

R.                                                                                            T

At the conference of Thorn a Danish special envoy, Baron Christian Rantzau, also appeared to congratulate the victor of Poltava. The Danes had lost no time in joining the enemies of Sweden. At the end of May King Frederick IV. of Denmark, on his way home from Italy, visited Augustus at Dresden, and on June 28 concluded with him an alliance "to restore the equilibrium of the North, and keep Sweden within her proper limits." The allies solemnly engaged not to lay down their arms till Augustus had been reinstated in Poland, and the King of Denmark had secured from Sweden all the territories wrested by her from his forefathers. Nevertheless, for fear of the Western Powers, who were amicably disposed towards Sweden, and not at all inclined to part with the Danish and Saxon mercenaries in their service so long as the war of the Spanish succession continued, the two princes agreed to exempt Sweden's German possessions from attack unless their own possessions in the Empire were attacked by Sweden.

Frederick IV. and Augustus II. then proceeded to Berlin to persuade Frederick I. of Prussia to accede to the new alliance. Magnificent festivities attended the meeting of "the three Fredericks,"* medals were struck to commemorate it, champagne and hock flowed in streams, yet very little came of it. The Prussian prime minister, Ilgen, restrained his royal master from taking any decisive step until he was promised the Polish province of West Prussia, by way of compensation for his services, and to this Augustus, who had already resolved to partition Poland on his own account, would not consent. Consequently, the alliance of the three Fredericks was of so general a character that it did little more than engage the King of Prussia to prevent the passage through his territories of any Swedish troops bent on invading the territories of Denmark or Saxony.

Still more anxious was the Danish Government to obtain subsidies from Russia, with whom negotiations had been renewed ; but on this point great difficulties suddenly arose. Now that he had vanished his once formidable assailant by his own might, the Tsar was not inclined to pay as liberally as heretofore for the

* Augustine's electoral title was Frederick Augustus.

co-operation of allies who had hitherto been more of a hindrance
than a help, and could now do nothing without him. Moreover,
in regard to Denmark he shrewdly calculated that she would
now attack Sweden in any case. The Russian ambassador,
Prince Dolgoruki, therefore informed King Frederick IV. that
the Tsar could no longer engage to give the 300,000 rix dollars
agreed upon during the negotiations at the end of December, 1708,
for the renewal of the alliance of 1699, or, indeed, supply the
Danish Government with any timber for building vessels. When
Frederick IV. expressed his painful surprise at this very unpleasant intelligence, Dolgoruki curtly declared that the Tsar
could terminate the war with the King of Sweden whenever he
liked, as Charles had actually sued for peace, but his Tsarish
Majesty would not grant it till he had learnt the dispositions of
the King of Denmark. This absolutely mendacious statement
operated instantly. On October 22, 1709, Frederick IV. of
Denmark concluded an offensive and defensive alliance with
Peter the Great against Sweden without receiving any subsidies
from him.

Thus Frederick IV. of Denmark, against the advice of his
wisest counsellors, and despite the angry remonstrances of Great
Britain and Holland, had resolved to attack Sweden at the very
time when the Tsar was harrying the remnant of her Baltic
provinces. Success was taken for granted; but Sweden was
once more to show the world that a military state whose martial
traditions and strong central organisation enabled her to mobilise
troops more quickly than her neighbours, was not to be overthrown
by a single disaster, however serious. Despite her terrible losses
in Russia, she could still oppose 16,400 well-disciplined troops to
the Danish invader; and these troops were commanded by Count
Magnus Stenbock, the last, but not the least of the three great
Caroline captains.* Her fleet too, was a little stronger than the
fleet of Denmark-Norway; and besides her garrisons in Stralsund,
Wismar, Bremen, Verden, and other places, she had Krassau's
army corps of 9,000 men, which, on receiving intelligence of the
Poltava catastrophe, had prudently retired, with King Stanislaus,
from Poland to Pomerania. On November 12, 1709, 15,000

---

* The other two, Rehnskjöld and Levenhaupt, were now prisoners in Russia.

Danes landed in Scania, at Raa, south of Helsingborg; a Norwegian army corps, advancing from the north-west, was to co-operate simultaneously. At first the Swedes were too weak to offer any resistance, and allowed the Danes to advance into the heart of Scania; but the non-appearance of the Norwegian auxiliary corps compelled the Danish commander to retreat, and on March 10 he was attacked and routed by Stenbock at Helsingborg, whereupon the Danes hastily evacuated Sweden. Yet, failure though it was, the short Scanian campaign had been of material assistance to the Tsar. It had prevented the Swedish Government from sending help to the hardly-pressed Eastern provinces, and thus given Peter a free hand in that direction. Riga, into which "accursed hole" he had the satisfaction of hurling the first bomb with his own hand, was starved into surrender on July 15, 1710; in the two following months fell Pernau and Reval, and with them all the Swedish dominions south of the Gulf of Riga. Finland was also invaded, and the fortress of Viborg, "the bolster of Petersburg" as Peter called it, was captured in June.

But now alarming news from the south suddenly interrupted the Tsar's career of conquest in the north. Even before Poltava Tolstoi at Stambul had had the greatest difficulty in preventing the Porte from indirectly assisting the Swedes. Immediately after Poltava, Tolstoi demanded the extradition of Charles and Mazepa. This was a diplomatic blunder, as it irritated the Turks, who were already alarmed. Tolstoi now reported "great military preparations made in extreme haste," and advised that the Russian forces should be increased rather than diminished. He also recommended the abduction of Charles from Bender, where he had been received and entertained with royal honours. In August, Tolstoi offered the Grand Mufti 10,000 ducats and 1,000 sables if he would hand over the fugitives, but the Mufti gravely replied that such a breach of hospitality would be contrary to the religion of Islam. Evidently the Turks wished to prolong the Russo-Swedish war till they were ready to take the field themselves. Nor was Charles himself idle. For the first time in his life he was obliged to have recourse to diplomacy; and his pen now proved almost as formidable as his sword.

First, he sent his agent, Neugebauer, to Stambul with a memorial in which the Porte was warned that if Peter were given time he would attack Turkey as suddenly and unexpectedly as he had attacked Sweden in 1700.* The fortification of Azov and the building of a fleet in the Black Sea clearly indicated his designs, and a Swedo-Turkish alliance was the only remedy against so pressing a danger. "Reinforce me with your valiant cavalry," concluded Charles, "and I will return to Poland, re-establish my affairs, and again attack the heart of Moscovy." These arguments, very skilfully presented, had a great effect upon the Porte. At Varnitsa, whither he was now transferred, Charles was provided with a guard of honour of 500 janissaries, and 500 thalers a day were assigned to him for the maintenance of his suite. Charles's chief difficulty was want of money. But on the death of Mazepa (August 22, 1709) he borrowed 80,000 ducats from the Hetman's heirs, and subsequently he received 100,000 thalers from the Court of Holstein, besides a large advance from Cooks, the English bankers of the Levant Company at Constantinople. Neugebauer's arrival at Stambul seriously embarrassed Tolstoi, and when Neugebauer was reinforced by Stanislaus Poniatowski, Charles's ablest diplomatist, the situation became acute. Nevertheless, at first, the Moscovite prevailed. In November, 1709, the Russo-Turkish peace was renewed, and it was agreed that Charles should be escorted to the Polish frontier by Turkish, and from Poland to the Swedish frontier by Russian troops! But in January 1710, Poniatowski succeeded in delivering to the Sultan, personally, a second memorial by Charles, convicting the Grand Vizier, Ali Pasha, of corruption and treason, and in June he was superseded by Neuman-Kuprili, whose first act was to lend Charles 400,000 thalers free of interest. Kuprili, also, would have avoided war, if possible, but the patriotic zeal of the semi-mutinous janissaries was too strong for him, and he had to give way to the still more anti-Russian Grand Vizier, Baltaji Mehemet Pasha. Peter, encouraged by his Baltic triumphs, now thought fit to adopt a higher tone with the Porte, and in October, 1710, categorically demanded if the Sultan wanted peace or war,

* Compare Charles XII.: "Egenhändiga Bref"; Solovev: "Istoria Rossy," XVI., 1.

threatening an invasion unless he received satisfactory assurances forthwith. The Porte, unaccustomed to such language from Moscovy, at once threw Tolstoi into the Seven Towers, and the Grand Vizier was sent to the frontier at the head of 200,000 men. For the first and last time in his life Peter had lapsed from his habitual cautious prudence, and his impulsiveness was to cost him dear.

But there was no going back now. As soon as the intelligence of the rupture with the Porte was confirmed, Prince Michael Golitsuin moved into Moldavia at the head of ten dragoon regiments, and on February 25, 1711, in the Uspensky Cathedral, war was solemnly proclaimed, in the Tsar's presence, against "the enemies of the Cross of Christ." On March 6, Peter set out for the front, but he was detained at Luck, in Poland, by the severest attack of illness he had ever experienced, one of his "palaxisms,"* as he called them, lasting for thirty-six hours, during which his life was despaired of. An unwonted despondency clung to him after his recovery, and he wrote to Menshikov, whom he left behind to guard Petersburg, that God alone knew the end of the uncertain road which his feet were now destined to tread. But he grew more cheerful as he advanced, especially after a meeting with the ever-jovial Augustus at Yaroslavl, where he concluded a fresh offensive and defensive alliance, confirmatory of the Treaty of Thorn (May 30, 1711). The petitions and promises of the orthodox Christians in Turkey now induced Peter to accelerate his pace, and he concluded, *en route*, a secret treaty of alliance with Demetrius Cantemir, Hospodar of Moldavia, by which Moldavia was to be created into an independent state, whose fortresses were to extend to the Dniester and include Budziak. Peter had expected that a general insurrection of the Serbs and Bulgars would have compelled the Grand Vizier to re-cross the Danube, especially when, after the Russians had crossed the Dniester, Demetrius Cantemir openly declared for them. But unexpected difficulties suddenly began to accumulate. On June 8, the Russian commander-in-chief, Marshal Sheremetev, reported that the whole land had already been wasted by the Turks, so that he knew not whence to draw provisions and

* Paroxysms.

provender for his army.   He had, he said, only a month's supply
of bread, and 2,000 head of cattle.   At a council of war, held in the
middle of June, Peter and General Rönne, against the opinion of
the majority, decided to advance still further, in order to support
Sheremetev, and unite with the orthodox Christians.   On June 24
Peter reached Jassy, the capital of Moldavia, where he received a
Wallachian envoy, who offered to betray his Hospodar, Bran-
covenu, who was on the Turkish side.   But the question of
supplies had now become so pressing, that all strategical considerations had to be subordinated thereto.   On the rumour that
an immense quantity of provisions had been hidden by the Turks
in the marshes of Fulchi, near Braila, Peter crossed the Pruth and
proceeded in search of these phantom supplies through the forests
on the banks of the Sereth.   But on July 17 the advance guard
reported the approach of the Grand Vizier ; and the whole army
hurried back to the Pruth, fighting rear-guard actions all the
way.   On July 19 the Moscovites, now reduced to 38,000 men,
entrenched themselves ; and the same evening 190,000 Turks
and Tatars, with 300 guns, appeared and beleaguered them on
both sides of the Pruth.   An attack upon the Russian camp the
same day was repulsed, the janissaries alone losing 7,000 men,
but the position of the Russians, out-numbered as they were,
exhausted by marching and fighting in a semi-tropical summer,
with provisions for only a couple of days, and no hope of succour,
was absolutely desperate.   Had Baltaji only remained stationary
for a week, he could have starved the Moscovites into surrender
without losing a man or firing a shot.   Learning, however, from
a Turkish prisoner that the Grand Vizier himself was pacifically
inclined, Vice-Chancellor Shafirov, who had accompanied the
army, persuaded the commander-in-chief, Sheremetev, to send
a trumpeter to the Turkish camp desiring a renewal of peace on
the old terms.   It was the merest forlorn hope, and Sheremetev
himself remarked that the Grand Vizier would be the craziest
person in the world to take half, when, by waiting a little longer,
he would have the whole.   The trumpeter came back empty-
handed, but in reply to a second and more urgent message from
Sheremetev, the Grand Vizier professed his readiness to negotiate
if an honourable person came to him from the Russian camp.

The same day Shafirov, with three interpreters and two couriers, Michael Bestuzhev and Artemy Voluinsky, both of whom had brilliant careers before them, departed upon what everyone regarded as a fool's errand. Shafirov's instructions strikingly reflect the extreme depression of the Tsar. Peter was now ready to surrender practically all his Baltic conquests except Petersburg; to recognise Stanislaus Leszczynski as King of Poland; and to give complete satisfaction to the Sultan. He also authorised Shafirov to promise the Grand Vizier 150,000, his Kega 60,000, the chief Ciaus 10,000, and the Aga of the janissaries 10,000 rubles if his army were permitted to return home unmolested. Shafirov acquitted himself of his difficult task with consummate ability. The terms of peace he brought back with him on July 11 were, under the circumstances, amazingly favourable. In return for a solemn engagement to retrocede Azov, to dismantle Taganrog, and all the other newly-built Azovian fortresses, to avoid all interference in Polish affairs, and grant the King of Sweden a free passage to his domains, the Russian army received permission to retire. Shafirov was immediately sent back to the Grand Vizier to conclude peace on these conditions, and the treaty was signed and confirmed on the following day.*

This unlooked-for deliverance was at first received with the utmost incredulity by the Moscovites. The Comte de Lion, who was in the Russian camp at the time, tells us,† that, if anyone the day before had suggested the possibility of such terms, he would have been regarded as a hopeless lunatic. There was only one person who took no part in the general rejoicing, and that was the Tsar. His position was undignified, and even a trifle ridiculous. He had come loudly proclaiming his intention of delivering the Christian population of Turkey from the Mahommedan yoke, and driving the Turks out of Europe, and now he had signed a peace whereby he abandoned the Sea of Azov, and undertook to destroy the work of his own hands, his fortresses, and still worse, his costly, new-built fleet! And then, too, he had been guilty of inexcusable foolhardiness. How could he defend himself against the reproach of jeopardising his little army

* Solovev: "Istoria Rossy," XVI., 2.        † Lion: "Mémoires politiques."

by blindly leading it into a distant land on the vague hope of support from irresponsible Wallachs, Serbs, and Bulgars? He had committed precisely the same blunder as Charles XII., when he plunged into the Ukrain at the bidding of the Cossacks, and the result had been almost as disastrous. And this, too, after "the most glorious victory!"\* How was he to bear the shame of such a blunder? Peter's despondency is clearly reflected in the singular letter, which he addressed to the newly-instituted Senate† on July 10th, the very day when the negotiations with the Porte were proceeding. In this letter he informs his ministers that he is surrounded by a countless Turkish army, and without a special manifestation of God's grace sees nothing before him but a hopeless pitched battle, or Turkish captivity. "In the latter case," he continues, "regard me no longer as your Tsar and Gosudar, and obey no orders from me, though they may be under my hand and seal, till I appear among you in person. And in case of my death elect the worthiest as my successor."‡ After the peace was signed, however, he became more cheerful and confident, and from his letters to Apraksin and others it is plain that he intended to gain time by evading the performance of the conditions of the peace of the Pruth as long as possible.

Two days before the Russian army departed from the Pruth, Charles XII., who had provided the Grand Vizier with a plan of campaign beforehand, arrived on the scene of action to see the *coup-de-grâce* duly administered. Only then did he receive the unwelcome news that peace was concluded. Well might he denounce the conduct of Baltaji as a treason to the Sultan as well as to himself. "He seemed to have more regard," wrote Charles, "for the conservation of the enemy's army than for the advantage of the Ottoman Porte."§ Even now, however, Charles did not abandon the struggle. He was materially assisted by Peter's tergiversations. First the Tsar said he would not surrender Azov or raze the other fortresses till the King of Sweden had returned to his own country. When the Turks thereupon

---

\* The name Peter always gave to the Battle of Poltava
† See next Chapter.
‡ Solovev: "Istoria Rossy," XVI., 2. Solovev accepts this strange document as authentic, despite "a strong presumption against it."
§ Charles XII.: "Egenhändiga Bref."

threatened to cut in pieces Shafirov, whom the Tsar had been obliged to leave as a hostage in their hands, Peter ordered Apraksin to level Taganrog as low down as possible without injuring the foundations, " as God may at some future time order otherwise." Skilfully taking advantage of this shuffling, Charles at last procured the dismissal of Baltaji, and his friend, Jussuf Pasha, the Aga of the janissaries, became Grand Vizier in Baltaji's stead. War was then, once more, declared against Russia (November, 1711) ; and the Sultan announced that in the spring he would lead his army against Peter in person. Yet the Turkish ministers told Shafirov privately that the Tsar might still have peace if he evacuated Poland, concluded a three years' truce with the King of Sweden, and placed the Ukrain beneath the protection of the Sublime Porte. Shafirov replied that such terms were impossible and counselled Peter again to prepare for war (January, 1712). Then Peter so far gave way as to abandon Azov and raze Taganrog to the ground, without waiting for the dismissal of Charles XII. But the danger was not yet over. Early in 1712 the influential French ambassador at Stambul began urging the Sultan to declare war against Russia for the third time. Peter, he argued, was not to be trusted, and if only the Sultan sent Charles home with an escort of 30,000 Turks and 15,000 Tatars, all Poland would hail him as a deliverer.* But the British and Dutch ministers now came to Shafirov's assistance, and persuaded the Grand Vizier to accept a treaty drafted by themselves for a twenty-five years' truce between Russia and the Porte, Peter undertaking to evacuate Poland and acknowledge the sovereignty of the Porte over the Cossacks (April, 1712). This treaty cost Shafirov 84,900 Venetian ducats, of which the Grand Vizier got 30,000, the Grand Mufti 10,000, and the friendly Dutch and English ministers from 4,000 to 6,000 apiece. Tolstoi was now released, and at once petitioned Peter to deliver him from the " Turkish hell " in which he had languished seventeen months, without medical assistance and in constant fear of torture. But the Turks would not let him go

* Solovev : " Istoria Rossy," XVI., 2. Compare Charles XII. : " Egenhändiga Bref." The hope of obtaining such an escort was the true cause of Charles's long stay in Turkey

till the April treaty had been confirmed, and Peter's persistent evasion of its principal clause, the evacuation of Poland, not only imperilled the lives of his ministers, but armed his enemies at the Porte with a potent weapon against him. The French and Swedish ministers warned the Divan that the Tsar was bent upon dismembering Poland, and re-establishing the Greek Empire, and Charles sent the Sultan's mother, who had great influence at Court, a watch and diamond ear-rings worth 5,000 francs. But Shafirov outbid the Swedes by bestowing on the old lady 1,200 purses and a diamond girdle worth 6,000 francs. He could also boast of the steady support of the Grand Vizier, "who though a Mussulman has behaved better to me than most Christians," he gratefully reported. But once more, "the devilish King of Sweden," as Shafirov called him, proved the stronger. The continuance of the Russian troops in Poland could no longer be concealed, and Poniatowski succeeded in presenting a third memorial of Charles's to the Sultan, while on his way to the mosque, emphasising and commenting on this flagrant breach of the April treaty. On October 25 a Turkish courier returned from Poland with confirmation of the fact, and Shafirov, Tolstoi and Sheremetev, with 208 of their suite, were again sent to the Seven Towers and confined in such narrow quarters that they were almost asphyxiated. On November 29, 1712, the Sultan himself set out for Adrianople, and war was declared against Russia for the third time. Shafirov reported* that this change of front was entirely the Sultan's doing. He had never liked the Peace of the Pruth, and, egged on by the French ambassador, was resolved to reinstate Charles, to whom he had sent a present of 600,000 francs. In the beginning of 1713, however, better reports arrived from Shafirov. The Sultan declared war, it now appeared, by way of extorting territory from the Poles, but the Poles remaining firm, he concluded that the Tsar was stronger in Poland than his rival, and that the French and Swedish ministers had deceived him. He also feared that, in the present temper of the janissaries, disaster might mean his deposition. He therefore requested Charles to depart from Turkey, whereupon Charles entrenched himself in his camp at

* Despatches cited by Solovev : " Istoria Rossy," XVI., 2.

Bender and killed and salted for food the priceless Turkish full-bloods which the Sultan had sent him from his own stables.  On February 1, 1713, Charles was attacked by a whole Turkish army corps and made prisoner after a contest which reads more like an extravagant episode from some heroic folk tale than an incident of sober eighteenth century history.  Even Shafirov was moved to exclaim that the King was "the first and bravest soldier in the universe."  Shafirov was now released and sent to Adrianople, where the negotiations with Russia were resumed.  But the eyes of the Turks had now been opened for the first time to the fact that the Polish and the Eastern questions were inseparable, and to its inevitable corollary that Russia's predominance in Poland was a direct menace to the Porte.  The new Grand Vizier, Ali Pasha, now demanded tribute from Russia with the obvious intention of provoking a rupture (June, 1713), and Shafirov only averted war by bribing with 10,000 ducats the Grand Mufti, who thereupon refused, on religious grounds, to declare war against the infidel.  Finally, on June 24, 1713, the Peace of Adrianople, mediated by the maritime Powers, adjusted all the outstanding differences between Russia and the Porte.

Meanwhile, in Poland itself the gentry were in full revolt against the unheard-of extortions of the Russian and Saxon troops, so that when Charles sent Grudzinsky thither (in 1712) with 10,000 Tatars, whole regiments of Poles joined his standard, and the situation became so grave that Dolgoruki, the Russian ambassador at Warsaw, gave the country up for lost.  The rout of Grudzinsky by Vasily Dolgoruki at Vresna (June 11) extinguished the threatened conflagration, but the misgovernment and double-dealing of Augustus had united all parties against him, and armed confederations were repeatedly formed for the purpose of compelling the Saxon mercenaries to evacuate Poland, where they systematically levied blackmail on every farm and manor-house.  To such a depth of misery was the unhappy country reduced that the majority, not only of the peasantry, but of the smaller squires, subsisted on bread and pot herbs, and the Russian ambassador feared that in case of another bad harvest the bulk of the population would be obliged to seek sustenance elsewhere.  At last the Tsar himself had to intervene to protect the Poles against their own King, and the differences between Augustus and his subjects were settled provisionally by the compact of Warsaw (October 24, 1712).

On returning from the Pruth Peter had spent three weeks (Sept. 15/Oct. 3, 1711) at Karlsbad, to repair his shattered health. On October 22 he proceeded to Krossen, to concert measures with his allies for the vigorous prosecution of the Swedish War, which was now transferred to Germany, where the long struggle for the dominion of the North was to be fought out.

By this time Sweden's position had distinctly deteriorated. In March, 1710, the Swedish Senate had concluded a neutrality compact with the Emperor, Prussia, Hanover, Great Britain, and Holland, whereby Charles's North German possessions* were guaranteed against attack on condition that Krassau's army in Pomerania abstained from hostilities within the German Empire and was not employed either in Poland or Jutland. This guarantee treaty was, under the circumstances, a prudent act of statesmanship, but Charles incontinently rejected it as interfering with his Turkish plans, thereby greatly irritating the maritime Powers, who were already by no means so well disposed towards Sweden as heretofore owing to the depredations of the Swedish privateers in the Baltic. In 1712 the unwisdom of Charles in so summarily renouncing a compact intended for his special protection became strikingly apparent. Not only did the Tsar and King Augustus determine to proceed against the Swedish possessions in Germany, but they persuaded Frederick IV. of Denmark to join them. This was only natural, as Sweden's German territories were a perpetual menace to Denmark's southern frontier, to say nothing of the fact that for a century and a half the acquisition of Bremen and Verden had been the constant ambition of the Danish crown. The plan of the allies was for the Danes to fall upon Bremen and Verden, where Stade was the chief fortress, while the Russians and Saxons simultaneously attacked Stralsund. Stade capitulated (September 7) to the Danes, who thereupon occupied the bishoprics of Bremen and Verden, but the allies failed to make any impression on Stralsund, and the

* Compare "Sveriges Historia," IV., 580, 581: "Danmarks Riges Historie," V., 45.

abortive siege led to a violent quarrel between the Kings of Poland and Denmark which the Russian ministers only succeeded in composing with the utmost difficulty.

But now a fresh danger suddenly threatened Peter and his associates from the West. From the first the maritime Powers had been far more amicably disposed towards Sweden than towards Moscovy. We have already seen how all Peter's pacific overtures had been coldly and curtly rejected both at London and The Hague. This anti-Russian feeling was strongest in England. The disappearance from Central Europe of so disturbing an element as Charles XII. was, doubtless, a distinct relief to all the members of the Grand Alliance during the war of the Spanish succession ; but far more offensive to the allies than the arrogance of Sweden was the interference of semi-barbarous Moscovy in European affairs. Before Poltava, Sweden was held to be the counterbalance of Moscovy, and entitled, so far as she performed that useful political function, to the support of the maritime Powers. Hence Great Britain recognised Stanislaus as King of Poland, and in London the Russian ambassador, Matvyeev, was treated with the most contemptuous indifference. The Queen, he was told, could not afford to offend so powerful a potentate as Charles XII. by admitting the Tsar into the Grand Alliance.* And presently outrage was added to insolence. Matvyeev, who had already received his recall, was, on January 21, 1709, proceeding to Somerset House to hear the latest political gossip from the other foreign envoys, who habitually met together there to exchange news, when three men attacked him in his carriage, deprived him of his cane, sword and hat, and lodged him in jail on a warrant obtained against him by two shopkeepers and a lace merchant for a debt of £50. The ambassadors assembled at Somerset House were speedily informed of what had happened, and the Portuguese and Florentine ministers hastened to the Secretary of State to protest against what they described as an insult to the whole diplomatic corps. On the following day all the foreign ministers waited upon Matvyeev with the liveliest expressions of horror and indignation at such a violent breach of international courtesy. At the same time Matvyeev was assured

* Matvyeev's despatches, cited by Solovev : " Istoria Rossy," XVI., 1.

by Under-Secretary Walpole that the Chief Secretary had posted down to Windsor to report the matter to the Queen, and the much-ruffled ambassador was released and promised every satisfaction. We can understand Matvyeev's feelings when, from The Hague, he reported the crowning outrage of the "Christ-hating English nation" to Peter; but the Tsar was in such straits at the time that he was obliged to condone the offence. Even after Poltava the tone of the British Cabinet was distinctly and persistently unfriendly. The British and Dutch ministers at Copenhagen had done their utmost to prevent Denmark from acceding to the second coalition against Sweden, and the invasion of Pomerania by Russian troops, who wintered there in 1712, filled the Court of St. James's with the gravest suspicions. The interview between the Tsar and Lord Whitworth on this very subject at Karlsbad was so lively that the diplomatist had to quit the Tsar's presence somewhat hurriedly, and Bolingbroke told Van der Lit, the new Russian ambassador at London, that Russia's obvious intention of extruding the Swedish King from German soil was what Great Britain never could put up with. In the course of 1712 the maritime Powers offered their mediation in the Northern War in such a threatening manner that Peter declared it was not mediation, but intimidation. Nevertheless he expressed himself willing to make peace on the somewhat vague stipulation that all the ancient Russian lands which he had reconquered should be retroceded to him. As, however, Charles XII. refused to surrender anything, "whatever the conjunctures," all idea of mediation was finally abandoned.

Charles's obstinacy was to cost him dear. From Bender he had originated a fresh plan of campaign too heroic to be practicable. Magnus Stenbock was to form a new army corps in Sweden, convey it to Pomerania, and invade Poland from the north, to reinstate Stanislaus and drive out Peter and Augustus, while Charles and the Turks co-operated with him from the south. On September 24, 1712, Stenbock, escorted by a fleet of twenty-four liners, succeeded in transporting an army of 9,400 men, a park of artillery, and a quantity of transports, laden with stores, from Sweden to the isle of Rügen in Pomerania, despite the disturbing presence of a large Danish fleet under

Gyldenlöve, which subsequently destroyed the greater part of
the transports. After reinforcing himself from the garrison
of Stralsund, Stenbock had at his disposal an effective army
of 17,000 men, but what was he to do with it? He had
strict orders from Charles to move south-eastwards to attack
the Russo-Saxon army in Poland. At an earlier stage of the
war, a Swedish army of 17,000 men might not have regarded
such a task as impossible. Charles himself, under similar circumstances, would not have hesitated an instant. But Stenbock
knew that his army was Sweden's last army ; and that while a
victory was problematical at best, a disaster would be irreparable.
He therefore refused to accept the responsibility of plunging
blindly into Poland, leaving Sweden's German possessions to
their fate, especially as Prussia also now began to adopt a
threatening tone. It was equally impossible for him to remain
at Stralsund, where he was already suffering from lack of provisions. So to feed his soldiers he marched westwards into
Mecklenburg, reached Wismar in safety, and proceeded to live
upon the land. But even here he could not long remain in
safety. The Danes were advancing against him from the south-
west, the Russians and Saxons from the south-east, and to
prevent their junction he resolved to attack the weaker foe, the
Danes, whose army was little superior to his own. By forced
marches he overtook the Danes near Gadebusch, before the
Saxons could overtake him or join the Danes, and won a victory
(December 20, 1712) which well deserved the congratulations
bestowed upon the victor by Marlborough, but, unfortunately,
was of very little service to Sweden. Hoping to crush Denmark
to the earth, as Torstensson had done in 1643, by occupying
Jutland, Stenbock crossed the Holstein frontier on New Year's
Day, 1713, and after destroying the defenceless city of Altona,
an absolutely wanton act of barbarity, he marched northwards
through Holstein pursued by the Russo-Dano-Saxon armies
under the Tsar's own command. Cut off from Jutland and
surrounded on every side by enemies, Stenbock at last lost
courage, and took refuge (February 14, 1713) in Tönning, the
chief fortress of Holstein-Gottorp, Sweden's one ally. Three
months later, after an unsuccessful attempt to break through the

beleaguers, Stenbock, with the assistance of the Holstein minister, Von Görtz, succeeded in obtaining honourable terms of surrender for his army, now reduced to 11,000 men (capitulation of Oldenburg, May 6, 1713), though he himself remained in Danish captivity till his death, four years later.

No sooner was Stenbock safely shut up in Tönning, than Peter, leaving Menshikov with a large Russian contingent to support the Danes, went in search of fresh allies. The Elector of Hanover, whom he visited first, gave him good advice, but would pledge himself to nothing. At Berlin the new King of Prussia, Frederick William I., showed a keen appetite for slices of Polish territory; but as Peter would not consent to a dismemberment of the republic for fear of offending Augustus, the Prussian visit also proved abortive. Unable to obtain assistance at Hanover and Berlin, Peter determined to conquer Finland in order "to break the stiff-necks of the Swedes," and have something definite to surrender when the time for negotiation should have arrived. The necessary preparations were made immediately after his return to St. Petersburg in March, 1713. On April 29 the Russian fleet sailed. It consisted of 93 galleys and 110 smaller vessels, and carried with it an army of 16,000 men. Peter accompanied it in his capacity of rear-admiral. The defence of Finland had been entrusted by the Swedish Senate to the incapable Lybecker, who heaped blunder upon blunder, and his gallant successor, Karl Gustaf Armfelt, with hopelessly inadequate forces, could do little but retreat skilfully northwards. His own and Finland's fate were finally decided on February 19, 1714, at the bloody battle of Storkyrko, when the Swedish general stood at bay with his raw levies against threefold odds and was practically annihilated. After this catastrophe further resistance was useless, and by the end of 1714 the whole Grand-Duchy was in the enemy's possession.

Meanwhile in Germany, during the summer of 1713, the Swedish fortress of Stettin had been besieged by the Russians and Saxons under Menshikov and Fleming. It capitulated in September and was occupied by neutral Prussian and Holstein troops on the understanding that it was to be restored to Sweden at the conclusion of a general peace. This curious arrangement,

known as "the Stettin sequestration," was primarily the work of
the Holstein ministers Görtz and Bassewitz. Their object was
to tempt Prussia over to Charles, and the Prussian Court actually
agreed to drive the Danes out of Holstein and guarantee the
neutrality of Charles's German possessions in the hope of
receiving compensation from him subsequently. Peter approved
of the arrangement so far as it concerned Stettin, shrewdly
calculating that it must ultimately draw Prussia into the struggle,
though he strongly disapproved of its anti-Danish provisions.
But the diplomatists had reckoned without Charles XII., who
at once denounced "the Stettin sequestration," naturally refusing
to recognise the right of Prussia to occupy one of his fortresses
under any conditions whatsoever. Thus the whole result of
Görtz's super-subtlety was to saddle the monarch he wished to
serve with a fresh enemy.

During the summer of 1714, owing to the incurable jealousy
of Denmark and Saxony, the war languished, and fresh efforts
were made to bring about a general pacification at the Congress
of Brunswick. Peter was willing to make peace with Sweden if
all the territory ceded to her by Russia at the Peace of Stolbovo
were now retroceded. In case of emergency he was even willing
to restore Livonia to Sweden, provided that all its fortresses
were demolished ; but he threatened that, if his other demands
were not complied with, he would destroy Livonia so utterly as
to make it absolutely valueless. But Peter's principal object at
this time was to bind Denmark more closely to him. Now that
the tide of victory had carried the Russian arms in triumph right
up to the head of the Gulf of Bothnia, and the Swedes were
driven back to their native peninsula, any future operations
against them would largely depend upon the possession of sea-
power. But the Russian navy consisted for the most part of
galleys which could not hold the open sea against the Swedish
line-of-battle ships, and consequently, in any attack upon
Stockholm or the great arsenal of Carlscrona, where the military
and naval forces of Sweden were now concentrated, the co-operation of the Danish navy was indispensable. Peter therefore
offered Denmark 150,000 rubles a year in subsidies and a subsidiary army of 15,000 men, maintained at his own expense, for

a descent upon Scania, which Denmark now hoped to regain. But the Danes considered the proffered assistance inadequate, and they also imposed as a condition precedent the active co-operation of Prussia, who was to guarantee them the possession of Bremen and Verden in return for a Danish guarantee to Prussia of Stettin.

In April, 1714, the Elector of Hanover came forward with a fresh scheme of partition. According to this project Prussia was to have Stettin; Hanover, Bremen and Verden; and Denmark, Sleswick-Holstein; Denmark and Prussia undertaking to capture Stralsund while Hanover took Wismar, which was to be transferred to Mecklenburg. Peter warmly approved of the Hanoverian scheme, and ordered all his ministers abroad to support it; but it foundered on the hostility of Denmark, who refused to part with her own conquests, Bremen and Verden. A simultaneous attempt to bring about an undertaking between Peter and Charles by the Marquis de Chateauneuf, the French minister at The Hague, failed because of the Tsar's profound distrust of France. He could not, he said, negotiate apart from his allies. At this juncture an event of capital importance occurred which profoundly affected northern politics. On August 12, 1714, died Queen Anne; the Swedophil Tory ministry disappeared; and the most unscrupulous and least excusable of Charles XII.'s numerous despoilers ascended the English throne as George I. Three months later Charles XII. reappeared upon the scene. On September 20 he had quitted Turkey, and after traversing Austria, and making a long *détour* by Nürnberg and Cassel to avoid the domains of his enemy, the Elector of Saxony, arrived unexpectedly, at midnight on November 11, at Stralsund, which, Wismar excepted, was now all that remained to him on German soil.

The year 1715 was memorable for the conclusion of the so-called "English affair," which resulted in the formation of a third coalition against Charles XII. The author of this nefarious league of spoliation was the new King of England, and the preliminaries were arranged at Copenhagen in February, but not till after considerable pressure had been brought to bear upon the Danish Court by the Russian ministers. Pure rapacity was

the sole cause of this shameful conduct on the part of the Protestant Powers, who pretended to be Charles's allies, and from
whom he had a perfect right to expect, if not active assistance,
at least neutrality. Prussia had all along been playing a waiting
game, and as soon as the Swedish Empire began to crumble
away she made haste to enlarge her own domains out of its
ruins. Her final accession to the league of spoliation was
extorted by the categorical demand of the British minister at
Berlin whether she was going to join it or not.

Still more disreputable, if possible, was the conduct of
England-Hanover, for, though nominally at peace with Sweden,
and indeed very unwilling to provoke a quarrel with her, the
Whig ministry was obliged to support the foreign monarch of
their own choice ; and an English fleet was sent to the Baltic to
co-operate, to a limited extent, with the Danes and Russians
against Charles, under the pretext of protecting the English
trade from the Swedish privateers. The Treaties of Copenhagen,
May 2, 1715, between Hanover and Denmark, and of May 17,
between Denmark and Prussia, arranged all the details of the
projected partitions. Wolgast and Stettin were to fall to the
share of Prussia ; Rügen and Pomerania north of the Peene to
Denmark, who was also to have the absolute control of Holstein-Gottorp ; and the duchies of Bremen and Verden to
Hanover, which was to pay Denmark, their conqueror and present
holder, 600,000 rix-dollars for the transfer. Charles protested
against this iniquitous traffic in stolen property, of which he
was the real owner, and absolutely refused to have any dealings
with the robbers, whereupon Hanover formally declared war
against him (October, 1715). Thus, at the end of 1715, Sweden,
now fast approaching the last stage of exhaustion, was at open
war with England-Hanover, Russia, Prussia, Saxony, and Denmark. For twelve months Charles defended Stralsund with
desperate valour. It was as if he would wipe out the disgrace
of past disaster and long captivity by another exhibition of
superhuman heroism. Again and again, at the head of his
" blue boys," he drove the allies from the isle of Usedom, and
when at length it was captured at a heavy cost, the Kings of
Denmark and Prussia were so delighted at their hard-won

triumph that they danced round the table after dinner, and Frederick IV. smoked tobacco, though "it was contrary to his nature." But the hostile forces were overwhelming, and on December 23, 1715, the fortress, now little more than a rubbish-heap, surrendered, Charles having effected his escape to Sweden, after miraculously eluding the Danish cruisers, two days before.

But at this, the very darkest hour of his fortunes, the sudden discord of his numerous enemies seemed to offer Charles XII. one more chance of emerging from his difficulties. It had become evident to all the members of the anti-Swedish league that till Charles had been attacked in the heart of his own realm the war might drag on indefinitely. But when it came to the execution of the plan of invasion, insuperable obstacles presented themselves. To begin with, Denmark and Saxony, and Hanover and Denmark, jealous of each other, were also incurably suspicious of the Tsar; yet without Peter's active co-operation Charles was practically unassailable. And at the beginning of 1716 Peter seemed to justify their suspicions by his high-handed interference in purely German affairs. It was bad enough when, at the end of January, he punished Dantzic, a free and independent city, for trading with Sweden, even going the length of seizing all the Swedish vessels in the harbour, and compelling the Dantzickers to build him privateers for nothing; but when, on April 19, by the Treaty of Dantzic, he solemnly guaranteed Wismar and Warnemünde to the disreputable and tyrannical Duke Leopold of Mecklenburg, who had married Peter's niece, the Tsarevna Catherine Ivanova, the same day, the prospect of seeing Mecklenburg a Russian outpost infuriated George I. and Frederick IV.

There can be no doubt that the Mecklenburg compact was a political blunder on the part of Peter. The most capable and experienced of his own diplomatists, Prince Boris Ivanovich Kurakin,* now at The Hague, had from the first strongly dissuaded him from it. The Duke was of notoriously bad character. He was

---

* Kurakin was also Peter's cousin by marriage. He was sent abroad in 1697 to learn navigation, and from 1707 to 1722 represented Russia at nearly every European Court. His diplomatic services to Peter were inestimable. It was he, for instance, who prevented England from declaring war against Denmark in the crisis of the Northern War.

not even divorced from his first wife, so that a second marriage would be uncanonical. When Peter persisted, Kurakin counselled him at least not to imperil the profitable English alliance by aggrandising Leopold at the expense of Peter's own allies. The Tsar again disregarded Kurakin's advice, and complications immediately ensued. Prince Repnin, sent by Peter with an army corps to help Hanover and Denmark to reduce Wismar, was informed that his services were not required; and when the fortress capitulated, on April 4, the Russian contingent was refused admittance. Peter was highly offended. But his necessities compelled him to dissemble his wrath, and at a meeting between the Tsar and Frederick IV. of Denmark at Altona, on June 3, the invasion of Scania, where Charles XII. had established himself in an entrenched camp defended by 20,000 men, was definitely arranged. On July 17 Peter arrived at Copenhagen with his galley squadron; and 30,000 Russians and 23,000 Danish troops began to assemble in Sjelland in order to make the descent under cover of the English, Danish, and Russian fleets. But July passed by, and still the Danes held back. Even when the English admiral, Sir John Norris, proposed a reconnaissance in the direction of Carlscrona, they raised objections. In mid-August Peter cruised off the Scanian coast to examine the lie of the land, and discovered that the Swedes had very strongly entrenched themselves. A bullet from one of their batteries actually pierced the yacht on which he flew his flag. Peter was naturally cautious, and his caution had been intensified by the terrible punishment with which his one act of temerity had so promptly been visited, five years before, on the banks of the Pruth. Charles XII., he argued, always formidable, would be doubly dangerous at bay in the midst of his own people. Moreover, Peter was growing more and more suspicious of his allies, and their prolonged delay in striking at the common foe seemed to point at secret negotiations, or, at least, some understanding with Sweden. He submitted his doubts to two councils of Russian ministers and generals on September 12 and 16; and they unanimously advised him to postpone the descent to the following year. Such was the real cause of the sudden and mysterious abandonment of the Scanian expedition which so long mystified Scandinavian historians, and had such important political results.

Peter's resolution was duly communicated to the Danish and Hanoverian Governments, and produced a storm of indignation which almost blew the league of spoliation to pieces. The Danish ministers declared that the mask had fallen at last, and Peter stood revealed in all his native treachery. They even pretended to fear an attack on Copenhagen, and ordered Admiral Norris to attack and destroy the Russian warships and transports there, which he refused to do. In October the Russian troops quitted Denmark, and went into winter quarters in Mecklenburg. The same month Peter concluded a fresh defensive alliance at Havelsberg with Frederick William of Prussia, whose haunting fear of Charles XII. kept him unalterably loyal to the Tsar. From Havelsberg Peter proceeded to Amsterdam, where he was joined by his two chancellors, Golovkin and Shafirov, Peter Tolstoi, Vasily Dolgoruki, and Boris Kurakin. At the beginning of the Great Northern War it would have been held impossible that such a galaxy of super-eminent native Russian diplomatists could have been assembled together towards the end of it. This political Areopagus met in high good humour, and presently its satisfaction was still further increased by the tidings from London that the Swedish minister, Count Carl Gyllenborg, had been arrested for participation in a Jacobite conspiracy engineered by Charles XII., who was said to have sent, or to be sending, a fleet with an army of 17,000 men to Scotland. Peter at once believed the story. Such an escapade seemed to him just the sort of thing that Charles XII. was likely to put his hand to. He anticipated a war between Sweden and England at the very least. " Am I not right in always drinking to the health of this enterprising fellow ?"* he wrote, ironically, to Apraksin. "Why, he gives us for nothing what we never could buy at any price ! ' But the Tsar was wrong. The whole scheme turned out to be a fanciful idea of Baron von Görtz's, which Charles sternly discountenanced.† Shortly afterwards Peter himself was suspected of Jacobite tendencies by the nervous Whig Government, because Dr. Erskine, the Scotch physician in his service, happened to be a

* Nachinatel.        † See Charles XII.: " Egenhändiga Bref."

relation of the Earl of Mar. Peter himself openly repudiated
the absurd accusation, and sent Tolstoi and Apraksin to meet
George I. on his passage through Holland to Hanover. But
King George not only refused to receive the Russian ministers,
but declined to have any dealings with Peter personally till the
Moscovite troops had evacuated Mecklenburg. Unable to obtain
anything from England, Peter, by the advice of his Prussian
ally, now began to look towards France. Louis XIV. had been
consistently hostile to Russia as being a meddling interloper
with interests contrary to France, both in Poland and at the
Porte ; but Louis XIV. was dead, and the Duc d'Orléans, who
ruled France in the name of Louis XV., was less particular. In
view of the collapse of Sweden, the ancient ally of the French
monarchy, he thought that Russia might take her place in
France's political system ; yet for fear of offending England the
French Government was not disposed to guarantee to the Tsar
all the conquests made by him during the Great Northern War.
Nevertheless, Peter considered the outlook sufficiently promising
to justify a visit to Paris, where he arrived on April 26, 1717.
Apartments had been prepared for him in the Louvre, but he
rejected them as far too magnificent. He raised the same
objection to a hotel near the Arsenal, which was subsequently
chosen for him, preferring to lodge in a private house more
suitable to his simple tastes. On the day after his arrival he
received a visit from the Regent, who conversed with him for
half an hour, Prince Kurakin acting as interpreter. Four days
later, Louis XV., then seven years of age, called upon him, and
the Tsar is said to have been delighted at the sight of the handsome child. At the return visit Louis came out into the hall to
meet Peter, but Peter, leaping from his carriage, ran to meet the
little King, caught him up in his arms, and carried him into the
Salon. Immediately after returning the royal visit, Peter explored
Paris with Kurakin as his cicerone. For merely pretty things he
showed little interest. He gave but a glance at the picture
galleries, but spent much time in the gobelin-lace factories and
the *jardin des plantes*. Everything serving a useful purpose,
especially if it had to do with commerce or navigation, at once
excited his curiosity, and he astonished everyone by his technical

knowledge and quick intelligence.   On June 9 he quitted Paris for the waters of Spa.   The political outcome of this visit to Paris was the Treaty of Amsterdam (August 4, 1717), between France, Russia, and the United Provinces, guaranteeing each other's possessions and establishing favourable commercial relations between the three countries.   France, at the same time, undertook not to renew her treaty of alliance with Sweden, which was to expire in April, 1718.

But the Treaty of Amsterdam meant very little so long as Sweden continued to show a bold front against the divided league of partition.   Throughout the whole of 1717 the political situation was hopelessly complicated and problematical.   In the beginning of the year the Hanoverian and Danish Courts demanded the withdrawal of the Russian troops from Mecklenburg, and the Danes limited the Russian contingent which was to serve in Scania to twelve battalions.   Peter thereupon drew still nearer to Prussia, and once more guaranteed to her the possession of Stettin.   Finally Hanover gave way on the Mecklenburg question, but when Peter desired the active co-operation in the Baltic of fifteen English line-of-battle ships " to bring the King of Sweden to reason," King George's Government curtly refused to place any portion of the British navy at the absolute disposal of a foreigner, and a fresh coldness ensued.   Matters were not mended by the mysterious embassy of the Abbé Dubois to England, which gave rise to the rumour that England was negotiating a separate peace with Sweden through the mediation of France.

It was under these circumstances that Peter resolved, at last, to treat directly with Sweden.   The chief intermediary was the notorious Holsteiner, Baron Georg Heinrich von Görtz, a man of uncommon astuteness and audacity, who seems to have been fascinated by the heroic element in Charles's nature, and was determined, if possible, to rescue him from his difficulties.   He owed his extraordinary influence to the fact that he was the only one of Charles's advisers who believed, or pretended to believe, that Sweden was still far from exhaustion, or, at any rate, had a sufficient reserve of force to give impetus to a high-spirited, energetic diplomacy.   This was Charles's own opinion.   His fatal optimism utterly disregarded actual facts.   But misfortune had so far depressed him to the level of common-sense that he was now willing to negotiate, but on his own terms. He was willing to relinquish a portion of the duchies of Bremen and Verden, in exchange for a commensurate part of Norway, due regard being had to the differences of soil and climate. Thus Charles's invasions of Norway in 1716 and 1718, so far from being mere adventurous escapades, were mainly due to political speculation. It was obvious that with large districts of Norway actually in his hands, he could make better terms with the provisional holders of his ultramarine domains. But the exchange of a small portion of Bremen-Verden for something much larger elsewhere was the utmost concession he would make. This was an altogether inadequate basis for negotiation. Anyone but Görtz would have retired from the affair altogether. Nay, Görtz himself thought the position well-nigh desperate. " If we are to succeed at all,"he wrote to his friend Dornat,"we must not be over-particular about the means." Charles was to be coaxed into treating, first of all, and thus gradually brought over to Görtz's plans step by step. Thus, trusting to time and his own ability, the Holsteiner plunged into the adventure and wasted, on what was obviously a hopeless quest, an amount of *finesse* and *savoir-faire* which would have made the fortunes of half a dozen ordinary diplomatists.

Görtz first felt the pulse of the English ministry, who rejected the Swedish terms as excessive, whereupon he turned to Russia. Formal negotiations were opened at Lofö, one of the Åland Islands (May 23, 1718), Görtz being the principal Swedish, and Osterman the principal Russian commissioner. Osterman, a Westphalian by birth, had been introduced to Peter by Admiral Kruse, in 1704, as a young man who understood all the principal European languages, Russian included. He quickly gained the confidence of the Tsar, who was so impressed by the ability displayed by him during the negotiations on the Pruth, as well as on a subsequent mission to Berlin, that he engaged the young diplomatist not to quit the Russian service till the conclusion of a general peace. At the Åland Congress, Osterman came prominently forward for the first time, and laid the foundations of what was to become a European reputation.

Peter, in view of the increasing instability of the league of partition, sincerely desired peace with Sweden; but he was resolved to keep the bulk of his conquests. Finland he would retrocede, but Ingria, Livonia, Esthonia and Carelia, with Viborg, must be surrendered by Sweden. If Charles consented, the Tsar undertook to compensate him in whatever direction he might choose. The Russian plenipotentiaries were instructed to treat the Swedish negotiators with the utmost courtesy and to assure them that it was not merely a peace, but an alliance with the King of Sweden that the Tsar desired. " When all ancient grudges and sorenesses are over between us," wrote the Tsar privately, "we two between us will preserve the balance of Europe."* Görtz was promised a gratuity of 100,000 rubles if peace were concluded.

Two things were soon plain to the keen-witted Osterman —that Görtz was hiding the Russian conditions from Charles, and that the majority of the Swedes were altogether opposed to the Russian negotiations, rightly judging that nothing obtained elsewhere could compensate for the loss of the Baltic provinces. He opined that there was little chance of a peace unless, at least, Revel were retroceded.

Twice the negotiations were interrupted, in order that Görtz and Osterman might consult their principals. In October, Osterman, in a private report to the Tsar, accurately summed up the whole situation. The negotiations, he said, were entirely Görtz's work. Charles seemed to care little for his own interests so long as he could fight or gallop about. In the circumstances it might fairly be argued that he was not quite sane. Sweden's power of resistance was nearly at breaking-point. Every artisan and one out of every two peasants had already been taken for soldiers. She could not fight much longer. Osterman strongly advised that additional pressure should be brought to bear by a devastating raid in Swedish territory. There was, however, a chance that Charles might break his neck, or be shot in one of his adventures. " Such an ending," continued Osterman, " if it happened after peace had been signed, would release us from all our obligations; and if it happened before, would be equally

* Peter to Osterman. Solovev: "Istoria Rossy." XVII., 3.

beneficial to us by dividing Sweden between the Holstein* and
the Hessian factions, both of whom are eager to save Sweden's
German, and therefore willing to cede her Baltic possessions, and
bid against each other for our favour."

Osterman's anticipations were strikingly realised. On December 12, 1718, Charles XII. was shot dead in his trenches while
besieging the fortress of Fredericksten in Norway. The news
reached the Åland Islands on Christmas Day, 1718, and the
Congress was suspended to await events. The irresolution of the
young Duke of Holstein sealed the fate of a party already
detested in Sweden because of its identification with Görtz, who
was arrested the very day after Charles's death and executed for
high treason in February, 1719. In March, Charles's one surviving sister, the Princess Ulrica Leonora, was elected Queen of
Sweden, and immediately afterwards the negotiations at Lofö
were resumed. But the Swedish plenipotentiaries now declared
that they would rather resume the war than surrender the Baltic
provinces ; and in July, a Russian fleet proceeded to the Swedish
coast and landed a raiding force which destroyed property to the
value of thirteen millions of rubles. The Swedish Government,
far from being intimidated, thereupon broke off all negotiations
with Russia. On September 17 the Åland Congress was dissolved ; and pacific overtures were made instead to England,
Hanover, Prussia and Denmark. By the Treaties of Stockholm,
February 20, 1719, and February 20, 1720, Hanover obtained the
bishoprics of Bremen and Verden for herself, and Stettin and
district for her confederate, Prussia. The prospect of coercing
Russia by means of the English fleet had alone induced Sweden
to consent to such sacrifices ; but when the last demands of
Hanover and her allies had been complied with, she was left to
come to terms as best she could with the Tsar. The efforts
which England made at Vienna, Berlin and Warsaw, in the
course of 1720/21, to obtain by diplomatic methods some
mitigation of Russia's demands in favour of Sweden, proved
fruitless, chiefly owing to the stubborn neutrality of Prussia ; and

---

* Charles Frederick, Duke of Holstein, the son of Charles XII.'s eldest sister,
was at the head of the Holstein. Prince Frederick of Hesse, the consort of Charles's
second and sole surviving sister Ulrica, was at the head of the Hessian faction.

though an English fleet was despatched to the Baltic to protect
Sweden's coasts, it looked helplessly on when the Russian bands
again descended upon the unhappy country in the course of 1720,
and destroyed four towns, forty-one villages and 1,026 farms
"We may not have done much harm to the enemy," wrote Peter
on this occasion, "but thank God we have done it beneath the
very noses of Sweden's defenders, who were unable to prevent it."
In her isolation and abandonment Sweden had no choice but to
reopen negotiations with Russia at Nystad in May, 1720.  She
still pleaded hard for at least Viborg; but a third Russian raid,
in which three towns and 506 villages were destroyed, accelerated
the pace of the negotiations; and on August 30, 1721, by the
Peace of Nystad, Sweden ceded all her Baltic provinces (except
Finland, which was retroceded by Russia), receiving in return an
indemnity of two millions of thalers, free trade in the Baltic, and
a solemn undertaking of non-interference in her domestic affairs.

On September 3 a courier, with a sealed packet containing
the Treaty of Nystad, overtook Peter on his way to Viborg.
On opening the packet the Tsar declared, with perfect justice,
that it was the most profitable peace Russia had ever concluded.
"Most apprentices," he jocularly observed, "generally serve for
seven years, but in our school the term of apprenticeship has
been thrice as long.* Yet, God be praised, things could not
have turned out better for us than they have done."  And,
indeed, the gain to Russia by the Peace of Nystad was much
more than territorial.  In surrendering the pick of her Baltic
provinces, Sweden had surrendered along with them the hegemony of the North, and all her pretensions to be considered a
great Power.

* The Great Northern War had lasted twenty-one years.

# CHAPTER XI.

## The Reforms and the Difficulties of the Regenerator in the Internal Administration. 1700—1721.

The Internal Administration—The New *Prikazui*—The Rathhäuser and Trading Companies—The Reforms of the Currency—The Immigration *Ukaz*—Toleration of the Dissenters—Promotion of Education—Kopiewski—The First Gazette—The Drama—Civilising *Ukases*—Liberation of the Moscovite Women—Death of the Patriarch Adrian—The Patriarchate Dangerous—Stephen Yavorsky—Supersession of the Patriarchate—The Russian Prelates—Popular Disaffection—Peter regarded as Antichrist—The Costume *Ukases*—The Astrakhan Rebellion—New Men—Makarov—Osterman—Shafirov—Disgrace of Vinius—Kurbatov's Reports on Fiscal Corruption and Public Venality—Sanitary Reforms—Measures against Freebooters—Introduction of the "Civil Script"—Institution of the Senate and of the Colleges—Fiscal and Legal Reforms—The Custom of Primogeniture Introduced—Educational Measures—Measures to Promote Commerce, Manufactures, and the National Industries Generally—The Building of Petersburg—Condition of the Peasantry—Measures for their Protection—Universal Peculation—Its Causes—Measures against it—Appointment of Imperial Fiscals and other Informers—Archbishop Yavorsky's Protest—Venality of the Senate—Ober-fiscal Nestorov and the Gagarin Affair—Wholesale Depredations of Menshikov—The Solovev Affair—Disgrace of Menshikov—Death of Kurbatov—Police Regulations—Pososhkov, the first Russian Economist, and his Book on Poverty and Riches—Educational Measures—The Printing of Books—Promotion of Science—Collection of Art Treasures—Petersburg—Difficult Position of the Church—Peter's Attitude towards the Dissenters—Persecution of the Rationalistic Sects—Protestant and Catholic Propaganda—Measures for the Discipline of the Church—Archbishop Stephen Yavorsky—His Hostility to Peter—The Rise of Theophan Prokopovich—His Rivalry with Stephen—Institution of the *Dukhovnaya Kollegiya*, or Synod—The Real Reason of this Innovation.

HITHERTO historians have regarded the Great Northern War too exclusively from the soldier's point of view, yet it was not so much an arena for the strife of heroes as, in the first place, a training school for a backward young nation, and, in the second place, a means of multiplying the material resources of a nation as poor as she was backward. Peter the Great undertook the war with Sweden in order that Russia might gain her proper place on the Northern Mediterranean. The possession of an ice-free seaboard was essential to her natural development ; the creation of a fleet followed inevitably upon the acquisition of such a seaboard ; and she could not hope to obtain her due share of the trade and commerce of the world till she possessed both.

But, in the meantime, Russia had to be educated, as far as possible, up to the European level, in order that she might be able to appreciate and utilise the hardly-won fruits of Western civilisation. And thus it was that, during the whole course of the Great Northern War, the process of internal, domestic, re-formation had been slowly but unceasingly proceeding. The whole fabric of the state was gradually changing. New, brand-new, institutions, on Western models, were gradually growing up among the cumbrous, antiquated, worn-out machinery of old Moscovy, and new men, capable and audacious, brimful of new ideas, were being trained, under the eye of the great Regenerator, to help him in his herculean task, and carry it on when he himself had vanished from the scene. At first, indeed, the external form of the administration remained much the same as before. The old dignities disappeared of themselves with the deaths of their holders, for the new men, those nearest to Peter, did not require them ; yet a number of boyars, *okolnichie* and *dumny dyaks* still presided over their tribunals, delivered judgments, and issued *ukazes*. The *prikazui*, too, continued to exist, some retaining their old names, while others were transformed and re-christened, according as fresh branches of business required the institution of new departments of state. Thus, between 1701 and 1703, the naval, artillery, mining and coining directories sprang into existence. The great drag on the wheels of the Government was its penury, a drag which grew more and more sensible every day as the war proceeded. The expense of the fixed embassies at foreign Courts (one of the earliest Petrine innovations) was a particularly severe drain upon the depleted treasury. None of these ministers, not even the most important of them, ever received adequate salaries. Thus Matvyeev at The Hague got but 15,000 gulden a year, while his expenses amounted to 27,193 gulden. Every expedient to increase the revenue was eagerly snatched at. Taxation was made universal, all exceptions being abolished, the sale of spirits became a Government monopoly, the administration of which was at first entrusted to the newly instituted Rathhäuser, by means of which Peter hoped at first to accustom his people to local self-government. For the purpose of promoting trade, commercial companies were formed all over the country ; but it was soon discovered that commerce could not be created by *ukazes*, and most of these companies failed because the Russians did not know how to make use of them. Another impediment to commerce was the deplorable state of the currency. The ruble and the altuin\* were the units of account ; but neither of them existed, the only coins in circulation being the well-worn silver copecks and half-copecks, most of which were further deteriorated by bisection and trisection. In many places goods were paid for by leather and other tokens. The currency was reformed by the coinage *ukas* of March, 1700, which established mints for the stamping and testing of gold, silver, and copper coins by qualified masters. Previously to 1700, only from 200,000 to 500,000 coins had been annually struck in Russia. In 1700 the number rose to 1,992,000, in 1701 to 2,559,000, and in 1702 to 4,534,000.

Peter's two great objects at this period of his reign were external security and internal prosperity. The former he had obtained by the creation of the new army on a European model, the latter he hoped to promote by a whole series of administrative measures. In April, 1702, he issued his celebrated *ukas* for facilitating the immigration of intelligent foreign specialists into Russia, on a scale never before contemplated. In the preamble to this *ukas* it was explained that these foreigners were coming "to make our subjects better and prosperous," and the invitation was made as tempting as possible, all such visitors being allowed free ingress and egress into and out of the country, full liberty of worship, and permission to be judged by their own tribunals. To the better sort of Russian Dissenters, also, Peter was very tolerant. Religious persecution was indeed his abomination. Even when he could not prevent the Church from persecuting heretics, he always endeavoured to give the proceedings a political motive.

\* A three copeck piece.

His attitude towards the chief centre of the *Bezpopovshchina*,[*] founded at the end of the seventeenth century, on the banks of the Vuiga, between the lake of the same name and the lake of Onega, is characteristic of his general policy. The enterprise and organising genius of this wealthy community enabled it practically to monopolise the rich fisheries and hunting-grounds of the White Sea, while the abundant harvests which filled to overflowing the granaries of the *Vuigavskaya Pustuin*,[†] as it was somewhat inappropriately called, gave this colony the command of the corn market of Petersburg. All danger from without was avoided by a composition with Peter, the Vuigovtsui agreeing to pay double taxes, and work, at set times, for nothing in the state mines and foundries at Povyenets. In return for such services the tolerant and practical Tsar permitted these lucrative Nonconformists full liberty of worship (*ukaz* of 1703) with the use of the ancient rites and the old service-books. Peter, indeed, though undoubtedly orthodox, and even genuinely religious in his own peculiar way, was theoretically a respecter of conscience, though, as in the case of the unfortunate Bible-reading widow, Zima, he sometimes winked at terrible persecutions by the ecclesiastical authorities. The only people to whom he denied toleration were the Jews, whom he regarded with the liveliest hatred. " I would rather see Mahomedans and heathens than Jews," he said on one occasion. " They are scoundrels and sharpers. I would extirpate, not disseminate, *this* evil. They shall neither dwell nor trade in Russia, however they may try to bribe those who are near me."

From the first, Peter did much to promote education, especially education of a practical sort. Schools of mathematics and navigation were established, about 1702, at Moscow, three Englishmen being the first teachers, and in 1703 another school was founded by the German pastor, Glück, at which geography, ethics, politics, Latin rhetoric, the Cartesian philosophy, dancing, and the elements of French and German were taught. Great efforts were made to

---

[*] The popeless or priestless community.

[†] *Pustuin*, a monastery of hermits in the wilderness ; but as the monastery now stood in the midst of twenty-seven ancillary establishments, the term was scarcely appropriate.

provide cheap books for the schools.  In 1700 the brothers Tessing, of Amsterdam, obtained the monopoly of printing Russian books for fifteen years, but they made but little use of it, the chief worker in this field being the Protestant Pole, Ilia Kopiewski, a scholar of repute and a great admirer of Peter, who found him a valuable collaborator.  Kopiewski set up a press of his own at Amsterdam, about 1697, and, after receiving from the Dutch Government the privilege of printing all Russian books, produced a considerable number,* among which may be specially mentioned an abridgment of the Greek Emperor Leo the Philosopher's " Art of War," by the special command of Peter in 1698, and a version of " Æsop " in 1700, remarkable as being the first Russian translation from the ancient classical authors.  In 1703, Leonty Magnetsky, the teacher of arithmetic in the newly-erected (1701) School of Mathematics and Navigation at Moscow, composed a manual of arithmetic and mathematics, and published in the following year a Slavonic-Greek-Latin lexicon.  It was at this time, too, that the first Russian newspaper appeared.  Up to Peter's time extracts had been made from the foreign gazettes for the private use of the Tsar and those near him, but, by the *ukas* of December 17, 1702, these communications were made public, and, in 1703, the first Russian gazette appeared.  It was entitled : *Vyedomosti o voennuikh u inuikh dyelayakh dostoinuikh znanya i pamyati.*†

Nor was another means of education, the stage, forgotten. Scenic representations had hitherto been the private pastime of the Sovereign ; Peter made them popular.  A troupe of German actors was brought to Moscow by the player Fürst, and the clerks of the various *prikazes* were taught the art of acting.  A wooden theatre was built in the middle of the Red Square at Moscow, and there, on state occasions, long-winded histories concerning Alexander of Macedon and Scipio Africanus, as well as modern comedies like " Le médecin malgré lui," were acted before crowded houses.  The pupils of the Slavonic-Latin academy also gave dramatic representations of a religious

---

* In 1699 he printed no fewer than twenty-one Russian books.  See S. Pekarsky : " Nauka i literatura v Rossy pri Petrye Vel."

† "Tidings of military and other events worthy of knowledge and remembrance."

character. Yet the brutal old manners, even in the highest circles, persisted in spite of all these feeble efforts to soften them. The pupils in the schools could not very well be worse than they were. The foreign professors fought with the musicians at the dramatic entertainments, and the servants of the Tsarevich Alexius grossly insulted his preceptor, Professor Neugebauer of Leipsic. Neugebauer retaliated by calling the Russians dogs and barbarians, and was promptly dismissed from his post. He revenged himself by publishing his " Schreiben eines vornehmen Offiziers," sometimes cited as an authority on Peter the Great, but the testimony of its angry author, still smarting from recent ill usage, should be received with caution.

Undeterred by repeated failure, and the most discouraging relapses, Peter, though himself a semi-barbarian, laboured hard to civilise those who were even more barbarous than himself. In 1702 a whole regiment was sent to Kostroma to seize ten freebooters, who were also landed proprietors, for committing all manner of outrages and burning villages wholesale. In the same year, in order to minimise conflagrations, a *ukaz* directed that all houses were to be built of brick instead of wood, and firehose were introduced. In 1704 *ukazes* were issued forbidding midwives to kill misshapen children, and undertakers to bury corpses till three days after death; restricting the sale of herbs to apothecaries' booths, and ordering the construction of stone houses at Moscow. Other *ukazes* of the same period endeavoured to raise the tone of public morality, and inculcate self-respect. Thus the *ukaz* of April, 1704, sternly prohibited compulsory marriages, which had been one of the chief scandals and miseries of old Moscovite family life, released women from the captivity of the *terem*, and compelled their husbands and fathers to admit them to all social entertainments. Henceforth, no young person was to be married without her consent, and the clergy were strictly charged to protect children from the tyranny of their parents in this respect. The *ukaz* of December 30, 1701, forbade falling on the knees before the Tsar, or doffing the hat before the Imperial palace. "What difference is there between God and the Tsar, if equal honour be shown to both?" asked Peter on this occasion.

In October, 1700, died the patriarch Adrian, and Kurbatov, on

X 2

reporting the event to Peter, suggested the postponement of the election of his successor and the establishment of a new *prikaz* to look after the temporalities of the patriarchate, which he described as in a very bad way.   There is no reason to suppose that Peter intended to abolish the patriarchate in 1700.   It is far more probable that the idea matured in course of time when no inconvenience resulted from the suspension of the dignity, and the attitude of the hierarchy towards the Tsar in the affair of the Tsarevich Alexius convinced him that the majority of the prelates were hostile.   On the other hand, the patriarchate was undoubtedly a danger to Peter at this period.   The enemies of reform could always count upon the acquiescence of the arch-pastor of the Russian Church.   The patriarch Joachim had protested against the employment of foreigners.   The patriarch Adrian had written forcibly against the shearing of beards. Adrian, however, was a timid slothful man, of whom Peter had no fear.   When Peter imposed the beard-tax, Adrian had relapsed into sullen silence, and his administration had latterly been so negligent, that his enemies accused him of sleeping away his time, and eating up his revenues.   Adrian's dilapidations could be repaired only by a very energetic successor, but where was a patriarch in sympathy with the reforming Tsar to be found ?   An energetic but unfriendly patriarch would be the natural leader of a whole army of malcontents ; he would be a most dangerous rival, a second Nikon.   In January, 1701, the administration of the temporalities of the patriarchate was entrusted to a layman, Count Ivan Aleksyei Musin-Pushkin, who had already displayed considerable administrative and financial ability as Governor of Astrakhan.   He was now appointed President of the Monas-tuirsky Prikaz, and held his Court in the patriarchal palace.   His appointment was the first step towards a rigid inquisition into the government and revenues of the Russian monasteries, which resulted in the famous *ukaz* of December, 1701, depriving the religious houses of the control of their estates, and making the archimandrites, *igumens* and monks, the salaried officials of the Government.   The care of the spiritualities was confided to a Little-Russian prelate, Stephen Yavorsky, with the title of Exarch of the Most Holy Patriarchal See.   Yavorsky had been sent to Moscovy by his own metropolitan, Varlaam Yasinsky, Archbishop of Kiev, to be consecrated Bishop of Pereyaslavl, but Peter, who desired to have the learned Kievlyan well within reach, preferred him to the see of Ryazan, which was much nearer to Moscow than Perlyaslavl. The ignorant Great Russian clergy detested this more enlightened Little Russian interloper, and such pressure was brought to bear upon him that on the day appointed for his consecration he hid himself away in a monastery, declaring that he could not accept his new dignity so long as his episcopal brethren at Moscow accused him of simony, heresy, or wine-bibbing. But Peter, well aware that the same people who repudiated Yavorsky, called him, the Tsar, Antichrist, overruled Yavorsky's objections, and insisted on the consecration of the man whom he already regarded as a fellow-worker. As metropolitan, Yavorsky offered no opposition to the work of reform, and did much for education. It was he who, as Rector of the Moscow Academy, introduced the Latin element into that institution, which before that time had been exclusively Greek. Another learned Malo-Russian, Dmitry, became metropolitan of Rostov, a province which then included all the Great Russian dioceses, and was in great ignorance and disorder. A third Malo-Russian, Filothei Leszczynski, was made the first metropolitan of Tobolsk, and did much to convert the heathen Siberians. But while favouring the Kievlyans, Peter was in perfect sympathy with the best of the Great Russian prelates, some of whom were his personal friends. Thus Theophan, the saintly Bishop of Voronezh, was as zealous as the Tsar himself for the good of his country, and frequently sent packets of money to Peter, with the inscription : " For the soldiers." Loath as he was to part with his hobbies, Peter ordered the statues of the ancient heathen deities ornamenting his house at Voronezh, which he had procured at great expense, to be removed for fear of offending this holy old man, and wept bitterly when he heard of his death.*

All this time the popular disaffection against the Tsar was steadily growing. As the war proceeded, as the burden of taxation became more grievous, and the number of the recruits

* Solovev: "Istoria Rossy." XV., 2.

ever larger, the murmuring of every class of the population grew louder and louder. "What manner of Tsar is this," it was said, " who takes us all for soldiers, and gives us no rest, and makes our wives and children widows and orphans? If he lives much longer, he will ruin the whole land. Why has he not been killed long ago? If things go well, he is well enough; but if they don't, he tears and rages, and now he has turned against God also, and taken the bells away from the churches. He is a *miroyed*,* he eats up the whole world. The people explained to their own satisfaction Peter's fondness for the Germans by devising all kinds of fables. He was a supposititious child, the son of a German girl, substituted for the daughter really born of the Tsaritsa Natalia. He was the son of Lefort. The *real* Peter had remained abroad, and sent back a German stranger to turn the orthodox into Mahommedans. In fact Antichrist now sat on the Moscovite throne. A printer, Grisha Talitsky, encouraged by Ignaty, Bishop of Tambov, actually printed and circulated a pamphlet proving that Peter was Antichrist. Talitsky was executed and the bishop degraded into a simple monk, and banished to Solovka. But so deep was the popular impression on the subject, that Yavorsky, at the Tsar's command, wrote a book entitled "The Signs of the Coming of Antichrist." He might have saved himself the trouble, for the disaffected refused to read the book, and persisted in regarding Talitsky as a martyred saint, and Peter as Antichrist, because he tortured " the true-Christian stryeltsui" with his own hands and never observed the fasts of the Church. On January 4, 1700, the Tsar irritated the reactionaries still further by issuing the *ukaz* directing the general use of short Saxon or Hungarian jackets and French or German hose. This was followed in 1701 by the *ukaz* forbidding from henceforth, under heavy penalties, the wearing of the cumbrous old Moscovite garments. Models of the new costumes were hung up on all the gates of Moscow. The change of costume, so far from being a trifle, was a reform of the first importance, intended to mark a complete and final rupture with the semi-barbarous past. The European nations of the West had long since discarded the long, heavy flowing garments,

* One who enriches himself at the expense of the community.

which may suit well enough the indolent dignity of somnolent Asiatics, but are only in the way of more alert and energetic races.   Moscovy alone still clung to oriental costumes as well as to oriental ideas, and by substituting therefor occidental costumes Peter emphasised in the most public and striking manner his intention of completely Europeanising his still semi-Asiatic subjects.    But, as Catherine II. reminded Gustavus III., a century later, there is nothing more difficult than to change the traditional habits of a people, and Peter's latest innovation was bitterly resented as both indecent and irreligious.   In Moscow itself open resistance was out of the question.   There the most capable and enterprising people were in the ranks of the reformers; the stryeltsui had been extirpated, the clergy had no patriarch, enlightened reforming prelates from Kiev leavened the reactionary mass of the Great Russian hierarchy, even in the Tsar's absence sharp eyes kept vigilant watch, and at Preobrazenskoe the terrible Romodanovsky kept down evil-doers with an iron hand.

But if nothing could be done at Moscow, far away from Moscow it was another matter, and in the July of 1705 a dangerous rebellion broke out at Astrakhan, under the leadership of Cossack officers and ex-stryeltsui.   The governor, who had hidden in a fowl-house, was dragged forth and murdered, and a Dissenter. one Yakov Nosov, and the Burgomaster of Astrakhan, Gabriel Gonchikov, were placed at the head of a provisional government.   The Astrakhan rebels then sent a letter to the Cossacks of the Terek, urging them to co-operate.   "We of Astrakhan," runs this curious document,* "have risen for the Christian faith, and because of the beard-shearing and the German clothes and the tobacco, and because we and our wives and children are not allowed to go to church in the old Russian dress, and because the governors worship Kummerian idols,† and would make us do likewise, and because of the taxes on our cellars and baths, and because we cannot bear our grievous burdens, and will not give up our old religion," etc., etc.   The Cossacks of the Terek. Krasny and Chernuy Yar yielded to the arguments of the Astrakhan people when presented pike to

* Solovev: "Istoria Rossy," XV., 2.
† These idols turned out to be wig-blocks.

throat, but the Volgan districts in general remained neutral. It had been the intention of the rebels to capture all the Volgan fortresses, with the aid of the Don Cossacks, and then attack Moscow in the absence of the Tsar, who was supposed to be chained to a pillar in a Swedish dungeon. But the Don Cossacks did not rise, because the insurrectionary letters were addressed to their official headquarters at Cherkask instead of to the out-lying settlements on the Don, where the more unruly spirits were usually to be found, and in the meantime Admiral Apraksin, then at Voronezh, succeeded in localising the rebellion. Yet at one time there were grave fears for the safety of Moscow, and Peter, knowing the inflammability of the Astrakhan district, and acting on the advice of Golovin, to whom the Astrakhan people had presented a petition with a heavy list of complaints against the foreign Government officials, ordered a general amnesty to be granted, so that complications in the East might not interfere with his operations in the West. Nevertheless, Astrakhan would not accept the Tsar's terms, and Sheremetev took it by assault (March 13, 1706), after losing twenty killed and fifty-three wounded. Three hundred and sixty-five of the rebels were subsequently sent to Moscow, to be broken on the wheel and decapitated.

After 1705 the reform movement was necessarily interrupted. Peter, now constantly at war with foreign and domestic enemies, had no time to give to domestic affairs. The Astrakhan rising was speedily followed by the Bashkir revolt, Bulavin's rebellion, the treason of Mazepa, and the invasion of Charles. During the Tsar's frequent absences the boyars continued to hold sway, though they now went by the name of " ministers." Menshikov was still the most potent of Peter's counsellors, but he did not rule alone. There was now another person still closer to the Tsar, a very quiet, modest person, who was neither seen nor heard publicly, but whose advice and protection were constantly solicited by the most important people. This was Peter's cabinet secretary, Aleksyei Vasilevich Makarov, who accompanied him on all his travels, and opened and reported upon the hundreds of documents which daily followed him all over and beyond the Empire. Another quiet unobtrusive counsellor was the equally invisible German, Andrei Osterman, already mentioned, who was also a permanent member of the Tsar's suite, and conducted the foreign correspondence.  On the other hand, many once familiar figures begin to disappear, or fall into the background.  Amongst these failing lights was old Andrei Andreeivich Vinius, who in time past had rendered to his master inestimable services.  He had increased the revenue by hundreds of thousands; he had discovered and worked new copper and silver mines; he had built four factories; cast hundreds of cannon; opened up the China trade; invented a superior sort of gunpowder; founded a school of mathematics, and made his influence felt everywhere.  Unfortunately the old man was not clean-handed, and, in 1703, his defalcations were found to be so considerable that he was threatened with the loss of all his offices and dignities.  In his extremity he turned to the favourite Menshikov, and bribed him handsomely to say a good word for him.  Menshikov took the bribes, and gave Vinius a letter of exoneration, but, at the same time, with characteristic baseness, he wrote privately to the Tsar that Vinius, "for all his wriggling," could not be justified.  Vinius, in fine, never regained the favour of the Tsar, and had the mortification to see younger men, like the clever, jovial Jew translator, Shafirov, rise above him.  Another exceedingly energetic and capable public servant was Kurbatov, who, in 1705, was appointed Inspector of the Rathhäuser, in other words, head of the finances, the Rathhäuser's principal function being to adjust and levy taxation.  It was Kurbatov's duty to discover new sources of revenue, and reveal all fiscal abuses, and, strong in the protection of Menshikov, he did his duty manfully, not sparing the most powerful personages in the land.  His reports are demonstrations of the universality and shamelessness of Moscovite venality and corruption.  In 1706 he reported that 40,000 rubles had been stolen in Yaroslavl alone, and that at Pskov 90,000 rubles had been embezzled during the war with Sweden.  The people of Pskov had offered him 20,000 rubles to hush the matter up, and he begs Peter to save him from their vengeance now that he has resisted the temptation and informed against them.  He also reported gross tyranny on the part of the newly-appointed burgomasters towards the poorer citizens, whom they oppressed and plundered in every conceivable way, even refusing to receive petitions and redress grievances. Thus Peter's well-intentioned plan of introducing local government in place of the despotic old governorships had resulted in a still more grinding oppression. Another and very frequent complaint of Kurbatov's related to the unaccountable disappearance of the tax-money during the process of collection. Many places were thousands of rubles in arrear; in the case of Astrakhan the deficit amounted to 150,000 rubles. Kazan was as bad. Some governors sent in nothing at all. Others who admitted having collected as much as 70,000, forwarded only a seventh part of that sum to Moscow. In 1711, to his infinite disgust, Kurbatov was made Vice-Governor of Archangel. Scenting disgrace in this new appointment, he asked the Tsar, point blank, why he pretended to be angry with him. "If I wanted to be angry with you," replied the Tsar, "I should make no pretence about it." "But at least make me governor," insisted Kurbatov. "Build me three ships, and *you* *shall* be governor," replied Peter.

Every expedient was snatched at to raise revenue so as to pay for the war, and meet the ever-increasing expenses of a Government that was too progressive to be economical. Fresh taxes were imposed on fish offered for sale; on oak coffins, to be collected at the monasteries; on beards and moustaches, graduated according to rank and means, every person being now obliged to pay at least two *den'gi** per beard, on entering or leaving town. Tobacco and salt were made Government monopolies, and the price of salt was doubled. The salaries of civil servants and the pay of soldiers were also taxed. But the amounts raised by these and other shifts fell far short of the requirements of the treasury.

Yet never for a moment was the great work of reform and amelioration suspended. In 1706 the first modern hospital and medical training school was built on the river Yaniza, close to the German settlement at Moscow. In 1705 a *ukas* ordered the paving of Moscow, but the necessary funds could not be procured, so Peter had to be content with keeping his capital clean. In February, 1709, sanitary inspectors for every ten

* A *den'ga* was half a copeck.

houses in Moscow were appointed, whose duty it was to see that all accumulations of filth were removed from before the doors of the dwelling-houses, at the expense of the proprietors.    Everyone disobeying or evading this ordinance was to be punished with a fine of from five to ten rubles and a flogging.

In 1707 a commission of boyars was appointed to devise the best means of dealing with the wholesale vagabondage and highway robbery which had always been one of the curses of Moscovy.   One typical instance of this reign of ruffianism may suffice.   In 1710 it was reported to the Monastuirsky Prikaz that a robber chieftain, Gabriel Stavchenok by name, with sixty armed confederates, had invaded the Ipatevsky Monastery near Kolshchevo in broad daylight (and monasteries were semi-fortresses in those days) and, after drinking themselves drunken till nightfall, they had made off with everything they could lay their hands upon, after horribly torturing the overseers.   This same band waylaid all chapmen passing from town to town, and became the terror of the whole countryside.   They were finally tracked down and destroyed by a regiment of dragoons.   And if the eighteenth century Moscovites had little scruple about living on their own countrymen they naturally had still less as to how they made money out of their country's enemies.   Thus, in 1706, Dositheus, Patriarch of Jerusalem, reported to the Tsar that hundreds of Swedish prisoners were regularly sold to the Turks in the slave markets, which caused a great scandal among the Christian population.

Such evils could be only gradually eradicated by the spread of enlightenment, and this Peter perfectly well understood.   He had already done much to promote education ; in 1707 he proceeded a step further by introducing into Russia the so-called " civil script."*  Hitherto the old Cyrillic alphabet of forty-eight letters (still used for the liturgical books) served for all Russian books.   Peter deleted eight of the most cumbersome letters,† simplified the remainder by approximating them as nearly as possible to the Latin alphabet, and sent to Holland to have the new alphabet

* Grazhdansky Shript.

† At present the Russian alphabet consists of thirty-five letters, three of which might very well be dispensed with.

cast into type. It was brought back to Russia in 1707 by the typographer, Anton Dernei, and, with some few later modifications, has been used there ever since. This simplification of the old Cyrillic alphabet was the first step towards the composition of the modern Russian written language, and therefore a cultural reform of capital importance. The first three books printed in the new script appeared at Moscow in 1708. They were a treatise on land surveying, a book on etiquette, and a manual for the regulation of rivers. The same year Peter commanded Polikarpov, the superintendent of the new printing office, to compose and publish a history of Russia from the days of Tsar Vasily Ivanovich to his own times, besides translations from Quintus Curtius, and various classical books on the science of war. Peter himself corrected the proofs and supervised the translations. Simplicity and clearness were what he chiefly aimed at, and in these respects many of the versions presented to him fell far short of his requirements. Some he pronounced to be unintelligible.

In 1708 Russia was divided into the eight "governments" of Moscow, St. Petersburg, Kiev, Smolensk, Archangel, Kazan, Azov, and Siberia, in order that the country might be administered "in a more orderly and peaceful manner." At the head of each "government" was a governor, one of whose chief duties it was to see that the taxes were duly collected and transmitted to Moscow. On January 27, 1710, the first Imperial budget was framed, when it was discovered that the annual revenue amounted to 3,016,000 rubles, or, taking a three years' average, 3,133,000 rubles, while the total expenditure came to 3,834,000 rubles. According to these estimates the army cost 1,252,000, the fleet 444,000, the diplomatic service 148,000, artillery and stores 221,000, ordnance 84,000, and the garrisons 977,000 rubles.* Thus expenditure exceeded revenue, but it was also indubitable that the revenue would have been much larger but for the wholesale peculation, which diminished the amount in transit. Absorbed as he was at this period by the Swedish and Turkish Wars, which required his prolonged absence from Russia, Peter could not attend to the details of the domestic administration

* A ruble was the equivalent of five shillings English of the day.

personally ; but, as it could no longer be neglected, he instituted
(by the *ukaz* of February 22, 1711) a supreme governing board,
to which he gave the name of " The Administrative Senate." On
March 2 a fresh *ukaz* was issued defining its functions. It was
to take the place of the Tsar during his absence, and receive
the implicit obedience due to himself. It was to be a court of
ultimate appeal, with power to punish by fine or forfeiture. It
was to control the public revenue, collect imposts, and prevent
waste. It was to select officers for the army and navy from
among the young boyars. It was to inspect all goods offered
for sale, regulate the salt tax, and supervise the Persian and
China trade. It was to appoint all the fiscal officers. It was
to receive regular reports from all the local governors, and communicate with them by special commissioners. In a word, it
was responsible for the whole burden of the administration.

But the Senate was not merely to issue *ukazes*, it was also to
see to their prompt execution, bearing in mind that " time wasted
is as irrevocable as death." In order to facilitate the communications of the Senate with the governors and the fiscal functionaries, the office of Revisor-General of *Ukazes* was instituted in
November, 1715. The first of these revisor-generals was Vasily
Zotov, the son of Peter's old tutor, the mock-patriarch Nikita
Zotov. In 1718, the Senate was adorned and fortified by the
accession of Menshikov, Apraksin, Golovkin, James Bruce,
Shafirov, Tolstoi, Dmitry Golitsuin, Andrei Matvyeev, Dmitry
Cantemir, in their capacities of presidents of the new colleges or
departments of state, which, in 1717, superseded the confusing
and cumbersome *prikazui*. The idea of this administrative
reform was first suggested to Peter by Leibnitz. By the *ukaz*
of April 18, 1718, all the colleges were to be in all points exactly
on the model of the Swedish " services," so that Peter may be
said to have learnt the science of government as well as the
art of war from his Scandinavian rivals. As finally constituted,
these new public offices were nine in number, and corresponded
roughly with the ministries of Western Europe. Andrei Matvyeev,
who had now completed his diplomatic career, took charge of the
College of Justice ; Golovkin and Shafirov, as chancellor and
vice-chancellor respectively, presided over the College of Foreign

Affairs, Menshikov was War minister, and Apraksin controlled the Admiralty. Most of the presidents of these colleges were Russians, most of the vice-presidents foreigners, Peter invariably acting on the patriotic principle, not always followed by his immediate successors, that natives should always fill the highest posts, and that no alien should occupy any place that a Russian was equally capable of filling.

By 1720, the college system was in full operation, but it soon became patent that, instead of harmoniously working together, as contemplated by its author, the various parts of this new machinery of government too often impeded each other, and violent collisions between the heads of the various colleges were of scandalous frequency. This was eminently the case in the department of Foreign Affairs, where Shafirov refused to obey Golovkin, and abused him publicly in the most discreditable manner.

Efforts were also made to simplify local government as much as possible by subdivision of labour. Thus the various governments were split up into counties or districts (*uyesdui*), each district having its own president assisted by a council of assessors, called *landsraths*, elected by the gentry. In 1720 *nadvornuie sudbui*, or courts of justice, with jurisdiction in both civil and criminal cases, were established in every town, and *zemskie kontorui*, or land-offices, where public account books had to be regularly kept, were established in every district. The land offices were to supervise the taxpayers, and report regularly to the *Kammer Collegium*, or chief fiscal Board of the Empire. In April, 1718, the old *uloshenie*, or code of laws, which was found in many respects to be incompatible with the new reforms, was remodelled according to the existing Swedish code. By the *ukaz* of June 15, 1718, insolvent debtors were to be compelled to work off their debts in public institutions, at the rate of a ruble a month, during which time they were to be fed at the expense of the state like convicts, obtaining a receipt in full discharge of their debts at the end of their term of service. A new law of succession was also introduced. After consulting the best English, Scotch and Venetian authorities, the old practice of partitioning real estate was abolished, and the custom of primogeniture was introduced. The reasons alleged for this innovation were threefold (1) the better regulation of taxation and the amelioration of the condition of the peasantry ; (2) the prevention of the pauperisation of the great families, and (3) the encouragement of the military profession. In the preamble to this remarkable *ukas* we get a glimpse of the recklessness of Moscovite hospitality and of the reformer's views thereon. "If a man have a thousand farms, and five sons, he will have a comfortable house, a splendid table, and see good society. If, after his death, his property be divided among his family, and each of the five sons have only two hundred farms, the sons, mindful of the glory of their father, and the honour of their family, will have no wish to live sparingly, their poor serfs will have to support five tables instead of one, and an estate of two hundred farms will be obliged to pay out almost as much as an estate of one thousand farms, so that such subdivision will tend to the detriment of the treasury and the ruin of the peasantry. In case of further subdivision, the gentry may even sink down to the level of poor villagers, of which degradation there are many instances in Russia." Henceforth, however, younger sons were to be allowed to buy landed estates after seven years' civil, or ten years' military service. By the *ukas* of January 16, 1721, all officers in the army, whatever their origin, and their children after them, were declared to be noble, and entitled to patents of nobility. But education had previously been declared to be the indispensable qualification for advancement in every branch of the service. Thus the famous *ukas* of January 20, 1714, ordered professors from the mathematical schools to go the round of the provinces, and teach the children of the gentry arithmetic and mathematics. No gentleman was henceforth to marry unless he had first been properly educated. The Guard was to serve as a training school for inferior officers, while the sons of eminent persons were to be sent abroad to learn the science of war from famous generals. Thus Prince Repnin sent his sons, Vasily and George into the Austrian army and in 1717 twenty young gentlemen volunteers entered the French, and twenty-seven the Venetian navy.

Now, as formerly, the poverty of the Government was its chief impediment. There was no money to pay carpenters and ship-builders, yet ships had to be built if the sea were to be held, and the command of the sea was necessary for the increase of commerce, while the increase of commerce would eventually recoup the Government its expenses. But if trade is to be promoted, traders must be encouraged and taken care of. Peter fully realised this. In November, 1711, half a dozen mercantile experts, who best understood the nature of Russian trade, were transferred from Moscow* to Petersburg, to advise and assist the Government in concluding a new commercial treaty with England and Holland. A further effort to promote trade and industry is seen in the institution of the *glavnuy magistrat* or chief magistracy (*ukas* of January 26, 1721), a supreme local government board, subordinated to the Senate, consisting of the members of the Petersburg civic authorities, half of whom were foreigners, the Tsar himself nominating the President. The " chief magistracy " was to appoint and superintend the magistrates in all the Russian towns, which were now divided into categories, according to wealth and population. At this very time a controversy was proceeding as to whether Petersburg should be made the staple of Russia's foreign trade instead of the remote and inhospitable port of Archangel. Peter was in favour of the change, but the Dutch merchants, who had long been settled at Archangel, and feared above all things lest Russia should monopolize the Baltic trade, strongly protested against the transference, mainly on economical grounds. They represented that the expense of living at Petersburg was prohibitive. A wooden hut there, far inferior to the humblest Dutch cabin, could not be had under 800 or 1,000 florins, while at Archangel or Moscow a comfortable wooden house cost only 200. Food too, especially fresh meat, was both bad and dear at Petersburg. From these and other accounts it is quite plain that " the earthly paradise," as Peter fondly called his new capital, was not the sort of place in which any lover of personal comfort would live from choice. He was in such haste to build it up that the erection of stone buildings elsewhere in Russia, till it was completed, was forbidden. The result was a stately array of fine mansions,

* The best Russian merchants of those days were the Archangel traders, the next best were the traders of Vologda. Dorpat and Narva.

which did very well in the short summer, but exposed their inhabitants to all sorts of dangers during the endless winters. We hear, for instance, of splendid banquets in gilded chambers at Petersburg being spoiled by cracking walls, gaping floors, and leaking roofs, and the boyars and bishops, to use the vigorous expression of an English envoy, "wished it at the devil." More-over, access thereto was at first by no means easy. The roads between the old capital and the new were so bad that it often took foreigners eight weeks to traverse them, and they had fre-quently to wait for a week at a time for post-horses at the squalid and ill-served post-stations.

Great efforts were made by the Regenerator to utilise Russia's latent resources. All landed proprietors were urged to search for and work the minerals on their estates, "that God's blessings, under the earth, may not be in vain," or the Government was to do it for them. In 1719 we find the silver mines of Nerchinsk, the iron mines of Tobolsk and Verkoturya, and the copper mines of Kungura, in full working order. At Tula and Kashirsk, about the same time, Aleksyei Naruishkin founded iron works. Still more lucrative were the Lipski iron works, which were bound by contract to turn out 15,000 small arms of all sorts, including 1,000 pistols, per annum. In 1717 Tomelin and Rynmin were granted the monopoly of the needle manufacture for thirty years. The Olonets iron foundries were important because of their proximity to Petersburg, and the ability of their director, Hen-ning, one of Peter's most zealous co-operators. It was one of the duties of the *Kammer Kollegium* to keep the Government well informed as to the resources and productivity of every province of the Empire, and to populate waste lands with useful colonists. No improvement was too small for the attention of the Tsar. Thus, in May, 1725, he ordered that corn should henceforth be reaped with scythes instead of with sickles. Peter was also the first to cultivate tobacco for commercial purposes, but he gave particular attention to the flax and hemp trade, both import and export. But no branch of industry was overlooked. In 1716, Captain Nosov was sent abroad to hire shepherds and workers in cloth. The cloth manufactory of Moscow had engaged Peter's attention since 1705, and he at last committed it entirely to private firms, both to save expense and to accustom the Russians to industrial enterprises. The uniforms of the Russian soldiers and the liveries of gentlemen's lackeys were henceforth to be of cloth made in Russia. The manufacture of sails was introduced into Moscow in 1702, but languished till taken in hand in 1716 by Prince Odoevsky. The leather trade had always been of the utmost importance. In 1716 alone, 135,467 poods* were sent to Archangel for export. Peter did much for the leather industry. By the *ukaz* of 1715 he ordered that the leather should henceforth be prepared with train-oil instead of with tar as heretofore, as experience had shown that tar-prepared leather let in the wet and soon rotted. Master-tanners were sent from Reval to Moscow, to teach the people there how to tan the leather properly, and, after two years of such instruction, those of the Moscow tanners who persisted in the old way were to be punished by imprisonment and confiscation of their property. The manufacture of writing-paper was introduced in 1714. The manufacture of silk and lace was a monopoly in the hands of Apraksin, Tolstoi and Shafirov, who worked it very successfully. To encourage the lace industry, the import of European lace into Russia was forbidden.

These commercial innovations and reforms naturally affected the position of the peasantry, and with the beginning of manufactures a new class of peasants arose, attached not to the soil but to factories. The needs of the Government compelled it to use forced labour, and recruit its artisans as well as its soldiers from the peasantry, and the period of reform was too close to the old Moscovite period of peasant serfdom to admit of any amelioration in the general condition of the serfs as regards the state. We cannot wonder, therefore, if the misery of the peasantry frequently drove them to revolts (there was a notable rising in 1713), which were cruelly suppressed. Yet the Government did what it could to protect the serfs from "their worst enemies, those drunken and disorderly masters who deteriorate their estates, laying all sorts of unbearable burdens on their peasants, and beating and tormenting them, so that they run away from their grievous burdens, for which cause waste lands

* A pood equals 40 lb.

multiply, and the arrears of taxation increase." All such
"masters" were to be placed under restraint as lunatics,
and their property was to be administered by their nearest relatives
or by the state. Moreover, by the *ukaz* of April 21, 1721, proprietors were forbidden to sell their serfs separately; they were
only to be sold in families. The price of a peasant family
differed according to circumstances. Thus we find thirty-five
rubles* paid for a peasant family transferred from the country
to town for smith's work, whereas such an *article de luxe* as a
family of dwarf peasants sold for as much as fifty rubles.

As already indicated, financial difficulties harassed the Regenerator at every step. The most important undertakings had
frequently to be abandoned for want of money, and the whole
country being very poor and sparsely populated, the taxable
people either ran away, or resorted to every imaginable expedient
for evading the payment of the taxes. But there was worse
than this. Peter knew well that the emptiness of the treasury
was very largely due to peculation, that ancient and ineradicable
vice of Russian society. The Russian official had in the course
of ages come to regard the public service mainly as a source of
personal income, and ages were to elapse (they are still to elapse)
before he could get rid of this idea. Having no regular salary,
he looked to his underlings "for nourishment,"† as the phrase
went, and he took from them according to his needs, most
liberally interpreted. Peter was not the man to leave the
improvement of public morals to the gradual operation of time,
and, as he always adopted the most violent measures by preference, he was very speedily committed to a struggle with the
robbers of the treasury almost as bloody as his struggle with
the rebellious stryeltsui. A poor yet progressive state, as
Russia was at the beginning of the seventeenth century, which
is unable to recompense its public servants adequately, must
let them "nourish themselves" somehow. Peter therefore was
obliged to wink at the taking of bribes within limits; the
difficulty was to fix those limits. The vileness of some of the
remedies which he found it necessary to adopt is eloquent of

* A ruble was equivalent to about five shillings of the English money of the day.
† *Na Kormlenyi.*

the extent and virulence of the evil with which he had to cope. By the *ukaz* of August, 1713, informers were invited to report all cases of defalcation to the Tsar, and promised the rank and the property of those whom they denounced. The *ukaz* of December 24, 1714, further encouraged delators to come forward fearlessly, and not to be afraid to report against even their official superiors. The *ukaz* of January 28, 1721, instituted an order of official public accusers, the so-called Imperial ober-fiscals and fiscals, whose principal duties were to protect the revenue and supervise the administration of the Senate. The fiscals were to warn the senators thrice of any dereliction of duty, and the third warning disregarded, they were to report the matter to the Tsar direct. That the Senate resented this system of tutelage is plain from the reports of those of the fiscals who complain that it is no longer safe for them to appear in the Senate, inasmuch as they had been called "gutter judges" by Senator Plemyannikov, and "rogues and Antichrists" by Senator Prince Yakov Dolgoruki.

But it was not only the Senate which complained of the fiscals. On March 17, 1712, Archbishop Yavorsky vigorously attacked them, and, indeed, the whole system of official espionage, in a sermon which caused a sensation. "They lay traps for their brethren, and calumniate them at their good pleasure," exclaimed the indignant prelate, "and it is accounted no fault in them that they cannot make good the accusations so brought by them. Not one word is said to them. They are free to accuse as often as they will. This should not be. If a man seeks my head, and lays a lying accusation against me, and does not prove it, that man should forfeit his own head. If he lays a trap for me, he should fall into it himself." Much of this sermon could not be gainsaid, and it was not without effect. The *ukaz* of March 17, 1714, imposed upon any fiscal or delator convicted of a false accusation the same penalty which would have been imposed upon the alleged delinquent if he had been found guilty, but mistakes arising from carelessness were only lightly punished.

Villainous as the system was, it certainly brought much rascality to light. One of the most active and courageous of these public delators was the ober-fiscal Aleksyei Nestorov, who, besides convicting several senators of dishonesty, reported very badly of the merchants of Moscow.   According to him, the richer traders systematically robbed their poorer brethren, under the pretext that they were supplying the wants of the Gosudar.   Other traders secured exemption from taxation by living under the protection of powerful boyars, whose debtors they pretended to be.   Others took posts as clerks or managers, though they had independent fortunes.   Others even went the length of seeking refuge in hospitals, as if they were seriously ill.   But Nestorov's most signal triumph was the Gagarin process, which, after a six years' struggle, he won against a combination of the chief dignitaries of the Empire, who were all more or less implicated in the gigantic fraud.

As early as 1711 Nestorov reported to the Tsar that the Governor of Siberia, Prince Gagarin, was plundering the treasury, and had succeeded in monopolising the lucrative China trade for the exclusive benefit of himself and his friends.   Nestorov sent a whole chestful of incriminating documents to the Senate for investigation, which Senator Count Musin Pushkin, whom Nestorov had already reported to the Tsar for malversation, promptly ordered to be destroyed.   But the indefatigable ober-fiscal immediately set about collecting fresh evidence, and in 1717 he presented a second and stronger accusation against Gagarin and his abettors, the wealthy mercantile house of Evreimov.   Peter entrusted the further examination of the affair to Senator Prince Yakov Dolgoruki, but, becoming suspicious of him also, ultimately transferred the case to a committee of the officers of the Guard, whom he could trust implicitly.   A number of merchants were now examined, and they confessed not only that Gagarin had systematically corrupted all the Siberian officials to wink at his depredations, but that many senators and heads of colleges were his tools, including Menshikov, Apraksin, Field-Marshal Sheremetev, and Prince Yakov Dolgoruki, all of whom had been bought by Gagarin and his creatures.   Peter, now thoroughly aroused, despatched Major Likharev, of the Guard, to Siberia, to examine Gagarin on the spot.   The prince was tried and convicted of every sort of dishonesty.   He had bought large quantities of Government stores with Government funds, and then sold them on his own account at an enormous profit. He had also burnt his account books, and established a system of intimidation which was perfect of its kind. Finally, Gagarin made a full confession of his crimes, and threw himself upon the Tsar's mercy. He petitioned for leave to pass the remainder of his days in a monastery ; but Peter sent him to the gallows, and he was hanged without ceremony.

Some of the Tsar's bitterest moments were due to the discovery of peculation on the part of those whom he loved and trusted the most. His own integrity in money matters was above suspicion. He spent little or nothing upon himself. His pastimes, if rude and coarse, were simple and inexpensive. Every penny he could spare was devoted to the service of the state. He had a right to expect that those whom he had exalted and enriched should keep their fingers out of the public coffers. If there was one man in particular from whom Peter had a right to expect faithful service, it was Menshikov, his most intimate friend, "mein Herzenskind," "Little Alec," as he fondly called him, whom he had raised from the gutter and loaded with riches and honours.* Yet every time the Tsar returned to Russia he received fresh accusations of peculation against "his serene highness." Peter was deeply irritated by such inexcusable transgressions, and more than once Menshikov narrowly saved his head. The Tsar's first serious outburst of indignation against the greedy favourite (March, 1711) was due to the prince's shameless looting in Poland. Poland, indeed, had by this time become a sort of happy hunting-ground where, as Catherine II. once phrased it, you had only to stoop down in order to pick up anything you liked ; but Menshikov's rapacity on this occasion seems to have shocked the very Russians themselves. He had pillaged whole provinces systematically, and carried off waggon-loads of loot, and this, too, in a country actually in alliance with the Tsar. Menshikov at first pooh-poohed the whole business as a mere trifle. "It is no trifle," retorted Peter, "for it destroys our credit with the inhabitants, and does us no good." "Besides," he added,

* Menshikov was now a prince of the Holy Roman as well as of the orthodox Russian Empire.

"your conduct is the more outrageous, as you have deliberately disobeyed my *ukazes*." On his return to Russia in 1712 Peter discovered that even in the new province of Ingria and Petersburg, of which he was Governor-General, Menshikov had winked at wholesale corruption. "You have represented honest men to me as rogues, and rogues as honest men," wrote the indignant Tsar on this occasion. " For the last time I warn you : change your ways or you will come to grief. Mind you do not behave in Russia as you did in Poland. You shall answer with your head for the slightest complaint against you." At this very time Debey, the Dutch resident at Petersburg, informed his Court that another high official, Zotov, was fleecing the foreign merchants unmercifully, and sharing the booty with Menshikov. In 1713 the famous Solovev process began, in which our old friend, Kurbatov, came into collision with Menshikov. We have seen how Kurbatov had been in the habit of denouncing the highest functionaries to the Tsar, relying on the support of his serene highness, whom, with more gratitude than veracity, he described in his letters to Peter as " the chosen vessel, the one man without reproach before your Majesty." There had been a slight disagreement between them when Kurbatov had indignantly refused to transfer an unjust judge to a higher tribunal, to suit Menshikov's convenience, but the Tsar had intervened on this occasion, and reconciled the two friends. Shortly afterwards Kurbatov was transferred to Archangel, as vice-governor, where he made the acquaintance of Demetrius Solovev, who was supposed to superintend the shipping of corn abroad on Government account. Demetrius had two brothers, Joseph, who was the agent of the Russian Government at Amsterdam, and Theodore, who was the confidential manager of Menshikov's vast estates in Ingria. As a matter of fact, the three brothers were at the head of a combination for selling Menshikov's corn in preference to the corn of the Russian Government, and the bulk of the proceeds went into his serene highness's pocket. It is only natural to suppose that so acute an observer as Kurbatov must from the first have had an inkling of the real state of things. But the fact remains that, for some months, he and Demetrius Solovev worked

amicably together as joint commissioners of export, no doubt
very much to their advantage, till in May, 1713, the Senate,
eager to gratify a long-standing grudge against Kurbatov for
revealing its irregularities to the Tsar, deprived him of his
commissionership on the ground that one commissioner was
sufficient. A month later Kurbatov, suspecting the hand of
Menshikov in the affair, retaliated by reporting to the Tsar
that, from 1709 to 1711, Demetrius Solovev, acting in col-
lusion with his brother Joseph at Amsterdam, had exported
22,766 quarters of his own corn, as well as 32,709 quarters of the
Gosudar's corn, whereas the *ukaz* of 1705 had, under pain of
death, forbidden the export of any corn from Russia except on
account of the treasury. The natural inference was that the
Solovevs had been selling Menshikov's corn and keeping the
Tsar's corn back, and this was confirmed by letters intercepted
from Joseph Solovev, at Amsterdam, telling his brother to send
no more corn till the old stocks had been sold out. " How,"
pertinently asked Kurbatov, " is the Tsar's corn to be sold, if
Solovev sends so much corn of his own out of Russia ?" Senator
Prince Volkonsky, a friend of Menshikov, was sent to Archangel
to inquire into the matter, and the result of his inquiry was
an accusation for malversation against Kurbatov himself, who
was tried at Ustyug, the central town of the Archangel government. But nothing definite could be proved against him,
and he quickly countered by informing Secretary Makarov
that Prince Menshikov had been pillaging all the Baltic
provinces, and had defrauded the Government of 100,000 rubles.
Kurbatov's denunciation resulted in a rigid examination (1714)
of the business transactions of the chancellery of Ingria, and
Menshikov and his principal colleagues and subordinates,
including Kossakov, Vice-Governor of Petersburg, Alexander
Kikin, the head of the Admiralty, Senyavin, Chief Commissioner
of Public Works, and Senators Opukhtin and Prince Volkonsky
were implicated in astounding frauds upon the treasury. The
exasperated Tsar did not spare his hand. Kossakov was
knouted publicly, the two senators had their tongues seared
with red-hot irons, and Prince Volkonsky, as the worst offender,
was subsequently shot. Menshikov seems to have owed his

life to a sudden and dangerous illness caused by panic terror acting on a constitution enfeebled by years of debauchery. At one time the doctors gave him up, and, on his recovery, Peter's fondness for his friend overcame his sense of justice, and the penitent scoundrel was at last forgiven. A pound of tobacco from Dantzic was the olive-branch sent to him by his too indulgent master, whereupon his serene highness ventured respectfully to express the hope that the Almighty might send down His Holy Spirit upon the waters of Carlsbad, which the Tsar was about to take for the benefit of his health.

The duel between Menshikov and Kurbatov continued for some years with varying success. His serene highness was palpably hit when Kurbatov bribed Menshikov's servant, Dyakov, to purloin his master's private papers containing damning evidence against the Solovevs. Armed with these treasures, Kurbatov, in October, 1716, accused them to the Tsar of wholesale malver-sation, and, twelve months later, Joseph Solovev was arrested at Amsterdam and conveyed to Petersburg, when an examination of his books revealed the fact, confirmed by a subsequent vigorous application of the question extraordinary in the torture-chamber, that the Solovevs had systematically robbed the treasury of 675,000 rubles, and accumulated a fortune of nearly half a million. The affair dragged on till 1721, when Kurbatov died. His ideas about public morality, judged from the Western standpoint, were certainly rudimentary, and he appears to have misappropriated 12,000 rubles of public money, yet relatively he was an honest man, and, compared with the gigantic frauds of Menshikov, his defalcations were insignificant enough.

The recrudescence of highway robbery, especially after the death, in 1717, of the terrible "King of Pressburg," Prince Theodore Yurevich Romodanovsky, into whose bloody hands the most hardened desperadoes feared to fall, led to the policing of the Russian towns, and civic guards were chosen from among the male inhabitants over twenty years of age. The police were also to see that no wares unfit for food were exposed for sale,[*] examine and test all weights and measures, and act as firemen. In order "to prevent the violence of Vulcan," all houses were

---

[*] All salesmen were now ordered to wear white aprons and keep them clean.

henceforth to be built of less combustible material, and be wider apart. That such precautions were not unnecessary is plain from the great fire of Moscow in 1712, which destroyed 9 monasteries, 35 hospitals, 86 churches, 32 Imperial châteaux, and 4,000 private houses.

The social morality of all classes was still very low. Both the boyar and the peasant had to be regenerated against their will, and the process was necessarily a violent one. Yet the most enlightened of Peter's contemporaries approved of and applauded his violence. Some of them even believed that his most energetic measures were not violent enough. " If any land be overmuch cumbered with weeds, corn cannot be sown thereon unless the weeds first be burnt with fire. In the same way our ancient inveterate evils should be burnt with fire." These words are taken from a work entitled : " Books on Poverty and Riches,"[*] by the first Russian economist, Ivan Tikhonovich Pososhkov.[†] Of this truly remarkable man we know little more than the dates of his birth (1670) and of his death (1726), and, oddly enough, so far as we can tell, he was neither recognised nor employed by Peter the Great, though in many respects his views anticipated and even went beyond the intentions of the Regenerator. A self-taught man, brought up upon Church literature, he had nevertheless thoroughly grasped the fact that Russia's salvation depended upon her complete development in every direction. The " Knigi o skudosti," to which he chiefly owes his fame, would be remarkable if only for its lucid style and originality, but when we reflect that its author was abso- lutely ignorant of the very elements of Western European economical science, it must be pronounced an astounding per- formance. Pososhkov is, above all, an advocate of peasant rights, a nationalist, an advocate of democratic centralisation subordinated to the principle of absolute monarchy. But I have not to do with Pososhkov's economical theories, however inter- esting. I would simply cite him as an unexceptionable eye- witness of the condition of the Russian country-people of his

* " Knigi o skudosti i bogatetvye," etc.

† See works edited by Pogodin, 1842 63; and biography by Tsarovsky: " Pososhkov i ego sochineniya," 1883.

day.   So deeply convinced was he of the necessity of wholesale
reform, that he would have hastened it on by the most drastic
measures.   Peter himself does not denounce the national vices so
fiercely as does this peasant's son.   Nothing good can ever be
done, he exclaims, till the rascality which abounds everywhere
is rooted out.   There are hundreds of squires like Theodore
Pustoshkin, who has never rendered a day's service in his life,
and who evades every sort of obligation by bribery or by feigning
madness so successfully that the recruiting officers leave him on
the roadside as a worthless lunatic, "whereupon he returns to
his own mansion, roars like a lion, and all his neighbours cower
before him."   Another type of the contemporary squire is Ivan
Zolotarev, also a lion to his neighbours, but an ass from the
point of view of utility.   The usual practice of this gentleman
was to send poor kinsmen to serve in the wars in lieu of himself,
while he remained at home to harry and despoil his defenceless
villagers.   The universality of this malingering evokes from
Pososhkov a passionate apostrophe to the Tsar.   "What is the
use of your Majesty pulling us in one direction with ten-men
power, when millions are pulling us in the contrary direction ?"
Equally scathing are his denunciations of the apathy of the
peasantry, the result of centuries of sloth and stagnation.   There
were many peasants, he tells us, who lived at ease upon the
profits of mendicancy.   Others, engaged in lucrative trade, sent
out their children to beg.   Fires were so destructive and robbers
so dangerous because none took the trouble to extinguish the
one or resist the other.   Frequently robbers would descend on a
village of thirty houses or more, select a victim, burn and torture
him, rob him of all his property, and decamp in safety, because
the other villagers remained in their houses without raising a
finger to help their suffering neighbour.   Ignorance was another
universal defect.   In a village of thirty houses not a person
could be found able to read or write, so that if anybody appeared
among them with or without an *ukas*, everyone in the village at
once believed him, and allowed the most exorbitant taxes to be
levied upon them, "because they are so blind and ignorant that
they know no better."   The peasants ought to be compelled,
he says, to send their children to the *dyak* to be taught.   Another

crying evil was the brutality of the gentry to their serfs.   There
were some squires so inhuman that they would not allow their
peasants leisure to till their own plots of land.   " Some proprietors
say : ' Don't let the fleece of the peasant grow thick, shear him
like a sheep, to the very skin.'   And so they do to the great
harm of the Tsardom, not leaving the countryman so much as a
goat, wherefore the peasants quit their homes, and fly into the
Ukrain, or abroad."

But Peter, meanwhile, was doing what he could to spread
education.   Schools, especially technical schools, were being
established everywhere.   In the new capital a marine academy
was founded under the charge of a Frenchman.   In 1719 thirty
young men were sent abroad to learn medicine from the famous
Dr. Blumentrost.   In 1718 Konon Zotov was ordered to enter
the French naval service and record his experiences in Russian
for the benefit of his countrymen.   Suvorov Tuvolkov went to Spain
to study the science of canalisation there, and wherever harbours
or docks were in process of construction young Russians speedily
appeared, so as to gain a practical knowledge of these things on
the spot.   In 1716 five of the pupils of the Latin school settled
in Persia to learn Persian, Turkish, and Arabic.   The printing
presses also were at work, under the superintendence of Theodore
Polikarpov.   Amongst the books first published by him should
be mentioned Marsov's " Account of the Warlike Exploits of the
Tsar," Shafirov's " Inquiry into the Causes of the Great Northern
War," which is little more than a brief for Peter, and the archimandrite Gabriel Buzhensky's translation of Puffendorf's " Introduction to European History."   In those days it was a question
into what language translators were to translate.   Peter preferred
the popular modern spoken tongue, but the majority of scholars
still clung to the old Church Slavonic.

Science was promoted by the *ukaz* of February, 1718, recommending the collection of natural objects.   The preamble of this
interesting ordinance runs thus : " If anyone find in the earth, or in
the water, any ancient objects, such as unusual stones, or the bones
of man or beast, or of fishes or of birds, unlike those which are
now with us, or such as are larger or smaller than usual, or any
old inscriptions on stones, iron or copper, or any ancient weapon

not now in use, or any vessel or such like thing, that is very ancient or unusual, let him bring all such things to us, and an ample reward shall be given him." Especial attention was paid to geographical science, and in 1719 the geodesists Evreimov and Luzhin were sent to survey the Kamschatka district, and decide the question whether North-east Asia and America were united or not.

The strong desire of Peter to embellish his new capital induced him to search Europe for art treasures. His agents at Paris, Konon Zotov and Lefort, the son of the old favourite, were instructed to purchase curiosities, and also to find some great historical painter to immortalise the exploits of their master, Peter shrewdly arguing that, the King of France being dead, and his successor a minor, both masters and masterpieces would now be going a begging, and might be got cheaply. Some of his commissioners seem to have made marvellous bargains. Thus Raguzinsky secured two large statues of Adam and Eve, by the Venetian master, Bonatsi, so good "that even splendid Versailles can show few better." In 1719 Kologrivov bought, for 196 efim thalers, an ancient marble statue of Venus. recently excavated, worth 10,000 rubles, and "superior to the famous Florentine Venus because it is unmutilated." One hundred thousand planks of the best walnut wood were also sent from Venice, for the wainscotting of the Tsar's summer palace. By this time Petersburg was emerging from its scaffolding, and foreigners began to speak well of it. Already it could boast of some fine buildings, such as the Admiralty, the Bourse, the Post-office, and Menshikov's palace on the Vasilevsky Island. The imposing Nevsky Prospect, built entirely of stone by gangs of Swedish prisoners, who also had to clean it every Saturday, was especially admired.

Extraordinarily difficult during this period of transition and transformation was the position of the Russian Church. As the sworn guardian of orthodoxy, she was bound in many respects to observe a conservative attitude, yet patriotism equally obliged her not to oppose the beneficent civilising efforts of a reforming Tsar. At the same time, she could not remain indifferent to the intrusive influence of Catholics and Protestants who came to Russia with the foreign teachers, while the wealthy and influential

communities of the *Raskolniki* planted schism in her very midst.
The most notable of these dissenting establishments was the
great monastic settlement on the river Vuiga, in the province
of Olonets, which the organising genius of Daniel Vikulin and
Andrew Denisov had raised to such an unprecedented degree of
opulence that Peter thought it worth while to tolerate them for
the benefit of the treasury. "What sort of traders are these
Dissenters?" inquired the Tsar when he first heard of them.
"Are they honest and diligent?" "Yes, Gosudar, they are both
honest and diligent." "Then let them believe what they like,"
replied Peter. "If it is impossible to convert them by argument,
fire and sword will never do it." We have already seen how
he favoured them, and in 1711 Denisov obtained a *ukaz* from
Menshikov forbidding all persecution of the community under
the severest penalties. This *ukaz* did not, however, prevent Job,
the influential Archbishop of Great Novgorod, from seizing
Andrew's brother Simeon and detaining him a prisoner for four
years. Peter forbade the torturing of Simeon, but he left him in
jail, despite the urgent and reiterated entreaties of his brother
Andrew, a remissness which proves either that the Church was
still in some respects stronger than the state, or that the Tsar,
averse to persecution on principle, was not prepared to imperil
his own reputation for orthodoxy by consistently championing
the Dissenters. Moreover, from the way in which he counte-
nanced Peterim, Igumen of Pereyaslavl, one of the most acute of
the orthodox disputants, it is clear that Peter regarded dissent as
an error at best, and therefore could not allow it to be propa-
gated, though he might countenance for a time its least offensive
manifestations. He was well aware that not all the Dissenters
were as peaceable and industrious as the community on the
Vuiga, but that many of them were dangerous fanatics and
malignant opponents of every species of reform, openly denouncing him as Antichrist, and depleting the state of its best blood
by flocking in thousands to the forests and deserts. At first he
was inclined to make a census of all the Dissenters in his realm,
to discover which of them were harmful and which were harmless;
and even when, in 1718, he gave Peterim inquisitorial powers in
the diocese of Lower Novgorod (of which he was now bishop,

and where Dissenters abounded) as well as the assistance of the secular arm in the person of Major Rhzevsky, the Tsar was careful to write across the *ukaz*, with his own hand, the words: "If possible, try to find some patent offence against them, other than mere dissent." In 1719 Peterim informed Peter that he had reconverted 3,000 Dissenters, and, in 1721, Rhzevsky reported that 9,194 out of 46,965 Dissenters had been recovered to orthodoxy, but as those who refused to be convinced by argument were sent to the galleys minus their noses, the dialectic of the orthodox champions must have been singularly deficient.

While Peterim was thus successfully contending against the *Raskolniks* in the diocese of Lower Novgorod, Archbishop Stephen Yavorsky was combating Protestantism at Moscow. Here also, when argument failed, the ingenuities of the torture-chamber were freely employed. The most obstinate sufferers were the rationalistic sects, as represented by such men as Ivan Maksimov, a professor of the Latin-Slavonic school, his accomplice Tveritinov,* and the iconoclastic gardener, Ivanov, who mutilated the sacred images in the Chudov Monastery. Ivanov preferred to be hanged rather than take the benefit of the merciful *ukaz* of February 22, 1716, which allowed recanting heretics to become the archbishop's serfs. Some poor sects of Bible-readers were also mercilessly rooted out, about the same time, at Moscow, the chief sufferer and offender being a widow, Nastasia Zima, whose house the Dissenters frequented, and who exhibited under pro-longed and indescribable torture the heroism of a true martyr. The Roman propaganda was less formidable to the orthodox Church, because the Tsar himself distrusted the Catholics. As the influx of foreigners into Russia increased, the Jesuits estab-lished themselves in Moscow, but Peter ordered their books to be confiscated, and themselves to be expelled the realm, by the holograph *ukaz* of April 18, 1719.

Meanwhile efforts were being made to extend the dominion of the Russian Church eastwards. In 1711 the Siberian metro-politan, Theodore, was commanded to destroy the idols of the

* They all refused to recognise the Real Presence in the Blessed Sacrament and ridiculed obeisances to ikons.

heathen Voguls, Votiaks, Tatars, Tunguses and Yakuts, and bribe the savages to adopt orthodoxy by reducing the *yasak*, or fur tax, and presenting them with money and linen.* One of the cheapest of these speculative conversions stands to the credit of the hieromonakh Alexius, who in 1719 succeeded in baptising 379 Cheremisses, in the province of Kazan, at a total cost of 30 rubles.

But the Church herself was very much in need of discipline. The number of unworthy priests had greatly increased in consequence of the influx into the ministry of many gentlemen who evaded military service by becoming candidates for holy orders. This abuse was met by the ordinance directing the bishops not to ordain anyone under twenty-five a deacon, and anyone under thirty a priest. Efforts were also made to raise the status of the clergy, which had fallen very low. Pososhkov† tells us that in the whole diocese of Great Novgorod there was not half the piety there used to be, and that in Moscow itself he had met with men of sixty years and upwards who had never been to confession. This, he says, was due not to the spread of dissent, but to the negligence of the presbyters. The *ukaz* of 1716 attempted to obviate this by commanding everyone to go to confession at least once a year under heavy penalties. The *ukaz* of 1718 went further still. It compelled all parishioners to go to church every Sunday and holiday, and absentees were henceforth to be ineligible for public offices. But the real motive of this ordinance was that the people might hear the *ukazes* read after divine service, as, in those days of general ignorance, comparatively few could read the *ukazes* posted up on the gates of the towns. Talking in church was punished by a fine of a ruble a head, the proceeds of which were to form a fund for the building of churches.

The patriarchate still remained unoccupied, and Archbishop Stephen Yavorsky, "the guardian of the patriarchal see," found some difficulty in filling up the vacant bishoprics, because he could not always agree with his co-optors, the members of the administrative Senate. Stephen's position was at this time somewhat anomalous. He had alienated

---

* Solovev: "Istoria Rossy," XVI., 3.       † "Knigi," etc.

the Tsar by openly espousing the cause of the unfortunate Tsarevich Alexius.* He had protested cryptically, but still unmistakably, against such patent irregularities as the putting away of the Tsaritsa Eudoxia. He had frequently alluded in his discourses to the "raging waves" beating continually against "the solid shore"; and after he had explained "the solid shore" to mean "the law of God," his hearers readily guessed whom he meant by "the raging waves." Peter at last thought it expedient to put himself right with the Church on minor points by obtaining a dispensation from Jeremiah, Patriarch of Jerusalem, for himself and his soldiers to eat meat on all fast-days except during the week before communion, but even after this "the raging waves" still continued to beat against "the solid shore" in the homilies of Archbishop Stephen. Presently Peter lent his ear to denunciations against the archbishop, who was accused, amongst other things, of embezzlement, peculation, condoning the murder of a drunken abbot, and ordaining thieves and runaway soldiers to be priests. As nothing came of these accusations, it is charitable to suppose that they were the inventions of Stephen's enemies. But Peter, now more than ever suspicious of him, compelled the unfortunate metropolitan to quit the comforts of Moscow and reside at Petersburg in a house which Stephen described as unfit for human habitation. At Petersburg Yavorsky had the crowning humiliation of seeing close to the Tsar's person, and high in his favour, the very man whom, shortly before, he had denounced as a dangerous heretic. This was Theophan Prokopovich, prefect of the Kiev Academy, who had been recommended to Peter by Prince Golitsuin as the only man of the Kiev clergy who was devoted to the Russian Government. Theophan subsequently won Peter's favour by his brilliant sermon on "the most glorious victory,"† and accompanied him to the Pruth as one of his chaplains. At last the Regenerator had found among the clergy a priest after his own heart, a man of vast learning, brilliant gifts, and great force of character, who fully sympathised with the reform movement, and was determined to promote it. Naturally, as Peter drew away from Stephen, he drew closer

* See next Chapter.                    † Poltava.

to Theophan, but irritated, as he continued to be, with the
Metropolitan of Ryazan, he valued his services so highly that
he treated his remonstrances, and even his impertinences, with
singular patience.    Thus, when Stephen, in his celebrated
sermon, in March, 1712, with obvious reference to the Tsar's
neglect of ecclesiastical discipline, reminded his audience that
those who neglected to hear the Church were to be regarded by
the faithful as heathens and publicans, Peter not only recognised
the right of the prelate to rebuke the vices of the mighty, but he
demonstrated his own superior knowledge of the Scriptures in the
most striking manner.    For when a copy of Yavorsky's sermon
was submitted to him, he wrote in the margin, opposite the
quotation, "if he neglect to hear the Church, he shall be unto
thee as a heathen and a publican," the words, "*first* between him
and thee, and *then* in the presence of witnesses," * and sent it
back to Stephen, whom he thus convicted of acting unscrip-
turally by publicly denouncing a sinner before remonstrating
with him privately.

But if Peter spared Stephen, he at the same time promoted
Theophan, for, by his command, "the Light of Kiev" was consecrated bishop of the opulent see of Pskov, despite an accusation of crypto-Calvinism brought against him by the indignant
Stephen.    Henceforth, though Theophan was twenty-three years
the junior of Stephen, he was the Tsar's chief counsellor among
the clergy, and enjoyed his unbounded confidence, while his very
reverend brother of Ryazan had to be content with the sympathy
of the clergy of the old capital and the arch-conservative party,
and as much of their support as they dared to give him.

After Theophan's consecration, Peter formally reconciled the
two prelates, and their antagonism disappeared from public view,
though it worked subterraneously.    When Peter, for the better
regulation of Church affairs, proposed the establishment of
a *dukhovnaya kollegiya*, or "spiritual department," Theophan
alone was entrusted with the drafting of the project, so that he
may be regarded as the creator of what was subsequently known
as "The Holy Synod."    In January, 1721, an Imperial manifesto
announced that inasmuch as the Tsar must fear the divine

* Thus epitomising Matthew xviii., 15—17.

vengeance if, after reforming the civil and military, he neglected to reform the ecclesiastical administration, "and we would not be found speechless when the Most High calls us to account therefor," and inasmuch as the government of the Church by a single person could not be carried on "without passion," therefore his Majesty deemed it expedient to entrust the conduct of spiritual affairs to a synodical administration, as being more in keeping with the spirit and traditions of the orthodox Church. But the real reason for this important innovation is obviously to be found in the following sentence justifying the substitution of a collegial for a personal rule. The Synod was established: " because simple folk cannot distinguish the spiritual power from the sovereign power, and suppose that a supreme spiritual pastor is a second Gosudar, the spiritual authority being regarded as higher and better than the temporal."

The new college was to spread enlightenment and the knowledge of God's law, and extirpate superstition by composing and publishing three books, the first on the dogmas of the faith, the second on the duties of every order of men, while the third was to be a collection of sermons from the holy fathers, explanatory of dogmas and duties generally. Moreover, the bishops were to have seminaries attached to their palaces for the training of the clergy, and the curriculum was to include such temporal subjects as geography, arithmetic, history, physics, and politics. The rival prelates, Stephen and Theophan, sat side by side in the Synod, along with Theodosy, Archbishop of Novgorod, and other ecclesiastical dignitaries. Henceforth, in filling up a vacant see, the Tsar was to select one out of two candidates presented to him by the Synod.

# CHAPTER XII.

## The Case of the Tsarevich Alexius.
### 1690—1718.

Peter's First Marriage—Character of the Tsaritsa Eudoxia—The Tsarevich Alexius
—His Early Training—And Character—Antagonism between him and his
Father inevitable—Mischievous Influence of the reactionary Protopop Ignatev
—The Marriage of Alexius—Is Employed by his Father—Wounds himself to
escape further Service—Deepening of the Tsar's Hatred—Alexius confident of
the Future—The Mass of the Nation on his Side—His Partisans—The
Dolgorukis—The Golitsuins—Sheremetev—Kurakin—Kikin—Death of the
Princess Charlotte—Peter's Solemn Letter of Warning and Remonstrance to
his Son—Alexius offers to relinquish his Succession to the Throne and enter a
Monastery—Flight of Alexius to Vienna—Throws himself on the Protection
of the Emperor—Is sent to Naples—Peter Tolstoi despatched by the Tsar
to recover him—Tolstoi at Naples—He succeeds in constraining the Tsare-
vich to depart—Return of Alexius to Moscow—The First Examination of
Alexius—He resigns the Succession and reveals his " Accomplices "—Their
Torture and Execution—The Arrest of the ex-Tsaritsa Eudoxia, and the so-
called " Moscow Process "—Humiliation of Eudoxia—Examination and Con-
fession of Afrosina—Trial of Alexius—Peter's Appeal to the Spiritual and
Temporal Members of the Tribunal—Their Replies—Alexius Tortured—The
Senate condemns him to Death—He is Tortured a Second Time—His Death
—Alexius undoubtedly removed by his Father for the Good of the State.

THE strong and terrible reforming Tsar had triumphed over
every obstacle, triumphed so thoroughly that any interruption of
his work during his lifetime was inconceivable. But in the
midst of his triumph the thought persistently haunted him : " Will
my work survive me?" And Peter's anxiety was reasonable.
His health was uncertain, his half-taught pupils were few and
divided, the adversaries of his reforms were many and of one
mind, and they believed, and believed rightly, that in the heir
to the throne, the Tsarevich Alexius, they possessed a secret
sympathiser who would one day reverse the whole policy of the
Tsar-Antichrist and restore the old order of things. It was
tragic enough that Peter's only son should be his father's worst
ill-wisher and the would-be destroyer of his father's creation ;
but it is too often forgotten that Peter himself was to a large

extent responsible for the beginnings of this unnatural hostility. His premature and unconquerable dislike of his own son anticipated, and to a certain extent justified, the son's horror of his father. Peter, as we have already seen, in the case of Menshikov, and, as we shall see presently, in the case of Catherine, could forgive everything to those whom he loved. But to those whom he disliked he was inhumanly severe, and he pursued the objects of his hatred with a murderous vindictiveness which was rarely satisfied with anything short of their absolute extermination. Such, in brief, is the true explanation of the terrible fate of the Tsarevich Alexius, the details of which I will now endeavour to set forth as impartially as possible.

On January 27, 1689, in the Week of the Prodigal Son, the young Tsar Peter married, at his mother's command, the *boyaruinya* Eudoxia Lopukhina, who was three years his senior. We know nothing of the bride, except that she was beautiful, modest, and had been "brought up in the fear of the Lord."[*] The Tsaritsa Natalia seems to have thought that a pious and virtuous wife[†] was the best means of weaning her riotous son from the debauchery of the German settlement, and there can be no doubt that the unfortunate bride herself really loved her handsome, stalwart young husband. Eudoxia would have made a model Tsaritsa of the pre-Petrine period, but, unfortunately, she was no fit wife for such a vagabond of genius as Peter the Great. Accustomed from her infancy to the monastic seclusion of the *terem*, her mental horizon did not extend much beyond her embroidery-frame or her illuminated service-book. She was of those Moscovite princesses who were not allowed to receive the foreign ministers lest they should inadvertently commit themselves by saying something silly. From the first her society bored Peter unspeakably, and, after the birth of their second, short-lived, son Alexander, on October 3, 1691, he practically deserted his wife, taking no notice whatever of the pathetic letters in which she complains that "her light" never tells her of his health, and implores him to come and see her,

---

[*] See Selitsuin: "Preobrazhenskoe."
[†] Subsequently, according to Prince Boris Kurakin, she got to hate her daughter-in-law.

and " not despise her petition." Peter, indeed, had by this time got to hate Eudoxia as the living embodiment of the stupid, detestable, old Moscovite system, which he would fain do away with, and he extended this hatred to all her relations, most of whom were implicated in conspiracies against him and banished or degraded. Her uncle, Peter Lopukhin, was tortured so savagely by Peter's orders, some say by Peter's own hands, that he died of collapse on the following day. Peter's sole surviving son, Alexius, born on February 19, 1690, was utterly ignored by his father till he was nine years old. Peter was a rare and unwelcome guest in his own family, and a son who loved his mother could have little affection for a father who had ever been that mother's worst persecutor. No doubt, too, the iniquities of his father were familiar to him from childhood, for the denizens of the German settlement, among whom Peter's mistress, Anna Mons, figured conspicuously, could not have had the best of reputations in the *terem* of the pious Tsaritsa Eudoxia. When Alexius was six years of age he was taught his letters by Nikifor Vyazemsky, a pedantic scholar who excelled in that diffuse and florid rhetoric which passed for eloquence among the old Moscovites. Vyazemsky remained with his pupil for some time after the removal of the Tsaritsa Eudoxia to the Suzdal Pokrovsky Monastery; but Peter, eager to instruct his son on modern lines, now confided the care of his education to learned foreigners like Neugebauer and Huyssens, who taught him French, history, and geography, "the true foundations of politics," and mathematics. In 1703, in order that he might practically apply his lessons, Alexius was ordered to follow the army to the field as a private in a bombardier regiment, and in 1704 he was present at the capture of Narva. On the second occasion Peter wrote to his son, now a lad of fourteen, as follows : " I have taken you on this campaign to show you that I shirk neither trouble nor danger. I may die any day, but all the same you will have very little comfort if you don't follow my example. You ought to love everything which tends to the honour and welfare of your country. You ought to love faithful counsellors, whether they be your own subjects or foreigners. If my advice be thrown away and you will not do what I wish, I shall not acknowledge you as my son, and I will pray God to punish you both in this world and the next."* This stern epistle, headed " Son," is a fair specimen of Peter's epistolary correspondence with Alexius.

At this period the Tsarevich's preceptor, Huyssens, had the most favourable opinion of his pupil. He reported that the Tsarevich was of a precocious intelligence, and a singularly amiable disposition. He had already read the Bible six times, five times in Slavonic, and once in German; he had mastered the works of the Greek fathers, read all the spiritual and temporal books translated into the Slavonic tongue, and could speak and write French and German with facility. Of the ability of Alexius there could be no question, but unfortunately it was not the sort of ability which his father could make use of. The Tsarevich was essentially a student, with strong leanings towards archæology and ecclesiology. He took after Tsar Alexius, though, with his knowledge of modern languages, his intellectual vista was wider, and he would doubtless have gone much further than his grandfather. Nevertheless, the quiet seclusion of a monastic library was the proper place for this gentle, emotional dreamer, who clung so fondly to the ancient traditions, and was so easily moved by the beauty of the orthodox liturgy. We get a vivid glimpse of his character in a letter written shortly before his marriage to his confessor, Ignatev, who had counselled him to convert his foreign bride. The faith and fervour of Alexius rejects all such precautions as unnecessary. " I have not compelled her to accept our holy orthodox faith," writes Alexius, " but when she comes to Moscow and sees our holy conciliar, apostolic church, and the ecclesiastical adornment of the holy ikons, and the magnificence of the vestments of the archbishops and archimandrites, and the decency and splendour of the Church services, then methinks, she will require no pressure to accept our orthodox faith."

To a prince of the temperament of Alexius, the restless, vehement energy, the racket and bustle of his abnormally energetic father, were very offensive. He liked neither the labour itself, nor its object. Yet Peter, not unnaturally, demanded that his heir

* Solovev: " Istoria Rossy," XVII., 2.

should dedicate himself heart and soul to the service of new Russia, and help to fashion his future inheritance. He demanded from a youth with the nature of a recluse practical activity, unceasing labour, unremitting attention to technical details, the concentration of all his energies upon the business of government, upon the herculean labour of maintaining the new state at the high level of greatness to which it had already been raised. In consequence of these stern demands on the one hand, and an invincible repugnance to execute them on the other, painful relations between father and son, quite apart from the personal antipathies already existing, were inevitable. Alexius was bound to regard his father in the light of a tormentor, for can there be any greater torment than to be forced to change completely one's very nature?

It was an additional misfortune for Alexius that he should have been left to his own devices just as he was growing up from boyhood to manhood. In 1705 his tutor Huyssens was sent abroad on a diplomatic mission ; the Tsar was constantly absent from Russia, and a timid, hesitating council of boyars was left behind to rule a people whom never-ending impositions and ceaseless levies of recruits had driven to the verge of desperation. All the forces of reaction and rebellion turned instinctively towards the heir to the throne, who, it was rumoured, loved neither the war, nor the sea, nor the ships, nor indeed any of the detested novelties which had been forced upon the reluctant nation by the Tsar-Antichrist. Moreover, Stephen Yavorsky and the other archpastors openly expressed their disapprobation of the Tsar's new and strange ways, and, as a loyal son of the Church, the Tsarevich gladly listened to those who had the power to bind and loose, pleased, no doubt, to find that his duty and his inclinations pointed in the same direction. But the person who had most influence with him at this time was his confessor, the protopop Yakov Ignatev, whom, in the confessional, he promised to obey as "an angel and apostle of God." Ignatev, a man of considerable force of character and some education, was a fair type of the uncompromising clergy of the day who prayed earnestly for the removal of the troublesome Tsar, and it is to be feared that he familiarised the Tsarevich with the idea of parricide. Thus, on one occasion, Alexius confessed to Ignatev that he had wished for his father's death. "God forgive thee!" answered the priest, "yet we all desire his death because there is so much misery in the nation." Ignatev also encouraged Alexius to think more of his mother, the innocent victim of his father's lawlessness, and in 1708 the Tsarevich ventured to visit Eudoxia in her monastery. The wrath of Peter when he heard of this was terrible. He instantly summoned his son to Zolkow in Poland, and, after reprimanding him for his folly, sent him to Smolensk to collect provender and recruits, and from thence to Moscow to fortify it against Charles XII., who had just crossed the Russian border. At the end of 1709, Alexius went to Dresden for twelve months for finishing lessons in French and German, mathematics and fortification, and, his education completed, he was married, greatly against his will, to a German princess, Sophia Charlotte of Blanckenburg-Wolfenbüttel, whose sister, almost simultaneously, espoused the heir to the Austrian throne, the Archduke Charles. Alexius would have preferred to wed one of his own countrywomen, and he tried to gain time by all sorts of excuses ; but the Tsar would hear of no delay. The utmost he conceded was the choice between two or three foreign princesses. Charlotte pleased Alexius the most. He describes her to his confessor as the best princess there, "and a good creature," while the princess herself alluded to her prospective groom as " sensible, upright and amiable." The wedding was celebrated at Torgau on October 14, 1711, in the house of the Queen of Poland, and three weeks later the bridegroom was hurried away by his father to Thorn to superintend the provisioning of the Russian troops in Poland. For the next twelve months Alexius was kept constantly on the move. His wife joined him at Thorn in December, but in April, 1712, a peremptory *ukas* ordered him off to the army in Pomerania, and in the autumn of the same year he was forced to accompany his father on a tour of inspection through Finland. Evidently Peter was determined to tear his son away from a life of indolent ease, and make a man of him. Partly for the same reason, no doubt, and partly, perhaps, to compel the princess to hasten on her journey to Russia, the young people were made to feel that their future comfort depended entirely on the Tsar's good pleasure. Although Peter had solemnly engaged by the marriage contract to allow the princess 50,000 rubles a year for her maintenance, Menshikov, when he visited the couple at Thorn, in the spring of 1712, found them in such a state of destitution* that he was moved to lend them 5,000 rubles, which had been set apart for the payment of the uniforms of the Ingrian regiment. In December, 1712, Charlotte returned to her mother because she had not money enough to take her to Russia, till a letter from Peter, styling himself "your affectionately inclined father," and enclosing a draft for 25,000 efim-dollars, removed both her fears and her difficulties, and she proceeded to Petersburg, where she was kindly welcomed by the new Tsaritsa Catherine Skovronskaya, whom Peter had espoused the year before,† and the rest of the Imperial family. Of her husband she at first saw but little. Immediately on his return from Finland, Alexius was despatched by his father to Staraya Rusya and Ladoga to see to the building of more ships. This was the last commission entrusted to him, for, on his return to the capital, Peter, in order to see what progress his son had made in mechanics and mathematics, asked him to produce for inspection his latest drawings. Presumably Alexius had taken the liberty of neglecting this branch of his education, for his father's command threw him into a state of panic, and in order to escape the ordeal of such an examination, he resorted to the abject expedient of disabling his right hand by a pistol shot. The bullet missed its mark, indeed, and the only injury inflicted was a bad burn, but even this was sufficient for his purpose. In no other way could the Tsarevich have offended his father so deeply. He had behaved like a cowardly recruit who mutilates himself to shirk military service. At first Peter stormed and swore, and cursed his son, and struck him. But soon his indignation turned to indifference. He seemed to take no further interest in Alexius. He left him entirely to himself. He employed him no more. He no longer pressed him to attend public functions. Alexius rejoiced at this welcome

---

* They had barely money enough for their table, and none at all for equipages.
† For details, see the following chapter and R. N. Bain : "Pupils of Peter the Great," I., 2.

change, but he had cause rather to fear it. It marked the deepening of a hatred which might have been overcome. Peter seems to have made a strong effort at this time to like his son, and be kind to him, but from henceforth he seems to have regarded him as both useless and dangerous. Alexius was evidently consoling himself with the reflection that the future belonged to him, and Peter felt that that future might not be so very far distant. It is true he was not an old man counting by years ; but his illnesses were now more frequent, and he did not recover from them so quickly. Besides, Alexius was well aware that the mass of the Russian nation was on his side. With the single exception of Archbishop Theodosy, all the prelates were devoted to him. Equally friendly were the two great families of the Dolgorukis and the Golitsuins. The Dolgorukis, who had first come prominently forward in the reign of Tsar Alexius, were well represented in Peter's service. Two of them occupied important diplomatic posts. A third was one of the best of the Tsar's generals. A fourth was an exceptionally energetic senator. All of them detested the domination of the upstart Menshikov. and disliked his all-powerful protectress the new Tsaritsa Catherine. The Dolgorukis lost no opportunity of encouraging and flattering the Tsarevich. Prince Vasily Dolgoruki, the diplomatist of the family, once said to him : " You are cleverer than your father. Your father is clever, but he does not understand clever people.* You will be able to understand them better."

The Golitsuins were even more illustrious than the Dolgorukis. So far back as the days of Ivan III. (1462-1505) their ambition had become a tradition. Prince Dmitry Mikhailovich Golitsuin, the head of the family, a man of austere character and flawless probity, was the most enlightened of the reactionary leaders. Though he had served Peter diligently, he still remained in a subordinate position, completely overshadowed by the favourite Menshikov. Golitsuin naturally attributed the singular and distressing elevation of such low-born adventurers to their unscrupulous use of the basest expedients to which a gentle-man like himself would be incapable of stooping. As a loyal,

* I.e., themselves.

arch-conservative Churchman, he regarded the marriage of Peter and Catherine as uncanonical. The only canonical Tsaritsa, in his eyes, was Eudoxia, and all his sympathies were with Eudoxia's son, the heir to the throne, like himself a *laudator temporis acti*. Golitsuin's family was also well placed. His brother, Field-marshal Prince Michael Golitsuin, was one of the bravest and most capable, and indisputably the most chivalrous of all Peter's captains. His cousin, Prince Peter Aleksyevich Golitsuin, was Governor-General of Riga.

Most of the other magnates were equally dissatisfied with Peter, and equally devoted to Alexius, especially such malcontents as old Field-marshal Count Boris Sheremetev, who thought that his life-long services had been inadequately recompensed, and that his master treated him, a Knight of Malta, "far too unceremoniously." He, too, hated Menshikov rancorously. Another very important partisan of Alexius was the veteran diplomatist, Prince Boris Kurakin, who was also his kinsman. "Is your step-mother good to you?" he asked Alexius on one occasion. "Yes," was the reply. "Well," returned Kurakin, "so long as she has no son of her own she will be good to you, but when she has a son, she will be different." Thus the patricians were the natural allies of Alexius.

Another influential friend of the Tsarevich was Alexander Kikin, who had once stood high in Peter's favour, which he had forfeited by gross dishonesty. Intense hatred of Menshikov, who had sinned far more than himself and had yet been forgiven, was at the bottom of Kikin's devotion to Alexius, whose favourite he hoped to be when the Tsarevich ascended the throne. Finally Alexius could count among his partisans all those, and they were many, who longed for the repose that was impossible under a Tsar who was always on the move, and compelled everyone else to be moving likewise.

Alexius had the great advantage of knowing that, anyhow, the future belonged to him, and would amply compensate him for his past sufferings. All he had to do was to sit still, keep out of his father's way as much as possible, and await the natural course of events. But with Peter the present was everything. He could not afford to leave anything to chance. All his life long he had been working incessantly with a single object—the regeneration of Russia—in view. The more difficult portion of that work was done; a band of fellow-workers, carefully trained for the task under the master's eye, was at hand to help the successor of the Regenerator to put the finishing touches to the great achievement. All that was required of the successor was sympathy and good-will. But what if the successor were hostile, or even indifferent? What if he refused to tread in his father's footsteps, or still more, tried to destroy his father's work? By some such process of reasoning as this must the idea of changing the succession to the throne by setting aside Alexius have first occurred to the mind of Peter the Great.

Peter had hoped much from the influence of his daughter-in-law upon her husband; but the unhappy princess, so far from being able to help him, was herself very much to be pitied. She was surrounded by Russian ladies whose language she did not understand, and whose ways were strange and barbarous. Her expenses were regulated by a niggard hand. She never seems to have had an adequate establishment, and was often hard put to it to pay her domestics and her tradespeople.* Her husband was rarely with her, and her existence must have been dull and miserable. When she was not weeping, or writing irritated and irritating letters to her father-in-law, she shut herself up in her apartments with another German lady, her bosom friend, the Princess Juliana Louisa of East Friesland, who, so far from reminding her of her duties and obligations to her adopted country, jealously intervened between her and the rest of the Court. In July, 1714, Charlotte was delivered of her first child, the Tsarevna Natalia. On the occasion of the lying-in, Peter confided his daughter-in-law to the care of Muscovite midwives of the old school, whose meddling fussiness, ignorant interference, and ridiculous precautions could not fail to strike a princess used to the more civilised customs of the West, as offensive, and even indecent. On the birth of the child she received very affectionate congratulations from both Peter and Catherine, and so far recovered her equanimity as to apologise to the former for failing

---

* According to Pleier, the Imperial ambassador at Petersburg, her allowance was doled out to her by driblets of £100 at a time.

on this occasion to bear a prince. She hoped, she said, to be
more fortunate next time ; and fourteen months later (October 18,
1715) she did indeed give birth to a son, who was christened
Peter.* Everything now seemed to promise a happier future,
when Charlotte caught a chill from rising too soon to receive the
congratulations of the Court, and died four days after the birth
of her son.

The Tsarevich, naturally affectionate, was inconsolable. He
had attended his young spouse to the last, and when the end
came, fainted three times from emotion. On the very day of
the funeral (October 11), Peter gave Alexius what was evidently
meant to be a last chance, by addressing to him a stern letter †
of warning and remonstrance. " My joy (at our past successes),"
begins this impressive document, " is swallowed up by grief when
I look around me and see in you a successor very unfit for the
administration of affairs of state, and above all determined not
to give any attention to military affairs, by means whereof we
have emerged out of darkness into the light, and have become
honoured and respected. You may argue that fighting may be
left to the generals. It is not so. Everyone, naturally, follows
the example of his chief, and besides, if you know nothing of
warfare, how will you be able to command those who do ? Nor
is ill-health any excuse. It is not work I want from you, but
good-will, which is quite independent of sickness. Ask anyone
who remembers my brother (Tsar Theodore), who was incon-
testably much sicker than you,‡ and for that reason could not
ride on swift horses. Yet, having a great love of horses, he was
continually inspecting them, and kept them constantly before
his eyes, so that there were not, and to this very day never have
been, such stables in Russia as he had. I feel that I am leaving
my inheritance to one who resembles the slothful servant in the
Gospels, who hid his talents in a napkin. Here have I been
cursing, and not only cursing, but striking you all these years,
and it has been all in vain. You will do nothing, but simply sit

---

* Twelve years later he ascended the throne as Peter II. See R. N. Bain:
" Pupils of Peter the Great."

† Abridged from the Russian original in Solovev : " Istoria Rossy," XVII., 2.

‡ As Tsar Theodore was a helpless cripple, the irony of this comparison is
obvious.

at home enjoying yourself, however contrary things may be going. Sorrowfully reflecting upon all this, and perceiving that I cannot in any way incline you to do good, I have thought well to address this last appeal to you, and wait a little longer to see if, perchance, you will turn from the error of your ways. If you do not, be quite sure that I will deprive you of your succession ; I will cut you off as though you were a gangrenous swelling. For do not think because you are my only son, that therefore I say this only to frighten you. Verily I will do as I say; God is my witness. I have never spared, I never will spare, my life for my country and my people. How, then, shall I spare a useless thing like you ? Far better outside merit than one's own rubbish."

Peter had naturally expected that this final appeal to the self-respect of his son would have led to a personal explanation, followed by repentance and an effort at amendment, especially as the Tsarevich was not asked to do anything but acquiesce in his father's plans. After all, the first duty of Alexius was to the nation he was one day to rule ; and private tastes should always be sacrificed to the call of public duty. But it was now that he showed what a poor creature he really was. After consulting his old tutor Vyazemsky, his friend Alexander Kikin, Theodore Aprak-sin and Vasily Dolgoruki, he wrote a pitiful reply to his father, offering to renounce the succession in favour of his baby half-brother Peter* (who had been born the day after the Princess Charlotte's funeral), on the plea of ill-health and general incompetence. Peter's first impulse on receiving this craven reply to his appeal was to order his son to the block incontinently, but Prince Vasily Dolgoruki intervened, and saved the Tsarevich.† But rage and mortification, and the effort to drown them at a banquet given by Apraksin, brought on a serious attack of his old malady. So ill was he, that the senators were hastily summoned and slept all night at the Palace, and the last sacraments were administered to the Tsar. On Christmas Day, however, Peter was able to attend divine service in the Cathedral, but for some time afterwards he was very weak and ill. Only on January 19, 1716, was he able to reply to his son's letter, and he

* The little prince died a few months afterwards.
† Solovev : ' Istoria Rossy," XVII., 2.

now offered Alexius the choice between amending his ways or
becoming a monk. " It must be one or the other," wrote the Tsar;
"it is impossible for you to be neither fish nor flesh for ever."
Again Alexius consulted his friends, and they advised him to
submit to the tonsure, and await better times in a monastery.
"The Klobuk* won't be nailed to your head," said Kikin, "you
can take it off whenever you like." Then Alexius wrote to his
father for permission to become a monk, signing the letter:
"Your slave, and useless son, Alexius." Thus the last means of
compulsion had failed. The apathy of the son had triumphed
over the indignation of the father. Even a monastery had no
terrors for a prince determined, at all hazards, to shirk the duties
of his high calling. Still Peter did not despair. On the eve of
his departure for the Pomeranian and Mecklenburg campaigns
he visited Alexius, who was ill at the time, and urged him to
think the whole matter over once more, and do nothing in a
hurry, and on August 26, 1716, he wrote to him from abroad
urging him, if he desired to remain Tsarevich, to join him and
the army without delay.

Alexius at once saw a chance of escaping from his false
position altogether. Two years previously, while taking the
waters of Carlsbad, his friend, Kikin, had advised him not to
return to Russia while his father was alive, but place himself under
the protection of his brother-in-law, the Emperor, or of Louis
XIV., the willing protector of fugitive princes. Alexius's affection
for his wife had, however, brought him back to Charlotte at the
time of her first confinement; but his wife was now dead, the
urgency of his father had grown disquieting, and his fears for his
own safety had greatly increased since his aunt, the Tsarevna
Natalia, had advised him on her death-bed (January, 1716) to
keep out of harm's way, and take refuge with the Emperor.
Peter's letter from Pomerania decided him. He informed Menshikov, who had been left behind as Governor of Petersburg,
that he had made up his mind to join his father, and on September
26, 1716, he departed from Riga accompanied by his mistress,
a pretty Finn girl, Afrosina by name, her brother Ivan, and three
servants, ostensibly for Copenhagen. At Libau he encountered

* Hood.

his high-spirited great-aunt, the Tsarevna Maria, returning from
abroad. As one of the Miloslavskis, Maria hated Peter, and
sympathised with his son, though she half despised Alexius for
his egotism and cowardice. To her he confided the secret of
his flight, but the old lady took a gloomy view of his prospects.
" Wherever you may go," said she," your father will find you out."
Much more encouraging was Kikin who had been attached to the
Tsarevna's suite during her tour abroad. He privately informed
Alexius that the authorities at Vienna had been prepared for his
arrival, and that he would be perfectly safe from the pursuit of his
father in the Emperor's dominions. He advised him to pay no
heed to any messages or promises from his father, as Peter
would most certainly kill him if ever he succeeded in laying hold
of him again. "But what am I to do, if anyone overtakes me
at Dantzic or Königsburg?" asked the panic-stricken wretch.
"Why, depart at night with the girl only, and if there are two
messengers, feign illness, send off one of them with the news and
dodge the other."

On October 21 Peter received a despatch by courier from
Menshikov informing him that his son had set out to join him,
and had not since been heard of. Peter at once instructed
Veselovsky, his minister at Vienna, to request the Emperor to
deliver up Alexius if he were to be found in any part of the
Austrian dominions. He had guessed at once that the Tsarevich's most probable place of refuge would be the Court of his
brother-in-law.

Meanwhile, a strange scene was being enacted at Vienna.
Late in the evening of November 10, 1716, an agitated fugitive,
calling himself Kokhausky, knocked at the door of the Austrian
vice-chancellor, Count Schönborn, and introduced himself as
the Tsarevich Alexius. The terror of this strange intruder was
pitiable. He ran round and round the room looking for spies
in every corner, gesticulating wildly, and implored Schönborn to
protect him. He explained that his father sought his life, and
that he had fled to his brother-in-law to avoid entering a
monastery or forfeiting his inheritance. Then falling exhausted
into an armchair, he exclaimed: " Conduct me to the Emperor!"
Count Schönborn did his utmost to soothe his terrified visitor.

R.                                                                    A A

He gave him a glass or two of Moselle, assured him that he was perfectly safe, but explained that it was too late to see the Emperor, who must first be informed of his errand. Alexius then declared that had he accompanied his father to Pomerania he would have been ruined, body and soul, by drink* and hard labour ; but that for fear of exasperating his father still further he had not taken refuge in Sweden, though it offered a nearer asylum. Besides, the Emperor, as his near kinsman, had a prior claim upon him and would not be likely to give him up to what would be utter destruction, for his father was surrounded by bad people, and was himself very cruel and never sparing of human blood, and had, like God, the power of life and death in his hands.

Meanwhile Peter had succeeded in tracing Alexius to Vienna, but there every vestige of him was lost. The Austrian Government denied all knowledge of the fugitive Tsarevitch, but Captain Alexander Rumyantsev, of the Russian Guards, discovered that a dirty-looking young Russian, called Kokhausky, had recently arrived there, and he finally tracked him to the Tyrolian fortress of Ahrenberg, where he was being detained as a state prisoner. The Russian ambassador, Veselovsky, thereupon informed the Emperor that the Tsarevich had been discovered, and desired his extradition. The Emperor, to gain time, promised to communicate with the Tsar on the subject, and sent Alexius and Afrosina to Naples, where they were placed under the charge of Count Daun, the Governor-General of Naples, in the Castle of St. Elmo. That the Emperor sincerely sympathised with Alexius and suspected Peter of harbouring murderous designs against his son is plain from his confidential letter to his ally, George I. of England, whom he consulted on the delicate affair. In this letter he explained that he was harbouring the unfortunate Tsarevich to save him from the tyranny of his father, who was quite capable of employing poison, or "similar Moscovite gallantries" to get rid of him. To Peter himself Charles VI. sent an ironical and declamatory letter, the meaning of which the Tsar professed to be unable to understand.

* This is not so extravagant an accusation as it seems at first blush. There is evidence at hand to show that Peter encouraged Menshikov to make the Tsarevich drunk, saying to himself, no doubt, that this was the best way of knocking the monkish nonsense out of him, and making a man of him.

Peter's agitation was extreme. The flight of the Tsarevich to a foreign potentate was a reproach and a scandal. He must be recovered and brought back to Russia at all hazards. But the operation was likely to be one of exceptional difficulty, and it was therefore confided to the most subtle and astute of all the Moscovite diplomatists, Count Peter Tolstoi, with Captain Alexander Rumyantsev—who had already given striking proofs of his detective ability, by tracing the Tsarevich to Naples— as Tolstoi's assistant. The two diplomatists were to protest against the tone of the Emperor's letter and demand permission to see Alexius.

Three days after his arrival at Vienna, Tolstoi had an audience of the Emperor, and delivered his master's commands so forcibly that Charles VI., in some alarm, submitted the whole matter to the consideration of three of his most confidential ministers, who, after a prolonged conference, advised the Emperor to allow Tolstoi to proceed to Naples to see the Tsarevich, and not to prevent the Tsarevich's departure if he went willingly. They gave this advice in view of the defenceless position of Bohemia and Silesia, against which the Russian troops actually in Northern Germany might easily be diverted. Tolstoi and Rumyantsev were accordingly informed that the Emperor would not object to the voluntary departure of the Tsarevich, but that it would be barbarous and contrary to international comity to force him to go.

On September 24, 1717, Tolstoi and Rumyantsev arrived at Naples. Their instructions were grimly precise. They were to assure the Tsarevich that if he returned home with them at once everything would be forgiven, and he would be restored to favour and have perfect liberty ; but, if he refused to return, his father, as his sovereign, would publicly denounce him as a traitor, while the Church would simultaneously excommunicate him as a disobedient son, in which case he might be sure that he was damned, and fit material for the tormentors, both in this world and the next. They were also to impress upon him the futility of hoping to escape from his father's vengeance for long. However strongly guarded he might be, his father could always find the means of compelling the Emperor to deliver him up, and he

356 THE FIRST ROMANOVS.

could judge for himself what would happen to him after that. Peter also wrote to Alexius in much the same strain, reproaching him bitterly for thus exposing his father to shame; but, at the same time, swearing solemnly "before God and His judgment seat," that if he came back he should not be punished in the least, but be cherished as a son.

On September 26 Tolstoi and Rumyantsev had their first interview with Alexius in the presence of Count Daun. They found him almost insane with terror and possessed by the fixed idea that they had come to kill him. At a second interview, two days later, he declared outright that he was afraid to face his father's wrath. Then the pressure of lying threats was roughly applied. He was told that his father would come and fetch him by force if he did not return willingly. Still he held out. Tolstoi now grew impatient. He reported that only the most extreme compulsion could, as he brutally phrased it, " melt the hard-frozen obstinacy of this beast of ours "—and we can imagine what such words meant in the mouth of a man who had not hesitated to remove an inconvenient secretary by poison. The unfortunate Tsarevich, who knew instinctively that he was fighting for his life against merciless enemies, had but a feeble chance against the craft and subtlety of his father's sleuth-hounds, and there is something coldly diabolical in the zest with which Tolstoi evidently gave himself up to the congenial task of breaking this bruised reed. At first, however, relying on the Emperor's solemn promise of protection, Alexius stood firm and refused to depart. But Tolstoi won over both the Viceroy and the Viceroy's secretary, and they pulled away the poor creature's last prop by assuring him that the Emperor, already involved in a war with the Ottoman Porte, would think twice before engaging in another war with the Tsar simply because he, Alexius, was obstinate and unreasonable. While he was still reeling from the effects of this blow, Tolstoi utterly crushed the last feeble remnant of his resistance by secretly persuading the Viceroy to threaten to take away Afrosina, whose pregnancy was now imminent. Rather than be parted from his mistress, whom he loved passionately, Alexius instantly surrendered. He promised to return at once to Russia with Tolstoi, but on two conditions. His father was to allow him to live quietly on his estates, and marry Afrosina. To these terms Tolstoi agreed verbally, and Peter himself solemnly confirmed them in a letter to his son, dated November 18, 1717. We shall see that these promises were never kept: there is good reason to assume that they were never meant to be kept.

Alexius was now hustled out of Italy as rapidly and as stealthily as possible. Before departing from Naples he visited and adored the relics of St. Nicholas at Bari, but this was the only respite allowed him. He was prevented, how we know not, from meeting Charles VI. at Venice, though they were both in the place at the same time, and when the Emperor, too late suspecting that force was being used, and knowing that the prisoner must pass through Brünn on his way home, secretly instructed the governor, Count Morawski, to have a private interview with the Tsarevich and ascertain his real wishes, Tolstoi took good care to be present throughout the interview, and Alexius, whose dirty, neglected condition painfully affected Morawski, said only what he had been told to say beforehand. On January 31, 1718, without any further adventure on the journey, the Tsarevich reached Moscow.

But what was to be done with the Tsarevich? That was the question, a question the solution of which admitted of no delay. To allow him to live quietly in his country-house was to establish in the heart of Russia a centre of disaffection; yet this had been one of the Tsarevich's conditions of surrender, and the Tsar had solemnly sworn to observe it. And there was another and still more serious difficulty to be faced. It was inconceivable that a dreamy weakling like Alexius could, of his own accord, have ventured upon such a bold step as flight to a foreign potentate. He must have had counsellors and abettors. Who were they? Peter, nervously apprehensive of the designs of the forces of reaction, scented a wide-spread domestic conspiracy, fed perhaps by foreign gold, and certainly suggested by foreign foes. He determined to institute a most searching inquisition in order to get at the bottom of the mystery.

The first step was to extort a full confession from the Tsarevich. On February 18, Alexius, without his sword, was brought before an assemblage of magnates and prelates presided over by the Tsar. It is evident on this occasion that Alexius was not only not a free agent, but so paralysed with terror that, face to face with his terrible father, he was as clay in the potter's hands. The Tsar had no sooner opened his mouth to upbraid him, than he fell upon his knees, confessed himself guilty of everything, though no crime had yet been imputed to him, and abjectly begged for mercy. For the second time, Peter promised him full forgiveness if he revealed the names of all his accomplices, and this Alexius immediately proceeded to do, retiring for the purpose alone with his father into another room.

The whole assembly then proceeded to the Uspensky Cathedral, where, at his father's command, the Tsarevich, standing before the Gospels, most solemnly renounced the succession to the throne in favour of his little half-brother, the Grand Duke Peter Petrovich. A manifesto to that effect was issued by the Tsar the same day. In this manifesto Peter further declared that, though his son deserved death for putting his own father to shame before the whole world, "yet, nevertheless, our fatherly heart having taken compassion on him, we promise him immunity from all punishment." This third promise of pardon was no doubt calculated to allay the apprehensions of the patricians friendly to the Tsarevich as to his ultimate fate.

On the following day Alexius was ordered, under pain of death, to put down in writing, as minutely and conscientiously as if he were in the confessional, an account of his flight and the motives thereof. He was told that if he omitted anything that might come to light afterwards, the pardon already promised him would be no pardon at all. This tantalising promise of pardon, ever present, yet ever elusive, advanced repeatedly to elicit fresh incriminating confessions, and withdrawn again immediately afterwards, was certainly as potent a means of pressure as the physical torture ultimately superadded.

Of course Alexius confessed everything suggested to him. Of course his wretched confederates, torn from their hiding-places and dragged to the torture-chamber, supplied the prosecution with evidence which nowadays would never be accepted in any court of justice.* Alexander Kikin, inhumanly delivered into the hands of his deadliest enemy, Menshikov, was horribly tormented three times, and, after confessing in writing that he had advised Alexius to seek refuge at Vienna, was condemned to "the cruel death."† Other "accomplices" shared the same fate. Alexius's old tutor, Vyazemsky, only escaped because he could prove that, since 1711, he had been in disfavour with the Tsarevich, who had even kicked and cuffed him at Wolfenbüttel. Prince Vasily Vladimirovich Dolgoruki, who was sent in chains from Petersburg to Moscow, escaped with banishment to Solikamsk because the Senate refused to accept the testimony of Alexius against him—a significant indication of what they thought of the evidence in general. Nor did the clergy escape scot free. Peter was well aware of their dislike of him and his ways. "If there had been no monks and nuns," he said to Tolstoi on one occasion, " Alexius would never have dared to commit such unspeakable evil. My father had to deal with one of these *borodachies*,‡ but I have to deal with thousands of them. However, I mean to clip their wings very soon, and then they will not be such highflyers." And he was as good as his word. Knowing that the eyes of the orthodox clergy were reverently fixed upon the Suzdal-Pokrovsky Monastery, where the ex-Tsaritsa Eudoxia was imprisoned, Peter resolved to strike a blow at the hierarchy, through her, which should terrorise all opposition. Accordingly, soon after the execution of Kikin, Captain Pisarev of the Guards was sent without warning to the monastery to arrest Eudoxia, and bring her to Moscow. He found "the nun, Elena," going about in ordinary costume and held in high honour by the archimandrite and the nuns, who persisted in regarding her as the lawful Gosudaruinya. By Pisarev's advice, "in order that many villainies might be revealed," Eudoxia's kinsman, Abraham Lopukhin, Major Stephen Glyebov, Dosithy, Bishop of Rostov, and other friends of the ex-Tsaritsa were arrested and haled away to Moscow. But all that prolonged

---

* Perhaps nothing shows how immeasurably superior in humanity Charles XII. was to his rival than his abolition of torture in legal process at the very beginning of his reign.　　　　　† Impalement, or breaking on the wheel.

‡ *I.e*, the patriarch Nikon. *Borodach* means the wearer of a long, full beard.

and oft-repeated torture could extract from these unhappy creatures was the fact that they sympathised deeply with Eudoxia. Some of them believed in her future restoration and reconciliation with her husband, and the bishop had even prophesied that this glad event would one day happen. Dosithy was at once degraded to the rank of a monk, in order that the question extraordinary might be applied to him. He, and many of the other prisoners, confessed under torture that they had desired the death of Peter and the elevation of Alexius, but even this extorted "evidence" failed to substantiate the suspected conspiracy. Peter had to be content with a public confession of adultery with Major Glyebov from Eudoxia, who was thereupon banished to the still more remote monastery of Ladoga. Her alleged paramour, who is said to have been the handsomest man in Russia, after being submitted to unspeakable torments, was left all night on the stake on which he had been impaled, expiring at sunrise. He endured his sufferings with heroic silence. His one request that the sacraments might be administered to him was refused. Finally Peter himself approached and adjured the dying man, as he would answer for it to that God before whom he was about to appear, to confess his crime. "You are as stupid as you are cruel," replied Glyebov coldly. "Do you suppose that after I have endured all your torments I would, now that you can hurt me no more, appear before my Maker with a lie upon my lips, and stain the honour of an innocent woman?"* Another victim was broken on the wheel. The rest of Eudoxia's sympathisers were hanged, or flogged and banished.

On the conclusion of the "Moscow process," as it was called, Peter hastened back to Petersburg to be nearer to the Åland Islands, where the peace congress was still sitting. There was a lull in the prosecution of the Tsarevich's affair, and Alexius, naturally sanguine, and conscious that something was owing to one who had unhesitatingly confessed everything required of him, bent all his efforts to obtaining the fulfilment of his father's promise that he should marry the Finn girl, Afrosina, who was now on her way home from abroad after her confinement. Like

* Solitsuin : "Preobrazhenskoe."

everyone else who was in trouble, he begged the omnipotent Tsaritsa Catherine to intercede for him in this matter, and Catherine, always good-natured, promised to do what she could. Little did either of them anticipate the frightful *dénouement* that was now rapidly approaching.

In April, 1718, Afrosina arrived at Petersburg, but instead of being taken to the arms of her lover, as she had expected, she was suddenly brought before the Tsar's inquisitors.   As the mistress and confidante of Alexius she was the depositary of all his secrets, and those secrets the prosecution was determined to get hold of.   Of course they succeeded.   What could a timid, helpless, ignorant girl do except tremble and babble when suddenly confronted by such merciless and interested ruffians as Alexander Menshikov and Peter Tolstoi?   Afrosina obsequiously answered every leading question, and recollected instantly everything she was asked to remember.   All the thoughts, hopes, fears, confidences and day-dreams of her unfortunate lover were speedily in the Tsar's possession.   They did not amount to very much, but they were sufficient to destroy Alexius.   He had told her, amongst other things, that there was a revolt in the Russian armies and a mutiny at Moscow.   He had rejoiced at the illness of his supplanter, the little Grand Duke Peter.   "You see what God is doing," he had said on this occasion.   "Dad does his work, but God is working also." Living largely as he did on his hopes of the future, he had freely confided these hopes to the girl who was to be his Tsaritsa. When he was Tsar, he had told her, he would order things very differently.   He would live at Moscow and let Petersburg remain a mere provincial town.   He would have no ships, and keep the army solely for defensive purposes.   He predicted that on the death of his father a civil war would break out, between his own partisans and the partisans of his little brother, in which he would ultimately prevail, because the Russian people would not endure the government of women.*

Immediately after this "confession" had been obtained, Peter sent for Alexius, confronted him with it and reproached him for concealing material facts, and thereby forfeiting his pardon.

---

* *I.e.*, his step-mother Catherine and her daughters.

The Tsarevich might very well have retorted that he had been inveigled home by a solemn promise of absolute and unconditional forgiveness which had been most ruthlessly and hypocritically broken, but at the sight of his father he collapsed. Nor should we too hastily reproach him with cowardice during this horrible ordeal. We have abundant testimony to the fact that Peter in his wrath was so appalling that the manliest and sturdiest of his subjects, when brought before him, shook as if in the grip of an ague.* Alexius, who was naturally rather a poor creature, must have been half-dead with terror. All he could do now was to try to save the miserable remnant of life that his tormentors might allow him to call his own, and this he obviously thought might be done by saying " yes " to everything. Yes, he *had* wished for his father's death ; he *had* rejoiced when he heard of plots against his father ; he *had* been ready to accept his father's throne from rebels and regicides. All had now been said. At last the worst was known. It is true there were no actual facts to go upon. The Tsarevich had done nothing yet,whatever he might intend to do. His "evil designs " were still *in foro conscientiæ* and had not been, perhaps never would be, translated into practice. But all such considerations as these weighed not at all with the Tsar. In the eyes of Peter his son was now a self-convicted and most dangerous traitor. His life was forfeit. The future welfare of Russia imperatively demanded his speedy extinction.

But now a case for casuists arose, and Peter himself was casuist enough to recognise that it was a case of unusual and peculiar difficulty. Even if Alexius deserved a thousand deaths, there was no getting over the fact that his father had sworn " before the Almighty and His judgment seat," to pardon him and let him live in peace if he returned to Russia ; and it was only on these conditions that Alexius (very foolishly, in the opinion of his friends) had placed himself once more in his father's hands. From Peter's point of view the question was : Did the enormity of the Tsarevich's crime absolve the Tsar from the oath which he had taken to spare the life of this prodigal

* *E.g.*, old Admiral Apraksin on the mere rumour that the Tsar was wroth with him had a fit of apoplexy.

son? This question was solemnly submitted to a grand council of prelates, senators, ministers, and other dignitaries, on June 13, 1718. First the Tsar addressed the clergy. Although, he said, he had a perfect right to punish his son's crimes without consulting anybody, yet, nevertheless, lest he should sin against God unwittingly, and also because in all doubtful matters a man should never be his own sole counsellor, but especially because he, the Tsar, had bound himself by an oath, subsequently confirmed by writing, to forgive " this my son," therefore, being mindful of all these things, he exhorted the archbishops and clergy, as the teachers of the Word of God, to search and find from Holy Scripture " what punishment was meet for this son who had wrought after the manner of Absalom," and give their opinion in writing " as became the guardians of the divine commandments and the faithful pastors of Christ's flock."

The temporal members of the council were exhorted to judge without fear and without respect of persons, fearing not to pronounce a lighter sentence than death if they thought such sentence just. " Do justice," proceeded the Tsar's declaration, " lest ye jeopardise your souls and mine likewise, that our consciences may be clear on the terrible Day of Judgment, and our country may at this present time be secure."

Five days later the clergy presented their memorial, which was signed by the Metropolitan of Moscow, two Greek metropolitans, five Russian bishops, four archimandrites,* and two hieromonakhs.† It was a cautious non-committal document, plainly inspired by fear,‡ but unmistakably inclining to mercy. After citing various examples of filial obedience and disobedience from Holy Scripture, it offered the Tsar an alternative. If he would punish the fallen sinner, he would find numerous precedents for so doing in the Old Testament, though, on the other hand, the much injured Tsar David would have forgiven his persecutor Absalom. But if he were pleased to pardon, he had the example of Christ Himself, who said, I will have mercy and not sacrifice; while the voices of the apostles bade mercy

---

* Abbots.                    † Monks in holy orders.

‡ We must recollect that the terrible "Moscow process," in which a bishop had first been degraded to the level of a common monk, and then tortured and slain, and all for his sympathy with Alexius, was only just over.

prevail over judgment. "But," concluded the memorial, "the heart of the Tsar is in God's hand; let him choose what part he will."

Thus, by pointing to the highest of all examples, the example of Christ Himself, the clergy indirectly counselled forgiveness. But it is a significant fact, which says very little for the courage of the clergy on this unique opportunity for asserting themselves and saving their friend the Tsarevich, that they entirely passed over the strongest, the most irrefragable of the arguments in favour of Alexius, namely, the Tsar's solemn promise of forgiveness to his son, in reliance upon which Alexius had returned to Russia. On this crucial point they had not a word to say, although the Tsar had explicitly exhorted them to relieve his conscience on this very point.

Peter was in a dilemma. There can, I think, be little doubt that he had at last determined to rid himself of his detested son; but he certainly shrank from a public execution, the scandal of which would have been enormous and its consequences incalculable. The temporal members of the council helped him out of his difficulty by expressing a desire to be quite convinced that Alexius had actually meditated rebellion against his father. If this were a genuine desire, it was no doubt a last effort of the Tsarevich's friends to save his life; but, in view of what ensued immediately afterwards, I am inclined to suppose, though I admit that there is no available evidence supporting the hypothesis, that it was a pretext for bringing the Tsarevich to the torture-chamber where he might very easily expire, as if by accident, under legal process. The most ordinary mode of administering the question extraordinary was by the terrible knout. The knout was a whip made of parchment cooked in milk, and so hard and sharp that its strokes were like those of a sword. Those who were to be flogged with the knout generally had their backs bared, their arms tied behind them, and were then hoisted up by one arm to a sort of gallows. The executioner, with the knout in his hand, then took two or three running springs, the impetus of which enabled him to cut to the bone at each stroke. Practised executioners in Russia could kill a man with three strokes. There were few instances of anyone

surviving thirty strokes.*    It was to this torture that the
Tsarevich Alexius, never very robust, and severely reduced by
mental suffering and prolonged anxiety, was now to be submitted.
It was hardly possible that he could survive it ; the natural inference is that he was not intended to survive it.    On June 19,
Alexius received five-and-twenty strokes with the knout, and
betrayed his confessor, Ignatev, who was also savagely tortured.
On the 22nd Tolstoi was sent to see Alexius at the fortress of
St. Peter and St. Paul, where he had been confined since the 14th,
but beyond a vague confession of unworthiness and incompetence
he could get nothing more out of his victim, simply because he had
nothing more to tell.    On June 24 Alexius received fifteen more
strokes, but even the knout could now extract nothing.    The
mangled wretch could only feebly protest that he had revealed
everything he knew.    On the same day the Senate condemned
the Tsarevich to death for *imagining* rebellion against his father,
and for *hoping* for the co-operation of the common people and
the armed intervention of his brother-in-law, the Emperor.    The
solemn promise of the Tsar, which the clergy had ignored, was
sophistically explained away by the senators.    The Tsar, they
said, had only promised his son forgiveness if he returned
willingly ; he had returned unwillingly, and had, therefore, forfeited the promise.    This shameful document, the outcome of
mingled terror and obsequiousness, was signed by all the senators
and ministers, and by three hundred persons of lesser degree.
Among the signatures we find the names not only of such deadly
enemies of the Tsarevich as Menshikov and Tolstoi, but the
names of his secret friends and sympathisers, the Dolgorukies
and the Golitsuins.    Two days later, June 26, 1718, the Tsarevich
died in the Trubetskoi guard-house of the citadel of Petersburg, at six o'clock in the evening, while still under arrest,
and on June 30 he was buried in the Petropavolsk Cathedral by
the side of his consort, in the presence of his father and his step-
mother.    The precise manner of his death is still something of
an enigma, most of the existing documents relating to it being
apocryphal, the outcome of popular excitement and exaggeration.

* Juel: " En Rejse til Rusland, etc." Juel had opportunities of seeing the
punishment inflicted.

So far as I am aware there are only two extant genuine documents
which throw any light upon the subject. These two documents are
(1.) a "record" of what took place in the chancellery of the
garrison-fortress between the hours of eight and eleven on the
day of the Tsarevich's death, and (2.) the official account of the
last moments of Alexius in the "rescript" sent by Peter to his
ministers abroad for communication to foreign Powers. Taken
separately, these two documents only mystify, but taken together
they are mutually explanatory and bring us within measurable
distance of this awful mystery. I present them consecutively.
First let us take the "record," which runs as follows: "At eight
o'clock in the morning of June 26 there assembled his serene
highness Prince Yakov Dolgoruki, Gavriil Golovkin, Theodore
Apraksin, Ivan Musin-Pushkin, Tikhon Stryeshnev, Peter
Tolstoi, Peter Shafirov and General Buturlin. A *zastyenok** was
set up and remained in the garrison till eleven o'clock, when
the party separated."

Take next the Imperial "rescript": "Moved, on the one hand
by natural pity, and, on the other hand by the necessity of
guarding the integrity and safety of our realm, we had come to
no resolution; but the Almighty desiring by His own act and
by His righteous judgment to deliver us from such doubts, and
our house and realm from such danger and shame, cut short the
life of this our son Alexius, by sending upon him, after the
declaration of his sentence, and the detection of so many of his
great crimes against us and the realm, a cruel disease like
apoplexy. But, when once more he recovered his senses, and, as
was his bounden Christian duty, had confessed and communicated,
he called us to him, and we, putting aside all our anger, went to
him with all the senators and ministers present, and he acknowledged all his offences with repentance and tears and asked our
pardon which we gave him as an affectionate father and a
Christian man, and thus about six o'clock in the afternoon of the
26th, he ended his life after a Christian sort."

Now what do we gather from a comparison and combination
of these two documents? Surely this: At eight o'clock in the

---

* A *zastyenok* was the partition within which prisoners under arrest were
tortured.

morning of June 26, 1718, the Tsar, accompanied by some of the chief dignitaries of the Empire, proceeded to the fortress, and Alexius was produced and placed before them within the walls of a *zastyenok*.  His death-sentence was then suddenly read to him. The shock, acting upon an enfeebled frame, and crushing the last hope of life with which the poor wretch had hugged himself in the midst of his awful sufferings, brought on a fit which lasted some hours, and on his recovery he was carried into the close-adjoining Trubetskoi guard-room, where he died.  One does not like to think that the natural consequence of such a shock was deliberately premeditated ; but it could easily have been fore-seen, and, from the point of view of the Tsar, it was eminently desirable.  The account of the " rescript " of the final interview between father and son is, probably, quite correct.  Alexius had indeed committed no crime, unless intentions and expectations are to be judged in the same way as actions ; but self-willed and indolent he certainly had been, and his conscience, always tender, would, at the hour of death, be more than usually sensitive and contrite.  No doubt, therefore, he *did* ask for his father's forgiveness, let us hope he obtained it.  Abominable, unnatural, as Peter's conduct was to his unhappy son, there is no reason to suppose that he ever regretted it.  Why should he ?  He would argue, he *did* argue, that a single worthless life stood in the way of the regeneration of Russia, and was therefore forfeit to the common-weal.  That life he cunningly removed, and, all rhetoric and exaggeration apart, we may safely say, taking all the circumstances into consideration, that Peter the Great deliberately cemented the foundations of his Empire with the blood of his son.

# CHAPTER XIII.

## WESTERN DIPLOMACY, AND THE FAR AND THE NEAR EAST.
### 1719—1725.

Peter proclaimed Emperor of All Russia—Relations of Russia with Austria, Prussia, Sweden and France—Proposed Marriage between Louis XV. and Elizabeth Petrovna—Predominance of Great Britain—Futile Efforts of France to reconcile Peter and George I.—Peter and the Jacobites—Peter's Relations with China—Izmailov's Mission to Pekin—The First Trans-Caspian Expedition—The Calmucks and the Kuban Tatars—Voluinsky's Mission to Persia—The Persian War—Peter's Dealings with the Armenians—Acquisition of the Caspian Provinces—Uneasiness of the Porte—Alarming Despatches of the Russian Ambassador Nepluyev—Treaty of Constantinople.

BUT, however cemented, the Russian Empire was now, at any rate, an established and imposing fact. Its official birthday dates from October 22, 1721, when, after a solemn thanksgiving service in the Troitsa Cathedral at Petersburg for the Peace of Nystad, the Tsar proceeded to the Senate and was there acclaimed: " Father of the Fatherland, Peter the Great and Emperor of All Russia," the grand-chancellor Golovkin acting on this occasion as the spokesman of his fellow senators. The threefold *vivat !* was taken up by everyone inside and outside the cathedral, amidst the ringing of bells, the firing of salvoes, the flourish of trumpets and the roll of drums. Some would have preferred to proclaim Peter Emperor of the East, but Peter himself adopted the more patriotic title. In the hour of his triumph, he would not deprive the Russian nation of its proper share in the great event; his first thought was for the glory of his country. In a brief reply to the chancellor, Peter consented to accept the Imperial title, at the same time modestly disclaiming all personal merit, and solemnly attributing the final victory of Russia, after a struggle of twenty-one years, to the will of the Almighty. In conclusion he exhorted his hearers not to allow the peace they had so hardly earned to soften and enfeeble them, lest they should one day share the fate of the imbecile and degenerate Byzantine Empire.*

Prussia, the nearest ally, and the Netherlands, the oldest friend of the Tsar, were the first of the European states to recognise Peter's Imperial title, but elsewhere the novelty was received with disfavour, especially at Vienna, where the emergence of a second Empire which threatened to overshadow the Holy Roman Empire gave great offence. The Austrian ministers were also alarmed at Peter's progress in Persia,† and found it hard to endure the just reproaches of the English ambassador for their foolishness in neglecting to curb Russia at the right time when Sweden, though in extremities, was not yet extruded from the Baltic. "Russia," exclaimed the English minister, on this occasion, "is now well on the way to India, and likely to found another Empire larger than that of Rome."‡ Curiously enough, the friendship of Prussia, which might have counterbalanced the hostility of Austria, was imperilled by Peter's withdrawal from Berlin of the gigantic grenadiers whom he had previously lent, or given, to Frederick William I. The Prussian King, whose partiality for these Goliaths was notorious, almost broke his heart at the enforced departure of his finest specimens, and for some time afterwards the Russian ambassador at Berlin was not permitted to see him, even on urgent business, on the plea that "the rankling wound was still too recent."

Peter indemnified himself for the defection of his Prussian ally by contracting an offensive and defensive alliance, for twelve years, with his ancient enemy, Sweden, which, under the prudent pacific administration of Count Arvid Horn, was being gradually nursed into political convalescence. By the Treaty of Stockholm (February 22, 1724) Russia contracted to assist Sweden, in case she were attacked by any other European Power, with 12,000 infantry, 4,000 cavalry, nine ships of the line, and three frigates ; while Sweden undertook, under similar circumstances, to assist Russia with 8,000 infantry, 2,000 cavalry, six liners, and two frigates.

---

* Solovev: "Istoria Rossy," XVII., 3.          † See *infra*.
‡ Solovev: "Istoria Rossy." XVIII., 2.

The relations between Russia and France had also become much more cordial than heretofore. It was Peter's pet ambition to marry his second surviving daughter, the Tsesarevna Elizabeth, to the young King of France, Louis XV. That such a proposition should have been made at all shows to what heights the aspiring young Russian Empire had already risen. Under Louis XIV. it would have been regarded as an impertinence; the guardians of Louis XV. simply waived it aside with ironical smiles. The delicate mission of negotiating the marriage was entrusted to the eldest and most experienced of the Russian diplomatists, Prince Boris Kurakin, who informed Peter in 1723 that Louis had no desire to marry the young Spanish Infanta, who had been expressly educated for him in France since her childhood, and she was now to be sent back to her own country. Kurakin broached the subject of the Russian alliance on his arrival at Paris in 1724; but the leading French minister, the Duke de Bourbon-Condé, proposed, instead, an alliance between his own son, the Duke de Chartres, and the Tsesarevna on condition that Peter supported the candidature of his proposed son-in-law on the occasion of the next Polish interregnum. Peter, however, was by no means satisfied with the son of a royal duke for his Imperial daughter, when a young King was in the matrimonial market, and he urged Kurakin to bring about a marriage between Louis XV. and Elizabeth by every means in his power. But Bourbon pride proved an insuperable obstacle, and equally abortive were the efforts of successive French ministers to bring about a better understanding between Great Britain and Russia.

For some years after the termination of the war of the Spanish succession, Great Britain was, indisputably, the dominant Power of Europe. The French Government, painfully conscious of its own poverty and weakness, was very apprehensive of hurting the susceptibilities of a Power strong and wealthy enough to be a dangerous enemy, especially in combination with the Kaiser, the hereditary foe of the House of Bourbon. To prevent a renewal of the Anglo-Austrian alliance, and to isolate the Kaiser, were now the chief aims of the French ministers, especially in view of the anticipated break-up of the Austrian dominions on the death

of the sonless Charles VI., who, by the Pragmatic Sanction of
1713, had irregularly transferred the succession to his daughter,
Maria Theresa, now a child of eight. France, moreover, was
anxious to keep Russia free from complications elsewhere, so
that her mercenaries might be available against Maria Theresa
at the proper time, and a reconciliation between Great Britain
and Russia was considered at Versailles to be the best way of
steadying and restraining Peter. But such a reconciliation was
extremely difficult. King George had an ancient grudge against
the new Emperor of All Russia, and the mere mention of Peter's
name irritated him to frenzy. Peter's supposed friendship for
the Jacobites was an additional obstacle. But the adroit and
supple Fleury,* the governor of the young Louis XV., and since
the death of Cardinal Dubois (1723), the omnipotent Minister of
Foreign Affairs, believed himself capable of performing successfully the part of political peace-maker. He assured Prince
Kurakin that, though both the interests and the conscience of
the King of France must compel him, sooner or later, to support
the Chevalier de St. George, nevertheless, it was evident that the
best thing for Russia at the present time was reconciliation with
England ; indeed, he made an Anglo-Russian reconciliation the
condition precedent of a Franco-Russian alliance. Peter himself
was anxious to come to terms with England ; but on the other
hand, he did not want to quarrel with the Tories, who, as the
enemies of his enemy, were his friends. Indeed, the extreme
Tories, or Jacobites, now hailed Peter as their prospective
deliverer, and expected more from him than from any other
European potentate. In April, 1722, the Pretender's agent,
Thomas Gordon, informed the Tsar that the English nation was
ready to rise for its lawful King, if only they had 6,000 men and
arms for 20,000 more. In June, the same year, Prince James
Stuart wrote to Peter expressing his unspeakable gratitude for
the sympathy of his Imperial Majesty, and transmitting a plan
for the invasion of England. But as Peter would not embark
upon such a vast enterprise without the co-operation of France,
and as France desired to unite England and Russia instead of
dividing them, the Jacobite project never had the remotest

* Not yet cardinal.

chance of success, even if the Persian campaigns of Peter had not, at this very time, engrossed all his attentions and energy. It should also not be forgotten that the Tsar had got all he wanted in Europe. During the last four years of his reign his policy was predominantly oriental.

Well aware that Russia was the natural commercial intermediary between the East and the West, Peter never lost sight of the necessity of establishing and extending his influence in Asia. In 1692 the Dane Eleazer Isbrandt was accredited to the Chinese Emperor, Shing-Su, the protector of the Jesuits; but his presents were returned to him because the name of Peter preceded the name of the Grand Khan in his credentials. Nevertheless, he was favourably received at Pekin, and the Grand Khan declared his willingness to be at peace with the White Tsar and trade with him. In 1719, Captain Lev Ismailov, of the Preobrazhensky Guard, was sent to Pekin as the first Russian Minister Extraordinary. To avoid disputes, on this occasion Peter took the precaution of omitting all his honorific titles and signing his name *after* that of the Grand Khan. Those nearest to the Khan advised Ismailov to be very polite at his audience, and beware of imitating the former Russian minister, Spafari, who, when asked by the Grand Khan if he had learnt astronomy, replied he had, but when the Grand Khan thereupon inquired whether he knew of a star called " The Golden Nail," he had answered very rudely: " How can I know the names of the stars, who have never been to Heaven ? " Ismailov was not dispensed from kneeling before the Grand Khan during his audience, but he was courteously treated, and the Son of Heaven asked many polite questions concerning the White Tsar. He had heard, he said, of Peter's wars and victories, and how he had made himself terrible to his enemies by his ship-building. "Why should we quarrel ? " he continued ; " the Russian Empire is so cold and distant that an army sent against it would perish by the way, while my Empire is so hot that a Russian army sent against us would also perish. We both have so much land that a little more or less would be of no profit to either of us." But Ismailov was not allowed to establish an embassy or consulates, nor could he obtain a commercial treaty. Trade, the

Grand Khan explained, was such a paltry thing that only the poorest people ever took it up. It was not worth while to establish a Russian consular service in China on that account.

Peter, always in want of money, was first attracted to Central Asia by the report of the still unhanged Governor of Siberia, Prince Gagarin, of valuable gold deposits near the Calmuck town of Erketi on the Daria. The first Russian expeditions into Central Asia were disastrous failures owing to the ignorance and incapacity of their leaders. In 1716 Colonel Buchholtz was sent to build a fortress on Lake Yamuish, but was driven back by 12,000 Calmucks. In 1716 Prince Alexander Cherkasky set out to explore the mouths of the Amu Daria and the shores of the Sea of Aral ; to win over the Khans of Khiva and Bokhara to the Russian interest, and to attempt to open up a way to India. In the course of 1716 he proceeded with a small army of 4,000 men across the Caspian from the mouth of the Volga to Tyak, Karagan, and from thence to Krasnuie Vodui, at each of which very unsuitable places he built a small fort. In February, 1717, he returned to Astrakhan. This expedition excited a general rising of Tatars, Bokharans and Khivans, and in attempting to suppress it, in 1717, Cherkasky was slain, and his little army dispersed. Hundreds of Russian prisoners were carried to Khiva, where many of them were flayed, and their skins stuffed with straw. And there for the next three years the matter rested.

The Calmucks, as the last representatives of the Central Asian nomadic hordes pushing westward, also gave considerable trouble to the Russian Government, whose nominal subjects they were, and the so-called Tsaritskin lines, a vast trench guarded by troops and extending from the Volga to the Don, were dug to prevent the Calmucks from proceeding to the Crimea, and uniting with their kinsmen the Tatars. On the hordes of the Kuban district, still further south, on the slopes of the Caucasus, Russia had also to keep a watchful eye, especially during the Turkish War, when they invaded the provinces of Saratov and Penza, but were defeated. But in 1717 they again raided the Penza district and carried off thousands of prisoners. In the vast district lying between the Black Sea and the Caspian, which at that time was infested rather than inhabited by savage nomads, three great Powers, Russia, Turkey, and Persia, were equally interested. Russia could not permit the extension of Muhammadanism in these regions, and her commercial interests were also very largely involved therein. The beginning of the Russian influence in these parts dates from the appointment of the capable Artamon Petrovich Voluinsky as Russian minister at Ispahan in 1715. It is clear from his instructions, written by Peter's own hand, that he was sent rather as a pioneer than as a diplomatist. He was to find out what rivers fell into the Caspian, "and to which places on these rivers we can get by sea, and whether there are any rivers flowing into this sea which rise in India."* He was also to take note of Gilyan and the other Caspian provinces, and record his impressions in a regular and copious diary; and he was to divert, if possible, the raw-silk trade from Turkey to Russia through Persia with the assistance of the Armenians. Voluinsky arrived at Ispahan in March, 1717. The Shah, he reported, was a mere tool in the hands of the brutal and stupid favourite, Ekhtnia-Develet, who was equally impervious to bribery or persuasion. The country was in a shocking condition and so badly governed that another Alexander the Great and his army could not injure it more. Rebellion was everywhere rampant, and the Shah could not defend himself against his rebels, let alone outside enemies. There was nothing to be feared from Persia, a small Russian force could conquer a considerable portion of it easily. Voluinsky quitted Ispahan in September, 1717, after concluding a commercial treaty with the Shah very advantageous to Russia. On his return journey he wintered at Shemak, where he had excellent opportunity for still further spying out the nakedness of the land. He also won over to the Russian cause a Georgian renegade, Forsedan Bey, who, after becoming a Christian, had once more accepted "the abominable Moslem faith," as he called it, to save his family from captivity; but was quite willing to be reconverted to Christianity for a handsome consideration. For the next four years Voluinsky continued to urge Peter to invade Persia, but this was impossible during the continuance of the

* Solovev: "Istoria Rossy," XVIII., 1.

Swedish War.   In September, 1721, however, an event occurred
in Persia which forced the hand of the Russian Government.
Two Lesghian princes, Daudbeck and Surkai, revolted against
the Shah, seized Shemak and plundered Russian merchandise in
the bazaars to the value of 500,000 rubles.   Again Voluinsky
urged war, especially as the Russian invader could now pose as
the friend of the Persian Government, and, the Swedish War
being over, nothing prevented the Russian Emperor from taking
measures for the protection of Russian commerce on the shores
of the Caspian.   In the beginning of 1722 the state of affairs in
Persia became still more favourable for Russian intervention, for
the Afghans invaded the devastated country; defeated the
Persian troops in two pitched battles; seized Ispahan and
dethroned the Shah in favour of his third son Tokmash.   Peter
hesitated no longer.   On May 3rd the Guard left Moscow, and
on July 18th Peter sailed from Astrakhan to Derbent with an
army of 22,000 infantry, 9,000 cavalry, 20,000 Cossacks, 20,000
Calmucks, 30,000 Tatars and 5,000 sailors.   On August 23rd the
Governor of Derbent, on his knees, delivered up the silver keys
of the city to the Russian Emperor.   But difficulties of transport
had greatly impeded the Russian army *en route*, and provisions
grew scarce when a fierce and persistent north wind delayed the
departure of half the transports from Astrakhan and wrecked
the other half on the sandbanks of the Caspian.   At a Council
of War held at Derbent (August 29) it was decided to proceed
no further, and very cautiously Peter retraced his steps to
Astrakhan, building on his way the new fortress of Svety Krest,
between the rivers Agrakhan and Sulak.   On returning to
Russia, Peter, through his consul, Semen Avramov, notified the
Persian Government that he would clear out all the Kurds and
Afghans who were still ravaging the territories of the Shah, if
the Caspian provinces of Persia were ceded to him by way of
compensation, and in December, 1722, a Russian army corps,
under Colonel Shipov, began the work of deliverance by seizing
the great trading centre of Rescht.   But in the meantime the
Government of the Shah had succeeded in re-establishing itself
and Shipov was requested to withdraw, as his assistance was no
longer required.   This the Russian colonel refused to do, and

when the Persians besieged him in the Caravanserai of Rescht, he made a sortie and severely defeated them. Simultaneously General Matyushkin was operating against Baku, which Peter was very anxious to capture, as being the key of the south-western Caspian district. The town protested that it had always been loyal to the Shah, and could defend itself against rebels, but it was stormed none the less, and by the Treaty of Petersburg (September 12, 1723) was ceded to Russia along with Derbent, and the provinces of Gilyan, Mazandevan and Astrabad. The Persian Government refused, however, to ratify the treaty, and the Tsar's envoy, Lieut. Boris Meshchersky, was attacked by the Persians on his way to and from Ispahan. Only by the threat of a league of partition against her between Russia and Turkey was Persia finally compelled to consent to the cession of provinces thus extorted from her misery.

The conquest of the Caspian provinces brought the Russian Government into direct communication with the Armenians. During the seventeenth century Russia's relations with this race had been purely commercial, but from the beginning of the eighteenth century relations of another sort began. In June, 1701, three Armenians, headed by one Izrael Oria, appeared at Smolensk with a project for liberating the predominant Armenian population of Shemak, Tabriz and Erivan from the Persian yoke. Nothing came of this plan, and in 1707 Oria died on a tour through Persia, where, in the disguise of a papal legate, he was busy sowing rebellion. An interval of nine years elapsed, and then the negotiations were resumed by one of Oria's companions rhe archimandrite, afterwards archbishop, Minas Vartapet; but as on this occasion the two Armenian patriarchs could not agree as to the expediency of a general rising of the Armenians against the Persians, again nothing was done. Another seven years elapsed, and then the hopes of the Armenians revived at the spectacle of a Russian army on the southern shores of the Caspian. They now petitioned Peter for leave to settle in the newly acquired provinces of Gilyan and Salyan as Russian subjects, and in October, 1724, came a further petition from the two Armenian patriarchs, Narses and Isaiah, imploring

Peter for instant help lest they should be exterminated by the Turks.*

But, in any case, Peter's acquisition of, and his efforts to Christianise his new possessions by a wholesale importation of orthodox Georgians and Armenians, were bound to drive the Mussulman inhabitants of these provinces into the arms of the Sultan, and therefore threatened to bring about a rupture between Russia and the Porte. Even before this, in 1722, at the very time when he was preparing for his Persian campaign, Nepluyev, his minister at Stambul, informed Peter that the Lesghians were petitioning the Padishah for a Mussulman governor. The friendly French ambassador at Stambul simultaneously advised Nepluyev that Russia would do well to be content with the Caspian provinces, and not irritate the Porte by drawing Armenia and Georgia also within her orbit. On the other hand, the English, Austrian and Venetian residents used the Russian invasion of Persia as a means of terrifying the Porte, and insinuated that the Moscovite might penetrate as far as Trebizond, to the great detriment of the Turkish Empire. In August, 1722, the Grand Vizier told Nepluyev that Russia had better declare war against the Porte at once, and then they would know where they were. The whole of the Tsar's reign, he added, had been one uninterrupted war, in which he had given no rest to his neighbours. Subsequently Nepluyev reported to his Court that the Turks intended to conquer Persia and Georgia, and drive the Russians out of Daghestan. He earnestly advised the Emperor to be ready for war, as immense stores of ammunition were being constantly sent to Erzerum and Azov from Stambul. Indeed, so menacing did things seem at this time that Nepluyev destroyed his papers, solemnly recommended his little son (who was smuggled off to Holland by the French ambassador) to the Tsar's fatherly protection, and prepared for the worst. Fortunately Turkey was not ready for war, and the acquisition of the Caspian provinces by Russia was a matter of comparative indifference to the Sultan, it was the spread of Russian influence in the Caucasus that he really dreaded. In

* This letter Peter never received. It reached Petersburg shortly after his death.

the beginning of 1723, however, the political horizon again became overclouded, and the Grand Vizier mendaciously informed Nepluyev that as the Porte had now taken the Persian pretender, Daud Bey, under its high protection, any Russian claims upon Persia must first be submitted to the Padishah. This change of front was due to a communication from Berlin, handed to the Divan by the English ambassador at Stambul,* to the effect that Peter, with an immense army, was about to proceed against Daghestan and extend his dominions to the Black Sea. But Peter was not so easily frightened. He regarded the Caspian provinces as indispensable, and rather than abandon them, was prepared to risk a third war with the Porte. Accordingly he began to assemble another army, and Prince Michael Golitsuin was appointed its commander-in-chief. On April 9 Nepluyev was instructed to inform the Grand Vizier that the Russian Emperor would allow no other Power to approach the Caspian, and if the Porte wanted war, the Porte should have it. Then the Russian troops sailed to Baku, and still the Porte did not declare war, though the English ambassador urged it to do so by holding out the hope of simultaneous co-operation on the part of Great Britain and Denmark. In the beginning of 1724 war still seemed probable and Nepluyev demanded his passports; but ultimately, by the Treaty of Constantinople (June 12, 1724), a compromise was arrived at. It was arranged that Shemak should belong to a vassal of the Porte; but that the region extending, in a straight line, from Shemak to the Caspian should be divided into three parts, two of which, adjacent to the Caspian, should belong to Russia, while the third part, stretching southwards from Derbent, should be divided between Russia and Persia. A special envoy, Alexander Rumyantsev, sent to Stambul to exchange ratifications, was instructed to inform the Porte that Peter had promised to give the Armenians an asylum, and now proposed that they should migrate into his new territories, "as it is impossible for us, as a Christian ruler, to refuse protection to fellow Christians." This noble ambition, so worthy of an orthodox Emperor, Peter never lived to accomplish.

* Despatches of Nepluyev, cited by Solovev: "Istoria Rossy," XVIII., 1.

# CHAPTER XIV.

## INTERNAL ADMINISTRATION AND THE SOCIAL CONDITION OF RUSSIA IN THE LAST YEARS OF THE REGENERATOR.

### 1721—1725.

Progress of the Internal Reforms—Institution of the Offices of the " Procurator-General." the " Herald-Master." and the " Master of Petitions "—Prosecution and Fall of Shafirov—Prosecution and Execution of Nestorov—Peter's Justification of his Severity—The Finances— Trade—Obstacles in the Way of it—Curious Case of the Merchant Bogomolov—Manufactures—Efforts to Promote them—Reform in the Local Administration—Police Measures—Social Reforms—Court Receptions—Public Assemblies—Prevalence and Increase of Drunkenness—Persistence of the Old Pastimes—Dwarfs—Jesters—Anecdote illustrating the Brutality of Manners—Promotion of Education—Foundation of the Academy of Sciences—Re-constitution of the Synod—The Dissenters—The Succession to the Throne fixed in the Female Line—Coronation of the Empress—Consort Catherine—Her Character—Her alleged *Liaison* with Wilhelm Mons—Death of Peter the Great—Review of his Work—Results of his Teaching—He creates a new Russia—Estimate of his Character.

ONE of the most momentous events in the history of the world had been consummated. The eastern portion of Europe had at last entered into the common life of the West, and henceforth every movement of the armies of Russia was to awake apprehension or speculation in every Continental cabinet. Thus as early as 1720, only two years after the proclamation of Peter as Emperor, Prince Kurakin reported from The Hague that all the Western potentates rejoiced that the Russian Emperor was occupied by the Persian War, and prayed most fervently that it might last long enough to exhaust his resources. The ambition of Russia had already become a menace to the West.

But there is another aspect from which these wars of aggrandisement should be regarded if they are to be properly understood. It is true, as the Grand Vizier reminded Nepluyev,* that Peter's whole reign had been an interminable chain of wars,

* See preceding Chapter.

but the reason of this we have already seen. It was to restore to Russia her natural frontiers, it was to provide her with a seaboard, that she might thereby obtain her fair share of the commerce and consequently of the wealth, of the world. Moreover this incessant warfare had a moral as well as a material purpose, which was perhaps its best justification. It was to accustom the slothful and imbecile population of Russia to exertion and adventure—it was to be educational as well as acquisitive. It was thus only a means to an end, and the Regenerator was careful that the progress of domestic reform should keep pace with the triumphal advance of his armies abroad.

The reform of the internal administration engaged Peter's attention immediately after the termination of the Swedish War. He began with the highest tribunal of all, the administrative Senate. Experience had already shown that the senators, following the old Moscovite *laissez-aller* principle, were apt to neglect business, disregard the laws, and quash all complaints from inferior tribunals against themselves personally. To prevent this, Peter, at the beginning of 1722, instituted the office of Procurator-General, whose duty it was to sit in the Senate and see to it that the senators performed their duties "in a faithful, zealous, and orderly fashion, according to the direction of the standing rules and *ukases*, inasmuch as nothing is so necessary for the government of a state as the observance of the laws, and it is a vain thing to make laws if they are not kept, or if people play at cards with them." Whenever the procurator-general observed anything irregular or illegal in the proceedings of the Senate, he was instantly to admonish the senators thereof, in the plainest terms, and if they neglected his admonition and the affair was of sufficient importance, he was to report it to the Gosudar forthwith. "He is, in fact, to be our Eye," ran the *ukaz*. It required no ordinary courage and resource to occupy an office which must necessarily embroil its holder with all the highest dignitaries of the state, but Peter found the man he wanted in Paul Ivanovich Yaguzhinsky, the son of the Lutheran organist at Moscow, whom the Tsar, probably, first encountered in the German settlement, where he attracted

Peter's attention by his immense capacity for spirituous liquor, his perennial good humour, and inexhaustible vivacity. Yaguzhinsky was as capable as he was jovial, and the only man in Russia who could stand before the Emperor, even in his worst moods, without trembling.*

To keep a watchful eye upon defaulters and malingerers among the gentry, the office of Herald-Master was instituted in 1721. This functionary had to draw up lists of all the land-owners in the Empire, showing who were in the service of the state and who were not, and giving the fullest details as to their families and occupations. He was also to establish schools for the better education of the squirearchy, and see to it that not more than two members of each family remained private citizens, " lest the state suffer."

A third newly-established functionary, "the Master of Petitions," had to examine all the petitions presented to the various departments of state, and see that they were properly attended to. He was to report all gross cases of neglect to the Senate, " so that the poor and helpless be not wronged by undue delays."

But it was of small avail to simplify and specialise the administration, and fence it about with safeguards, so long as the new institutions were infected by the fatal maladies of the old. The most inveterate of these maladies was the universal corruption for which Moscovy had ever been so notorious, and Peter himself, though he cauterised it freely, could not wholly eradicate the evil. In the course of 1723 and 1724 he made terrible examples of two of his most confidential and meritorious servants, Vice-Chancellor Shafirov and the ober-fiscal Nestorov. Both these great processes, which profoundly impressed con-temporaries, originated from very trivial causes. In the autumn of 1722, the ober-procurator of the Senate, Skornyakov-Pisarev, complained to the Gosudar that Vice-Chancellor Shafirov was constantly reviling him, and brawling in full Senate. Peter appealed to Yaguzhinsky, who confirmed Pisarev's complaint, and described the Senate as little better than a bear-garden.

* For further details concerning this remarkable man, see R. N. Bain: "Pupils of Peter the Great."

Shafirov prevailed, however, on this occasion, but his triumph made his enemies, among whom were his superior, the chancellor Golovkin, and Prince Menshikov, doubly watchful, and he was convicted at last of using his senatorial authority to procure for his brother Michael a superfluous increment of salary on being transferred from one post to another.   Such jobs were clearly illegal, and Shafirov would have done wisely had he admitted his fault when it was first pointed out to him by Pisarev.   But instead of doing so he fell to hectoring and cursing not only the procurator, but the other ministers of state, whereupon Menshikov carried through a motion that the vice-chancellor should be excluded from the Senate for disorderly conduct, and that his irregularities should be reported to the Gosudar.   In January, 1723, Peter appointed a special tribunal to sift the matter thoroughly, and on April 17, 1723, the vice-chancellor was condemned to death " for infringing the laws of the realm."   He was reprieved on the scaffold itself, in consideration of his past services, which certainly were considerable ; compelled to live at Novgorod on something less than two shillings a week ; and kept under such strict surveillance that he was not even permitted to go to church.

In the following year ober-fiscal Nestorov, who had made a spèciality of tracking down evil-doers, and had especially distinguished himself in the great Gagarin malversation case,* himself fell beneath the sword of justice.

In 1718 a subordinate of Nestorov's, the fiscal of Yaroslavl, Savva Peptsov, grossly swindled and maltreated a merchant of that city, Ivan Sutyagin by name.   Sutyagin presented a petition to the Senate for redress against Peptsov, which petition, after going the round of all the tribunals for four years, returned to its original place of issue at Yaroslavl, and was simply pigeon-holed.   But the plaintiff, a man of determined character, persevered, and in 1722 he petitioned the Gosudar direct. Peter entrusted the unravelling of the tangle to Yaguzhinsky, with the result that both Peptsov, the original oppressor, and his official chief, Nestorov, who was proved to have shielded Peptsov's iniquity for a large sum of money, and confessed everything to

* See Chapter xi.

avoid torture, were condemned to death. Nestorov's execution was made a public spectacle. All the public officials at St. Petersburg, and especially Nestorov's subordinates, were under strict orders to be present. Peter himself looked on from a window in the Revision Department. The criminal was slowly broken on the wheel, conveyed from thence, still breathing, to the scaffold, and there beheaded.

Peter's justification for this act of severity, which profoundly impressed Nestorov's contemporaries, is the *ukaz* of February 5, 1724, wherein we read as follows: " Whosoever offends in his calling (of judge) does an injury to the whole realm. Venality and injustice on the part of a superior takes away all fear of consequences from inferior officials. When these latter perceive their superiors enriching themselves with impunity, it would be strange indeed if they also did not yield to the same temptation. Wherefore wilful neglect of official duty should be punished as severely as neglect of duty in time of war. It should be treated like treachery, and even worse than treachery, for it is a species of treachery which cannot be guarded against so easily."

An attempt was also made to remedy the disorders in the Senate brought to light by the Shafirov affair. Thus the *ukaz* of January, 1724, ordained that senatorial vituperation should be punished in the first instance by a fine of ten rubles, in the second instance by a fine of 100 rubles and arrest, while a third repetition of the offence was to be still more severely chastised by deposition and the confiscation of one-third of the delinquent's property.

Despite a constant if gradual increase* in the revenue, the financial needs of the Government, owing to the expenses of the long war, happily now over, and a series of bad harvests, led to all sorts of ingenious but oppressive fiscal experiments.† It was even found necessary at last to cut down all official salaries by one-half, and other and similar retrenchments were made. The difficulty of housing the soldiers properly led to the introduction

* In 1710 the revenue had amounted to 3,134,000 rubles; by 1725 it had risen to 10,186,000 rubles.

† At the first census, taken at this time, there were found to be 5,967,313 persons, of whom 172,385 were traders

of barracks into Russia. At the end of Peter's reign the army numbered 210,000 men, including the 2,616 Guards. There were besides 109,000 irregulars. The fleet consisted of 48 ships of the line, and 787 galleys and smaller vessels, whose full complement of crews was 27,939 men. There was also a considerable increase in the mercantile marine, and Russian merchants began to appear in the principal non-Russian Baltic ports, where they too frequently brought disgrace upon their country by their drunken, lawless ways. Nor was the condition of the country people very satisfactory. One of the most inveterate obstacles to Peter's reforms was the ingrained habit of the official and land-owning classes of regarding the commercial and industrial classes as a fair booty. When these unhappy traders received powers of self-government from the crown, they were hated more than ever by "their big brethren," who tormented them in every conceivable way. The new burgomasters and town councillors were frequently beaten to death by the soldiers or the local magnates, and the traders were deprived of their warehouses, and obliged to store their goods as best they could. The following is a typical instance of the rapacity of the upper classes, even in the later years of the Regenerator.

Gospodin Bogomolov was one of the wealthiest and most considerable merchants in the city of Moscow. He had stores of gems and precious stones, stacks of gold and silver plate, and much money. Men of all ranks and nations borrowed gladly of this rich merchant, who dwelt in a many-roomed house surrounded by a strong wall, which he had built at a cost of 5,000 rubles. One of Bogomolov's best customers was his neighbour Prince Boris Golitsuin, with whom he lived on terms of intimacy. On the death of the old prince, his son and successor, Prince Sergy, taking advantage of the age and loneliness of the old merchant, who had neither wife nor children, nor near kinsfolk, dismissed all Bogomolov's servants and substituted for them ten retainers of his own, under the pretext that his father's old friend required protection. These retainers had strict orders never to let Bogomolov leave the house alone, and never to admit anyone to see him. Even when the old merchant begged with tears for leave to go to the House of God the prince's people went with him, and never let him out of their sight for a moment. In 1713, by which time Bogomolov had grown still more infirm, Prince Sergy boldly appropriated all his goods, and shut him up in the Bogoyavlensky Monastery. How the matter ended we are not told, but it is evident that when even wealthy merchants ran such risks it required some courage to engage in trade at all. It is, therefore, not surprising to find that manufactures did not prosper as much as Peter had anticipated, and that, with some few exceptions, they thrived best in the hands of the upper classes. Yet the Government did all it could to encourage industrial enterprises by exempting from the onerous obligation of public service all who engaged therein. The most important branch of trade at this time was the cloth manufactory of Moscow, which had 150 looms going, worked almost entirely by Russians. The writing-paper manufactory was also so great a success that in 1723 an *ukaz* commanded that all the stationery used in the public offices should henceforth be made in Russia. The copper foundries of the new town of Ekaterinaburg, in the Urals, also did well, and in 1724 no fewer than 1,500 poods of pure copper were ready to be transported to Moscow. Iron foundries were also worked profitably at Alapaevsk, and cannon was cast at the factories of Kamensk. At the end of Peter's reign the native factories, all told, numbered 233.

Much also was done to develop and improve the local administration. Magistracies were formed in all the towns, consisting of a president, two burgomasters, and four rathmen, or councillors, whose duty it was to gather all the traders and artisans together into the *posad* and prevent them from drifting into the ranks of the untaxable by flying to the steppe or the forest. Thus this new institution was a determined attempt to meet a difficulty with which old Moscovy had been altogether unequal to cope. The magistrates had also to provide for the security of the towns, guard them against fires, keep a census of the inhabitants (to be sent annually to the chief magistrate at the capital), compel rogues and vagabonds to work, and see that the children of all classes were taught reading, writing, and arithmetic. The whole body of citizens was divided into three classes: (1) the first guild, consisting of the chief merchants,

R.                                                                                    C C doctors, apothecaries, and cloth manufacturers ; (2) the second guild, consisting of the petty traders and artisans ; and (3) the common people. The members of the two guilds were to elect *starshinas*, or elders, to help the magistrates in the local administration, and the *starshinas* were to elect a *starosta*, who was to look after the interests of the community, and prevent the small and rich families from shifting the burden of taxation from their own shoulders to the shoulders of their poorer brethren with large families, as had been so frequently the case in the præ-Petrine days. Unfortunately for the peasantry, the largest and most long-suffering portion of the community, Peter, with the best will in the world, could do but little. But he did what he could by minimising their obligations to their masters, and by depriving landowners who killed or tortured their peasants of the management of their estates. Something, too, was done to improve the means of communication, upon which the success of trade and industry so largely depended ; but natural irremovable obstacles, such as the poverty of the Government, the vastness of the country, and the sparseness of the population, thwarted all the efforts of the Regenerator in this direction. In the autumn of 1722 it took the Dutch minister five weeks to get from Petersburg to Moscow, owing to the mud and broken bridges. At one place he had to wait for post-horses a whole week. But these inconveniences were as nothing compared with the danger besetting travellers from highwaymen. Writing at the end of 1722, the Dutch minister says that twenty-four highwaymen were executed in a single day at Petersburg. But though they were made to feel they were dying long before they died, by being impaled, broken on the wheel, hung up by sharp hooks thrust between their ribs, and still more inhuman punishments, the evil was increasing rather than diminishing. The Danish minister, Juel, gives similar testimony.

The police regulations introduced at the beginning of the reign were extended and more stringently enforced. It was ordered that the houses in Moscow were henceforth to be built of stone with tiled roofs. At night movable barricades were set up at the end of the principal streets, and guarded by the better sort of the inhabitants furnished with cudgels and rattles.

Famine was provided against by the *ukaz* commanding that all surplus corn should be taken from the foreign merchants, and distributed, at fixed prices, to the needy. The corn so borrowed was to be returned at the next harvest. Precautions were also taken against any attempt of the corn merchants to profit by the distress of the people by raising prices in bad times. Weekly reports of the state of the crops were ordered to be sent from every government and province to the *Kammer-Kollegium*, or Board of Trade, at the capital.

With the moral shortcomings of the nation it was still more difficult to grapple. Hearing, on one occasion, of a gross piece of peculation in the Senate, Peter furiously ordered Paul Yaguzhinsky to draw up an *ukaz* inflicting capital punishment on everyone who henceforth stole so much as a rope's end. But Paul, on this occasion, showed himself to be wiser than Peter. "Surely, Gosudar," he said, "you don't want to be an Emperor without any subjects to rule over? We all rob you, the only difference being that some of us are bigger and bolder thieves than others." At which Peter laughed heartily, and the matter dropped.

Peter also did what he could for the manners of his people by ordering his Empress to hold receptions on the European model, and by making social gatherings compulsory. Catherine's receptions were generally held after dinner, at about five o'clock, in the gardens of the Summer Palace, the bands of the Preobrazhensky and Semenovsky regiments supplying the music.* Close to one of the fountains stood the Empress supported by her family, and attended by her ladies-in-waiting in European costume. Foreigners were amazed at the polish and civility of Catherine's Court. It was not inferior, they declared, to the best of the petty German Courts. Peter, on the other hand, affected extreme military simplicity. He was waited on entirely by orderlies. The entertainment, however, was not without a smack of old Moscovy. Everybody was perpetually drinking to everybody else, and the higher clergy, invariably present on these occasions, were the merriest of the whole company.

---

* Somewhat incongruously, Peter himself brought them wine and beer. in wooden beakers, in the course of the evening.

Dancing went on till about twelve o'clock, in an open gallery on the north side of the gardens overlooking the Neva. The *fête* generally concluded with a splendid display of fireworks.

Of still more importance, in Peter's estimation, were the ordinary public assemblies at the mansions of the nobles. The object of these curious institutions was to accustom Russian society to Western ways. Persons of means were henceforth compelled to receive company at their houses, between the hours of five and ten p.m., periodically, to promote social intercourse and the open discussion of events of the day. The host was not obliged to receive his guests in person, or even to be present on such occasions; but he was obliged to have two or three rooms cleared out, and tables ready, on which were to be placed candles and packs of cards, pipes and tobacco, wine and spirits, for anybody who might wish to smoke, drink, or play. These assemblies were supposed to be as free-and-easy as possible. Every affectation of superiority or *hauteur* was to be promptly punished by "the spread-eagle," *i.e.*, the compulsory draining of a huge bumper sufficient to intoxicate the offender. Bows and curtsies were permissible only on entering and leaving the room. All classes, including merchants and the better class of tradesmen were to be admitted, but the lackeys and servants were to remain in the side apartments till called for.

In one respect, however, as will have been seen, Peter was incorrigible. He made no attempt to curb the national vice of drunkenness and its degrading consequences. Indeed, it was far worse in his days than ever it had been before. The Danish minister, Juel, tells us* that even at the Tsar's drinking-parties tricks were played which would never have been tolerated in the lowest society in Denmark. The guests began by eating ten times as much as was necessary, and then drinking went on till four o'clock in the morning. On his way home from these banquets Juel frequently saw the frozen river and the snow-covered fields black with the bodies of drunken men and women sleeping off their carouse under the open sky, like the slain on a battle-field. Juel was obliged to be present at many of these banquets, as they afforded the best opportunities for transacting diplomatic

* " En Rejse til Russland, *etc.*,"

and other business.  But he did so very unwillingly because of the unavoidable potations, for Peter always insisted on his guests drinking a full skin in order that their tongues might wag the more freely and he might benefit by their indiscretions. Juel had to resort to the most extraordinary expedients to avoid drinking his fair share.  On one occasion he bribed the Tsar's confessor, and on another he begged the Empress to get him excused from over-indulgence.  But it was all of no avail. Even when he knelt before Peter and asked to be let off with one pot and a half of wine instead of the regulation couple, the Emperor only laughed, and, kneeling down by Juel's side, vowed he would not rise from his knees till the Dane did.  The upshot was that Juel was forced to swallow half a dozen bumpers while he knelt, so that by the time he was allowed to stand up he could not keep his feet.

In all other respects, however, we notice some improvement, although the people at bottom were still Moscovite rather than Russian.  This is very evident when we consider the amusements of even the most enlightened of the magnates.  Thus dwarfs continued to be indispensable requisites of great houses, and the present of a good dwarf was often rewarded by the emancipation of a whole family.  In 1716 Menshikov wrote to a friend, asking him to obtain the consent of the Empress Catherine to the transference of one of the dwarfs left by the deceased Tsarevna Martha, to his younger daughter, who was still unprovided with one, and he did not want her to be worse off than her sister.  Parrots who could talk well were also in request, but their place was sometimes taken by little barbarian girls.  Thus in 1708 Menshikov wrote to his wife : " I am sending you as a present, two little Shlyaktan girls, the smallest of whom may serve you as a parrot.  Such a chatterbox I have rarely met with among children, you will be much amused."  Jesters, too, occupied their old place in public favour.  Peter's favourite jester was a foreigner, Lacosta by name, who evidently exercised great influence, for at his petition Dr. Lestocq, afterwards so famous as the favourite of the Empress Elizabeth, was banished to Kazan.

The tyrannous old principles of the *Domostroi*,* though frowned

* See Chapter I.

upon by the Emperor, still persisted.   Even in the highest circles
wife-beating was a common occurrence, as witness the case of the
*kravchy*, or grand-pantler, Count Saltuikov, who was accused by
his father-in-law, Gregory Theodorovich Dolgoruki, of starving
his wife, robbing her, and flogging her till she was half-dead.
The husband indignantly explained that his spouse had been so
cross and contrary, that he was obliged to flog her, but that he
had done so in moderation.

This brutality of manner even asserted itself at convivial
gatherings in the most illustrious houses.   Thus at the end
of December, 1722, Prince Ivan Romodanovsky gave a banquet
to a distinguished company at Preobrazhenskoe, at which the
Emperor also was present.   Peter departed early, but he begged
Romodanovsky to continue the entertainment, although most of
the guests had already drunk more than was good for them.
Now an old enmity had long been smouldering between the host
and the eminent diplomatist and privy councillor Prince Gregory
Theodorovich Dolgoruki, and it burst into full flame when the
latter ostentatiously refused to respond becomingly to a toast
proposed by the former.   Abusive epithets were freely inter-
changed, both the old men lost their tempers, seized each other
by the hair, and well pummelled each other with their fists before
any of the party took the trouble to separate them.   The host,
who was the drunker as well as the weaker of the two, and
had therefore come off worst in the encounter, as soon as he
could speak at all, shouted for the guards, and placed Dolgoruki
under arrest, while Dolgoruki protested against the outrage thus
committed upon the person of a privy councillor and senator
who was also a Chevalier of the Order of St. Andrew.   Brawling
and fighting were so usual on these festive occasions that in all
probability no notice would have been taken of the incident but
for Dolgoruki's indignant protest.   That indeed was a novelty,
and pointed, however feebly, to a growing respect for social
courtesy and human dignity.

But if privy councillors were not exempt from personal affront,
if princes and *sanovniks** assaulted and vilified each other in
public, we cannot be much surprised if the merchants, and the

* A high dignitary of state, just as a *chinovnik* is an ordinary official.

lower classes generally, greatly added to the miseries of their already unenviable position by the insensate violence of their enmities. The following case is typical. Gospodin Shein was a merchant of Vyatka, worth 100,000 rubles, and paying 3,000 rubles a year in taxes. In an unlucky hour he quarrelled with his wife, and, like the typical old Moscovite husband he was, threatened her with a lifelong incarceration in a convent. But the spouse, a woman of spirit, appealed for help to her father, who had a potent friend in Nestorov, the *dyak* of the Preobrazhensky *Prikaz*, and that terrible tribunal was set in motion against the tyrannical husband. Shein was seized, hauled before the inquisitors, who had a well-equipped and highly efficient torture-chamber at their disposal, and a *ukaz* was there and then recited to the astonished merchant, pronouncing sentence of death upon him for calumniating his father-in-law. The general amnesty consequent upon the Peace of Nystad saved his head, but he was knouted, banished to Siberia, and all his property was confiscated, and no doubt divided between his energetic father-in-law and the complaisant *dyak* of the Preobrazhensky *Prikaz*.

Another case typical of the social degradation of the period is that of Captain Matyushkin at Astrakhan. This gentleman kept a drunken midshipman as a fool for his private amusement. He used to make the midshipman intoxicated, and then pour wine on his head and set it on fire, occasionally varying the entertainment by daubing the fool's face with soot in order to provoke from him extraordinary outbursts of vituperation and indecent profanity for the diversion of his guests.

And the women were not a whit better than the men. It is recorded of the Tsaritsa Praskovia, the widow of the semi-imbecile Ivan V., that on one occasion she broke into the Secret Chancellery of Moscow at night with her retainers to chastise an advocate, Derevnin by name, who had brought a civil action against her, and was detained there provisionally. By her command, her servants, after giving Derevnin a sound drubbing, singed him all over with candles, and then poured vodka over his face and head, and set them on fire. But for the intervention of the guard the unfortunate man would have been burnt to death.

Peter was by no means disposed that his daughters, the

Tsesarevnas Anne and Elizabeth, should grow up like their Aunt Praskovia. He took care to provide them with governesses, both native and foreign, from their tenderest years.* He was a great believer in the civilising power of education, and did much for its advancement in Russia, by the *ukas* of January 28, 1724, which laid the foundations of an academy of sciences, which was to be a university, a gymnasium and an elementary school at the same time. The tolls levied on merchandise in the ports of Narva, Dorpat, Reval and Arenberg, were set apart for its maintenance. Thus the benefits derived by Russia from her newly acquired Baltic provinces were intellectual as well as material.

Previously to the institution of the Academy, the Synod had been entrusted with the translation and circulation of books both sacred and profane. This was a branch of education in which Peter was deeply interested. In 1722, while at Astrakhan, on the eve of embarking on the Persian campaign, he wrote to the Synod for copies of Raguzhinsky's translation of Ortini's " Il regno degli Slavi," and Cantemir's translation of " The Religion of Mahomet." On October 24 he ordered a translation to be made of Pufendorf's treatise on the duties of men and citizens. Peter was, by this time, quite competent to criticise the methods and avoid the absurdities of his former teachers. This is very evident in another letter to the Synod, from which I quote a single passage. " Inasmuch as it is a practice of the Germans to fill their books with many useless details, in order that they may appear grand, see to it that such long-winded details be not translated. They only waste time and weary readers." Peter's own style, it may be added, though sometimes homely, was always forcible and precise.

The authority of the Synod had been officially recognised by the Patriarchs of Antioch and Constantinople in September, 1723. Shortly afterwards, Theodosy, Archbishop of Novgorod complained to Peter of the mischievous interference of the Senate in ecclesiastical affairs. Peter promptly took measures to protect the Synod by giving it a more independent position,

* For details see R. N. Bain : " Pupils of Peter the Great," and " Daughter of Peter the Great."

similar to that of its temporal partner, the Senate. After the death of its first president, Stephen Yavorsky, the office of President of the Synod was abolished, but it received a civil assessor in the person of the "Ober-procurator of the Synod," an office established on May 11, 1722. The object of this change was to differentiate the Synod from the colleges or ordinary departments of state, all of which had their presidents. The training of the clergy, especially of the Black clergy, the repression of dissent and superstition, and the promotion of the moral and religious enlightenment of the people, were henceforth to be the principal functions of the Synod. A newly created official, the proto-inquisitor, or "chief-fiscal in spiritual matters," was to exercise the same supervision over the Synod as the "procurator-general" already exercised over the Senate.

The spread of dissent, its increasing violence (one fanatic, the monk Varlaam, an ex-soldier, openly denounced Peter as Antichrist from the top of a shop in the bazaar at Penza), and the dominancy of its more Protestant elements induced Peter, towards the end of his reign, to endeavour to bring the schismatics once more within the fold of the Church. From the *ukaz* of April, 1724, it is clear that he preferred to do this by gentle and intelligent methods. In this document, addressed to the Synod, he urges the necessity of drawing up a short manual of instruction for the people, explaining what is the unalterable law of God, what are the counsels and traditions of the fathers, and what things are simply indifferent. "It seems to us," observes the Tsar on this occasion, "that these things should be set forth very plainly, so that the countryman may understand them. He ought to be shown clearly which is the narrow way of salvation, and especially ought he to be taught concerning faith, hope and love, matters as to which he is but little instructed, and that wrongly, or he would never put his whole trust in church-singing and fasting,* and such like things."

Towards the end of his reign the question of the succession to the throne caused the Emperor some anxiety. The rightful heir in the natural order of primogeniture was the little Grand Duke Peter, a child of six, but Peter decided to pass him over

---

* Yet Peter, as we have already seen, recognised the obligation of fasting.

because, as the son of the unfortunate Tsarevich Alexius, any acknowledgment of his rights would infallibly have excited the hopes of those people who had sympathised with his father, and the fears of those who had had a hand in Alexius' murder. But who, then, was to succeed the reigning Emperor? His own daughters, the Tsesarevnas Anne and Elizabeth, were still mere children, and his nieces, the daughters of his brother Ivan, had married foreign princes, and were living abroad. The Tsaritsa Catherine alone remained, and Peter resolved to secure the throne for her whom he loved best in all the world. That curious document, the *ustav*, or ordinance, of 1722, heralded this unheard-of innovation. Time-honoured custom had hitherto reckoned primogeniture, in the male line, as the best title to the Russian crown; in the *ustav* of 1722, Peter denounced primogeniture in general as a stupid, dangerous, and even unscriptural practice. It was a bad old custom, he said, of doubtful origin. History, both sacred and profane, justified, and even commanded, sensible parents to make alterations in this respect whenever necessary, and he concluded by making the succession to the Russian Empire, in future, absolutely dependent on the will of the reigning Gosudar. "Thus children, or children's children, will not be tempted to fall into the sin of Absalom, and this *ustav* will be a curb upon them." Thus was the little Grand Duke Peter deprived of his birthright. In the public prayer for the Imperial family, his name was henceforth recited after the names of his aunts, the Tsesarevnas Anne and Elizabeth.*

Not content with this manifesto, Peter ordered his faithful ecclesiastical henchman, Bishop Theofan Prokopovich, to compose an elaborate justification of this dynastic mutation, which appeared under the title of " Pravda voli Monarshei." Everyone was required to swear to uphold the new order of succession, but there was considerable opposition. The Dissenters, in some places, refused to kiss the cross to "a German Tsaritsa," and many monks, and not a few Cossacks, protested against the setting aside of the Grand Duke Peter. One Cossack and eleven of his comrades barricaded themselves inside a church, and blew

* The Austrian Court formally protested against the exclusion of the Grand Duke Peter from the throne

themselves up with gunpowder rather than subscribe the new oath of allegiance.

The marriages of the two Tsesarevnas now became a matter of primary importance. At first there was a rumour that the elder Tsesarevna, Anne, her father's favourite, was to be espoused to Alexander Naruishkin, who thereupon was to be appointed Peter's successor; but ultimately she was solemnly betrothed to Charles Frederick, Duke of Holstein, the nephew of Charles XII. (November, 1724). Both bride and groom at the same time solemnly renounced all their rights to the Russian throne.*

The *ustav* regulating the succession was but a preliminary step to a still more sensational novelty. In 1723 Peter resolved to crown his consort, the Tsaritsa Catherine, Empress. The whole question as to what were the proper titles of members of the Emperor's family had previously been submitted to the consideration of both the Senate and the Synod, who decided that Catherine should be called Imperatritsa, or its Slavonic equivalent Tsesareva, while the princesses were no longer to be Tsarevnas,† but Tsesarevnas.‡ On November 15, 1723, Peter issued a second manifesto, in which, after explaining that, from the days of Justinian and Heraclius to the present day, it had ever been the custom of Christian princes, both in the East and the West, to crown their consorts, he proceeded at some length, and in very affectionate terms, to cite the services rendered to him by his Tsesareva in the past, especially during the Turkish War, when, "with great self-sacrifice, she shared all the trials and discomforts of a soldier's life, encouraging us and our whole army by her valour and heroism. . . . Wherefore," proceeds the manifesto, "by the authority given to us by God, we have resolved to reward such great services of our consort by crowning her with the Imperial crown."

That Peter himself should have considered some sort of explanation necessary at all, is the clearest proof that he felt he was treading on dangerous ground. The whole nation listened aghast to the manifesto. The coronation of a woman was, in the

---

* The only child of this marriage, Peter Ulrich, ultimately reigned in Russia under the title of Peter III.

† The daughter of a Tsar or King.　　　　‡ The daughter of an Emperor.

opinion of the Russian people, a scandalous innovation. The
only princess who had ever enjoyed that distinction was Maria
Mnishka, the consort of the false Demetrius, in the sixteenth
century, and, heretic as she was, she had at any rate been of
noble birth.   But what sort of a Tsaritsa was this ?   Who was
she ?   Whence had she sprung ?   She had come to Russia not
merely as a stranger, but as a captive, a half-naked captive,
bandied about from owner to owner, who owed her very life to
the clemency of her Tsarish paramour, who had torn her from
the arms of his favourite, the vile Menshikov, her previous
possessor, and now, forsooth, this slave, this harlot,* was to wear
the Imperial crown, and sit upon the Imperial throne !   But on
this point Peter was utterly regardless of the feelings and the
prejudices of his people, and who shall say that he was wrong?
Peter was more than justified in elevating to the purple the
woman who had originally fallen to his lot among the spoils of
war.   Catherine Skovronskaya, coarse and ignorant as she was,
had inalienable claims upon his gratitude and affection.   An
uncommonly shrewd and sensible woman, with a magnificent
physique, an imperturbable good-temper, and an absolute indifference to the hardships of a roving life, she was an ideal wife
for a rough and ready peripatetic Russian soldier like Peter the
Bombardier.   But, more than this, she was, on the whole, the
least unsuitable of Peter's potential successors.   Her frank *bonhomie* had won for her the devotion of the army, every member
of which regarded her as a comrade, while a vivid consciousness
of the difficulties of her position had made her deliberately adopt,
betimes, the *rôle* of a habitual protectress of all who incurred the
displeasure of the Emperor, with the result that most of the
men of the new system had already made up their minds to
stand or fall with the new Empress.   On May 7, 1724, the
coronation of Catherine† took place in the cathedral of the
Assumption in the *kreml'* at Moscow, with extraordinary pomp
and splendour.   The crown of Catherine on this occasion was
the most costly and magnificent ever worn, hitherto, by a Russian

* I need not repeat the often-told story. For details. see R. Nisbet Bain :
" The Pupils of Peter the Great," chap. 2.
† See Zhmakin : " Koronatsy russkich imperatorov "; Semevsky : " Tsaritsa
Ekaterina "; and Andreev : " Ekaterina Pervaya."

sovereign.    It was made in Paris on the model of the old
Byzantine Imperial crown, and was studded with no fewer than
2,564 precious stones.    Each of the numerous pearls on it was
worth £500, and Peter had stripped his own crown of its finest
diamonds, the better to adorn his consort's.    But the most
remarkable jewel of all was a ruby as large as a pigeon's egg,
placed immediately beneath a cross of brilliants at the apex of
the crown.    This incomparable gem was purchased at Pekin,
at Menshikov's command, for 60,000 rubles.

In May, 1724, Catherine Aleksyeevna had thus been elevated by
her devoted consort to a pedestal of glory so lofty as, seemingly,
to place her, henceforth, quite beyond the reach of the slings and
arrows of outrageous fortune.    Yet, within a few months of her
crowning triumph, she was exposed to the very unpleasant consequences of a suspected intrigue with the administrator of her
private estate, Wilhelm Mons, a handsome, unscrupulous rascal,
the brother of Peter's former mistress, Anna Mons.    I have
elsewhere endeavoured to show that Catherine's relations with
Mons, though dangerously familiar, were perfectly innocent, * but
Peter, at first, took the opposite view, and his vengeance fell
furiously upon the minor offenders.    Mons, after being horribly
tortured, was beheaded for malversation, peculation, and usurp-
ing the authority of the Senate.    His head, preserved in spirits,
was placed in the private apartments of the Empress.    His
secretary, one of his sisters, Frau Balck, and the jester Balakirev,
were knouted and banished to Siberia.    Almost simultaneously
fresh gigantic frauds, on the part of Prince Menshikov, were
discovered.    His serene highness was thereupon deprived of the
lucrative administration of the War Office, and, for a short time,
his life was once more in jeopardy.    The supposed infidelity of
his beloved consort, and the shameless depredations of his most
trusted friend, seriously affected the health of Peter, who could
always be easily and deeply wounded through his affections.
His herculean labours and his gargantuan excesses had already
undermined what was originally the constitution of a Goliath.
Though not yet fifty-three, he was already an old man.    He
seems, however, to have anticipated a long life, but his days were

* R. N. Bain : " Pupils of Peter the Great," chap. 2.

already numbered.  On his return to Petersburg from the Persian campaign, in March, 1724, he seemed to be much stronger than when he started; but in the course of the summer the state of his health caused great anxiety, though, by the middle of September, he had so far recovered as to be able to indulge in his favourite pastime of sailing on the Neva.  On September 22 he had another very violent attack of his paroxysms, which left him so irritable that he drove all the physicians from his presence with curses.  Again, however, nature prevailed, and in October, ignoring the warnings of his cleverest medical attendant, Dr. Blumentrost, he undertook a long and fatiguing tour of inspection over the latest of his great public works, the Ladoga Canal, proceeding thence to visit the iron works at Olonetz, where he dug out a piece of iron ore, three poods* in weight, with his own hands.  In the beginning of November he returned to Petersburg by water.  Perceiving, near the village of Lakhta, a boat full of soldiers, on their way back to Cronstadt, stuck fast on a sand-bank, and in imminent danger of being drowned, he plunged into the water to render them assistance, and was immersed to his girdle for a considerable time.  His paroxysms immediately returned with redoubled violence, and he reached Petersburg too ill ever to rally again, though he showed himself in public as late as January 16, 1725.  After that date he never left his bed, and recognising that his end was approaching, he commanded that a movable chapel should be erected in his room.  On the 26th he confessed and communicated, and, shortly afterwards, the long and violent agony began.  On the evening of the same day, after extreme unction had been administered, he issued an order for the pardon and release of all misdemeanants.  On the 27th he directed that all those who had been condemned by court-martial, excepting murderers, and the worst kind of freebooters, should be set at liberty.  The same day he asked for ink and paper and tried to write something down, but the pen fell from his hands before he had finished.  All that could be deciphered were the words: " otdaite vse . . ."†  Then he called for his beloved daughter Anne, but when the Tsesarevna arrived, her father was speechless.  At six o'clock in the evening

---

* A pood = 40 lb.                          † " Forgive everything."

of the following day, he expired. His consort, with whom he was fully reconciled, never quitted his side during the crisis of the illness, and closed his eyes when he died.*

* * * * *

In frightful physical suffering, with the full consciousness of human weakness, demanding comfort from on high, and imploring the forgiveness of those around him, one of the very greatest of the world's great men had passed away. His career has been well compared to the course of a hurricane which purifies the air but leaves the earth devastated behind it, or, equally felicitously, to the operation of a drastic remedy which all but destroys the desperately diseased organism in the very process of healing it. In 1741 a shrewd and well-informed observer,† friendly to Russia, anxiously surveying the general condition of the country, thus expresses himself: "After all the pains which have been taken . . . to bring this country out of its ancient state, I must confess that I see it in no other light than a rough model of something meant to be perfected hereafter, in which the several parts neither fit nor join, nor are well glued together, but have only been kept so first, by one great peg, and now by another, driven through the whole, which peg pulled out, the whole machine would fall to pieces."‡ This gloomy prognostication was uttered sixteen years after the death of Peter the Great; how much more hopelessly uncertain and insecure must not everything have seemed to those who in 1725 stood around his death-bed? On Peter's death even the boldest and the most sanguine of Peter's pupils must have regarded the situation as desperate. The political machine, incomplete, almost fragmentary, had suddenly been deprived of its vital force, its motive power. Chaos or confusion met their gaze in all directions. Everything, the army, the navy, the administration, the diplomatic service, the civil service, the whole social and educational system, absolutely everything, was brand new, and only maintained with the utmost difficulty by the most

---

* For further details, see Bain: "Pupils of Peter the Great," chap. 2.
† Finch, the British ambassador at St. Petersburg.
‡ "Sb. of Imp. Russ. Hist., Soc.," vol. 91.

extraordinary expedients. Imposts in money and kind of exceptional and inconceivable severity, weighed upon every household in the poorest of empires. Everything had been taken from the people that could be taken, down to their oaken coffins, their one luxury. The Dissenters paid double for leave to remain Dissenters. All who chose to wear beards had to pay for the privilege. Every sort of restriction was imposed on trade and commerce. The very trade routes were arbitrarily altered. Merchandise had now to go westwards instead of northwards, as hitherto. A relatively insignificant armed force, itself an expensive novelty, was the sole restraint upon a population of millions on the verge of rebellion.

Nor was the moral any better than the material condition of the people. Superficially regarded, the bulk of the Russian nation was still pretty much the same as it had been in the bad old times. The coarse, violent manners, the disgusting vices of old Moscovy, still peeped forth everywhere from beneath the French costumes and the French perukes which were now universally worn by the higher classes. Senators and cabinet ministers habitually got drunk at each other's houses, and pummelled their guests at their own tables. It seemed, at first sight, as if the reforms of the Regenerator had but swept away the old foundations of society without substituting anything for them.

But it was not so. Peter's educational methods, if rough, were thorough, and they had already begun to leaven the seemingly still inert and sluggish mass of the nation. The Russian nation had really been taught not merely the arts and the trades of life, but its duties and obligations also. From the first the Regenerator, in his *ukases*, had been very careful to make everything quite plain. He was always explaining why he did this or that, why the new was better than the old, and so on ; and we must recollect that these were the first lessons of the kind the nation had ever received. What the educated Russian of to-day takes for granted, his forefathers two centuries ago first learnt from the manifestoes and *ukases* of Peter the Great. The whole system of Peter was deliberately directed against the chief evils from which old Moscovy had always suffered such as, dissipation of energy, dislike of co-operation, absence of responsibility, lack of initiative, the tyranny of the family, the insignificance of the individual. All his efforts were devoted to the task of releasing Russians from the leading-strings of an effete tradition, and making them act and think for themselves. They were to walk boldly with swords in their hands, not crawl along on crutches as heretofore. We have seen* that in ancient Moscovy to be without family connections was to be nobody and nothing. The tyranny of the family tended to individual atrophy both intellectually and morally ; for the old Moscovite, who was very punctilious on the score of family honour, was quite indifferent as to personal self-respect. The Regenerator gave the death-blow to this degrading dependence by paying exclusive regard to personal merit. Ability, wherever he found it, whether in the lowest ranks of his own people or among foreigners, was, during his reign, the sole qualification for employment and promotion, so that at last it was almost a recommendation for a candidate for office to say that he was of no birth, or of alien parentage. Personal liberty was also promoted by such ordinances as those which forbade children to be married without their consent, and released women from the degrading seclusion of the *terem*. Finally, the disgraceful old Moscovite proverb, " Byegstvo khot' nechestno da zdorovo,"† which was of universal application in the seventeenth century, died out of the language once for all during the stress of the Great Northern War, when Russia served her military apprenticeship.

As already indicated, Peter's campaigns were very largely educational. Although three-quarters of his reign were occupied in military enterprises, he was no mere military conqueror. Love of glory had not the least attraction for him. Half a dozen times during the course of the Great Northern War he would willingly have laid down his arms. When he had at last won sufficient to secure the independence of his country, when, by incredible exertions and sacrifices, he had succeeded in legitimating the just demands of the Russian nation for a sea-board which would enable her to export her produce and thereby give her

* Chapter I.

† " Though flight be contrary to honour, it is good for the health."

R.                                                                        D D

her fair share of the world's commerce, then Peter immediately sheathed his sword.

But Peter's claim to greatness rests mainly on the fact that from first to last he clearly recognised the requirements of the Russian nation and his own obligations as the leader of that nation. Foreseeing the inevitableness of a long and necessarily humiliating national apprenticeship, he nevertheless unhesitatingly subjected Russia, even in those days the haughtiest nation in the world,* to the bitter and scarce endurable ordeal of tutelage to the heretic West, but he compensated her ultimately with the inalienable gift of political greatness. How to civilise Russia without unduly subordinating her to foreign influence, was one of the most difficult problems that ever a ruler had to face. It would materially have lightened his task had he placed intelligent foreigners at the head of every department of state, and allowed them gradually to have trained up a native bureaucracy. But for the sake of the independence of the Russian nation, he resisted the temptation of taking this inviting but perilous short cut to greatness. He was determined that, at whatever cost, hardship, and inconvenience, Russia should be ruled by Russians and not by foreigners, and before his death he had the satisfaction of seeing every important office in his Empire in the hands of capable natives of his own training. But even in his most sweeping reforms he never lost sight of the peculiarities, the idiosyncrasies of the people he had to govern. Before all things he was practical and clear-sighted. The utopias of the latter end of the eighteenth century would have revolted his robust common-sense. He never destroyed anything which he was not able to replace by something better. To take a typical instance of this prudence, notwithstanding his strong and very intelligible dislike of the abuses of Russian monasticism, so far from abolishing the system, he endeavoured to give it a character more in accordance with the designs of its original founders, and better adapted to the needs of the nation.

Peter was born with a singularly alert and impressionable

---

* A century and a half earlier still, Gustavus Adolphus had described the Russians as "that haughty nation which would not learn from other nations."

intelligence. Well aware of his limitations, he kept well within them ; but he appropriated thoroughly everything to which he gave his mind or put his hand. He possessed, too, something of the heroic nature of the old Russian *bogatuirs*, or demigods, as we see them in the *skazki* and the *buílinui*. His expansive, impulsive genius loved width and space. If the *bogatuirs* of Russian fable longed after the wide steppe, the *bogatuir* of new Russia longed after the still wider sea. Places shut in between mountains had a cramping, stifling effect upon him. He called Carlsbad a hole, because there he could never see the sun. No doubt this last of the heroic *bogatuirs* possessed the violent passions as well as the wide views of his prototypes. All his qualities, indeed, were on a colossal scale. His rage was cyclonic, his hatred rarely stopped short of extermination. His banquets were orgies, his pastimes were convulsions. He lived and he loved like one of the giants of old. There are deeds of his which make humanity shudder, and no man equally great has ever descended to such depths of cruelty and treachery. Yet it may fairly be urged that the bright side of the Regenerator's character out-shines its darker features. It may generally be allowed that a strain of sublime nobility, of which we occasionally catch il-luminating glimpses, extorts from time to time an all-forgiving admiration. Strange, too, as it may sound to those who have followed his blood and mud-stained career, Peter the Great was at heart, profoundly religious. Few rulers have ever had an acuter sense of their responsibility to the Almighty, or a more intimate persuasion that they were but instruments for good in His hands. No other great ruler was ever so faithfully patient in the hour of adversity, so gratefully modest in the hour of triumph as Peter the Great. Listen to the words addressed by him to one of the ablest of his later *protégés*, Ivan Nepluyev, when, full of gratitude at his unexpected appointment as Russian ambassador at Constantinople. he fell on his knees before his benefactor. " Nay, my little brother, kneel not to me," cried Peter, raising him up. " God has set me over you, and it is my duty to see that 1 do not give places to incompetent, or take them away from competent, people. If you are a good man you will be doing good not so much to me as to your country. For

I shall have to give an account of all of you to God. I shall have to answer for it before His judgment seat if I do harm by promoting bad or foolish persons. Serve faithfully and justly, little brother, and first God, and then I also, will never forsake you."*

* Svinin : "Zhizn' Nepluyeva."

# INDEX.*

---

* Names other than personal names—*e.g.*, battles, treaties, etc.—are in italics.

## THE END.

BRADBURY, AGNEW, & CO. LD., LONDON AND TONBRIDGE;

Printed in the United States
94018LV00006B/447/A

9 781417 970766